D1274610

## THE URBAN IMAGE OF LATE ANTIQUE CONSTANTINOPLE

From its foundation in the fourth century to its fall to the Ottoman Turks in the fifteenth century, the city of Constantinople boasted a collection of antiquities unrivaled by any city of the medieval world. *The Urban Image of Late Antique Constantinople* reconstructs the collection from the time that the city was founded by Constantine the Great through the sixth-century reign of the emperor Justinian. Drawing on medieval literary sources and, to a lesser extent, graphic and archaeological material, it identifies and describes the antiquities that were known to have stood in the city's public spaces. Individual displays of statues are analyzed as well as examined in conjunction with one another against the city's topographical setting in an effort to understand how ancient sculpture was used to create a distinct historical identity for Constantinople.

Sarah Bassett is Associate Professor of Art History at Wayne State University. A scholar of late antique and Byzantine art, she has received fellowships from the National Endowment for the Humanities and Dumbarton Oaks. She has contributed to *Dumbarton Oaks Papers, The American Journal of Archaeology*, and *The Art Bulletin*.

# THE URBAN IMAGE OF LATE ANTIQUE CONSTANTINOPLE

## SARAH BASSETT

Wayne State University

CAMBRIDGE
UNIVERSITY PRESS

PUBLISHED BY THE PRESS SYNDICATE OF THE UNIVERSITY OF CAMBRIDGE
The Pitt Building, Trumpington Street, Cambridge, United Kingdom

CAMBRIDGE UNIVERSITY PRESS
The Edinburgh Building, Cambridge CB2 2RU, UK
40 West 20th Street, New York, NY 10011-4211, USA
477 Williamstown Road, Port Melbourne, VIC 3207, Australia
Ruiz de Alarcón 13, 28014 Madrid, Spain
Dock House, The Waterfront, Cape Town 8001, South Africa

http://www.cambridge.org

© Sarah Bassett 2004

This book is in copyright. Subject to statutory exception
and to the provisions of relevant collective licensing agreements,
no reproduction of any part may take place without
the written permission of Cambridge University Press.

First published 2004

Printed in the United Kingdom at the University Press, Cambridge

*Typeface* Bembo 11/15 pt. and Trajan      *System* LATEX 2ε [TB]

*A catalog record for this book is available from the British Library.*

*Library of Congress Cataloging in Publication Data*
Bassett, Sarah, 1954–
The urban image of late antique Constantinople / Sarah Bassett.
p.   cm.
Includes bibliographical references and index.
ISBN 0-521-82723-x
1. Sculpture, Classical.   2. Sculpture – Turkey – Istanbul.
3. Public spaces – Turkey – Istanbul – History.
4. Istanbul (Turkey) – Buildings, structures, etc.   I. Title.
NB85.B375   2004
733′.0939′8 – dc22       2004040673

ISBN 0 521 82723 x hardback

NB85
.B375
2004

i 052182723X

＄

"I never knew the old Vienna before the war, with its Strauss music, its glamour and easy charm – Constantinople suited me better."

Graham Green, *The Third Man*

＄

# CONTENTS

# CONTENTS

# ILLUSTRATIONS

*Figure numbers designate images accompanying the text. Plate numbers refer to images in the catalogue.*

ix

# PERIODICALS: ABBREVIATIONS

*AA = Archäologischer Anzeiger*

*ActaAArtHist = Acta ad archaeologiam et artium historiam pertinentia*

*ActaArch = Acta Archaeologica* [Copenhagen]

*AF = Archäologische Forschungen*

*AJA = American Journal of Archaeology*

*AM = Mitteilungen des Deutschen Archäologischen Instituts, Athenische Abteilung*

*AnalBoll = Analecta Bollandiana*

*AnalRom = Analecta Romana Instituti Danici*

*AnatSt = Anatolian Studies. Journal of the British Institute of Archaeology at Ankara*

*ANRW = H. Temporini, ed. Aufstieg und Niedergang der römischen Welt* (Berlin, 1972–)

*AntK = Antike Kunst*

*AntP = Antike Plastik*

*AntW = Antike Welt. Zeitschrift für Archäologie und Kulturgeschichte*

*ArchDelt = Arkaiologikon Deltion*

*ArtB = Art Bulletin*

*ASR = C. Robert et al., Die antiken Sarkophagreliefs* (Berlin, 1890–)

*AttiPontAcc = Atti della Pontificia Accademia romana di archeologia*

*AuChr = Antike und Christentum*

*AZ = Archäologische Zeitung*

*BCH = Bulletin de correspondance hellénique*

*BdA = Bolletino d'arte*

*Belleten = Belleten. Türk tarih kurumu*

*Boreas = Boreas. Münstersche Beiträge zur Archäologie*

*BSA = Annual of the British School at Athens*

*Byzantion = Byzantion. Revue internationale des études byzantines*

*BZ = Byzantinische Zeitschrift*

*CahArch* = *Cahiers archéologiques*

*CRAI* = *Comptes rendus des séances de l'Academie des inscriptions et belles-lettres*

*DOP* = *Dumbarton Oaks Papers*

*EAA* = *Enciclopedia dell'arte antica, classica e orientale* (Rome 1958–84)

*EchOr* = *Echos d'Orient*

*Ephesos* = *Forschungen in Ephesos veröffentlicht vom Österreichischen Archäologischen Institut in Wien*

*FelRav* = *Felix Ravenna*

*Germania* = *Germania. Anzeiger der Römisch-Germanischen Kommission des Deutschen Archäologischen Instituts*

*Helbig4* = W. Helbig, *Führer durch die öffentlichen Sammlungen klassischer Altertümer in Rom*, 4th ed. supervised by H. Speier (Tübingen, 1963–72)

*Hephaistos* = *Hephaistos. Kritische Zeitschrift zur Theorie und Praxis der Archäologie und angrenzenden Wissenschaften*

*Hermes* = *Hermes. Zeitschrift für klassische Philologie*

*Historia* = *Historia. Zeitschrift für alte Geschichte*

*HTR* = *Harvard Theological Review*

*IstArchMüzYill* = *Istanbul Arkeologi Müzerleri Yilligi*

*IstForsch* = *Istanbuler Forschungen*

*IstMitt* = *Istanbuler Mitteilungen*

*JAC* = *Jahrbuch für Antike und Christentum*

*JdI* = *Jahrbuch des Deutschen Archäologischen Instituts*

*JHS* = *Journal of Hellenic Studies*

*JMA* = *Journal of Mediterranean Archaeology*

*JÖBG* = *Jahrbuch der Österreichischen Byzantinischen Gesellschaft*

*JRA* = *Journal of Roman Archaeology*

*JRGZM* = *Jahrbuch des Römisch-germanischen Zentralmuseums, Mainz*

*JRS* = *Journal of Roman Studies*

*JSAH* = *Journal of the Society of Architectural Historians*

*JWarb* = *Journal of the Warburg and Courtald Institutes*

*Klio* = *Klio. Beiträge zur alten Geschichte*

*Latomus* = *Latomus. Revue d'études latines*

*LIMC* = *Lexicon iconographicum mythologiae classicae* (Zurich and Munich, 1974–)

*LTUR* = E. M. Steinby, ed. *Lexicon topographicum urbis romae* (Rome, 1993)

*MAAR* = *Memoirs of the American Academy in Rome*

*Marsyas* = *Marsyas. Studies in the History of Art*

*MdI* = *Mitteilungen des Deutschen Archäologischen Instituts*

*MÉFRA* = *Mélanges de l'École française de Rome, Antiquité*

*Milet* = *Milet. Ergebnisse der Ausgrabungen und Untersuchungen seit dem Jahre 1899*

*Nash* = E. Nash, *Pictorial Dictionary of Ancient Rome,* 2nd ed. (New York, 1968)

*NJbb* = *[Neue] Jahrbücher für Philologie und Pädagogik; Neue Jahrbücher für das klassische Altertum; Neue Jahrbücher für Wissenschaft und Jugendbildung*

*NTDAR* = L. Richardson, *A New Topographical Dictionary of Ancient Rome* (Baltimore, 1992)

*Palladio* = *Palladio. Rivista di storia dell'architettura*

*PBSR* = *Papers of the British School at Rome*

*PCPS* = *Proceedings of the Cambridge Philological Society*

*PECS* = R. Stillwell et al., eds, *Princeton Encyclopedia of Classical Sites* (Princeton, 1976)

*Platner-Ashby* = S. B. Platner and T. Ashby, *A Topographical Dictionary of Ancient Rome* (London, 1929)

*RA* = *Revue archéologique*

*RACrist* = *Rivista di archeologia cristiana*

*RE* = Pauly-Wissowa, *Real-Encyclopädie der klassischen Altertumswissenschaft* (1893–)

*RÉB* = *Revue des études byzantines*

*RepKunstW* = *Repertorium für Kunstwissenschaft*

*RM* = *Mitteilungen des Deutschen Archäologischen Instituts, Römische Abteilung*

*RömQSchr* = *Römische Quartalschrift für christliche Altertumskunde und Kirchengeschichte*

*Roscher* = W. H. Roscher, *Griechischen und römischen Mythologie* (Leipzig, 1897–1902)

*RSGR* = S. Reinach, *Répertoire de la statuaire grecque et romaine* (Paris, 1897–1924)

*TAPA* = *Transactions of the American Philological Association*

*TAPS* = *Transactions of the American Philosophical Society*

*TravMém* = *Travaux et mémoires. Centre de recherche d'histoire et civilisation byzantine, Paris*

*TürkArkDerg* = *Türk arkeoloji dergisi*

*ZfK* = *Zeitschrift für Kirchengeschichte*

# PRIMARY SOURCES: ABBREVIATIONS

*Anth. Gr.* = *The Greek Anthology*, 5 vols., ed. W. R. Paton (New York/ London, 1916–18)

Arethas, *Schol. Arist. Or.* = *Scholia Aristides Orationes* in *Scripta minor*, 2 vols., ed. L. Westerink (Leipzig, 1968–72)

Aristides = *Aelius Aristides Orationes*, ed. W. Dindorf (Leipzig, 1829)

Athenagoras = *Embassy for the Christians. The Ressurection of the Dead.* trans. Joseph Hugh Crehan, S. J. (Westminster, Md. and London, 1956)

Baillet = Jules Baillet, *Inscriptions grecques et latines des tombeaux des rois ou syringes*, 2 vols. (Cairo, 1926)

Buchanan/Davis = *Zosimus: Historia Nova*, trans. James J. Buchanan and Harold T. Davis (San Antonio, 1967)

Cameron/ Herrin = Averil Cameron and Judith Herrin, *Constantinople in the Eighth Century: The Parastaseis Syntomoi Chronikai* (Leiden, 1984)

Niketas Choniates = Nicetas Choniates, *Historia*, 2 vols., ed. Jan Louis van Dieten (Berlin, 1975)

*Chron. Pasch.* = *Chronicon Paschale*, 2 vols., ed. L. Dindorf (Bonn, 1832)

*CIG* = *Corpus inscriptionum graecarum*

*CIL* = *Corpus inscriptionum latinarum*

Constantine the Rhodian = "Description des oeuvres d'art et de l'église des Saints Apôtres de Constantinople, poème en vers iambiques par Constantin le Rhodien" *REG* 9(1896): 32–65

Cosmas Indicopleustes = Cosmas Indicopleustes, *Topographie chrétienne*, text and trans. Wanda Wolska-Conus (Paris, 1968)

Croke = Brian Croke, *The Chronicle of Marcellinus. A Translation and Commentary* (Sydney, 1995)

*CTh* = *The Theodosian Code and Novels and the Sirmondian Constitutions*, ed. and trans. C. Pharr (Princeton, 1952)

*Ek.* = Christodorus of Thebes, *Ekphrasis on the sculpture in the Baths of Zeuxippos* in *Anth.Gr.* I: 59–91

Eusebios, *VC* = Eusebius of Caesarea, *Eusebius, Life of Constantine*, ed.
   and trans. Averil Cameron and Stuart G. Hall (Oxford, 1999)
George Hamartolos = Georgius Monachus, *Chronicon*, 2 vols., ed. C. De
   Boor (Stuttgart, 1978)
Hesychios = Hesychios, *Patria Konstantinopoleos* in Preger
Himerius = *Himerii declamationes et orationes*, ed. Aristides Colonna
   (Rome, 1951)
Ignatius of Smolensk = Ignatius of Smolensk, "Journey to
   Constantinople," in George P. Majeska *Russian Travelers to Constantinople
   in the Fourteenth and Fifteenth Centuries* (Washington, D.C., 1984)
Jeffreys = E. Jeffreys, trans. *The Chronicle of John Malalas* (Melbourne,
   1986)
Jerome, *Chron.* = *Hieronymi Opera Omnia* in Migne *PL* 27
Julian = Flavius Claudius Julianus, *The Works of the Emperor Julian*,
   3 vols., ed. Wilmer Cave Wright (London/New York, 1923)
Kedrenos = Georgius Cedrenus, *Historiarum Compendium*, 2 vols., ed. I.
   Bekker (Bonn, 1838–39)
Anna Komnena = *The Alexiad of the Princess Anna Comnena*, trans.
   Elizabeth Dawes (London, 1928)
*Leo Choirosphaktes* = *Leo Choirosphaktes* (another anacreontic poem of the
   same magistros Leo on the bath built by the emperor Leo in the imperial
   palace), ed. and trans. Paul Magdalino, *DOP42* (1988): 97–118
Leo Gramm. = Leo Grammaticus, *Chronographia*, ed. I. Bekker (Bonn,
   1842)
Michael Glykas = Michael Glycas, *Annales*, ed. B. G. Niebuhr (Bonn,
   1836)
Magoulias = Harry Magoulias, *O City of Byzantium: Annals of Niketas
   Choniates* (Detroit, 1984)
Malalas = John Malalas, *Chronographia*, ed. L. Dindorf (Bonn, 1831)
Constantine Manasses = *Brevium historium metricum* in Migne, *PG* 137
Constantine Manasses, *Ek.* = Constantine Manasses, *Ekphrasis*, ed.
   Sternbach in *Jhb. Oest. arch.* I, V (1902) Bleibatt, col 75.
Mango, *Sources* = Cyril Mango, *Art of the Byzantine Empire AD 324–1453*
   (Englewood Cliffs, N.J., 1976)
Mansi = J. D. Mansi, *Sacrorum conciliorum nova et amplissima collectio*,
   31 vols. (Venice, 1759–98) reprint edition (Paris, 1901–1927)
Marc. Com. = Marcellinus Comes, *Chronicon* in *Chronica minora saec. IV.
   V. VI. VII*, ed. Th. Mommsen (Berlin, 1894)
Menander Rhetor = *Menander Rhetor*, ed. D. A. Russell and N. G.
   Wilson (Oxford, 1981)
Migne, *PG* = J. P. Migne, *Patrologia graeca* (Paris, 1928–36)
Migne, *PL* = J. P. Migne, *Patrologia latina* (Paris, 1879)

Nikephoros Kallistos. = Nicephoras Callistus, *Historia Ecclesiasticae* in Migne, *PG* 145

Niketas Paphlagonias = Niketas Paphlagonias, *Historia Ecclesiasticae* in Migne, *PG* 105

Overbeck, 1868 = J. Overbeck, *Die antiken Schriftquellen zur Geschichte der bildenden Kunst bei den Griechen* (Leipzig, 1868)

George Pachymeres = George Pachymeres, *De Andronico Paleologo* in Migne, *PG* 144

Palladios = Palladius, *The Lausiac History*, ed. Robert T. Meyer (London, 1965)

*Par.* = *Parastaseis syntomoi chronikai*, ed. and trans. Cameron/Herrin

*Patria* = *Patria Konstantinopoleos* in Preger

PLRE = A.H.M. Jones, *Prosopography of the Later Roman Empire*, 3 vols. (Cambridge, 1971)

Pollit, *Greece* = J. J. Pollit, *The Art of Greece, 1400–31 B.C.* (Englewood Cliffs, N.J., 1956)

Pollit, *Rome* = J. J. Pollit, *The Art of Rome, 753 B.C.–337 A.D.* (Englewood Cliffs, N.J., 1966)

Preger = *Scriptores Originum Constantinopolitanarum*, 2 vols., ed. Th. Preger, (Leipzig, 1901–07; reprint, New York, 1975)

Prokop. *De Aed.* = Procopius of Caesarea, *The Buildings*, ed. H. B. Dewing (London/Cambridge, Mass., 1940)

Prokop. *De bello goth.* = *History of the Wars: The Gothic War*, 2 vols., ed. H. B. Dewing (London/Cambridge, Mass., 1953–57)

Prokop. *De bello pers.* = *History of the Wars: The Persian War*, ed. H. B. Dewing (London/Cambridge, Mass., 1953–57)

Prudentius, *Contra Symm.* = *Prudentius*, 2 vols., ed. H. J. Thomson (London/Cambridge, Mass., 1953)

Robert de Clari = Robert de Clari and Geoffroy de Villehardouin in Albert Pauphilet, ed. *Historiens et chroniquers du Moyen Age* (Paris, 1932): 11–186.

Seeck, 1876 = *Notitia Dignitatum*, ed. Otto Seeck (Berlin, 1876)

Seeck, 1919 = *Regesten der Kaiser und Päpste* (Stuttgart, 1919)

Schaff/Wace = Philip Schaff and Henry Wace, Socrates Scholasticus and Sozomen Scholasticus, *Ecclesiastical History* in *A Select Library of Nicene and Post-Nicene Fathers of the Christian Church*, 2 vols. (Grand Rapids, Mich., 1952)

Socrates = Socrates Scholasticus, *Historia Ecclesiastica* in Migne, *PG* 67, 33–841.

Sozomen = Sozomenus Scholasticus, *Historia Ecclesiastica* in Migne, *PG* 67, 33–841.

Suidas = *Suidae Lexikon*, 5 vols., ed. A. Adler (Leipzig, 1928–38)

Symeon Magister = *Theoph. Cont:* 607–760

*Synax. CP* = *Synaxarium Ecclesiae Constantinopolitanae: Propylaeum ad Acta sanctorum Novembris*, ed. H. Delehaye (Brussels, 1902)

Themistios, *Or.* = *Themistii Orationes*, 3 vols., ed. G. Downey and A. F. Norman (Leipzig, 1965)

Theodoret = Theodoret, *Ecclesiastical History* (London, 1843)

Theophanes = Theophanes the Confessor, *Chronographia*, ed. C. de Boor, 2 vols. (Leipzig, 1883)

*Theoph. Cont.* = *Theophanes Continuatus*, ed. I. Bekker (Bonn, 1838)

Turtledove = *The Chronicle of Theophanes*, trans. Harry Turtledove (Philadelphia, 1982)

Tzetzes, *Chil.* = Joannis Tzetzes, *Historiarum variarum Chiliades*, ed. Th. Keissling (Leipzig, 1827)

Unger, 1888 = F. W. Unger, *Quellen der Byzantinishen Kunstgeschichte* (Vienna, 1888)

*Vita Euthymii* = *Vita Euthymii Patriarchae CP*, ed. and trans. Patricia Karlin-Hayter (Bruxelles, 1970)

Whitby/Whitby = *Chronicon Paschale 284–628 A.D.*, trans. Michael Whitby and Mary Whitby (Liverpool, 1989)

Zonaras = Zonaras, *Epitome Historiarum*, 3 vols., ed. M. Pinder and T. Büttner-Wobst (Bonn, 1841–97)

Zosimos = Zosimus, *Historia Nova*, ed. Ludwig Mendelssohn (Leipzig, 1887)

# PREFACE

This study owes its life to the 1979 publication of Ernst Kitzinger's book, *Byzantine Art in the Making, Main Lines of Stylistic Development in the Mediterranean World Second through Seventh Centuries*. Familiar to all students of late antique and early Christian art, Kitzinger's study describes the formation of Byzantine art as an ongoing dialectic between classical, mimetic traditions of representation and those of abstraction. When I first read this book in a graduate seminar shortly after its publication, two questions came to mind. Given the insistence in Kitzinger's work, and in almost all studies of Byzantine art, on the Hellenistic origins of the Byzantine tradition, I wanted to know two things: how did people in the Byzantine period know about antiquity, and what, if anything, did they think about it in a visual sense?

Those two questions led me to the gates of Constantinople and to a study of the antiquities that are the subject of this book. Originally the idea was to identify individual antiquities familiar to the Byzantines with the thought that it would be possible to derive from their visualization a corpus of works that would allow modern readers to know what the Byzantines knew of antiquity. In the way of all such projects, however, the terms of the discussion began to expand almost as soon as I set to work. In making the Constantinopolitan statuary the subject of my dissertation, it quickly became clear that there was a need to identify not only the basic components of the city's ancient holdings, but also the reasons motivating their collection in the first place. From there it became obvious that to reconstruct this context it would be necessary to understand both individual statues, and the discrete gatherings of antiquities that were distributed about the city. Thus, the aims and aspirations of the project have changed, becoming at once tidier and more focused, but at the same time opening up a whole new set of questions and problems, some of which will be addressed here. Specifically, this project aims to reconstruct the great urban displays of Constantinople by identifying the individual contents of the collection, and by addressing the context in which individual monuments came to be displayed. Thus, issues of urbanism, questions of group identity, and ideas of history form part of the larger discussion. At the same time, however, other questions will be dealt with cursorily, if at all. Those who would seek here a discussion of the history of sculptural reuse in preclassical and classical antiquity will do so in vain. Although fascinating in its own right, that subject is not and cannot be the focus of this book. It is far too broad a topic and any attempt to tackle it comprehensively here would be superficial at best. Nor is this a study of the history of collecting. Thus, although issues pertinent to that history are valid for this discussion, they hover in the wings rather than at center stage.

A word on terminology is also in order. Throughout this study, I refer consistently to a Constantinopolitan "collection." There are those who might reasonably disagree with such a designation, considering it a misleading shorthand given the diversity of the city's monuments and the wide chronological span over which they were brought together. I am sympathetic to that concern. At the same time, however, I do think that there is an argument to be made for its use. To be sure, any reference to the Constantinopolitan collection is a kind of abbreviation, but that does not make the designation incorrect any more than are references to the Louvre collections or those of the British Museum, themselves gatherings diverse in content and built up over time. In the case of Constantinople, what legitimates the use of the term is the question of intent. Clearly there was a systematic gathering and display of antiquities for didactic purposes that took place over time in the city. That the endeavor took place by fits and starts does not affect the equation. After the initial gathering of antiquities under Constantine, one of the driving forces behind the selection and placement of statuary was the urge to comment on and complement existing monuments in the group. It is this kind of self-conscious creation that supports the use of the term *collection*.

Finally, and most pleasurably, some words of thanks. Many institutions and individuals have contributed to the development of this project over the years, and it is my great pleasure to be able to acknowledge them here. The support of Bryn Mawr College brackets this project from start to finish. As a graduate student in the History of Art, I was supported generously with fellowships, among them a Giles Whiting Foundation grant for the final dissertation year. More recently I have been given safe harbor as a Research Fellow in the College's Center for Visual Culture. This support, together with funding from the National Endowment for the Humanities and a sabbatical leave from my home institution, Wayne State University, provided me with the time and setting to tackle the completion of this book.

Many other institutions have supported me in the build-up to this final effort, foremost among them the Trustees of Harvard University and the Dumbarton Oaks Research Library and Collection, which granted me a full-year fellowship in 1989–90 and a summer fellowship in 1999. Summer grants from Wayne State University (1998) and the National Endowment for the Humanities (1999) have also advanced this work.

Thanks also to the presses that have allowed me to quote from the translations that are the life blood of this study's documentation: the Australian Association for Byzantine Studies for Elizabeth Jeffreys; Columbia University for Averil Cameron and Judith Herrin; the estate of Harold S. Davis; the Trustees of Harvard University and the Dumbarton Oaks Research Library and Collection for Paul Magdalino and Cyril Mango; Liverpool University Press for Mary Whitby and Michael Whitby; Oxford University Press for Cyril Mango; and Wayne State University Press for Harry Magoulias. Full citations of the authors' translations are found in the primary source list of abbreviations.

Although no one would argue the necessity of scholarly institutions in the support of research and publication, I owe no less a debt to individuals. Among them Dale Kinney merits pride of place. Present at the creation of the dissertation, she has been a keen follower of the project these many years, and her friendship and intellectual engagement have been invaluable. Generous input from Brunilde S. Ridgway and the late Phyllis Bober have also improved this book immeasurably, together with the comments and editing of Kalliope Balatsouka, Franz Alto Bauer, Peter Brown, Terry Carbone, Jaś Elsner, Susan Harvey, Robert Ousterhout, Ilknur Özgen, Beatrice Rehl, and Ann Steiner. No scholarly endeavor is possible without library resources and I am especially grateful to Eileen Markson of the Rhys Carpenter Library at Bryn Mawr and to Irene Vaslef and Mark Zapatka at Dumbarton Oaks for help both on site and at long distance. And, finally, to Brian Madigan, cartographer extraordinaire, επιθυμώ να εκφράσω τις άπειρες και εγκάρδιες ευχαριστίες μου.

# INTRODUCTION

From its foundation in the fourth century by Constantine the Great to its sack by the army of the Fourth Crusade in the thirteenth, the city of Constantinople boasted a collection of ancient statuary unrivaled by any of the great medieval cities east or west. The self-conscious creation of the emperor and his advisors, this collection, composed largely of antiquities of pre-fourth-century manufacture, was created by transporting the sculptured riches of the cities and sanctuaries of the Roman Empire to the newly founded capital.[1] There, in a series of discrete yet interrelated gatherings spread throughout the city's public spaces, the sculptured patrimony of antiquity was marshaled to create a civic identity for the city, describing its history and in so doing explaining its unique right to urban preeminence.

What was initiated by Constantine was continued by his successors in the later fourth, the fifth, and the sixth centuries. Constantine's son, Constantius, appears to have completed a good deal of the initial work set in motion by his father, and over the course of the next two hundred years, additions continued to be made to extant gatherings around the city. With the expansion of the city limits and the concomitant development of new urban spaces under the aegis of the Theodosian house, new ensembles also were formed in the latter decades of the fourth and in the early fifth centuries. It was only in the sixth century, during the reign of Justinian, that the habit of reuse finally died out, by which time hundreds of ancient monuments graced the city's streets and public gathering places.

Although individual pieces inevitably were destroyed, felled by such natural and man-made disasters as fires and earthquakes or the occasional economic exigency that prompted the sacrifice of statuary for coin, the monuments that had been gathered for display in late antiquity stood largely undisturbed throughout the early middle ages.[2] Eventually, however, piecemeal attrition gave way to systematic, wholesale destruction as war replaced accident and imperial cupidity as the force behind the collection's demise. Two cataclysmic events shattered the city and with it the collection of antiquities: the 1204 sack of Constantinople by the army of the Fourth Crusade and the capital's fall to the Ottoman Turks in 1453.

In April 1204 the army of the Fourth Crusade, after having laid siege to and captured Constantinople, spent three days pillaging the city. Churches, palaces, and public buildings were raided, their sacred relics and riches scavenged. Public monuments also were assaulted: statues ancient and Byzantine were toppled, some to be destroyed, others to be carried away. There is no question but that the better part of the Constantinopolitan collection was destroyed at this time. Indeed, the wealth of Byzantine artifacts that first appeared in western Europe in the thirteenth century, among them not only relics and reliquaries but also the Horses of San Marco in Venice, confirm the extent of looting and destruction.[3]

What the Crusaders did not destroy was probably ransacked in May 1453, when the city fell to the Ottoman Turks. As in 1204, the conquering army was granted three full days of looting and slaughter. At the end of this period the central areas of the city are said to have been little more than rubble, a sight reported to have caused the conqueror, Sultan Mehmet II, to weep.[4]

The havoc wrought by these great sacks means that a gathering of antiquities that once numbered in the hundreds can now be counted on the fingers of one hand. In Istanbul only three monuments survive in situ: the Serpent Column of the Platean Tripod (cat. no. 141), the Theodosian Obelisk (cat. no. 138), and the porphyry Column of Constantine (cat. no. 109). Archaeological excavation, limited because of centuries of continuous habitation and the growth of the city in modern times, has expanded upon this picture only slightly. Excavations carried out in and around the city have yielded only a handful of antiquities associated with the collection: four statue bases (cat. nos. 31, 47, 75, 144), a sphinx (cat. no. 104), a dolphin (cat. no. 110), a portrait of Tiberius (cat. no. 116), a bronze goose (cat. no. 132), and the colossal head of a goddess (cat. no. 57).[5]

Although its destruction was virtually complete by the end of the fifteenth century, the Constantinopolitan collection has been the source of speculation and commentary from as early as the sixteenth, when it first began to pique the imagination of renaissance humanists. A general awareness of both the collection and the project for its development emerged as early as 1550 in two separate contexts: the intellectual world of Medicean Florence and the court of François I Valois. Although the Italian and the French interests developed simultaneously, their approaches to the gathering and the contexts in which they discussed it could not have been more different, with the Italians viewing the gathering as an artistic phenomenon and the French considering it under the rubric of philology.

The earliest published reference to Constantine's collecting activity appeared in the 1550 edition of Giorgio Vasari's *Lives of the Artists*:

> Thus, for this and many other reasons, one sees just how low sculpture and with it the other arts had fallen by the time of Constantine. And if anything else were necessary to bring about their final destruction, it was the departure of Constantine from Rome to establish the seat of his Empire at Byzantium by which act he brought to Greece not only all of the best sculptors and artisans of the age, whoever they might have been, but also an infinity of statues and other examples of the most beautiful sculpture.[6]

As the passage makes clear, Vasari used the fact of Constantine's collecting not as a gateway to any larger discussion of Constantinople and its newly massed gathering of statuary, but rather as evidence in a larger argument about the inexorable decline of Rome as an artistic center. Unsurprisingly Vasari viewed the removal of sculpture from Rome to Byzantium as the ultimate proof that Rome as an artistic center was dead, and with it, the artistic standards of the ancients. With the best artisans having been taken east, there was no one left in the city to produce art, and with the best art taken away, there was nothing left to appreciate. Rome had been denuded. Vasari went on to argue that this step was the last in a process of decline that had manifested itself first in a move away from the imitation of nature toward abstraction, and then in the pathetic reuse of ancient materials in building. As such, it was a definable moment that confirmed not only the death of an ancient artistic tradition, but also Vasari's own belief that the arts, like human beings, are born, grow old, and die.[7]

This negative tendency must have been nourished by the chauvinistic attitudes that underpinned his own literary efforts. As is well known, one of Vasari's own aims in the *Lives* was to establish the primacy of a reborn Italian art, and within that broader framework the seminal role of Florentine traditions in the development, promotion, and sustenance of that rebirth.[8] Thus, however lamentable the decay of ancient tradition Vasari documented, the Roman fall from grace was in a perverse sense felicitous as it paved the way for the Florentine reinvention and recovery of antiquity. As the signal event in that process of decline, Constantine's removal of statuary to Constantinople was key in this interpretation of history.

From the point of view of art-historical tradition, Vasari's interest in the Constantinopolitan collection was a dead end. No other art-historical author mentions the collection, and interest in the gathering passes into the realm of historical and philological study from the sixteenth century on. In fact most modern study of the collection is an outgrowth of the interest in Greek philology that occurred in humanist circles across Europe during the Renaissance. In the fifteenth and early sixteenth centuries the arrival of Byzantine scholars in the West in the build up to and wake of the Ottoman conquest accommodated this interest.[9] The presence of such great Byzantine intellects as Manuel Chrysoloras, John Argyropolos, and John Bessarion introduced western Europe not only to the language of classical antiquity, but also to the Byzantine literary traditions that had preserved and commented on the traditions of classical Greece. It was the study of these later texts that opened the door to an awareness of the Constantinopolitan collection, for it was here, in descriptions of the events of Byzantine history and the marvels of the Byzantine capital, that the gathering lived on.

The scholarly interest in Byzantium and its traditions that developed out of the initial philological interests of the humanists was also fueled by contemporary religious and political concerns. The ecclesiastical disputes of the Reformation and the Counter-Reformation made for an interest in the Orthodox church on the part of both religious groups, with Protestants lining up in support of the antipapist Orthodox clergy and Catholics calling for union with the eastern church in a bid to strengthen their ranks in the face of growing religious dissent.[10]

Equally important for the study of the Constantinopolitan antiquities were the alliances that grew out of western Europe's political infighting. The long-standing rivalry between François I Valois (r. 1515–47) and Charles V Hapsburg (r. 1519–58) led the French king to strike a military alliance with the Turkish Sultan, Süleyman the Magnificent (r. 1520–66), which in turn led to a series of diplomatic agreements that allowed the French open access to Constantinople and its environs. François took advantage of the alliance, not only in military terms, but also in cultural ones, sponsoring a series of studies on the seats of classical antiquity that included an overview of Constantinople and its history.[11] The man entrusted with this task was the French humanist Pierre Gilles (1490–1555), who, in accordance with his humanist roots, styled himself Petrus Gyllius for purposes of publication.

Gilles[12] was a contemporary of such noted French humanists as François Rabelais and Guillaume Budé, men who were themselves students of Erasmus and the Italian Humanists. The details of his education are unknown, but it is clear that like his contemporaries, he was not only a crack philologist, but also, by dint of his familiarity with authors such as Aristotle, Aelian, and Pliny, an important scientific observer. In the 1520s and 1530s Gilles wrote several books on natural history, dedicating at least one, a study of Adriatic marine life, to François I.[13] In addition to his scientific publications, he translated, edited, and commented on a variety of Greek texts and produced a Greek–Latin lexicon.[14] His interest in and command of Greek, coupled with his proven ability as a researcher in the natural sciences, must have made him an ideal candidate for a fact-finding mission to the eastern Mediterranean mounted by François I in 1544.

Gilles appears to have been in Constantinople between 1544 and 1547, and again in 1550.[15] Two important studies resulted from these visits: *De Bosporo Thracio libri tres* (Lyon, 1561; Leiden, 1632 and 1635) and *De topographia Constantinopoleos et de illius antiquitatibus libri quatuor* (Lyon, 1561; Leiden, 1661). The latter is Gilles' best-known and most important work. The text describes the city of Constantinople in four books. It is organized by city ward and proceeds from east to west, moving from the tip of the peninsula to the city's defensive land walls in the west. A general account of Constantinople and its setting introduces the project, followed by Book I, an outline of the mythological and historical background of the city that describes the city's mythical foundation under Byzas and its early growth in the late Roman and Byzantine period before ending with a survey of its contemporary layout. Gilles then examines Constantinople district by district and monument by monument, giving an overview of the city in his own day. Book II goes over the same territory in the same order, but with the aim of reconstructing lost monuments, especially those in the ancient city's monumental core. Books III and IV concentrate on the rest of the city, always with the intent of reconstructing the lost monuments of Constantinople. A survey of contemporary Ottoman monuments completes the book.

Gilles' work is interesting, not only because it is the first scholarly account of Constantinople, but also because of his working method. As the first person to map the city and describe it, he applied the lessons of the Greek sources to an interpretation of modern Constantinopolitan topography. His basic source was the fifth-century regionary catalogue the *Notitia Urbis Constantinopolis*,[16] which mapped out the city district by district. Following the scheme of the *Notitia* he observed the architectural and sculptural remains of Constantinople as they survived in the various regions. As befit his humanist bent, his intent was to recover the city's lost antiquities, an aim that set him apart from previous urban commentators, crusaders, and clerics for the most part, whose main interest was in the city's religious sites and their relics.[17]

*De topographia* is not only the first topographical study of Constantinople, it is also the first modern text to include references to the collection of ancient statuary. Naturally, Gilles observed the surviving monuments such as the Serpent Column and the Theodosian Obelisk. More importantly, he also used Byzantine texts to reconstruct destroyed buildings and sculpture. He did so, however, not as an end in itself, but rather as one piece in the larger topographical discussion. Thus, descriptive reporting identifies monuments and their location but offers no interpretation or analysis of either individual statues or the collection as a whole.

The French interest in Byzantium continued into the seventeenth century at the courts of Louis XIII (r. 1610–43) and Louis XIV (r. 1643–1715).[18] As in the sixteenth century, the interest has its origins in philological study. The systematic editing of Byzantine texts was the primary undertaking, and it is in the context of this enterprise that the real founder of Byzantine historical studies emerged, Charles Du Fresne Du Cange. Du Cange was a prodigious editor of and commentator on Byzantine historical texts. He also undertook research and writing on such related subjects as Byzantine history, genealogy, topography, and numismatics, and he is probably best known for his medieval Greek and Latin dictionaries;[19] however, his great work, the *Historia byzantina duplici commentario illustrata* (Paris, 1680), is an important marker in Constantinopolitan studies. The book is written in two parts: *Constantinopolis Christiana* and *De familiis byzantinis*. The former, a topographical study, deals with the city's structure and monuments, while the latter, a genealogical survey of Byzantine aristocratic families, is more purely historical.

Like Gilles, the foundation for Du Cange's interest was philological and historical; however, unlike his predecessor, Du Cange had no thirst for on-site investigation and study. In fact, *Constantinopolis Christiana* is the work of an armchair historian: Du Cange never once visited Constantinople and relied completely on Gilles and the Byzantine sources for his topographical information. Nevertheless the book is not simply a repetition of previous labors. Although largely similar in structure and content, Du Cange does offer new information gleaned from his study and observation of texts. As with Gilles, the interest in antiquities is part of the larger project of reconstructing Constantinopolitan topography and with it the stage set for Byzantine history. The material included is reported on the basis of textual references, and as with his predecessor the aim is descriptive and informational rather than analytical.

Gilles and Du Cange made the observation of antiquities an integral part of the discussion of Constantinopolitan history and topography, and in so doing, they established a precedent for all future topographers and historians.[20] For all their awareness of the material, however, discussion remained largely superficial, as observations regarding ancient monuments were always subsumed into the larger topographical project.

The first person to focus on the collection itself was the German classical scholar Christian Gottfried Heyne. In an article published in 1792, Heyne offered a hand-list of the city's ancient monuments.[21] Like Gilles and Du Cange before him, Heyne mined the Byzantine sources for information regarding antiquities. Unlike his predecessors, who consistently subordinated an interest in ancient statuary to the overall aims of history and topography, Heyne focused exclusively on sculpture. The result was a two-part census of monuments. Part I offered a list of male figures organized first by subject matter (gods, heroes, men of letters) and then by location. Using the same structure, Part II presented the evidence for female figures before concluding with a survey of nonrepresentational monuments such as tripods, obelisks, and columns, which he published together with a list of animals and mythical creatures. This project offered the most systematic and detailed study of the Constantinopolitan antiquities to date; however, for all its focus on the statuary, the work was in some senses identical to that of Gilles and Du Cange in that it remained essentially informational. Heyne expressed no awareness of or interest in the gathering as an actual collection or any desire to consider the motivation behind its conception.

It was only in the nineteenth century that interpretive studies of Constantinopolitan antiquities became of interest. With the development of classical archaeology as a discipline and the concomitant urge to establish a corpus of classical statuary based on recognizable sculptural typologies, scholars began to be interested less in the collection as a list and more in the details of its individual components. The claims made by Byzantine authors for the presence of such famous works of ancient art as the Olympian Zeus (cat. no. 157) or the Aphrodite of Knidos (cat. no. 151) led German scholars such as Otto Jahn and Wilhelm Gurlitt to search for other famous classical statues in the Constantinopolitan corpus with the result that a cottage industry associating individual statues with some of classical antiquity's most renowned works of art sprang up as scholars vied to identify the city's treasures.[22]

A second strand of interpretive study developed in the early twentieth century in the context of anthropology. In a paper presented to the British Folklore Society in the spring of 1924, R. M. Dawkins took up the problem of reception.[23] What interested Dawkins was the afterlife of classical statuary in the postclassical world, and his paper considered the attitudes that medieval observers brought to bear on the remains of antiquity, that is, anything of pre-seventh-century manufacture. On the basis of the textual evidence Dawkins noted a desire on the part of post-seventh-century viewers to interpret sculpture in terms of local, nonclassical history, to attribute to it mystical powers, and to interact physically with statuary, either to prevent wrong-doing on the part of an image or to punish a statue for crimes already committed. Drawing from these observations he concluded that one unifying idea characterized the approach to statuary in the postclassical world, a sense of the power, the knowledge, and the magical skill of the ancients.

Dawkins's use of statuary to explore medieval ideas and attitudes toward antiquity set the stage for Cyril Mango's influential study of classical sculpture in Constantinople.[24] Like Dawkins before him, Mango was interested in the problems of afterlife and reception, and like Dawkins, Mango observed the Byzantine propensity for reinterpretation in ways that had little or nothing to do with classical ways of seeing and thinking. At the same time, however, Mango went beyond Dawkins to observe what he felt were two different ways of seeing: one that preserved classical modes of seeing and thinking, and another defined by the folkloristic reinterpretation of images. It is this interest in perception and afterlife that has informed most recent studies of the Constantinopolitan collection.[25]

For all the awareness of and interest in the Constantinopolitan collection, there has been little desire to study the gathering during the initial period of its formation or to understand it as a consciously developed ensemble. Following the lead of Dawkins, most modern interest has centered on the questions of reception and afterlife. Publication of a series of articles on individual collections within the city has shifted the focus of this discussion somewhat, bringing the contextual and thematic questions associated with the reuse of ancient statuary to the fore.[26] This book is an attempt to continue that discussion by examining the collection in the initial period of its formation, the fourth, fifth, and sixth centuries. Its aim is threefold: to reconstruct its contents from the combined evidence of literary, graphic, and archaeological sources; to identify, describe, and analyze individual displays of statuary in terms of chronological development and topographical distribution; and to examine the collection as a whole, not in the warm glow of the afterlife, but in full light of the late antique ideals and assumptions that informed it. In so doing it also hopes to contribute to a growing body of literature on questions of collecting, reuse, and appropriation.[27] To this end, the book is arranged in two parts. Part I is an overview of the collection's chronological development from its formation in the fourth century under Constantine through the sixth-century reign of Justinian. Part II, a census of works known to have been in Constantinople, provides the documentation for the discussion undertaken in Part I. Arranged alphabetically by location and within each locus by subject matter, the census presents the monuments known to have been in the city together with the pertinent literary, graphic, and archaeological testimonia.

A word on the documentation for the collection is in order. Of the available testimonia, literary sources have proved most valuable in the creation of the census. Surviving monuments are the exception, and archaeological materials virtually nonexistent, with the result that almost all knowledge of the city's antiquities derives from texts. The nature of these sources is varied. For the most part Greek, the texts range in date from the fourth century through the fourteenth and include, in addition to histories, such diverse genres as chronography, panegyric, and ekphrasis. Non-Byzantine sources supplement these texts. Foreign visitors to the capital occasionally left records of the Constantinopolitan marvels, and scattered sources in ancient authors add historical and descriptive dimension to monuments attested by Byzantine writers.

Native or foreign, contemporary or ancient, these accounts are invaluable as the basic documentation for the collection: they have allowed identification of the greater number of antiquities, provided information about their topographical distribution, and offered details about the history and appearance of individual monuments. At the same time, however, the sources are not without their difficulties. Consistency in reporting is unheard of. Some authors make description their primary aim, while others mention antiquities only in passing. In both instances the kinds of observations made are entirely unpredictable. More often than not, ancient and medieval ideas of what constitutes description bear no resemblance to the modern conception of the exercise with the result that observations about the physical properties of a given monument that would form the backbone of any modern account are often only haphazardly observed, if at all. Thus, issues of size, medium, pose, and provenance, details that are useful to the modern observer wishing to reconstruct the actual contents of the collection, often go unremarked, with the result that the identification of individual statues must rely more often than not on the occasional bit of evidence casually observed, a remark about pose, an iconographic aside.

This is the case, for example, with a fifth-century description of one of the major thermal foundations in Constantinople, an ekphrasis on the statuary in the Baths of Zeuxippos by Christodoros of Koptos.[28] As it survives, the ekphrasis describes eighty-one statues or statue groups in the late fifth-century complex. Although some descriptions offer detailed accounts of pose that allow identification with known classical statue types, this kind of observation is rare. Instead, the notion of what constitutes description is defined less by the desire to record physical appearance than by the need to document the perceived sensations of emotion and intellect experienced by the individual figures displayed. The result is that individual passages are often long on interpretation and short on documentation. Consider, for example, the description of the orator Demosthenes (cat. no. 53). In the florid language admired by the age, Christodoros identifies and describes his subject with only passing reference to physical appearance. Instead, the author concentrates on re-creating the orator's mental state by alluding to past historical events. This technique allows Christodoros to infer a state of mind from which the orator's thoughts are duly extrapolated. Far more interpretive than factual, this verse is conceived less as an exercise in physical documentation than as the stirring evocation of a moment. Indeed, the real subject of Christodoros's poetry is not so much observed physical reality as the ephemera of thought and feeling.

Although fascinating in its own right and perfectly consistent with the aims of late antique ekphrasitic writing as a genre, this type of description provides only small pieces of the larger puzzle for most statues. In the case of the Demosthenes, for example, the opening verse describes the figure as standing, and the last suggests in a reference to "brazen silence" that the statue was bronze. These comments are not much to go on, and fuller reconstruction must by necessity depend on outside evidence when available. In this instance, surviving portraits of Demosthenes offer possible examples. In other instances, however, no such comparanda exist and the absence of viable comparative material means that the picture of individual statues will be incomplete.

Texts including detailed physical descriptions can be equally problematic, albeit in different ways. This is the case with Niketas Choniates's thirteenth-century de-scription of a statue of Athena in the Forum of Constantine that was felled during a riot in 1202 (cat. no. 107). In terms of physical observation, Niketas's description is as precise as Christodoros's is vague.[29] From it we understand that a standing bronze figure of Athena stood in the Forum of Constantine. Her right arm was outstretched, and the goddess wore a plumed helmet and long gown girdled with the aegis. Apart from outlining a general iconography, the description also suggests style and date of manufacture. Specifically, reference to the deep folds of drapery and the figure's dilated veins suggests a comparison with fifth-century B.C. classical styles. On the face of it, this is a treasure trove of information, and scholars have responded to it by identifying the figure with any one of a number of fifth-century B.C. statues by the Athenian sculptor Pheidias. It is, however, a clear-cut case of a little knowledge being a dangerous thing, for Niketas observes properties that are generally those of any classical or postclassical representation of Athena with the result that it is impossible to identify this statue with any particular image.

Although problematic in terms of descriptive detail, the texts by Christodoros and Choniates are valuable in terms of clear iconographic definition. Other texts are not so forthcoming. Reinterpretation of classical statuary over the course of the middle ages often resulted in the loss of original identities and the creation of new ones. Thus a statue group of Herakles and the Hesperides sisters (cat. no. 134) in the Hippodrome became a statue of Adam and Eve with the personifications of Famine and Plenty, while a Hekate (cat. no. 159) at the Milion metamorphosed into a representation of Constantine and his two sons, and a statue of Askleipios (cat. no. 16) became a bishop. Recapturing the classical identities of these statues depends almost exclusively on the inclusion of iconographic observation. In the case of the Askleipios statue, for example, identification hinges on a remark that the statue was equipped with one of the characteristic Askleipian attributes, a snake-entwined staff.

The difficulties in working with these texts are hardly insurmountable, but until recently they have been enough to force the question of reliability. Faced with non-modern descriptions and strange identifications, scholars have wondered whether the accounts of the city's antiquities were nothing if not invented.[30] There are, however, various reasons to accept the texts at face value. Now and again external evidence will redeem a text condemned as fiction. This was the case with the Zeux-ippos ekphrasis: only when excavation at the site recovered two bases (cat. nos. 31, 75) inscribed with the names of statues mentioned by Christodoros was the poem accepted as an actual description.

Textual autopsy can also legitimate the sources. One of the common complaints about many of the references is that they postdate the actual existence of sculpture by centuries and therefore cannot accurately account for the city's monuments. Increasingly, however, understanding of the ways in which Byzantine authors drew upon and recycled sources demonstrates the extent to which later texts incorporate the observations of earlier authors, thereby legitimating the claims of later writers. This is the case with the Lausos collection, a gathering of statuary destroyed in 476 and documented only by the tenth-century historian Georgios Kedrenos. Analysis of Kedrenos's text traced his sources to late antique authors contemporary with the installation of the collection, thereby lending his commentary a new legitimacy.[31]

Also crucial in the evaluation of the texts is the question of balance. Although it is increasingly clear that textual evidence should be relied on in the reconstruction of the collection, it is also important to bear in mind that the extant sources are likely to be selective in their reporting. As such they offer only a partial view of the gathering. That said, it should also be borne in mind that that view, lacunary though it may well be, is probably a good reflection of general trends of selection and display as well as ways of thinking about antiquities.

Finally, changes in the scholarly environment of the past half-century have contributed greatly to the ability to mine these sources profitably. Developing understanding of the problems of shifting mentalities from age to age has allowed an appreciation of materials once dismissed as debased on their own terms, and this new consideration in its turn has facilitated an approach to the understanding of the great monuments of Constantinople. Analyses of texts such as the *Parastaseis syntomoi chronikai*, the *Patria Konstantinopoleos*, and Niketas Choniates' *De Signis* have allowed a two-tiered understanding of these documents that at once recognizes their documentary value in terms of the recording of antiquities and respects the idiosyncratic aspects of period interpretation that once condemned these writings to the dust bin.[32]

The documentary materials that are the backbone of the census intersect with a wide range of broader, contextual subjects. As always, topography remains a key issue in the discussion of Constantinopolitan antiquities.[33] The collection was formed in the urban context for purposes of civic definition. Thus issues of location are important to an understanding of the gathering's development and aims. At the same time, however, Constantinopolitan topography is a notoriously difficult study. Because most of the evidence for the city has long since been destroyed, and the surviving texts remain open to interpretation, the city, although reconstructable in broad outline, resists secure description on any detailed level, with the result that some of the discussion will, by necessity, be speculative.

Urbanism also plays a role in the discussion.[34] Enough information is available to envision the city's monumental components and their placement, an exercise that in turn allows an understanding of the design principles at work in the creation of the capital. As in other urban centers in the late classical Mediterranean world, cities such as Rome, Antioch, and Alexandria, an established architectural image formed out of the components of the classical orders shaped the city and in so doing infused it with meaning. The articulation of space in terms of grand public forums and wide, colonnaded boulevards created a generic urban image of power that expressed the city's participation in the ongoing enterprise of empire. At the same time, individual institutions and the buildings that housed them specified the nature of that power. As in all major cities, the major reference point was Rome. Inclusion of such requisite institutions as a Capitolium made that point explicit in Constantinople as it did in any late Roman city with pretensions to urban status. At the same time, the Constantinopolitan approximation to Rome was far more intense than in any other city, a point driven home by the continued and consistent imitation of Roman models in the fourth and fifth centuries.

This evocative setting formed the backdrop for the city's great sculptured display, and, indeed, the deployment of statuary was an aspect of that urbanism. In the Greco-Roman world, sculpture carried a weight and significance that largely has been lost in modern times. All manner of statuary was displayed in public places, and these images were closely associated with a given city's identity and self-image. For example, in the fourth century B.C., the south Italian city of Tarentum commissioned a colossal bronze image of its patron god Herakles from the renowned Greek sculptor Lysippos (cat. no. 21). This statue was displayed on the city's acropolis, and images of it were reproduced on Tarentine coin issues. In a way that is difficult for the modern viewer to appreciate, this statue was the focus of city pride, an emblem of civic virtue. Thus, when Tarentum fell to Rome in the second century B.C., the great prize of conquest was the colossal bronze Herakles that was taken off to the Roman Capitol where it was displayed as booty, an emblem of conquest and Roman might.

The example of the Tarentine Herakles is particularly germane to the experience of Constantinople. Not only was the statue eventually brought to the city, but its own particular history of reuse also throws the questions pertinent to that issue into sharp relief. As with any discussion of statuary, issues of meaning stand at the fore. The case of the Herakles, or any reused monument, poses the question on two levels: the primary meaning vested in the initial creation and installation of a monument, and the secondary meaning accorded it through the history and experience of transport and reinstallation. These questions in turn engage the problem of appropriation, its role in the creation of new meaning and with it a collective civic identity that expresses a larger cultural interest. In the case of Constantinople the gathering of monuments from the cities and sanctuaries of the Roman world stood at the end of a long line of ancient acts of appropriation. As the example of the Tarentine Herakles makes clear, the Roman habit of reuse had a long and distinguished pedigree.[35] Nor was this tradition unique to the Romans. In the Hellenistic age, the Ptolomies adorned their capital at Alexandria with treasures brought from the sacred sites of pharaonic Egypt,[36] and well before these interventions, Xerxes, himself heir to a long tradition of reuse in the territories of Mesopotamia, wrestled statues from the Greeks.[37] In each of these instances, the plunder and subsequent display of statuary in a new setting was a way to express a hierarchical relationship between one population and another. Thus, as in the case of the Tarentine Herakles, Xerxes' removal of statuary from Athens was a visible expression of Persian triumph. In a similar but slightly different vein, the Ptolomaic display of Egyptian antiquities at Alexandria expressed not simply Greek control of Egypt, but also the successors' desire to claim continuity with the legitimating thread of pharaonic tradition.

The display of statuary in Constantinople was also an act of collecting. Thus, although there was a kind of inevitability to the fact of the gathering's existence that derived from and depended on time-honored beliefs about what constituted fit urban decor, the circumstances of the city's foundation and the speed with which it was built made the manner of its decoration unique. Unlike Rome, the city against which Constantinople measured itself and a place where sculpture had been massed for centuries to vivid urban effect, Constantinople saw the initial formation of its public displays in the short span of six years. Further, it is clear that the individual gatherings around the city that took shape in this period were created with an eye not only to internal coherence appropriate to a discrete civic space, but also with a sense of the larger, global project of urban self-definition. Thus, across the city individual collections of sculpture were conceived as parts in a larger whole that would work together to create a larger identity.[38]

Although this panurban impetus was particularly Constantinian and had as its basis the desire to create an urban history through the display of statuary, an urge to maintain continuity with the overall structure of the collection continued into the later phases of the gathering's development. Thus, although the collection of antiquities was more important for Constantine and the foundation of the city, it remained an aspect of urban activity throughout the Theodosian and Justinianic periods. Even though the aims and aspirations that drove the acquisition of monuments were sometimes different for these later emperors than those of Constantine were, there remained throughout the history of the collection's development an awareness of and reference to the initial Constantinian construct. As a result, the Constantinopolitan gathering, unique among the cities of the later Roman world, should be considered a collection in the true sense of the word.

Also important to the understanding of the Constantinopolitan collection are the question of imperial power and the definition of authority current in the late Roman social context.[39] Again and again the sculptural installations of Constantine and Theodosios appeal both implicitly and explicitly to the traditions of the paideia that were so much a part of the Roman élite's habit of self-definition. In so doing they created an image of power that was designed to legitimate the emperor's personal claims and those of his capital city.

Awareness of the religious culture of the later Roman world also is important for an understanding of the collection. With the legalization of Christianity and its embrace as the religion of choice by Constantine, scholars have puzzled over the emperor's apparently contradictory decision to deploy ancient statuary in the decoration of the capital, but the Constantinian decision to reuse monuments from the cities and sanctuaries of the Roman world took place outside the arena of religion. It was a choice made on the basis of civic tradition and symbolic association rather than questions of faith, and, as noted, it was one that drew a great deal of its meaning from the military tradition of conquest and plunder.

The social and religious background against which the collection grew raises the issue of audience. To whom was the Constantinopolitan collection addressed? In the absence of a consistent body of contemporary comment this is a difficult question to answer; however, the evidence of the collection itself suggests that the audience was broad. On the one hand, the repeated appeal to the traditions of the paideia that underpin the collection indicates that in its most profound and detailed sense the gathering was directed very specifically to the full range of assumptions and expectations that made up the mental and emotional world of the empire's ruling élite. On the other hand, the legion of bronze and marble monuments must have been designed to appeal to all people at all levels, dazzling through the sheer force of numbers and material splendor. In both instances, the end result was the same: the construction of an image of power.

Although very much a material presence in the city, the Constantinopolitan collection was first and foremost an intellectual construct. Thus, as much as the historical setting of late antiquity with its particular set of social and religious conditions shaped the development of the collection, so too did an idea of history. In the initial, Constantinian phase of its formation, the gathering grew up around the intersection of history and myth, claiming the latter for the former, to build a unique Constantinopolitan identity that made the city the last link in a chain of destiny that stretched from Troy to Rome. By the sixth century, when the reuse of antiquities was in decline, the mythical underpinnings of the city's identity remained, although the terms by which they were expressed had changed. Together with the protagonists that forged them, the unique set of events that defined the fall of Troy and the foundation of Rome in fourth-century public consciousness became less of an identifying factor by the sixth century as the actors in the great drama of Christian history took their place at center stage. This shift from pagan to Christian points of reference created a new sense of urban identity that for all its apparent novelty was based on the same blurred distinction between history and myth.[40]

In the annals of western thought, the antiquities of Constantinople have achieved something of a mythic status. Because the events of history have transformed the Constantinopolitan collection from a gathering of carefully selected and displayed antiquities that seduced spectators as much by the sheer force of their material splendor as by subject matter and theme into a collection of textural references, the gathering has in effect been dematerialized. The ephemeral nature of the material makes it difficult to imagine its importance and extent. Evidence suggests, however, that among all the activities associated with the foundation of the capital, it was the gathering of antiquities that struck the most profound chord in the hearts and minds of contemporaries. Consider, for example, Jerome's trenchant report on the city's 324 foundation, a single sentence in the compendium of world history known as the *Chronicle*: "Constantinople was enriched with the nudity of almost every other city."[41] It is a curious record. Contrary to expectation, there is no mention of the events surrounding the actual foundation or to the protagonists that shaped them. Instead, without once mentioning statuary or any other type of public monument, Jerome makes the decoration of the city his subject, describing the undertaking in the metaphorical language of the age. Because the remark is one about cities, the reference to "nudity" can only refer to one thing: civic decor, the architecture and sculpture that were the raiment of classical antiquity's great urban centers. As the emphasis on the stripping away of this raiment makes clear, it was the act of collecting in all of its empirewide rapaciousness, rather than the relatively circumscribed event of the foundation, that seized Jerome's imagination and with it that of his contemporaries.

This study is an effort to recognize that fact and in so doing to reclaim that pride of place for this great urban collection. To this end the essays in Part I will attempt to integrate the evidence for statuary in Part II with the larger, conceptual problems through which modern scholarship understands the age. By tradition and necessity, Chapter One will deal with the collection's urban setting, describing the fourth-century development of Constantinople in topographical terms. Chapter Two will set out the evidence for the mechanics of the collection's creation by examining the legal and administrative structure that allowed for the gathering's formation together with attitudes toward public monuments that contributed to the collection's particular development. Chapters Three, Four, and Five will address the Constantinian and Theodosian development of the collection, while Chapter Six will present the evidence for the Justinianic approach to reuse, noting a decline in the interest in antiquities and positing an explanation in changing attitudes toward the Hellenic past.

## ONE

# THE SHAPE OF THE CITY

O N SEPTEMBER 18, 324, WITH THE FINAL DEFEAT AT CHRYSOPOLIS IN BITHYNIA of his co-emperor, son-in-law, and arch-rival, Licinius, Constantine the Great became sole ruler of the Roman Empire for the first time since his proclamation as Caesar nearly twenty years before. This event, momentous in its own right, also had great significance for the urban history of the Roman world. Two months after his victory, on November 8,[1] after having considered and rejected at least one other possible location,[2] the emperor founded the city that would become known as Constantinople on the site of the old Greco-Roman town of Byzantium.[3] With the selection of Byzantium, a town that had been founded in the seventh century B.C., razed by Septimius Severus in the late second century A.D., and then partially rebuilt, Constantine launched one of the greatest projects of urban renewal the ancient world had ever known. City limits were drawn, and an armature of colonnaded streets strung with rich palaces and monumental public gathering places was imposed on Byzantium's extant plan.[4] Six years after this initial burst of building activity, on May 11, 330,[5] the emperor and his attendant court oversaw the city's official dedication in a series of extended ceremonies that took place against the backdrop of a newly outfitted urban core of monumental architecture and sculpture.

The exact nature of this city and its dedication remain one of the open questions of Byzantine historiography. Although the main lines of Constantinopolitan development in the years leading up to the dedication are known, there is much about the fourth-century city that remains conjecture, both with respect to the concrete issues of urban topography and in regard to the ephemera of intent. In large part this state of affairs is because of the fragmentary nature of the surviving evidence. The little that was left of late antique Constantinople at the end of the fifteenth century has been absorbed into the modern fabric of Istanbul long since, and the literary and archaeological sources that allow its reconstruction are often lacunary and opaque, making any but the most general observations regarding topographical development difficult if not impossible.

A similar lack of evidence hampers the assessment of intent. From as early as the fourth century, various claims have been made about Constantinople and its dedication. As befits the age, the discussion was carried on in terms of religion with some claiming the city for Christianity and others for pagan tradition. Shortly after the actual dedication, Eusebios of Caesarea wrote that Constantine had offered the city to "the god of all the martyrs," and by the sixth century when Christianity was the empire's dominant religion, a tradition of Christian dedication had grown up complete with a sense of the ritual associated with the event.[6] At the same time, however, other sources describe the foundation ceremonies in terms of established pagan rite and state that Constantinople was dedicated not to Jesus Christ, but to the traditional Roman deity Tyche/Anthousa.[7]

The competing claims of the medieval historiographers echo throughout modern scholarship, with some arguing the case for Christian dedication and others for the pagan.[8] All discussion has been resolutely partisan in its stance, assuming a correct answer lying on one side of the issue or the other. The purpose of this chapter is to build on and rethink some of the assumptions that drive these investigations to propose a new way of thinking about late antique Constantinople. Reexamination of the main lines of the city's fourth-century topographical development suggests that although religious concerns were indeed a component in determining urban structure, religious allegiance was never meant to be understood as an either/or proposition. Nor was it intended as the defining element in the urban mix. Far more important was the manipulation of site and plan to create a city that expressed not the primacy of a single religion, but a truth far more compelling, that of unrivaled imperial rule.

## THE PRE-CONSTANTINIAN CITY

Byzantium was long in the making. Although the medieval Greek historiographers that record the beginnings of the Constantinian city emphasize the act of creation and in so doing obliterate any real sense of an urban past, the city that was conjured at the foundation and dedication ceremonies came into being on a site that had been occupied for nearly one thousand years. Founded in the early years of the seventh century B.C. on a peninsula jutting into the Sea of Marmora at the confluence of the Golden Horn and the Bosporos, the city had had a long, if unremarkable, history by the time Constantine turned his attention to development of the site. According to tradition, Byzas of Megara, the legendary founder, established a colony around 660 B.C. Over the centuries this foundation developed into a successful center of trade and commerce, deriving its wealth from fishing and, at intermittent points in its history, from customs tariffs levied on ships passing through the Bosporos.[9]

Little is known of this early city's physical disposition. The original Megarian settlement appears to have been located on the high ground at the tip of the peninsula. As it developed, the settlement took hold on the northern side of the peninsula, leaving the southern shore relatively unpopulated. Temples dedicated to Artemis, Aphrodite, and Apollo stood on the acropolis together with their dependent buildings, and there was a temple to Poseidon at the point. Two harbors, port facilities on the Golden Horn, nestled at its foot. A military parade ground, the Strategeion, stood to the west of the acropolis cluster and probably served as the city's original forum. There were also theaters, baths, and residential quarters on the hills sloping down to the sea. A fortification wall ran from the Golden Horn on the north across the promontory's hilly terrain before turning and terminating at the southeastern end of the promontory on the Marmora shore.[10]

Although prosperous, Byzantium was never distinguished in any military or cultural sense, and its political development was largely unremarkable for the better part of its early history. This situation changed in the last decade of the second century A.D. when the city found itself embroiled in a civil war between the emperor Septimius Severus and a rival imperial claimant, Piscennius Niger. At the time of the dispute, Byzantium came out in support of Piscennius. Thus, after Septimius defeated and killed the would-be usurper, the town was duly punished. From 193 to sometime in 195 or 196, the emperor laid siege to Byzantium. When the city eventually fell, he not only executed those who had sided with the usurper, but also destroyed the place outright, burning it and razing its walls.

Though radical, the destruction of Byzantium gave way to a monumental urban renewal (Figures 1 and 2). After stripping the city of its ancient name and identifying it with a new title, Colonia Antonina, in honor of his own dynastic line, Septimius Severus began the process of rebuilding, not, as might have been expected, with the reconstruction of the city walls, which appear to have been left in their ruined state, but rather with a development of an area to the south and west of the old acropolis that included five monumental components: colonnaded streets, or emboloi, a forum, or agora, a basilican complex, a public bath, and a circus, or hippodrome.[11]

The colonnaded streets formed the backbone of the new development. Two avenues were built, one at the western and another at the southern limit of the

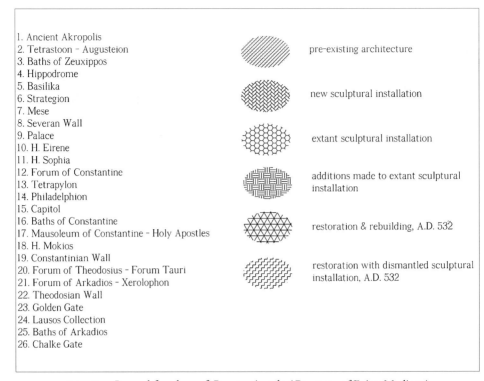

1. Ancient Akropolis
2. Tetrastoon - Augusteion
3. Baths of Zeuxippos
4. Hippodrome
5. Basilika
6. Strategion
7. Mese
8. Severan Wall
9. Palace
10. H. Eirene
11. H. Sophia
12. Forum of Constantine
13. Tetrapylon
14. Philadelphion
15. Capitol
16. Baths of Constantine
17. Mausoleum of Constantine - Holy Apostles
18. H. Mokios
19. Constantinian Wall
20. Forum of Theodosius - Forum Tauri
21. Forum of Arkadios - Xerolophon
22. Theodosian Wall
23. Golden Gate
24. Lausos Collection
25. Baths of Arkadios
26. Chalke Gate

pre-existing architecture

new sculptural installation

extant sculptural installation

additions made to extant sculptural installation

restoration & rebuilding, A.D. 532

restoration with dismantled sculptural installation, A.D. 532

FIGURE 1: Legend for plans of Constantinople (Courtesy of Brian Madigan)

archaic city. The western avenue ran uphill from a point midway above the shore of the Golden Horn toward the center of the peninsula where it met with the second avenue, a shorter road that ran on an east–west trajectory at the southern edge of the old city settlement. A third street, the Mese, formed at the confluence of these roads and ran west to the city wall.[12]

Within this armature, the centerpiece of the Severan restoration was the forum known as the Tetrastoon.[13] Built between the western and southern emboloi on a previously undeveloped track of land at the city's southwestern edge, the Tetrastoon was a large rectangular space surrounded on four sides by the stoas, or porticoes, that gave it its name. Other buildings clustered around this complex. To the west, on the other side of the embolos that ran north to the Golden Horn, stood another portico-enframed complex, the Basilika.[14] An imperial bath, known as the Zeuxippos,[15] rose on the south side of the complex, while the last component of the Severan redevelopment project, a circus or hippodrome,[16] stood next to the Zeuxippos on its southwest side.

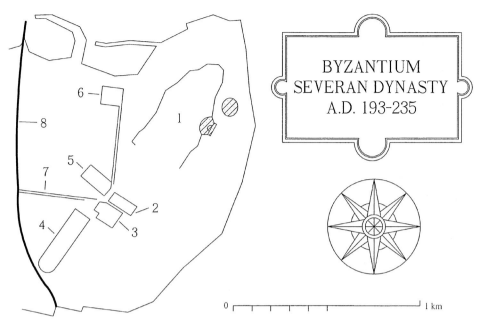

FIGURE 2: Byzantium under the Severan dynasty (Courtesy of Brian Madigan)

For reasons that are unclear, the Severan restoration was never completed. At least two of the five major projects, the Hippodrome and the Baths of Zeuxippos, remained unfinished at the time of the emperor's death in 211, and whether through lack of interest or some more practical reason like finance, Septimius's heirs abandoned the job. Nevertheless, even in its unfulfilled state, the project must have transformed the city. To begin with, construction of these buildings created a new urban appendage the monumentality and lavishness of which must have contrasted sharply with the narrow streets, confined spaces, and more modest buildings of the pre-Severan city. Although Constantinople doubtless remained small by comparison to Rome, the sheer scale of the Tetrastoon, with its unencumbered open space and enveloping marble peristyle, must have been startling in the context of the city's established architectural environment. Further, the controlled, systematic aspect of these spaces together with the institutions they housed are likely to have reframed the urban experience. Popular institutions like the public baths and the circus would have created new focal points for urban activity on the city's western edge that would have drawn the populace out of the archaic center. Finally, the nature of these institutions would have been transformative. In providing Byzantium with this complex of imperially sponsored foundations, the Severans dowered the city with spaces and institutions that were essentially Roman and, as such, alien to the city's Greek experience.

Both the building typologies and the lavish nature of the construction in Severan Byzantium were in line with projects undertaken during this period in other cities of the Roman world. Colonnaded streets and plazas coupled with imposing public works projects such as baths and circuses characterized the revitalization of cities in the eastern Mediterranean and North Africa in the second and third centuries. Centers such as Ephesos and Miletos in Asia Minor, or Septimius's own home town of Leptis Magna in North Africa, saw similar types of development transform their urban spaces.[17] The distinctly public nature of such enterprises created new centers for human interaction on a grand scale. Further, the similarity in design and material from one city to the next engendered a sense of cultural cohesion that described shared participation in an urban society under the aegis of imperial Rome.[18] Thus, in providing Byzantium with its new set of monumental forms, Septimius brought the city into the orbit of Rome, at once forgiving and obliterating the memory of civil insurrection. In short, through construction, urban development, and the concomitant introduction of imperial institutions, Septimius Severus redefined Byzantium as a typical Roman city, loyal to the emperor and his cause.

This then was the city that captured Constantine's imagination: an ancient settlement with a modern face that claimed participation in the traditions and destiny of imperial Rome through the very stuff of its building material. Apart from the obvious reasons of situation and strategy that made Byzantium a desirable setting for the emperor's new foundation, this built environment must have been part of the city's great appeal. Even in its incomplete state, it would have given the city the look of *romanitas*, that is of the common culture of the Roman imperial ideal, so essential for any urban center with the pretensions to grandeur implied by imperial patronage. What Byzantium offered was a springboard for the implementation of Constantine's urban vision.

## THE CONSTANTINIAN CITY

The building activity attendant upon the foundation and dedication of Constantinople suggests the nature of that vision (see Figures 1–3). In the years between 324 and 330, a flurry of construction activity transformed Severan Byzantium. The emperor's first undertaking was to define the city limit by walking the perimeter, lance in hand. This act, a traditional *limitatio* of the type associated with Roman foundation

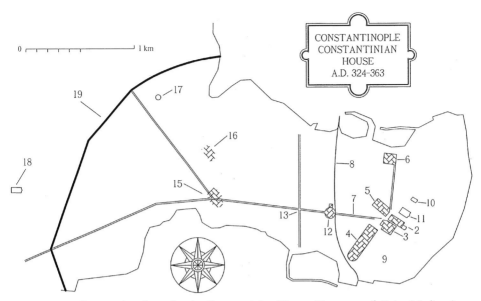

FIGURE 3: Constantinople under the Constantinian House (Courtesy of Brian Madigan)

rituals, extended the city's western boundary nearly three kilometers beyond the limit of the old wall almost quadrupling the urban territory.[19] In the aftermath of this event and in keeping with the traditional protocol of city foundations, it is likely that divinations were made and a horoscope cast.[20] These rituals set the stage for construction of the Constantinian defensive circuit, a project that appears to have both renewed and extended the city's existing fortifications by restoring the extant sea walls along the Golden Horn and Propontis to the point at which they joined the new construction that in turn plugged into the land wall traveling in an arc across the peninsula.[21]

With the city girded, the emperor turned his attention to the adornment of its monumental core, focusing first on the potential of the languishing Severan projects. The monumental development that included the emboloi, the Tetrastoon, the Basilika, the Baths of Zeuxippos, and the Hippodrome became the cornerstone of the Constantinian plan. The extant streets and buildings were either completed or remodeled, thereby providing the city with a magnificent new center in and around which the institutions of the Constantinian city might coalesce.

As in the Severan city, the framework for this development was the series of monumental colonnaded streets. First among these arteries was the Mese, which was probably maintained in its Severan form, as were the avenue's shorter branches, its eastern extension running along the southern edge of the Tetrastoon and its northern fork leading to the Strategeion. In recognition of its importance, Constantine marked the point at which these various avenues began with a large four-way arch or tetrapylon, the Milion.[22]

The streets spreading out from the Milion created the framework around and along which the city developed. Standing at the western terminus of the Mese and bounded by the lesser emboloi to the south and west, the Severan Tetrastoon, rededicated as the Augusteion in honor of the emperor's mother, the Augusta Helena, stood at the heart of the Constantinian refurbishing. The extent to which Constantine and his planners actually remodeled the space remains unclear. The addition of a silver honorific statue of the Augusta gave the place its name.[23] Beyond this addition, however, there is no mention of any peristyle remodeling or modification of the building's footprint. Whether maintained in its Severan form or adjusted to Constantinian needs, the forum's scale remained grand. Exact dimensions are not known, and estimates range between 17.500 and 3.500 square meters.[24]

This imposing space functioned as a place of public assembly and ceremonial display.[25] Its locus at the heart of the city made the forum a place of convergence, a true civic center where the community as a whole could meet, interact, and exchange information.

To the west of the Augusteion, separated from the forum by the embolos running north from the Milion, stood the complex known as the Basilika.[26] Like the Augusteion, the Basilika was an inheritance from the Severan era. Designed as a rectangular peristyle court, it accommodated a variety of institutions, a public library, the university, and a law court among them. Two temples erected by Constantine also stood in the complex, one dedicated to Rhea/Kybele, the other to Tyche/Fortuna. These buildings may have stood on the eastern side of the courtyard,[27] framing the doorway that led out of the complex, down a flight of steps, and across the road into the Augusteion itself.

The Basilika was only one of several complexes to develop around the nodal point of the Augusteion. A second important group grew up to the south, the triad comprised of the Hippodrome, the imperial palace, and the Baths of Zeuxippos. The Hippodrome[28] (Figure 4) stood south and west of the forum. Although it may have been in use from as early as the second century, the building was finished only in the fourth century with the extension of the cavea. The Hippodrome followed the standard circus form, which stemmed ultimately from that of the Circus Maximus in Rome. Characteristic features included a U-shape with starting gates (*carceres*) at one end and a central barrier (*euripus* or *spina*)[29] that bisected the track along its central axis.

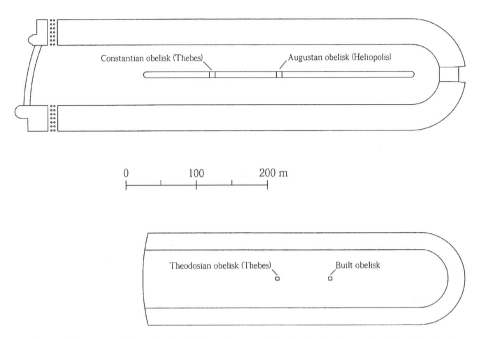

Circus Maximus in Rome (top) and Hippodrome in Constantinople (bottom), each oriented with adjacent palace at top

FIGURE 4: Comparative plans of the Hippodrome, Constantinople and the Circus Maximus, Rome (Courtesy of Brian Madigan)

In conjunction with the completion of the Hippodrome, Constantine began work on construction of the imperial palace.[30] The complex abutted the circus on its south side and was given a direct link to the racetrack through the kathisma or imperial box. The palace spread across the southern flank of the peninsula in a series of terraced gardens and pavilions that spilled down the sloping terrain to the Sea of Marmora. Its major ceremonial entrance, the Chalke Gate, on the northeast side of the complex, stood at the terminus of the road running to the south of the Augusteion, the Regia.

The third building in this group, the Baths of Zeuxippos[31] (Figure 5), stood between the Hippodrome and the palace immediately south of the Augusteion. Architecturally the Zeuxippos appears to have been a bath-gymnasium. Common as a bath type in western Asia Minor from the second century A.D., the characteristic features of this type included an integration of vaulted bathing chambers with open, rectangular exercise grounds.[32] Surrounded by the palace on two sides and Hippodrome dependencies on a third, the main entrance to the complex was from the Regia. At the time of the Constantinian development, the building must have been substantially complete in terms of structure, and Constantine's main contribution to its revitalization appears to have been its ornamentation with polychrome marbles and sculpture.[33]

Knowledge of the city in the area to the north of the Augusteion is less complete. The avenue running north from the Milion led to the military parade ground known as the Strategeion[34] that stood on a level, terraced area just above the harbors on the Golden Horn. Little is known of the Strategeion's appearance beyond the fact that it was an open, rectangular space suitable for military exercises. Its placement at the terminus of the northern avenue at once brought the area into the orbit of the city center but also kept it at some remove. Far more crucial was its ready access to the port facilities below it.

East of the Strategeion and north of the Augusteion lay the city's oldest section, the acropolis of Byzantium. Numerous temples, which appear to have been abandoned in the fourth century, are attested; however, the area was not a religious precinct as such. Theaters and other urban buildings also are mentioned, but there is no evidence for the location of individual buildings or the plan into which they were integrated.[35] It was in this area that Byzantium's first Christian ecclesiastical foundations were established, probably in a residential neighborhood. Constantine enlarged one of the foundations, possibly a domus ecclesia, to create the city's first cathedral, Hagia Eirene.[36] Consecrated by the bishop of Constantinople in 337, the appearance of this early church is not known, although it was likely to have been a basilica.

## THE LATE ANTIQUE URBAN CONTEXT

The Constantinian manipulations of the extant Severan buildings created a monumental set of interrelated yet independent public spaces that responded to and defined urban life in its most public aspects. It did so in two complementary ways. On the one hand, the creation of the monumental street system and the placement of buildings within it worked on a purely pragmatic level to provide the kinds of spaces and settings that would accommodate the institutions of Roman urban life. On the other hand, the carefully mapped design and the painstaking detailing of this armature drew deliberately on the traditions of late Roman visual culture to go beyond the mere facilitation of the practical to shape an idea of urban life that was itself expressive of the relationship between city and empire.

The overall planning of Constantinople worked to create a set of monumental public spaces linked by a series of wide, easily navigable avenues that accommodated

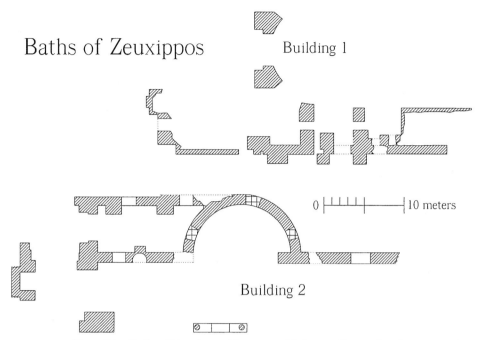

FIGURE 5: Plan of the Baths of Zeuxippos (Courtesy of Brian Madigan, after Casson, 1929)

the requisite urban institutions and facilitated movement within the city. Apart from these practical aspects of accommodation, access, and crowd control, however, it was the underlying choice of institutions and the concomitant manipulation of design traditions that gave Constantinople its particular urban character. To wit, the concentration of no less than five major imperial foundations, the Augusteion, the Basilika, the Hippodrome, the Great Palace, and the Baths, in a relatively confined area signaled the elaboration of a Roman imperial city.[37] Like Septimius Severus before him, Constantine created a city that downplayed indigenous Greek tradition in favor of the overarching magnificence of Rome, its empire, and its institutions.

Nowhere is this appeal to *romanitas* more evident than in the elaboration of the complex accommodating the Baths of Zeuxippos, the Hippodrome, and the Great Palace. Each of these institutions was the manifestation of a singularly Roman mentality. Great thermal foundations, an expression of imperial beneficence and favor toward a given population, were a uniquely Roman institution that had been transplanted from the city of Rome to the outlying territories of the empire. So too was the phenomenon of the circus and its associated palace, a combination evident in the Tetrarchic capitals of the Roman world that derived ultimately from the relationship

27

between the Circus Maximus and the imperial residence at Rome.[38] Finally, as the name suggests, the Milion, the great tetrapylon marking the intersection of the city's major thoroughfares, was conceived on the model of the Roman *miliarum aureum*,[39] and like it was meant to mark the start of the highways radiating from the city to points across the empire. Thus at the same time as it marked and made comprehensible the confluence of city streets and in so doing channeled the comings and goings of urban visitors, the Milion worked symbolically, directing the imagination beyond the city itself, to evoke the Roman world as a whole and the city's place within it.

The image of *romanitas* conjured by the city's institutions and monuments was at once general and specific. On the one hand, the outfitting of the city with places such as the Hippodrome and the Zeuxippos was of a piece with large-scale development in other cities of the Roman world, and it created a sense of participation in the Roman imperial experience. On the other hand, the specific conjunction of Hippodrome and Palace or the introduction of a monument such as the Milion created a more specifically Roman link that bound Constantinople directly and intimately to the city of Rome in ways not common to other cities of the Empire.

Whether general or specific, it was the visual language of late Roman architecture, particularly the prominent use of trabeated building systems made of rich, elaborately carved marbles, that gave ultimate expression to the concept of *romanitas*. Synonymous with the splendor and grandeur of the east, this architectural style was co-opted for imperial use in the second and third centuries when rising columnar facades and colonnaded avenues became the norm in urban design and the means by which the cities of the Roman world, increasingly under the sway of imperial authority, forsook their sense of autonomy to express, instead, an idea of participation in the enterprise of empire.

The most visible means by which this image was projected was the colonnaded street. In cities such as Palmyra, Gerasa, and Antioch in the east, as well as Timgad and Leptis Magna in North Africa, the embolos became the prime expression of *romanitas*.[40] Deployment of this motif in the armature of Constantinople was thus a deliberate appeal to and expression of this idea. The grand colonnaded avenues radiating out from the Milion would have functioned in a variety of ways. Formally these emboloi would have acted as a kind of connective tissue that bound the city together by creating a single monumental environment that directed movement and controlled access to individual buildings and public spaces. In turn, this environment, with its rich display of marbles and overwhelming sense of control, was an expression of power.[41] Like the Milion, which conjured images of Rome and empire, the architecture of the colonnade placed the seal of *romanitas* on the city and its inhabitants.

The redevelopment of the old city center set the stage for the city's westward expansion. With the construction of the new defensive wall, Constantine and his planners brought heretofore undeveloped areas into the urban territory, thereby enlarging the space available for building and development. The resulting expansion took place around an armature of streets and public spaces that grew up around the western extension of the Mese. The avenue ran west in a straight line from the now obsolete Severan fortification wall. About halfway between the old defensive wall and the new, it split, one arm veering north and west to connect with the Adrianople road, the other carrying on to the southwest where it met the Via Egnatia. A second, north-south avenue connecting the Propontis with the shores above the Golden Horn crossed the Mese at right angles at the midpoint between the Severan and Constantinian fortifications. In a manner similar to the Milion at the city center, a tetrapylon arch, the Chalkoun, or Bronze Tetrapylon, marked the intersection. Finally, a rectangular street grid set down in defiance of the peninsula's irregular terrain was marked out within the larger framework of the emboloi.[42]

Construction of the street system established a context for urban growth. The first and most important development along the extended artery of the Mese was the Forum of Constantine.[43] Although the Forum has long since been destroyed, its location is well known as its centerpiece, a porphyry honorific column known as the Column of Constantine (cat. no. 109), survives as modern Istanbul's Çemberlitaş. The Column and the forum over which it rose straddled the Mese at the point immediately to the west of its intersection with the old city wall.

The new space around the column was round. A pair of two-story, semicircular colonnades in Proconnesian marble opened out from the Mese just beyond the point where it passed through the old wall to frame the space north and south. Triumphal arches marked the entrance to the plaza on its east and west sides. A Senate House stood at the center of the north colonnade, a nymphaeum at the south. Somewhere near the southeast area of the Forum was the Praetorium, or courthouse, to which a prison was attached.[44]

The distinguishing feature of the Forum was its round shape. Although unusual among the public spaces of Constantinople, rounded public spaces delimited by colonnades were familiar from the cities of the Empire. As with tetrapyla, round forums were a means of marking important intersections. This was the case at both

Bosra and Gerasa where circular forums were inserted into the extant city plan in the second century and later articulated the intersection of the cities' cardo and decumanus. In both instances, further addition of imposing tetrapyla at the center of these newly articulated intersections created a focal point that not only anchored and aggrandized these spaces, but also lent them a decorative and ceremonial air.[45]

Rounded and oval shapes could also mask planning difficulties in that circular forms gave architects and planners the means to join irregular elements in seemingly regular ways. At Bosra,[46] for example, an oval forum across the main axis of the road leading from the west gate to the center of the city disguised a seven-degree angle that the decumanus was forced to take. Similar tactics were used in the development of the plan of Gerasa.[47] This capacity made such shapes ideal for linking disparate areas of a city that it might not otherwise be possible to join. Such was the case at Constantinople, where the Forum of Constantine stood at the juncture of the old city and the new. Built around the city's main thoroughfare, the space represented an elegant and practical solution to the problem of grafting the old city onto the new. The Forum also marked progress through the city. For those moving east toward the center, the space was a gateway into the old city. For those moving west, it signaled arrival in the city's new territories. In this sense the place served as a hinge between old and new.[48]

The grandiose development of the Forum was a function not only of location, but also of use. The place is described as a forum or agora, which suggests a commercial function.[49] This activity is borne out by the development around the Forum rather than in it: the Artopoleion, or Bread Market, grew up around the Mese immediately to the west and the silversmith's quarter was along the avenue to the east. It was not, however, this commercial focus that lent the Forum its distinctive look, but rather, Constantine's decision to make the space the site of a Constantinopolitan Senate House and, as such, a locus of government and its rituals. The building stood at the center of the colonnade on the north side of the Forum. Four porphyry columns supported a rising entablature and pediment. The contrast between the dark stone of the columns and the lighter Proconnesian marble of the Forum's encircling colonnade at once defined the entrance and created a sense of visual unity with the great column at the Forum's center. The building itself was a centrally planned domed structure. The combination of a classical, trabeated porch façade with domed interior structure made the building a miniature version of the Roman Pantheon.[50]

Although the building itself must have been impressive, it was the institution of the Senate that called for this type of grandiose architectural development and defined the place within the city. Founded by Constantine,[51] the Constantinopolitan Senate was in some respects the final manifestation of a series of reforms enacted by the emperor that were designed to refortify the Senate as an institution after its all but virtual suppression under Diocletian. Although most of the Constantinian legislation was directed at the Roman Senate, the institution of a Constantinopolitan body, albeit at a lesser rank than that of the Roman, was a radical move in and of itself. The creation of a second body was unprecedented: No other city in the Empire was accorded such an honor, and the move set Constantinople apart, although the function of the Senate was largely an advisory and ceremonial one. Given the importance of this act, the location of the Constantinopolitan Senate was no idle matter. Logically and logistically the building probably should have been erected in the old Severan core near the palace and the Augusteion. Its placement in the new Forum and the concomitant aggrandizement of that space must therefore have been in an effort to establish a new ceremonial center that would pull the city west.

Monumental development of the area around the bifurcation of the Mese underscored the emphasis on the city's western growth. Constantine oversaw two projects at this point, the Capitol, a temple dedicated to the triad of Roman state gods, Jupiter, Juno, and Minerva, and the Philadelphion. The Capitol stood on the tract of land between the two branches of the Mese. Its design was probably similar to those of other Capitoline temples in cities throughout the Empire: that of the traditional Roman temple with a high podium with a single flight of steps on one side leading up to a portico that both shaded and articulated the entrance to the inner chamber.[52]

The exact location and nature of the Philadelphion is not fully understood.[53] Technically speaking, it was not a public square, but rather a lavishly decorated stretch of the Mese that appears to have been situated in the area immediately to the east of the bifurcation. This segment of the street may well have opened up into a triangular plaza on the ground in front of the Capitol itself. The purpose behind this decorative articulation, which included porphyry columns and statuary, was doubtless to signal the approach to the Capitol.[54]

Inclusion of a Capitoline temple in the fourth-century city plan was a developmental and institutional choice consistent with Roman urban tradition.[55] Since the earliest days of imperial expansion, incorporation of a Capitol, the prime expression of the State, into the design of the Empire's cities was a means of expressing the binding relationship between Rome and its dependant territories. Capitoline temples generally stood at the heart of the city in the Forum and were an expression of the presence of the Roman state in the life of the local polity. For any city with pretensions to urban stature, they were one of the ultimate expressions of *romanitas*.

Construction of the Philadelphion and the Capitol represent the last major Constantinian developments along the Mese. Thereafter the focus of the emperor's building activity shifted north and west to the territory bordering on the newly established city limit where he established the site of and began construction on the last major monument to occupy his imagination, his own mausoleum, a centrally planned domed structure that was either circular or octagonal in form with radiating niches for the placement of sarcophagi. This structure stood in the middle of a peristyle, and the whole complex rose just to the east of the Mese's northern extension.[56] Thus, although its location near the wall distanced the mausoleum from the city center, proximity to the main artery offered access to the site and drew it into the city's orbit.

The inclusion of the mausoleum within the city walls was unusual. Only in exceptional cases was burial permitted within the walls of a city in the Roman world. The prime example of such an exception was the Mausoleum of Augustus in Rome, and it is possible that in the placement of his own mausoleum Constantine was imitating his predecessor.[57]

The comparatively restricted development of the western territory's monumental aspect was a function of two circumstances: the undeveloped nature of the terrain and use. Unlike the city center, which was the locus of public life, the area to the west of the Forum of Constantine was dedicated largely to private activity. Thus, development of the area around the armature that spread west from the Forum of Constantine appears to have been largely residential.[58] The nature of the housing is, however, conjecture.[59] Posh, single-family residences probably dominated the development; although there may also have been apartment buildings to accommodate lower income families. In addition to housing, institutions sprang up in these areas that would accommodate the rituals of daily life, fountains and privately owned and operated bathing establishments prime among them.

Although limited, the public projects that were undertaken in the new territories were of a piece with those in the old city. Like them, they were dedicated to shaping and articulating public space in a way that summoned an image of *romanitas*. Institutions such as the Senate and the Capitol fostered the sense in symbolic terms, while the very stuff of the architecture, its richly carved marbles and classical forms prevailing, expressed the sense of unity with empire in its most concrete aspect.

## SPATIAL CONTENT AND ORGANIZATION

Six years after the initial perimeter walk that set the limits of the new city's development, a lengthy *processus* from Rome to Constantinople inaugurated the events associated with the 330 dedication. In Constantinople itself, ceremonies that are said to have unfolded over the course of forty days took place against the backdrop of the newly restored and expanded city.[60] Cut by Constantine and his planners from the cloth of Greco-Roman antiquity, that city contained, in ways ephemeral and concrete, all of the elements of late classical urban design. At its creation, the rites and ceremonies that tailored the urban fabric were those associated with Roman foundations and dedications from time immemorial. In the years that followed, the institutions and administrative structures that organized life within this polity were unarguably Roman. So too were the design principles that underpinned the larger network of the city's streets and public spaces and the individual buildings within it. As the fifth-century historian Sozomen commented, Constantinople was provided with all of the "requisite edifices."[61] In this sense then, it was no different than any late Roman city with any claim to prominence or hope for preeminence.

For all of its conventionality, Constantinople was, however, a city like no other. At the same instant it drew meaning from and participated in the traditions of late Roman urban design, it also manipulated those traditions in ways that were unfamiliar. The development of the Augusteion is a case in point. Transformation of the Tetrastoon created a magnificent colonnaded space in the grand manner of Roman civic forums, and location at the heart of the new city's development further underscored the traditional sense. Yet appearances and placement aside, the Augusteion was unlike any forum in the Mediterranean world. Befitting their function as a civic center, most Roman forums were dedicated to mixed use and, as a result, were home to a variety of public institutions. Buildings dedicated to commercial, civic, and religious activities stood cheek by jowl, accommodating the various needs of Roman communal living. At Constantinople, however, there is no evidence for the variety of building or the rich layering of activity attendant upon the diversity of building function seen in other cities. Instead, the Augusteion seems to have been an open, almost neutral point of convergence outside of which a series of independently framed single-use complexes accommodating the variety of civic, commercial, and religious functions grew up. This development constituted a variation on a traditional theme of urban space that at once depended on but deviated from tradition.

The patronage and placement of religious foundations appears to reflect a similarly split sensibility. On the one hand, the emperor's support of such institutions continued a tradition of imperial patronage as old as the empire itself. On the other hand, the choice of institutions and their placement within the city represented a departure from these same traditions.[62]

Beginning with Augustus, it was the pious duty of emperors to endow cities with religious foundations. Constantine was no exception and no less than four institutions are associated with his development of the city: the two temples in the Basilika, the Capitol, and the church of Hagia Eirene. Together with the Capitol, the temples dedicated to Tyche/Fortuna and Rhea/Cybele represented the traditional type of Roman state religious patronage in that they were both temples dedicated to deities associated with the divine destiny of the state.[63] Unprecedented, however, was the inclusion of a Christian religious foundation, the church of Hagia Eirene, in the mix.

Although Constantine had shown himself an active patron of church-building in cities such as Rome and Jerusalem in the years leading up to and including the period of the development of Constantinople, his incorporation of Christian buildings into these centers was substantially different from that of Constantinople. In each of these places church-building was undertaken in well-established urban centers with strong historic identity. This circumstance meant that church-building responded not only to the needs of Christian cult, but also to the particular history of the place and the need to establish a Christian identity within a preexisting structure. In Rome, for example, construction of the Lateran basilica on the grounds of the Sessorian Palace, an imperial property with strong associations with the imperial guard, was not, as once thought, a bid to define a Christian presence in the city by building unobtrusively on its outskirts, but rather an aggressive act of architectural appropriation that was intended to obliterate the memory of an imperial guard that had been allied with Constantine's rival Maxentius.[64] Likewise, in Jerusalem, construction of the church of the Holy Sepulchre on the alleged site of Christ's burial and resurrection was one of a series of building events designed to mark sites sacred to Christian history and in so doing sacralize the region.

Each of these events treated Christian building as a separate, defining activity designed to reshape the urban landscape and with it civic sentiment. By contrast, the construction of Hagia Eirene was part of a much larger building campaign that included simultaneously the erection and decoration of pagan temples. As such, the project was unique as it established Christianity not as an overwhelmingly triumphant, conquering force, but as one option, albeit an important one, among many.

Building distribution appears to have confirmed this claim. The Capitol, traditionally the lynchpin of any civic forum in the heart of a Roman town, stood nowhere near the center of the city. Instead, it was relegated to the outskirts of the new territories. To any visitor accustomed to the conventional lay of Roman towns, this repositioning must have been startling. Its effect can only be estimated, but by and large it must have relegated the traditional tutelary gods to a secondary role within the urban system.

This is not to say, however, that their role was immediately taken over by others. Although located at the center of the city, the remaining temples and the one Christian church stood detached both from the Augusteion and from each other. In a sense, Constantinople was infused with the sacred, but in spaces carefully removed both from each other and from the flux of urban life. This organizational choice must have been deliberate and in a very real way was the concrete manifestation of the policy of toleration that was stated nearly two decades before with the legalization of the Empire's religions, Christianity included.[65] Constantinople created the ground on which that imperial vision could stand. In the reshaping of ancient Byzantium, Constantine and his planners struck a balance between pagan and Christian in their organization of public space. The city plan that they devised accommodated each of the Roman state's main religious cults, be they pagan or Christian, in a set of discrete, yet monumental precincts. This act of accommodation was nothing if not shrewd in that it not only recognized the inevitable and fundamentally irreconcilable differences between key members of the empire's population, but also took steps to defuse them by creating the conditions for peaceful coexistence.

The unique accommodation of the empire's religious cultures arrived at in the Constantinian plan makes it tempting to focus on this aspect of development as its defining feature. Although undoubtedly important, and indeed crucial to the success of the city, this manipulation of public religious space was but one element in the overall plan. Temples and churches were after all but single elements in a grand imperial scheme. Far more important to the overall success of that scheme was the common ground on which these buildings and the institutions they housed stood. This communality, expressed in the very fact that pagan and Christian religious institutions were both accommodated in the capital, was proclaimed with as much if not more insistence through the common visual language of late Roman architecture. Throughout the city all buildings with any pretense to importance presented their faces to the city using the rich marbles and towering columns that were the defining features of imperial architecture. Using the shared visual language of *romanitas*, Constantine and his planners subsumed the interests of individual parties into the one overriding interest, the creation of a grand urban space that was itself the expression of Roman imperial rule.

## ✑ TWO ✑

# CREATING THE COLLECTION

T HE CITY SHAPED BY CONSTANTINE AND HIS SUCCESSORS IN THE AFTERMATH OF the 324 foundation ceremonies forged an urban space that expressed the single truth of imperial dominion. Although it was the organization of public space and the placement of institutions and the buildings that housed them in and around that space that laid out that idea in broad, if explicit, outline, it was the city's sculptured decor that articulated and legitimated the specific nature of this truth. In the years between the foundation and the dedication, Constantine and his planners outfitted the city with a formidable collection of public sculpture. Assembled in the capital's foremost public gathering places, spaces such as the Augusteion, the Baths of Zeuxippos, and the Forum of Constantine, this great collection was designed to enhance the generic claims for imperial status made through the manipulation of architecture by creating and giving visual expression to a unique civic history that in turn confirmed the emperor's urban vision.

The monuments assembled in the service of this vision were diverse. Prominent in the new urban displays were imperial portraits: Images of Constantine, his sons Constans and Constantius, and his mother, Helena, stood throughout the city.[1] At the same time, however, these modern works represented only a fraction of the capital's sculptured wealth. The mainstay of the public displays was a group of works of ancient, pre-fourth-century manufacture. Culled from the cities and sanctuaries of the Roman world, these antiquities presented a varied aspect both in terms of iconography and in terms of style. Subject matter included portraits of pre-fourth-century emperors (cat. nos. 8, 103, 116, 158) and culture heroes such as poets (cat. nos. 54, 55, 65, 66, 67, 68, 73, 81) and philosophers (cat. nos. 45, 52, 60, 82). These images stood side by side with statues of gods (cat. nos. 3, 5, 7, 11, 14, 16, 17, 19, 22, 24, 102, 106, 107, 108), demigods (cat. nos. 4, 21, 39–43, 46, 57, 85, 128), and fantastic creatures (cat. nos. 104, 142, 143). Nonfigural monuments such as tripods (cat. nos. 105, 141, 145, 148) and obelisks (cat. nos. 138, 167) joined these statues to complete the city's public decor.

In terms of formal preference, most of the city's antiquities were of late classical Hellenistic or Roman manufacture. Statuary of fourth- and third-century B.C. Greek conception (cat. nos. 31, 53, 55, 56, 69, 91–93, 166) stood together with such uniquely Roman creations as Julius Caesar (cat. no. 48) and Virgil (cat. no. 95). Many works, among them a Doryphoros after Polykleitos (cat. no. 26) and a Sandalbinder after Lysippos (cat. no. 63), probably were copies of or variations on standard sculptural types from the classical and late classical phases of Greek history that could have been produced at any time during the Hellenistic or Roman period. This use of copies was a standard and expected element in ancient public works projects where a repertoire of several dozen favorite works by the great artists of classical antiquity was displayed against such formidable urban backdrops as nymphaea, city gates, theaters, and baths. Far from carrying the stigma of bad taste that such a display would today, the public exposition of these works was embraced as a way to evoke the glory of the Hellenic past and celebrate its vitality in the Greco-Roman world.[2] For all of their popularity, however, copies were not the only images brought to the city. Original monuments such as the Serpent Column of the Plataean Tripod (cat. no. 141) or a statue of the wolf with Romulus and Remus (cat. no. 147) joined ranks with the copies, suggesting that contemporary taste admired and appreciated a wide range of style within the overarching armature of the classical representational tradition.[3]

Diversity of medium was also an aspect of the city's collections. All of the major gatherings displayed works in marble, and there is evidence for statuary of porphyry (cat. no. 159) and other Egyptian hard stones (cat. no. 152). There should be little doubt, however, that bronze, especially gilt or silvered bronze, was the preferred medium, and, accordingly, surviving descriptions emphasize the presence of such statues.[4] Whether this focus reflects the collection's actual makeup is arguable as the attention paid to such monuments may reveal less about actual numbers and more about the desire to document and record the precious statues that did exist. More costly than marble or any other stone, it was bronze that lent a city an air of elegance, wealth, and grandeur.

This rich collection derived from a wide range of sources. As with architecture, some antiquities, figures of the Dioscuri (cat. no. 128) in the Hippodrome among them, were taken over from the Severan phase of the city's history. In most instances, however, monuments appear to have been brought from outside of Constantinople. This was certainly true of a large number of statues in the Hippodrome, the Serpent

Column included. Holdings in the Baths of Zeuxippos also were imports, as were the major monuments in the Basilika, the Forum of Constantine, and the Strategeion.

Eusebios of Caesarea, the only contemporary observer to refer to the collection's development, offers some information regarding provenance. According to him, statuary was brought from some of the major sanctuaries of the Hellenic world: Apollo at Delphi, the Museion on Mt. Helikon, and the Temple of Apollo Smintheos at Chryse in the Troad.[5] Writing at the end of the fourth century, when the collection was already well established, Jerome expanded this circumscribed list by observing that all of the Empire's cities supplied the newly founded capital with statuary.[6] He did not, however, name names. Specification of provenance is left to later sources such as Zosimos[7] who reports that Constantine brought statuary from Kyzikos and Rome, or the eighth-century *Parastaseis syntomoi chronikai*[8] and its tenth-century derivative the *Patria Konstantinopoleos*.[9] In one of the more specific enumerations of provenance, the *Patria* names some of the cities from which statuary was gathered. Among the places listed are Athens, Tralles, Sardis, and Smyrna. More general references to the islands of Chios, Rhodes, and Cyprus also appear, as does a blanket reference to "all the cities of Anatolia."

Archaeological evidence both supports and complements the written word. The survival of the Serpent Column (cat. no. 141) confirms Eusebios's claim that statuary was brought from sanctuaries such as Delphi. In support of Jerome, other finds demonstrate the widespread civic origins of a great many works. The Parian marble used in the creation of a colossal head (cat. no. 57) of fifth-century B.C. manufacture found during the excavations of the Baths of Zeuxippos indicates a provenance in mainland Greece, while a statue base with a dedication to Theophanes of Mytilene (cat. no. 144) recovered from the Hippodrome points to a Lesbian origin.

The picture to emerge from the delineation of provenance is a coherent one. The lion's share of the Constantinian gathering was from urban contexts. At least twenty-two cities in addition to Rome provided monuments for display in Constantinople, and these centers were overwhelmingly those of Greece and the eastern Mediterranean world. Apart from Rome itself, no statuary appears to have been brought from the farther reaches of western Europe or North Africa.

The decoration of Constantinople with works of art taken from some of the later Roman world's most prestigious civic and religious centers must count as one of the most far-reaching urban design projects ever implemented. It was, after all, no small thing to orchestrate the selection, removal, and reinstallation of some of the Greco-Roman world's most renowned public monuments for reuse in Constantinople. Further, the magnitude of the enterprise was unheard of. Although there was ample precedent in Roman history for the removal and transport of public statuary, no city was known to have been decorated so overwhelmingly or exclusively with reused antiquities. Early examples of reuse, though admittedly spectacular, were far more contained, being limited to single installations in a delimited urban space.[10] None was executed with the fervor, intensity, or citywide bravura of the Constantinopolitan enterprise. This being the case, how was it that this unusual gathering came into being?

Chronologically the collection developed in three distinct phases, each characterized not only and most obviously by the reuse of ancient monuments in critical mass, but also by the application of a consistent agenda to the treatment of this material. The first and doubtless most intense phase of the collection's creation took place under Constantine between 324 and 330 as part of the rush of building activity leading up to the dedication. This period saw the initial identification of display venues as well as the first installations of statuary at these sites. With the notable exception of the Forum of Constantine, most of this activity was concentrated in the newly developed areas of the old city. Activity must have been frenetic as well over a hundred monuments appear to have been erected in most of the major settings, the Hippodrome, the Baths of Zeuxippos, the Augusteion, the Basilika, and the Strategeion among them. Although it is likely that these initial ensembles were substantially complete by the time of the 330 celebrations, there is also evidence that some statuary was added later, either by Constantine himself or during the early years of the reign of his son and successor, Constantius (cat. no. 25). Conservative estimate thus indicates that the initial phase of the collection's creation took place over a period of roughly twenty years.

A second, less-intense phase of development occurred at the end of the fourth and the beginning of the fifth century. Covering the period of Theodosian rule that began with the accession of Theodosios I in 379 and ended around 420 when his grandson, Theodosios II, attained his majority, this phase of the collection's development appears to have been much less intense than the Constantinian phase. Thus although the number of statues brought during the initial period of the collection's formation tops 100, no more than 30 individual monuments are mentioned for the whole of the Theodosian age. Further, although at least one new collection was created (cat. nos. 150–57), many of the works appear to have been additions to extant collections such as the Hippodrome gathering (cat. nos. 129, 138, 140, 142).

The last chapter in the development of the Constantinopolitan collection was written in the sixth century, during the reign of Justinian. Unlike the Constantinian and Theodosian eras of the collection's history, however, this period appears to have been as much about destruction as about construction. Although Justinian did add to the collection, his efforts in this direction were few. Only two sculpture venues are associated with the emperor: the Chalke Gate and a portico in the Baths of Arkadios. Both settings were comparatively restricted as was the amount of statuary used, and the efforts at citywide development seen under Constantine and the Theodosians were clearly a thing of the past. Evidence that the emperor oversaw the dismantling and redistribution of collections around the city confirms this trend.

Although the sixth century represents a decline in the fortunes of the city's antiquities, it is evident that in the aftermath of its initial creation the fourth and fifth centuries were witness to the collection's ongoing development. Indeed, although the mechanisms by which this activity was initiated and sustained are not altogether clear, it is obvious that the project was considered integral to the city's development. The fifth-century historian Sozomen suggests as much in his report that Constantine "imposed taxes to cover the expenses of building and adorning the city."[11] Mentioned in a single breath, both the architecture of the city and the sculpture that adorned it were considered part of the same enterprise. Almost all of the sources commenting on this activity confirm this point of view, noting not only the monumental building campaign, but also the inclusion of sculpture as a requisite element in the city's design and development. Consider, for example, the words of John Malalas on the city's construction:

> He [Constantine] reconstructed the earlier city wall, that of Byzas, and added another great extension to the wall and, joining this to the old city wall, he ordered the city to be called Constantinople. He also completed the hippodrome and adorned it with bronze statues and with ornamentation of every kind, and built in it a kathisma, just like the one in Rome, for the emperor to watch the races. He also built a large and beautiful palace, especially on the pattern of the one in Rome, near the hippodrome, with the way up from the palace to the kathisma in the hippodrome by the staircase known as the kochlias. He also built a column, all of porphyry. On this column he set up a statue of himself with seven rays on his head. He had this bronze statue brought from where it had stood in Ilion, a city in Phrygia. Constantine took secretly from Rome the wooden statue known as the Palladion and placed it in the forum he built, beneath the column that supported his statue. Some of the people of Byzantion say that it is still there. He made a bloodless sacrifice to God, and the tyche of the city which had been restored and built and named after himself he called Anthousa. . . .
>
> Constantine built from the entrance of the palace up to his forum two splendid colonnades decorated with statues and different kinds of marble, and he called the place with the colonnades the Regia. Nearby he built a basilica with great columns and statues outside; this he called the Senaton. Opposite this he set up a statue of

his mother Helena as Augusta, on a low porphyry column. This place he called the Augusteion.

Likewise he completed the public bath known as the Zeuxippon, and decorated it with columns and marbles of many colors and bronze statues. He had found the public bath unfinished; it had been begun formerly by the emperor Severus.[12]

As the passage indicates, architecture and sculpture were part of the same enterprise. For every street laid or building erected, there was a sculptured component, and it was as much statuary as architecture that defined the city's greatness. Sculptured imagery saturated the city as all of the major public spaces incorporated substantial collections of statuary.

Although direct evidence for the creation of this monumental collection is nonexistent, it is likely that the administrative mechanism of late Roman imperial government facilitated the undertaking. Like any major urban project of the late antique period, including the construction of Constantinople itself, the gathering and installation of antiquities doubtless would have fallen under the rubric of "public works," a category that included everything from road construction and major building campaigns to bath and sewer maintenance. As such the Praetorian Prefecture, the administrative unit responsible for the organization of such projects, would have overseen it and subjected the project to the rules and protocols that governed such enterprises. Financing would have been provided by the state from public funds.[13]

As Sozomen indicates, the project was financed through taxation. There is, however, no specific information as to the type of tax or its duration. Presumably, it would have been a one-time, irregular levy overseen by the Praetorian Prefecture. Under this system, the imperial representative would have received a tax mandate, which then would have been turned over to local administrators for collection.[14] Evidence suggests that the nature of the tax may have varied at the local level, with some provinces or municipalities being exempt and others paying heavily. The almost complete lack of evidence for statuary from the Empire's western provinces suggests that the eastern cities may in fact have borne the major burden. In most levies, cash payment was preferred; however, there is also evidence for payment in kind,[15] and it may be that in the case of sculpture, provision of monuments fulfilled at least part, if not all, of the tax obligation.

There was, however, more to the acquisition of antiquities than the cost of the monuments themselves. Statuary needed to be identified, selected, transported to the city, and, finally, erected. For these aspects of the collection's development, some kind of cash outlay would probably have been necessary, especially in instances where

the work necessitated services, such as shipping, that may well have been provided
through the private sector.

The first step in the collection's formation would have been the identification
of monuments. This task could have been accomplished in a variety of ways. Evidence suggests both that imperial representatives may have been assigned to canvass
the empire for suitable monuments and that the cities themselves may have been
asked to offer appropriate types of statuary. The two scenarios are not mutually
exclusive, and it is possible that the selection of monuments was achieved through
diplomatic channels that involved negotiations between imperial representatives and
local communities.

Epigraphical evidence points to the use of scouts. A graffito of A.D. 326 documents
the travels of Nicagoras, a daduch of the Eleusinian mysteries, to Egypt, noting his
visit to ancient sites:

> In the consulate of Constantine Augustus, (consul) for the seventh time, and Con-
> stantius Caesar, (consul) for the first time.
>     The daduch of the mysteries of Eleusis, Nicagoras, son of Minucianus of Athens,
> having visited the divine Syringes, I admired them.[16]

A related inscription indicates that this journey was undertaken at Constantine's
behest:

> I, Nicagoras, a daduch of the most holy Eleusinian Mysteries,
> son of Minucianus, Athenian, having visited
> the Syringes well after the divine Plato
> of Athens, have admired and given
> thanks to the gods and to the most pious
> emperor Constantine who has
> sent me here.[17]

Although hardly conclusive, this evidence suggests that the emperor may have appointed individuals such as Nicagoras to travel the Empire examining the state of
antiquities, identifying and drawing up lists of potential monuments.[18]

Criteria for the selection of such monuments is not known; however, the subject
matter of some monuments indicates that the choice could have been bound up
with issues of urban history and identity, an idea that hints at the participation of
cities in the selection process. A statue of the first-century B.C. historian Theophanes
of Mytilene (cat. no. 144) was a case in point. Although the figure itself no longer
survives, a base recovered from the Hippodrome records the original dedication of
Theophanes's portrait on Lesbos. That the citizens of Mytilene themselves had a

hand in the selection of this statue is suggested by their traditionally high regard for Theophanes, a man who single-handedly helped to rehabilitate the city's fortunes in the aftermath of its defection from the Roman cause during the Mithridatic Wars.[19] His image also appeared on the city's coin issues as late as the fourth century. Given Theophanes's importance to Mytilenean history and identity, it is possible that the city fathers, faced with a mandate to provide statuary for the imperial cause, earmarked the statue as a suitable offering. Conversely, it also may have been the case that outsiders, knowing the importance of the city's benefactor, may have identified the figure themselves.

As the statue of Theophanes suggests, identification with civic tradition appears to have been one of the selection criteria. Other statues suggest the lure of a less parochial imagery. Some works, such as the Serpent Column (cat. no. 141), itself only a small part of a larger monument commemorating the final Greek defeat of the Persians at the Battle of Plataea in 476 B.C., memorialized events of far more far-reaching significance than the localized patriotic efforts of Theophanes. With the defeat of the Persians the Greeks preserved the integrity of their homeland and way of life. Likewise, a monument to Octavian's victory at Actium in 32 B.C., the Ass and Keeper (cat. no. 122), recalls one of the seminal moments in the creation of empire. Thus, side by side with images reflective of civic identity stood a whole collection of monuments dedicated to the celebration of defining moments in the history of Greco-Roman civilization.

Once selected, it is not immediately clear how statuary was requisitioned. No Constantinian legislation survives, but later fourth-century edicts from the Theodosian Code[20] dealing with the preservation of urban infrastructures and the restoration of public works suggest a procedure consistent with the hierarchical administration of the tax structure. As with the imposition of taxes for the funding of public works projects, an initial mandate would have been sent to the Prefect with the proviso that requisition orders be executed at the local level under the auspices of provincial governors and other officials. Given the involvement of local officials in this part of the process, it may be that negotiations over particular statues took place at this point.

The transport of monuments was also a consideration. Removal of statuary from its established location was a difficult and time-consuming undertaking as all care needed to be taken to avoid damage. For any but the smallest scale works of art, heavy-duty equipment of the type used in lifting blocks for stone quarrying would have had to have been put in place. Any one of a number of hoisting machines would have been used to lift statuary: pulleys, winches, or capstans, depending on the size, weight, and shape of the sculpture involved.[21] Once removed from its base, statuary was packed and loaded onto carts for transport to loading docks and shipment via land or sea. Sea freight was preferable, as it was far less expensive than land transport.[22] Once in Constantinople, the process then was reversed as statuary was taken from loading docks to its point of installation.

How labor for the removal, transport, and reinstallation of these monuments was provided also is unknown. Again, there is no direct evidence. Analogy to the administration of public works suggests, however, that it was forced, either by the temporary conscription of local populations, or, as is more likely given the duration of the project, by the use of criminals. *Damnatio ad opus publicum*, condemnation to labor on public works for criminal offense, was one of the harsher punishments in the Roman legal system, and it was the preferred means of accomplishing major imperial projects because of the savings it offered on labor.[23] The work included a wide range of activity such as the servicing of public buildings, the cleaning of sewers, and the construction of roads and streets. Major building projects were also considered public works, and doubtless the Constantinopolitan undertaking would have fallen under this rubric. Although some degree of specialized supervision would have been necessary for the more delicate operations surrounding the removal and reinstallation of monuments, most of the labor surrounding the packaging and hauling of individual statues could easily have been accomplished using the brawn of unskilled workers.

It was the late Roman imperial system that brought the Constantinopolitan collection into being by marshaling the resources of the Empire at their most practical level. What, however, was the driving force behind this action? What, in other words, led Constantine and his successors to the wholesale reuse of antiquities? There are several possible answers to this question, none mutually exclusive. To a certain extent practical considerations were central to the collection's formation, especially in its earliest phases of development. In purely pragmatic terms, the reuse of antiquities made sense from two perspectives, the temporal and the fiscal. The relatively short span of time between the foundation and the dedication required that all programs for construction and decoration be accomplished with a fair degree of dispatch. Legislation granting tax and service exemptions to craftsmen working in the city, architects and sculptors included, suggests a shortage of skilled workers.[24] In an atmosphere such as this there was, therefore, a real practical advantage to recycling sculpture. Financial considerations also must have played a part, as illustrated by the specific example of the public bath. No public building was more expensive, and fully half of the expenditure for such a complex would have been occasioned by the purchase of sculpture.[25]

Prudent resource management was not, however, the sole determining factor. In many respects, the real mandate for reuse was generated not in the dry-as-dust atmosphere of the Empire's administrative offices and counting houses, but in the ephemera of late Roman society's desires and expectations, an imaginative realm that shaped not only the physical structure of cities and with it their image, but also the response to these places and the ideologies they embodied.

In a very real way, the impetus to the project derived from a larger set of late antique assumptions about the nature of cities and their appearance that saw sculpture, ancient or modern, as an essential element in urban design. Just as the inclusion of what Sozomen referred to as the "requisite edifices" signaled a city's claims to participation in Roman imperial culture, the presence of sculpture legitimated those claims by describing a particular urban identity. Nowhere was this phenomenon more evident than in the cities of western Asia Minor, where, in the public spaces of towns such as Miletos, Ephesos, and Aphrodisias, whole populations of statuary grew up. Images of deities and mythological heroes stood together with representations of founder kings and prominent local citizens.[26] These images created an urban identity in two ways: first, through the material aspect of sculpture, and, second, through its storytelling potential.

From a purely formal, materialistic point of view, the display of statuary was desirable as a demonstration of wealth and prestige. Sculpture was an expensive undertaking. Materials, whether stone or metal, were costly, as was the craftsmanship that transformed them.[27] The ability to establish and maintain a city's sculptured population was thus an index of financial well-being. It was also, by extension, a benchmark of status, inasmuch as the patronage of the men and institutions that underwrote a city's installations expressed the goodwill and favor of those in authority toward a given community. Finally, sculpture was, together with the architecture that framed it, an invaluable and essential component in the definition of urban beauty, or *kallos*, a notion that embodied not only physical appearance but also the underlying sense of virtue and worth expressed in the very act of patronage.[28] Thus, by the fourth century, when Constantine set about creating his capital, the visual impact of sculpture was such that it was unthinkable that the place earmarked to become the Roman Empire's premier city should forego its display.

The representational qualities of the medium further enhanced the notions of prestige and status conveyed by the mere presence of statuary. Sculpture was the great medium of visual communication in the Greco-Roman world. In the choice of subject matter for individual statues and the juxtaposition of images to create visual narratives, cities documented their histories and in so doing legitimated their claims to status within the territories of the Roman world by documenting their ties to the past. They did so through the depiction of their mythical origins and the representations of prominent citizens.[29]

It was with this layered understanding in mind that Constantine undertook the decoration of Constantinople. By adorning the capital with statuary the emperor not only lent his city an air of beauty that befit its claims to imperial status, but also described a unique historical identity among the cities of the Greco-Roman world that legitimated that claim. For the Romans, a people that self-consciously defined itself against the past, this legitimating strategy was underscored by the physical aspect of these gatherings, specifically, the reused status of the statuary.

The general phenomenon of reuse had its origins in the traditions of military conquest where the plunder of statuary and other works of art came to evoke an idea of power.[30] From as early as the Republican period, the wealth of a conquered nation was transported to the capital where it was presented to the public as part of a military triumph. In the earliest triumphs booty consisted largely of arms, armor, precious metals, livestock, and slaves. With time, the definition of plunder expanded to include works of art, and it was often the case that objects taken as booty were put on permanent public display.

The intention behind the capture and display of these goods, or *spolia*,[31] was complex. At its most basic level, plunder, whether animal, vegetable, or mineral, was a matter of finance. Goods taken in the wake of conquest had monetary value that enriched the state. This was no less true of statuary than of other types of loot. The cost of materials such as marble and bronze, or, more rarely, silver and gold, made statuary intrinsically valuable. In the case of metal pieces it could and often was melted for coin. Workmanship also was valued, however, with nearly half of the cost of metal sculpture entailed in production.[32] Thus, both materials and process were costly, making the reuse of materials appealing at a very basic economic level. In this sense, then, reuse overlapped with economic motivation.

As an adjunct to their financial value, however, *spolia* had the potential for enormous symbolic import. To begin with, spoils explained the riches of a conquered nation better than any possible description, thereby offering tangible proof that a campaign had been worth the undertaking. Even more important, however, was the very act of possession: ownership demonstrated dominion. The control of financial resources meant, of course, absolute regulatory power over public life. In the case of public monuments and works of art, the more ephemeral issues of civic pride and cultural identity often were at stake.

That this attitude was a feature of fourth-century response to the Constantinopolitan collection is evident from the only surviving contemporary reference to the project, a passage in Eusebios of Caesarea's *Life of Constantine*:

> The pompous statues of brass were exposed to view in all the public places of the imperial city: so that here a Pythian, there a Sminthian Apollo excited the contempt of the beholder: while the Delphic tripods were deposited in the Hippodrome and the Muses of Helikon in the palace. In short the city which bore his name was everywhere filled with brazen statues of the most exquisite workmanship, which had been dedicated in every province, and which the deluded victims of superstition had long vainly honored as gods with numberless victims and burnt sacrifices, though now at length they learned to think rightly, when the emperor held up these very playthings to be the ridicule and the sport of all beholders.[33]

What this passage spells out is the response of a Christian religious to the phenomenon of the city's decoration. For Eusebios the urban display of temple images "dedicated in various provinces" trumpeted the Christian triumph over Hellenic religious tradition. It was, of course, the ferocity of Eusebios's Christian belief together with his genuine loathing of pagan cult that led him to see the development of the city's sculptural installations in terms of religious polemic.

Evidence suggests, however, that the Eusebian approach was only one way of understanding the collection. The testimony of another Christian author, Jerome, comes at the gathering from a very different point of view. Consider, for example, his comment on the dedication: "Constantinople was enriched through the stripping bare of almost every city founded before Byzantium."[34] Unlike Eusebios who understood the Constantinopolitan project in overtly religious terms and couched his response to the collection in vitriolically anti-Hellenic terms, Jerome's trenchant remark interpreted it in specifically civic ones by referring not to the statuary itself, but to the cities of the Empire from which sculpture was removed. Thus, without mentioning sculpture or any other public monument outright, it is clear that the reference to urban nudity was meant to conjure a vision of the wholesale stripping of cities and with it an expression of Constantinopolitan hegemony. It is the experience of Tarentum and the great bronze Herakles that Jerome called to mind with this spare and unsparing prose, doing so not in a manner specific to place, but in one applicable to the Empire as a whole.

On the face of it, Eusebios and Jerome represent radically different responses to the collection, yet a shared assumption underpins both reactions. Specifically, both men understood that reuse in and of itself could be, and indeed, in this instance, was the expression of a power relationship in which the ability to commandeer sculpture expressed the dominance of one party over another. In this instance, and appropriately for the new capital of the Roman world, the relationship expressed was that between center and periphery. With the reuse of statuary from the cities and sanctuaries of the Roman world, Constantine and his planners accomplished several things. In bringing the best and most marvelous of the Empire's sculptured offerings to the city, they seized, both literally and metaphorically, the cultural capital of the Greco-Roman world. Each and every antiquity brought with it a sense of place and history. Thus, the removal of some of the ancient world's most famous and best-loved monuments from the territories of the Roman Empire, and their subsequent integration into the architectural fabric of the capital, not only brought material wealth to the city but also pulled together the threads of space and time to make Constantinople a museum of empire. It was this far-reaching enterprise that gave testimony to the absolute power of the state. Resplendent against the city's classical architectural armature the collection described not only the control of material goods and resources, but also, through that control, the desire for power over territory, time, and civilization itself that lay at the heart of the imperial enterprise. The evocative power of *spolia* gave visual life not only to the longing for mastery but also to its realization. In so doing it created the first broad definitions of Constantinople as a place. Together architecture and the statuary that inhabited it made the city the epitome of late classical urban planning, the flagship of *romanitas*.

## ⁀ THREE ⁀

# THE CONSTANTINIAN COLLECTIONS

ALTHOUGH THE ARCHITECTURAL SPLENDOR OF THE CITY AND THE MAGNIFICENCE of the sculptural installations laid out a vision of *romanitas* in bold coloristic strokes, it was the selection of monuments for individual gatherings that sketched the details of that Constantinian vision. Against the backdrop of colonnaded streets and public spaces, the display of statuary, its subject matter and themes carefully chosen, punctuated this grand vision of imperially shaped *romanitas* with images that were designed to lay out the specific details of a unique Constantinopolitan history, a history that in turn legitimated the claims to urban hegemony promulgated in broad outline both in the planning of the city and by the phenomenon of reuse.

The exact nature of this history was defined by the contents of the individual collections that grew up in the various spaces of the capital. In settings such as the Baths of Zeuxippos, the Hippodrome, and the Forum of Constantine, the choice of statuary around themes appropriate both to the individual places and to the larger environment of Constantinople created a series of diverse but related groupings designed to foster a vision of a Constantinopolitan past that would legitimate the city's claims to contemporary authoritative status.

Of the collections initiated by Constantine, the most thoroughly documented are those in the Baths of Zeuxippos, the Hippodrome, and the Forum of Constantine. Less well known are the gatherings at the Basilika and the Strategeion. Virtually unknown is the nature of the statuary in the Augusteion and the Baths of Constantine. In part, this hierarchy is because of accidents of survival. The existence of descriptions such as Christodoros of Koptos's *Ekphrasis* on the Baths of Zeuxippos has preserved that collection in memory if not in substance, while the corrupt and isolated nature of the sources pertinent to places like the Augusteion allows only the most fragmentary assessment of these collections. At the same time, however, the degree to which collections are commented on reflects the importance of the site and its urban function. Thus, the Hippodrome and the Forum are more lavishly documented than either the Basilika or the Strategeion because they occupied a far more prominent place in the ebb and flow of the city's life for a far longer period of time. That prominence appears to have been reflected in the size of individual collections as well. The more closely a given public space found itself tied to the rhythm of the city's life in all of its quotidian and ceremonial richness, the more heavily adorned it was with sculpture. Thus, the Baths of Zeuxippos and the Hippodrome, two of the city's more prominent locations, had the largest concentrations of sculpture, while the Strategeion, reserved essentially for the military, was comparatively spare in its decor.

What was the nature of these individual ensembles? The three major gatherings, those in the Hippodrome, the Baths of Zeuxippos, and the Forum of Constantine, were conceived largely in historical terms. Smaller groupings at the Milion, the Basilika, and the Strategeion appear to have conformed to this tendency. In each of these spaces, the selective deployment of sculpture organized around themes pertinent to the definition of a Constantinopolitan past laid the groundwork for a collective vision of the city's contemporary identity.

## THE BATHS OF ZEUXIPPOS

One aspect of this identity was articulated by the gathering in the Baths of Zeuxippos (Figure 5). Founded and built by Septimius Severus, the Zeuxippos was taken over by Constantine, who made it a showpiece by dowering it with freestanding sculptural decoration in bronze and marble. In his account of the rush of building activity leading up to the dedication of the city, the sixth-century historian John Malalas described this undertaking as the capstone of many such enterprises: "Moreover, he [Constantine] completed the bath known as the Zeuxippos, decorating it with columns and different colored marbles and statues made of bronze."[1] Thus outfitted, the Zeuxippos functioned as the oldest and most centrally placed of the capital's imperial baths during the fourth, fifth, and sixth centuries. Throughout this period it not only served the needs of public bathing, but also as a locus for all manner of public speaking and debate.

Although destroyed in 532 by the fires that ravaged the city in the wake of the Nika riots, the Zeuxippos collection is known from literary sources. The most complete evidence is a description, or *ekphrasis*, written at the end of the fifth century by the Egyptian poet Christodoros of Koptos.[2] Christodoros was an established poet in Constantinople, where he worked in official circles, and it is likely that the Zeuxippos description was written in some sort of official capacity, perhaps on the occasion of a restoration and dedication of new statuary that took place in 467.[3]

The *Ekphrasis* survives incomplete as a 416-verse poem recording freestanding statues or statue groups in three basic categories: gods and demigods, mythological figures, and portraits. That this description recorded actual pieces as opposed to some imagined gathering is clear from correspondences between named statues and archaeological finds. Statue bases inscribed with the names of Aischines (cat. no. 31) and Hekube (cat. no. 75), two figures mentioned in the *Ekphrasis*, were found during excavation of the site.

The iconographic breakdown of statuary into the three categories is consistent with the traditions of Roman bath decor. Large thermal establishments in Rome and the provincial centers of North Africa and Asia Minor show a more or less similar sculptural repertoire. As at the Zeuxippos, statues of gods associated with the four elements, healing, or pleasure were displayed side by side with mythological figures and portraits.[4]

The most popular deities in the sculptured Roman baths were Askleipios and Hygeia, Dionysios and his attendants, Aphrodite, Herakles, and Apollo with the Muses. All were associated with the bath and its activities through their connections with the element of water, the idea of health, or pleasurable social activity. Askleipios and Hygeia were the two most popular divinities, no doubt because of their associations with health. Dionysios and the sea-born Aphrodite were linked with water, as was Herakles, whose physical prowess also made him a logical denizen of the bath. In the case of Apollo, statues of the god in the company of the Muses acknowledged the intellectual and social stimulation expected as an ideal part of any thermal visit, while solitary representations of the deity referred to the god's own healing powers.[5]

In the particular case of the Zeuxippos, the gods and demigods numbered eleven. There were three statues each of Apollo and Aphrodite (cat. nos. 38–43), a single figure of Hermaphroditos (cat. no. 62) and two groups, one of Herakles with the nymph Auge (cat. no. 61) and a second showing Poseidon with Amymone (cat. no. 85). Herakles is ubiquitous as a paragon of physical fitness. Less obvious is the inclusion of Hermaphroditos, a figure popular in baths throughout the Empire. Presumably the figure was considered appropriate because of his associations with Aphrodite and Artemis, goddesses who were linked with water. It was this same connection that allowed the inclusion of the Poseidon group.[6]

Noticeably absent from the Zeuxippos were statues of Askleipios and Hygeia and of Dionysios and his attendant nymphs and satyrs. It is possible that these figures, which were so lively a part of the bath scene elsewhere, were mentioned in the missing verses of the *Ekphrasis*.

The collection of mythological figures at the Zeuxippos is also comparable to known bath collections where subjects from a wide range of classical myth and literature were displayed to the stimulation and delight of the bath's patrons. In the Constantinopolitan baths, figures were selected from at least two narrative sources, the great Theban and Trojan myth cycles.

Two figures from the Theban narratives were recorded, the seer Amphiaraos (cat. no. 34) and his son Alkmaion (cat. no. 33). Given the paucity of figures and the fact that the *Ekphrasis* is incomplete, this particular choice of characters is difficult to assess. It may well be that there was a larger, more complete group of figures depicting heroes from the Theban narratives. After the Trojan epic, these gruesome stories were the most popular of the ancient myths, and groups of the heroes were known in antiquity.[7]

By far the largest number of mythological statues, twenty-nine in all, were linked to the Trojan epic,[8] and their number is large enough to suggest that at least in the particular sequence described, the specific moment of the *Ilioupersis* was meant to be evoked. Lines 143–221 record a series of famous couples attendant at the fall: Aeneas and Creusa (cat. no. 27), Helenos and Andromache (cat. nos. 37 and 59), and Menelaos and Helen (cat. nos. 74 and 58). Several other pairs are noted: Odysseus with his concubine Hekube (cat. no. 75), Kassandra and her rapist the Locrian Aiax (cat. nos. 70 and 29), Pyrhhos and Polyxene (cat. no. 87), and, finally, the reunited Oinone and Paris (cat. no. 76). Many of the figures documented as single statues also were connected with the city's fall. In fact, of the characters mentioned, only two, Sarpedon (cat. no. 90) and Chryses (cat. no. 49), are without any connection to the sacking of the city.

Because the *Ekphrasis* survives incomplete, the significance of inclusion or omission is not clear. It may be that other characters from this and other stories were displayed. The presence of Sarpedon and Chryses suggests as much, and it may well be that surviving references to the city's fall represent but one aspect of the decor's overall mythological content.

Neither the subject matter nor the scale and consistency of the Zeuxippos imagery is without precedent. Characters from the Trojan epic were displayed together with other mythological themes in baths throughout the Empire, and extensive iconographic cycles were also a commonplace.[9]

In addition to the fact that episodes from the Trojan epic are present in other baths where they recalled literary themes related to such cultural events as lectures and poetry readings that were often associated with bathing establishments, it is also worth recalling the saga's immense popularity in Late Antiquity. The Zeuxippos collection was but one example of the treatment of a theme that cropped up on everything from household silver and toilet articles to shields.[10] It is likely, therefore, that the Trojan images at the bath were expected to entertain and delight in much the same manner, with the difference that they would have done so on a monumental public scale.

It is also possible that the statues related to the Trojan epic were intended to function on a more weighty, ideological level. That Constantine himself was interested in Troy as a possible location for his new city is clear from the fifth-century commentaries on the foundation written by Zosimos[11] and Sozomen. Both authors state that the emperor looked first at the site of Ilion before settling on Byzantium, and Sozomen specifies that he did so "above the tomb of Aiax where it is said the Achaians entrenched themselves when besieging Troy."[12]

What was at the root of this interest? Ilion was linked with the history of Rome and the Roman people. As every schoolboy knew from his labors over the *Aeneid*, it was the destruction of Troy and the dispersal of its people and their gods that brought about the foundation of Rome.[13] This history was given life in other cities of the Roman Empire from the Augustan period. At Troy itself, a relief of Romulus and Remus unearthed in the Roman theater hints at a larger sculptured program emphasizing Ilion's role as the mother of Rome, and, in a similar vein, Roman Imperial coinage issued from the mint of Ilion showed scenes of the Trojan War and the Lupercal.[14] Elsewhere in Anatolia, at Aphrodisias, imagery linking the destiny of Rome and Troy figured prominently in the Julio-Claudian decoration of the Sebasteion.[15]

That this vision of Roman origins so clearly articulated by Virgil in the Augustan age and thereafter integrated into the visual repertoire of the Empire's cities still had currency in the Constantinian era is evident both in the late Roman school curriculum, which still included Virgil, and in the hold that the poet had over late antique imagination in general.[16] No less a figure than Augustine evoked the memory of these lessons referring in *City of God* to "Troy, mother of the Roman people."[17] Thus Trojan history, mythic in its heroic grandeur, was in another, very real sense the legitimate prehistory of the city, the people, and the empire of Rome itself.[18] Its elaboration in the Baths of Zeuxippos was, therefore, a way to claim that history for the new capital at Constantinople and in so doing promulgate the notion of continuity between past and present.

The Zeuxippos collection also remained faithful to the traditions of thermal decor in its inclusion of portraiture. Throughout the Roman world this element was standard in bath displays.[19] Such collections commonly included statues of emperors and members of the imperial family, priests, magistrates, local benefactors and grandees, contemporary figures linked, more often than not, to the particular history of the place. This was the case, for example, in the Hadrianic Baths at Aphrodisias.[20] Of the thirty pieces of sculpture found, fifteen were portraits. Of these, possibly only one, a statue of Valentinian II, would have enjoyed empirewide recognition. The remaining fourteen male and female, were representations of important local citizens whose presence was at once honorific and descriptive. Through them, Aphrodisias paid homage to its benefactors and, by relying on a concept of the past that focused on the deeds of famous individuals, described the unique history of the place that allowed it, as a community, to take its place with pride among the cities of the Empire.

Although the Zeuxippos collection included portraits, the gathering at the bath was anomalous in that the characters shown had, for the most part, no particular connection either with Constantinople or Byzantium before it. Christodoros mentions thirty-four portraits, of which one, that of the fifth-century general Fl. Pompeius (cat. no. 84), was a contemporary figure. The remaining thirty-three showed historical figures from pre-Homeric times through the second century A.D. Subjects included poets, philosophers, military figures, historians, and statesmen. Within this group the overwhelming emphasis was on the representatives of classical Greek civilization: Sixteen of the portraits depicted fifth or fourth-century B.C. Greeks.[21]

As with the deities and mythological figures, the lacunary nature of the poem makes any judgment about the significance of inclusion or omission problematic. It is difficult to know just what to make of the overwhelming emphasis on historical characters. That Fl. Pompeius was the only contemporary figure to stand with the bath's historical portraits is unlikely. At the same time, however, its fifth-century date makes it obvious that the figure was a post-Constantinian addition, possibly one of several figures dedicated in the baths in 467.[22] This late date suggests that the initial fourth-century gathering was set up with a core of historical figures to which it was expected that, as in other baths, contemporary figures, themselves representative of Constantinople and its greatness, would be added over time.

The use of historical figures at the core of the Zeuxippos collection represented a shrewd manipulation of established trends in thermal décor. Tradition dictated that the Zeuxippos, the city's premier bath, should have been populated with characters representative of the pre-Constantinian city's history. To a certain extent that task was accomplished by the sequence of figures from the Trojan epic. It was also achieved by the representations of the great heroes of Greek and Roman culture, men and women who from the dawn of recorded history had shaped and achieved status within the distinctive Greco-Roman cultural canon.

The choice of this repertoire was likely to have been the product of Constantine's own aspirations for his city. Because of its imperial status, Constantinople was required to serve the Empire as a whole. Given these circumstances, and the Zeuxippos's status as the new capital's premier bath, the collection's emphasis on Greek and, to a lesser extent, Roman historical figures at the expense of locals should come as no surprise. Of what interest could the petty and obscure details of Byzantium's relatively banal and sometimes inglorious past have been to the citizens of the greater Roman Empire? In staking its claims to capital status, Constantinople needed to transcend the specificity of time and place to create a universal frame of reference. Only then could it stand unrivaled among the already distinguished cities of the Roman world.

It was given to the massed poets, philosophers, and statesmen to accomplish this task. By occupying the positions traditionally allotted to local citizens, these figures created a new version of events. With them, the petty, sometimes sordid details of local history were pushed aside and the monumental sweep of the Greco-Roman past was embraced as the city's own. This shift in focus exchanged parochial vision and sentiment for one that was more universal in scope. Through it the capital's history became not only that of the Roman Empire, but also, and more portentously, the history of Greco-Roman civilization itself. It was this sort of history that envisioned Constantinople as nothing less than the heir to and guardian of the cultural and historical legacy of Greece and Rome.

What was it that inspired Constantine, a man otherwise unknown for his intellectual leanings, to set such store by cultural tradition in creating this image of power? In part the answer lies in the nature of the place. The choice of the Zeuxippos as a setting for sculpture together with the categories of representation was predetermined by the traditions of Roman thermal decor. The sheer weight of urban tradition made it unthinkable that the premier bath in the Roman Empire's capital city should continue to stand unadorned. Less obvious is the reasoning behind the emphasis on the Greco-Roman past. On the one hand, the desire to claim continuity with a rich cultural heritage seems straightforward enough. In so doing the emperor established an indissoluble link with the past that lent dignity to his city by describing it as the steward of a noble tradition. On the other hand, it is less clear why such a position should have been necessary. What significant difference could the city's relationship to the intellectual patrimony of the Greco-Roman world have made to the efficacy of its rule?

The image of power consolidated at the Zeuxippos derived from Late Antique assumptions about the nature of authority. In the later Roman Empire, access to power was, by tradition, a function of education and its accompanying cultural polish. In this scheme of things education meant but one thing: mastery of the literary and rhetorical traditions of the Greek educational package known as the paideia. Such mastery found its ideal expression in the sophisticated control of language, gesture, and reference, which was itself emblematic of the decorous self-control that was so much the property of the Empire's ruling elite. Commanded by a few, paideia was, paradoxically, a unifying force, as it created an empirewide frame of reference that allowed members of the elite to recognize and interact with one another.[23]

East and west from the provincial level on up, it was on the basis of this high culture that claims to leadership and authority were pressed. The advantage in accepting them was clear: education in the paideia was understood as a guarantee of moral fiber. Only a man trained in this tradition could be relied on to possess the combined merits of duty and vision necessary to the governing task.[24]

It is in the light of this concept of authority that the Zeuxippos collection should be understood. The massed historical figures stood as the embodiment of paideia: These were the very men and women whose works and deeds had shaped the educational canon, upheld its distinctive traditions, and given the Roman elite its universal mode of discourse. As such their presence in the bath had considerably more far-reaching implications than their revisionist historical function might at first suggest. In addition to rewriting the history of Constantinople, these figures linked the city and its eponymous emperor to the true and indisputable source of power, the moral authority vested in the paideia.

With the weight of paideia behind it, the Zeuxippos asserted Constantinople's unquestioned right to authority over the cities of the empire and in so doing gave a new, but comfortably recognizable twist to conventional bath iconography. To the traditional mix of images centered on concepts of health and healing, mental delight, and local honor, the Zeuxippos added the more portentous imagery of empire. As part of the city's monumental imperial core, it was well placed to do so. Nor was it the only building to undertake such a task. Next door in the Hippodrome, sculpture was used to similar effect. There, in the military and political terms appropriate to the circus and its activities, the city was described as New Rome, the legitimate heir to the rights and privileges of Old Rome itself.

## THE HIPPODROME

Like the Baths of Zeuxippos, the Hippodrome (Figure 4) was an inheritance from the Severan era of the city's history. Although it appears to have been in use from as early as the second century, it was finished only in the fourth century with the Constantinian enlargement and completion of the *cavea*, or seating ranks. In addition to completing the Hippodrome's structure, Constantine initiated the first systematic ornamentation of the site.[25] This project appears to have been only partially complete at his death, and subsequent emperors carried on the decoration of the racetrack. As well, the collection of antiquities was supplemented well into the sixth century by the addition of contemporary works representing circus competitors and members of the imperial house.[26]

The collection amassed in the fourth century stood largely undisturbed until the thirteenth century. Although fires and riots swept the Hippodrome on various occasions, damage to the monuments seems to have been slight. It was only in 1204 with the city's sack by the army of the Fourth Crusade that the Hippodrome collection was destroyed.[27]

Archaeological, graphic, and literary evidence document the collection destroyed in 1204.[28] Moreover, the location of the circus has never been lost, and two of its fourth-century antiquities remain in situ: the Serpent Column and the Theodosian Obelisk. These monuments represent but a fraction of the Hippodrome's original wealth. Although excavation has uncovered little of the original decoration, the lost splendor of the site is attested by graphic and literary sources. A sixteenth-century engraving of the ruined circus by Onofrio Panvinio (Figure 6) shows a series of empty statue bases and honorific columns running along the central barrier. The view indicates the general arrangement and display of monuments, as does an anonymous sixteenth-century drawing of the lower rung of the now-destroyed Column of Arkadios (Figures 7 and 8). Literary sources indicate that there was also statuary above the *caraceres*, at the entrances, and in the *cavea*.[29] The disposition of monuments conformed to what was essentially the standard manner of display in Roman circuses.[30]

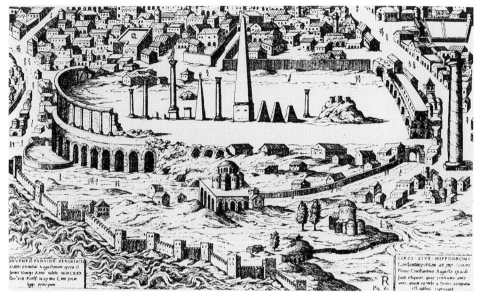

FIGURE 6: Onofrio Panvinio, view of the Hippodrome (from *De ludis circensibus, libri II*, Venice, 1600)

Literary documentation expands on the archaeological and graphic evidence. The sources are extensive but far less systematic than those related to the Zeuxippos. Instead of a single, exhaustive text produced at a more or less definable moment in Late Antiquity for the purpose of description, information about the circus depends on a series of references derived from a variety of literary contexts that range in date from the fourth century through the fourteenth. Epigrams, patriographic texts, chronographs, and histories all record statuary in the Hippodrome.[31] Taken together, these sources document at least twenty-five antiquities, most of which were figural sculpture. Of these antiquities, the majority, around twenty, appears to have been brought by Constantine.

The antiquities brought to the circus may be classed in four groups: apotropaia, victory monuments, public figures, and images of Rome. These categories are not hard and fast and sometimes overlap. What was the thinking that informed this particular assembly?

Of the various monuments collected, the apotropaia are perhaps the most straightforward in terms of function. Included in the ranks of these statues were pagan deities such as Zeus (cat. no. 148), wild animals such as hyenas (cat. no. 137), and fantastic creatures such as sphinxes (cat. no. 143). These monuments functioned either as representations of patron gods or as talismans to ward off evil. A god such as Zeus,

FIGURE 7: Drawing of the Column of Arkadios (south side). The *Freshfield Album*, Trinity College Library, Cambridge, MS 0.17.2, folio 12 (Courtesy of The Master and Fellows of Trinity College, Cambridge)

given the epithet "Hippias," found his way into the circus because of his ancient associations with horses and their breeders.

Although statues of deities were understood as patrons of racers and the races, images of wild animals such as the hyena and mythical creatures such as the sphinx were employed for their more general apotropaic value. Such creatures were believed to be evil in and of themselves. Captured and harnessed in a civilized setting such

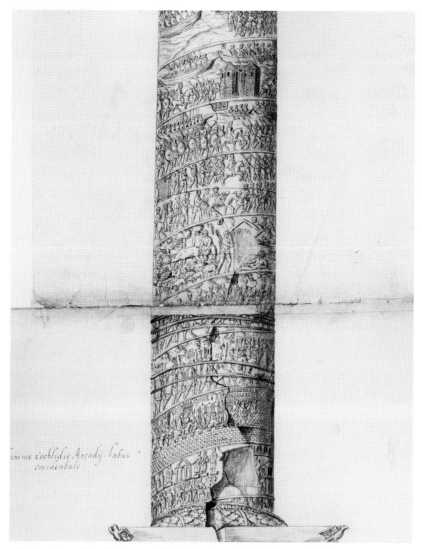

FIGURE 8: Drawing of the Column of Arkadios (west side). *The Freshfield Album*, Trinity College Library, Cambridge, MS 0.17.2, folio 13 (Courtesy of The Master and Fellows of Trinity College, Cambridge)

as the Hippodrome, their own nefarious powers were turned loose against the very forces that had spawned them. Thus the hyena, notorious as a trickster and killer of men, was actually turned into a force for good as its own dark powers were channeled into keeping other evil spirits at bay.[32] In this sense the apotropaia were the most useful and practical images to adorn the course, for by purging the circus of evil they kept the track and its personnel in good running order.

Images of victory were by far the most common type of antiquity brought to the circus. Within this general category, some monuments may be viewed as generic victory dedications, others as commemorative of military triumphs, and still others as exemplars for Hippodrome competitors.

Works classified as generic dedications are those that embody the general concept of victory without reference to any particular person or event. This was the case with a group of bronze tripods from the sanctuary of Apollo at Delphi (cat. no. 145). Traditionally tripods were used as awards and votive dedications in athletic and dramatic competitions. The common practice was to dower the victor, whether athlete or poet, with a tripod that he, in turn, could offer the god. At their initial dedication, then, these monuments had specific associations with specific individuals and the contests through which they were glorified. On removal to Constantinople, however, these associations were probably lost, and the tripods were transfigured to become anonymous images evocative of the idea of victory through genre alone.

In addition to these generic dedications, there were also monuments associated with specific military conquests. Works understood in this manner included the statue of an ass with its keeper and the Serpent Column of the Plataean Tripod.

In its original setting at Nikopolis in Epiros, the Ass and Keeper (cat. no. 122) commemorated Octavian's victory over Mark Antony at nearby Actium. The curious subject matter is explained by Suetonius[33] who reports that Octavian, having set out on the battle's eve to spy on the enemy, saw a man approaching him accompanied by a donkey. When asked to identify himself and his business the traveler introduced himself as Eutyches (Prosper) and his donkey as Nikon (Victory), explaining that they were traveling to the victor's, that is, Octavian's, camp. Accordingly, when the battle was won, Octavian, then Augustus, immortalized the travelers in a shrine at newly founded Nikopolis. Presumably the statue stood in situ until its removal to Constantinople in the fourth century.

The second monument associated with military triumph is the Serpent Column (cat. no. 141). Originally part of the support for a large tripod that stood in the sanctuary of Apollo at Delphi, the Serpent Column was dedicated by the Greek allies to commemorate their victory over the Persians in the 479 B.C. battle of Plataea. As Pausanias[34] reports, the actual tripod, which was made of gold, was carried off in 355 B.C. by a band of marauding Phocians. This left the entwined bronze snakes as the commemorative monument, and it was this curious object that Late Antique viewers understood as the emblem for the Plataean victory.

The third group of victory monuments included images of demigods and heroes that served as exemplars for circus competitors. Included under this rubric were statues of the Dioscuri and Herakles.

Statues of the Dioscuri (cat. no. 128) stood by the entrance and were an inheritance from the Severan circus that Constantine integrated into his own plan. By the fourth century the twins Castor and Pollux had long been associated with the circus and its games. Castor was known as a horse tamer, Pollux as a pugilist, and both were counted as charioteers. In their capacity as athletes, the twins were considered overseers of the games. Pindar[35] described how Herakles, having been assumed to Olympus, passed the mantle of the games along to Castor and Pollux, while Horace[36] notes that it was through justice and steadfastness of purpose that the twins attained such glory. The Dioscuri also were viewed as exemplars for those aspiring to circus victories in that they provided a model of strength and virtuous behavior for those who would themselves be victorious in the races.

A similarly exemplary figure is that of Herakles. At least two statues stood in the circus. One showed the hero struggling with the Nemean lion (cat. no. 135), a popular type of unknown authorship from the series of the Labors. The second Herakles statue is identifiable from a group described problematically as "Adam and Eve, Eutheria and Limos" as Herakles with the Hesperides sisters (cat. no. 134). Even though these statues originally were placed in different settings, their use in the Hippodrome was perfectly appropriate. Herakles was known for his successful completion of the twelve Labors. His accomplishment of these feats made him the model for male strength, and, not surprisingly, he was frequently associated with physical culture. Among the Greeks he was proclaimed patron of athletic contests, and the same association was maintained well into Late Antiquity by the Romans, who linked him even more specifically with the circus.[37]

Understood in the popularity of Herakles as a monument for the circus was a moral strength that complemented his physical prowess. To accomplish his Labors, the hero required not only muscle power, but also fortitude and wit. In this respect he was the perfect *exemplum virtutis* for the Hippodrome competitor. For the contestant, the race through the circus was analogous to the accomplishment of a Labor. It required the strength, wit, and fortitude of a Herakles to defy the odds, sustain the effort, and gain victory.

In addition to apotropaia and victory monuments, the Hippodrome was stocked with images of public figures. These monuments included overtly imperial images of the emperors Augustus (cat. no. 124) and Diocletian (cat. no. 127) and a probable representation of the dictator Julius Caesar (cat. no. 126). In addition there was a statue of Alexander the Great (cat. no. 120) and one of the Mytilenean civic hero Theophanes (cat. no. 144).

Images of Julius Caesar, Augustus, and Diocletian represented men who had ruled Rome from Republic to Empire and Tetrarchy, and their presence may have been intended to achieve for the Hippodrome what the reuse of the Trajanic, Hadrianic, and Antonine reliefs accomplished for the Arch of Constantine in Rome. In the Roman arch a sequence of images of sound rulers from the halcyon days of the Empire's past evoked at once the memory of a Golden Age and, by means of comparison, the idea of its resurgence in the present under the enlightened rule of Constantine, who appears both as the inheritor of tradition and as the catalyst for renewal.[38] In the Hippodrome this different but equally important group of Roman rulers would have functioned similarly by inviting comparison between the great rulers of the past and their modern counterparts. The statue of Alexander the Great (cat. no. 120) would have functioned to similar effect, pushing the equation even further back in time to imply the similarity not only between Constantine and Alexander as rulers, but also between the Macedonian and the Roman empires.

By contrast, an image of Theophanes of Mytilene (cat. no. 144) would have invited response to more purely local traditions. Theophanes was a friend and advisor to Pompey the Great. During his lifetime and throughout the Roman period, the Mytileneans, to whom he was a symbol of their reintegration into the Roman orbit in the aftermath of the Mithridatic wars, lionized him. The statue was, therefore, a monument to civic identity. Once removed to Constantinople, it retained that meaning, commemorating by its presence the Roman embrace of Greek Mytilene and with it the notion of the Empire as an agglomeration of cities.

First and foremost among these cities was Rome, referred to in a fourth group of monuments. A statue of the wolf with Romulus and Remus (cat. no. 147) called to mind the legend of Rome's foundation. The image was, of course, a reference to the legend of Romulus and Remus and their building of the capital. The choice of the figure can be explained on one level by the fact that the ancient festival of the Lupercalia was celebrated in the Hippodrome.[39] Thus, the wolf and the twins referred to events that took place in the circus. At the same time, however, the statue did more than refer to an isolated celebration. In the reenactment of the Lupercalia, Rome's foundation festival, Constantinople appropriated the old capital's history. The statue of the wolf with the twins was a permanent acknowledgment of this act of assimilation that described the Constantinopolitan absorption of Rome's own history. As a result the city was seen to partake of the destiny of Rome.

This idea of a Constantinopolitan succession to the traditions of Rome is borne out in the formal aspects of the circus. The seventh-century *Chronicon Paschale*[40] notes that the Hippodrome was built in imitation of the Circus Maximus (Figure 4), and, indeed, one of the very basic aims in the requisitioning of statuary must have been to make the place look like its Roman prototype. The reuse of antiquities may be considered an aspect of this imitation, for by using ancient monuments as decoration, the Hippodrome acquired a patina of age and respectability that an essentially fourth-century (i.e., modern) building would have lacked.

Non-Roman images in the circus supported this claim. A statue like the Theophanes made sense only in the context of an imperial city, because it described a relationship between capital and province. Monuments such as the Serpent Column and the Ass and Keeper could have been seen in a similar light. Although both referred to victory and so were appropriate for the sporting ambience, the specific nature of their reference was, on another level, descriptive of the city and its claims to authority and preeminence.

Although the Serpent Column commemorated the victory of the Greeks over the Persians at Plataea, it was more than a monument to the fortuitous outcome of a single battle. At Plataea, the Greek allies repulsed their would-be conquerors, the Persians, for the last time, thereby securing the safety of their homeland and way of life. For them, the monument celebrated nothing less than the triumph of civilization over barbarism, of the rational west over the irrational east. In the Hippodrome this memory lingers, for by its presence the Serpent Column described Constantinople as the new protector of these ancient values. Further the presence of the Serpent Column and other Delphic tripods may have reminded the spectators in the circus of the ancient belief that Delphi was considered to be the center of the civilized world.[41] Therefore, removal of these images to Constantinople also may have been intended to imply this status for the new city itself. This notion may well have been underscored by the cosmological symbolism that was an integral part of the imperial ceremonies that took place in the Hippodrome, ceremonies in which the structure of the circus and the workings of the races were understood as a microcosm of the universe, a microcosm over which the emperor himself held sway.[42]

The Ass and Keeper can also be understood as an evocation of Constantinopolitan primacy. In its initial setting the monument glorified Augustus, his victory, and the consolidation of his power. In the Hippodrome, the statue may have recalled these events and the ensuing evolution of Roman rule, claiming as it did so a mandate for Constantinople in the course of Roman history. By reason of its provenance and the moment it commemorates, the statue also may have gone one step further. It is possible that it suggested an analogy between Augustus and Constantine, Nikopolis and Constantinople. Like Augustus at Actium, Constantine consolidated his power by the defeat, in 324, of his last rival, Licinius, in a naval battle near Chrysopolis. Shortly thereafter, the emperor traced the walls of his new capital on the Bosporos. Like Nikopolis, Constantinople could be seen as a monument to victory and consolidation of one man's rule. Moreover, like Augustus, Constantine was repudiating a system of power sharing: his defeat of Licinius represented the final rejection of the Tetrarchic system in favor of the more traditional apparatus of the Principate, a mode of rule defined by Augustus himself.

The monuments displayed in the Hippodrome were designed to function on two levels. On the one hand, the circus decor reflected the athletic events that took place there. Statues of demigods, heroes, and charioteers honored the competitors and their games. On the other hand, many of these same images stood in conjunction with other monuments as part of a civic display that expressed not only the grandeur but also the supremacy of the city intended to become the premier city of the Roman Empire.

This population of the Hippodrome with statues whose imagery was pertinent to both athletic and political concerns was determined by the circus's function. From the start, games were always more than isolated sporting events. Most were associated with the great religious and civil ceremonies that shaped a city's annual calendar. Moreover, in Late Antiquity the Hippodrome became increasingly important as a locus for imperial ceremony. Constantinople was no exception in this regard. Practically all of the city's important ceremonies took place in the circus, which was the meeting spot between emperor and people.[43] It was therefore logical that the Hippodrome be adorned for its role as the premier gathering place of the Empire's first city.

In the context of Roman circuses, the kind of imagery seen at the Hippodrome was at once commonplace and unique. In the sense that it described a civic identity and that all circuses seem to have incorporated this type of imagery, the Hippodrome collection conformed to standard ideas about circus design and decoration. At Tyre, for example, statues of Herakles proliferated not only as straightforward circus imagery, but also because the hero was the city's patron god.[44] What is startling, therefore, in the Constantinopolitan display is not the existence of a civic imagery per se, but the claims made by this particular group of statuary and the intensity with which they are presented. No other circus in the Roman world incorporated so many images of Rome with such consistency as to proclaim itself unequivocally a New Rome. Although similar types of statuary existed in other circuses, the presence of uniquely Roman monuments was unknown elsewhere. The high concentration of such well-known works as the Delphic tripods, the Ass and Keeper, and the Serpent Column was unprecedented. It was the unique quality of this display that gave Constantinople its identity as New Rome. What was implied in this identity was contradictory in some senses. On the one hand, the name evoked the authority of the past. On the other hand, the very fact that the city was described as new invited a distinction. Constantinople may have based its claim to authority on the embrace of Rome's past, but it was, without doubt, a city built for present and future needs.

This ornamentation of the Hippodrome with *spolia* was a choice that doubtless represented a more deliberate appropriation of the past through reuse than that seen in the Baths of Zeuxippos where a strong tradition of sculptural recycling had long informed thermal traditions. Spoils are, by nature, Janus-like. Their value lies in their capacity to envision the future through evocation of the past. In the Hippodrome, in a clever combination of imitation and physical presence, the neat armature of the circus so lavishly hung with antiquities captured what in the history and tradition of Rome was pertinent to the Constantinopolitan present. The imagery of victory and sport was complemented by that of history and tradition to create an environment radiant with the idea of power on the Roman model. At the same time, the construct of the Hippodrome was patently artificial. It was Rome-like, but not Roman in the sense that the particular combination of images was unknown in the old capital. Thus, even as *spolia* referred to the authority of the past, they created a new vision for the future. It was this distinction that gave the Hippodrome its vitality and force. The arrangement was no banal imitation but a neatly crafted ensemble that described a vision of power in its past, present, and, by extension, future manifestations. With *spolia* the Hippodrome was ornamented for its role as the didactic centerpiece of the new capital of an ancient empire.

As in the Baths of Zeuxippos, however, the display of antiquities described an aspect of the city's identity through the fabrication of a unique Constantinopolitan history. In this particular instance, the history adduced was not one of heroic or intellectual tradition, but rather one of military and political prowess. This image, rooted in the appeal to Rome and the assimilation of its military and political preeminence, formed the perfect pendant to the notion of intellectual tradition and its accompanying moral authority outlined in the Zeuxippos.

## THE FORUM OF CONSTANTINE

The theme of Roman continuity echoed around the city. In the Forum of Constantine, a space dedicated to public ceremony and government administrative functions,[45] the display of statuary once again crafted a history that linked the old Rome to the new.

As with the Hippodrome, documentation regarding antiquities in the Forum of Constantine derives from a wide range of sources. Literary testimonia predominate, recording no less than thirty-three monuments.[46] These include the porphyry Column of Constantine and its associated bronze statue (cat. no. 109); the Roman Palladion (cat. no. 114); figures of Paris, Hera, and Aphrodite (cat. no. 113); a statue of Athena (cat. no. 107); a figure of Thetis (cat. no. 115); and an elephant (cat. no. 111). There were also twelve figures of "sirens" or "gilded seahorses" that were probably hippocamps (cat. no. 112). Archaeological evidence supplements this list. A fragment of a dolphin (cat. no. 110) and a head of Tiberius (cat. no. 116) were found during a 1963 salvage excavation at the site.[47]

The sources associate three of the Forum's monuments with Constantine himself: the porphyry column, the bronze statue, and the Roman Palladion. The porphyry column was the vehicle for the display of a colossal bronze statue that contemporaries identified as Constantine himself (cat. no. 109). This figure, which was put in place in 328, wore the *corona radiata*, carried an orb in its left hand, and a spear in its right. The statute was probably nude, and is likely to have been a reused ruler portrait of either a Hellenistic king or a Roman emperor.

The Palladion (cat. no. 114), an ancient guardian statue of the armed Athena that was associated first with Troy and its fortunes and later with Rome and its destiny, is also said to have been brought by Constantine from Rome. The statue is reported to have stood at an unspecified point beneath the column. The combination of scale and medium suggests that it may well have been kept under cover, perhaps in a shrine within the base of the column or in one of the porticoes ringing the Forum.

Two interrelated themes govern the Constantinian selection of monuments for the Forum: kingship and history. Because the Forum was dedicated to the emperor himself, the earliest imagery was designed to describe the nature of his person and his rule. That rule in turn was legitimated by the construction of a history that rooted Constantinopolitan tradition in the epic history of the heroic age.

The column with its portrait of Constantine stood dead center in the Forum where it articulated the theme of kingship. As an honorific monument, the column's function was enhanced both by its colossal scale and by its medium, porphyry.

Reserved exclusively for members of the imperial house by the fourth century, the medium defined the monument itself, the statue it bore, and the space it anchored as imperial.

To the contemporary viewer, the statue itself recalled through its iconography the theme of Hellenistic kingship. The scale of the figure, described as colossal, together with its nudity and its attributes, ultimately derives from and was doubtless meant to recall images of Alexander the Great and the Diadochs. It also must have called to mind the colossal statue of Nero in Rome, itself an appeal to Hellenistic precedent. It is possible that the figure, which is described as having come from Asia Minor, was reused from an actual Hellenistic dedication, and if, as Malalas claimed, the statue came from Ilion it might have been a reshaped imperial portrait from the period of the city's Julio-Claudian refoundation intended to evoke the image of the Hellenistic rulers. Thus, at the very least the colossal bronze would have presented Constantine in the superhuman guise of a new Alexander. The image may also have been overlaid with Julio-Claudian references to statues such as the Colossus of Nero in Rome. In either case, this identity complemented and refined the imperial imagery of the column itself.

Finally, there was the statue known as the Palladion. A statue of the armed Pallas Athena linked irrevocably with the history and destiny of Troy, the Palladion was understood as an image of divine origin.[48] Said to have fallen to Troy from heaven, it was kept in the citadel at Ilion as a guarantee of the city's safety. Odysseus and Diomedes carried the statue away, thus creating the conditions for the city's fall. Roman tradition states that Aeneas rescued the Palladion and brought it to Lavinium whence it was taken to Rome. There it was kept in the inner sanctum of the Temple of Vesta.[49] The cult of Vesta expressed the permanence of Rome, a notion bound up with the Palladion's pre-Roman history. Just as the statue guaranteed the safety of Troy through its presence, it also protected the city of Rome. Further, the embrace of the apotropaic power of the Palladion was in effect an assimilation of Trojan history to Roman that gave Rome and, eventually, its empire a history of unparalleled antiquity. The very antiquity of this history legitimated Roman rule by creating a sense of timeless permanence and unbroken continuity. In Constantinople, the statue must have been intended to function in a similar manner. Through the Palladion's numinous presence, Constantinople assimilated the history of Rome and before it Troy, embracing as it did so the legacy of these great cities as its own.

The theme of Trojan origins played out in other elements of the Forum's decor. Thus, although sources identify only three monuments as specifically Constantinian, the list can be lengthened on the basis of iconography. Bronze statues representing

Paris, Hera, and Aphrodite stood together in the forum along with figures of Athena and Thetis. Together these *dramatis personae* formed an ensemble depicting the Judgment of Paris (cat. no. 113), that fateful event engineered by Discord for the destruction of Troy. This display confirmed what the presence of the Palladion implied, that the Constantinopolitan past was one with the Trojan.

There is no evidence for the original display of the group; however, a likely spot would have been the nymphaeum on the Forum's south side.[50] Nymphaea were important features in any Roman city and as such were often subject to extensive architectural development. This was particularly the case in the cities of western Asia Minor to which Constantinople owed so much in terms of its architectural forms. The Miletos nymphaeum,[51] a second-century construction, suggests the possible form and appearance of the Constantinian Forum's. An elaborate columnar façade rose on three levels as the frame for a large rectangular pool fed by waters from the local aqueduct. In the third century an addition of sculpture depicting gods and goddesses, nymphs, heroes, and local dignitaries completed the ensemble. Images of gods such as Askleipios or Poseidon and his attendant nymphs embraced the theme of water and its life-giving properties. At the same time, there was a specifically Milesian cast to the imagery. Figures such as Dionysios referred to his local cult. Other statues, such as a portrait of Lallianus, Asiatic Proconsul under Gordian III, brought contemporary civic figures into the mix.[52]

On the model of a building such as the Miletos fountain, it is possible that the statues representing the Judgment of Paris were displayed at the Forum's nymphaeum. This setting would also have been the logical one for the hippocamps. Indeed, these marine figures could well have formed part of a larger group of a marine thiasos celebrating the marriage of Peleos and Thetis at which gathering the Judgment of Paris took place. The marble fragment of a dolphin (cat. no. 110) also may have belonged to such a display.

Although the proposed display of these figures is hypothetical, the image that their collective presence created is clear. The group recalled the events that created the circumstances for the abduction of the Palladion and the ensuing destruction of Troy. The fall of Troy and the removal of the Palladion to Italy brought about the rise of Rome. Finally, with the transferal of the Palladion, or what was believed to be the Palladion, to the Forum, the destiny of Constantinople was assured. By depositing this most ancient and sacred of images at the base of his statue in the center of his eponymous forum, Constantine not only secured the greatness and destiny of his own city, but also proclaimed Constantinople the heir to Roman permanence and stability.

The decoration of the Forum, the Hippodrome, and the Baths of Zeuxippos reinforced the image of *romanitas* articulated in the city's architectural development with the installation of sculptured ensembles around historicizing themes that legitimated the notion of Constantinopolitan antiquity and through it preeminence. Specifically, these three collections invented an urban history that linked the city to an epic past and in so doing made the steward of a great cultural tradition. These themes were played out in statements and their variations in the three great gatherings at the Hippodrome, the Baths, and the Forum. In each and every one of these spaces, Constantinople was described as the heir to the traditions first of Troy and then of Rome. The nature of the inheritance and the sense of stewardship that followed from it varied from place to place. In the Hippodrome, military prowess and political power were the dominant themes, while in the Zeuxippos intellectual hegemony took pride of place. Finally in the Forum, history entwined with the power of the sacred to ensure Constantinopolitan greatness.

## THE LESSER COLLECTIONS

The grand schemes of the city's major collections were reiterated on a smaller scale in nodal points around the city. At the Milion, the notion of continuity with Roman rule was articulated by placing equestrian statues of the emperors Trajan and Hadrian (cat. no. 158) side by side with images of Constantine. Here, in a manner similar to the emperor's great arch in Rome, the comparison of Constantine to Trajan and Hadrian not only emphasized themes of continuity, but also spoke of renewal and revival. In the comparison, Constantine drew on the ideas outlined in the grand, encompassing displays of the Hippodrome and the Zeuxippos to describe not his city but himself as a monarch with the military prowess of Trajan and the cultural sagacity of Hadrian.

Antiquities in the Strategeion were used to similar effect. Here Constantine set up a statue of Alexander the Great (cat. no. 166). In this instance the emperor reached back farther into the past, as he did in the Forum of Constantine, to draw upon the themes of Hellenistic kingship that were implicit in the reference to the Hellenic world's first true imperial ruler.

The Basilika was treated in a like manner. In this instance an assemblage of specifically religious images worked with the efficacy of the Palladion to bring the numinous power of Roman national cults and their traditions into the Constantinopolitan orbit. Like the Baths of Zeuxippos and the Hippodrome, the Basilika was an inheritance from the Severan period of the city's development. Constantine added to the Basilika by building two temples on either side of the entrance, one dedicated to the Great Mother, Kybele (cat. no. 22), the other to the Roman Tyche (cat. no. 24). In each, he placed a statue of the appropriate divinity. The image of Kybele/Rhea is reported to have been brought from the goddess's sanctuary in the mountains above Kyzikos. There is no word on the provenance of the Tyche, whose Roman origins were perhaps a given.

Kybele was connected directly with the Roman state religion. Introduced into Rome in 204 B.C. with the importation of a sacred stone from the goddess's sanctuary at Pessinous in Asia Minor, Kybele, the Roman Magna Mater, was associated in the Roman mind with the defense of the state and victory.[53] As well, the goddess was considered as both a generator and protector of cities. In this guise she was associated specifically with the well-being and fortune of Rome, a connection that was seen to coincide with the Trojan origins of Rome itself.[54] Worshipped at Troy itself, Magna Mater was the great defender of Aeneas, and for Virgil, his patron Augustus, and subsequent generations of Romans both the goddess and the hero came to realize their greatness at Rome. Further, it was Magna Mater that created the essential link between Rome's heroic past and her future greatness.

These sentiments were not restricted to poetic declamation. Under Augustus the connection between Rome and Magna Mater was given special emphasis. The emperor himself restored her Palatine temple (A.D. 3) and installed himself as the goddess's neighbor in his nearby residence.[55] Augustus's wife and consort, Livia, styled herself a kind of Magna Mater by claiming descent from the goddess through her own ancestors and adopting the mural crown and other attributes in her portraits.[56]

Although her origins were not as ancient as those of Magna Mater were, Tyche/Fortuna also was connected with the Roman state religion. Among the many guises in which she was worshipped was that of Fortuna Publica or Fortuna Populi Romani. As such she was, together with Magna Mater, one of the tutelary goddesses of the state. Another of her guises was that of Fortuna Caesaris or Augustus, the protectress of emperors.[57]

As with the Palladion, the notion behind the incorporation of these images into the urban network must have been to bring the power of Rome and its supernatural defenders to Constantinople. In so doing the emperor co-opted once again the guarantors of Roman power for his own purposes, at once legitimating Constantinopolitan claims to primacy and guaranteeing the city's future greatness. This emphasis was consistent with those in the city's other great displays. Connections to an epic Trojan past, to notions of victory and especially to ideas of Augustan triumph and restoration were implied, echoing the sentiments of the Hippodrome, the Baths, and the Forum.

Inclusion of one of Rome's most prominent spoils, the great Herakles by Lysippos of Sikyon (cat. no. 21), continued this theme to complete the Constantinian elaboration of the Basilika. Made by the Greek sculptor in the fourth century B.C. for the south Italian city of Tarentum, the Herakles stood on that city's acropolis before being captured and taken to Rome as a spoil in 209 B.C., where it was displayed on the Capitol as an emblem of Rome's military and political fortunes. Like other statues of Roman provenance, the Herakles, steeped as it was in the history and imagery of the old capital, gave testimony to the absorption of the old city's traditions into those of the new. In this case, however, the traditions referred to were not ancient, quasi-mythical events, but documented historical proceedings that proclaimed the triumph of Roman power. What was implied, then, in the presence of the Herakles was not only the Constantinopolitan absorption of Roman tradition, but also the assimilation of the old city's worldly power, authority, and prestige. In this way, the Herakles stood as testimony to the efficacy of the Kybele/Tyche cult.

The statue was also appropriate to the setting in terms of its simple iconography. The great Lysippan bronze showed the hero seated and resting in what is likely to have been the aftermath of his induction into the Eleusinian mysteries. Understood in this depiction of the hero was an introspective, contemplative bent that complemented his more active persona. This aspect in its turn was appropriate to the setting, for the Basilika was, among other things, the seat of the city's university and libraries. Thus, the image of the hero lost in thought functioned in much the same vein as he did in the circus with the difference that here he was an exemplar for the life of the mind.

Decoration of the imperial palace was also a concern. One of the largest and most complete of the individual Constantinian ensembles must have been the group of Muses statues from the Museion on Mt. Helikon (cat. no. 18). Eusebios reports that the statues were set up in the Palace. Later fourth- and fifth-century sources place them inside a Senate House built on the eastern edge of the Augusteion in the later fourth century. The two statements are not mutually exclusive. Two major Muse groups, both the products of fifth- and fourth-century B.C. manufacture, stood in the Helikonian sanctuary, and it is possible that both were brought to the city either at the same time or separately and eventually set up in different locations. Alternatively, it is possible that the Muses were moved to the Augusteion Senate from the Palace at the time of its late-fourth-century construction.

Eusebios does not state where the Muses stood. It is likely that they were given a very public setting at the entrance to the palace itself or in a prominent interior space such as the main audience hall. Whatever their locale, viewers probably would have understood these figures as reflections of imperial virtues. Themistios (cat. no. 18), writing at the end of the fourth century when one of the groups had been installed in the Senate House, considered the Muses models of virtue, associating them with philosophy and the qualities of mansuetude and clemency that he averred were the properties of the senators themselves. Placement of the figures in the palace would have invited a similar association of these same qualities with the emperor and, by extension, his rule. As such, the statuary not only described the qualities of the emperor, but also proclaimed virtue and its accompanying moral authority as the root of imperial power. In this sense, the statues reflected many of the same ideas and ideals as those in the Baths of Zeuxippos.

The last and arguably the greatest of the ancient collections in Constantinian Constantinople was that of the Augusteion. Unfortunately it is also the least well documented. A single source, the eighth-century *Parastaseis*, describes statuary that stood in front of the Hagia Sophia in the period before its Justinianic rebuilding (cat. nos. 7–15). That the space referred to is actually that of the Augusteion is suggested by the fact that later sources refer to the area as a kind of courtyard giving access to the Great Church. The Augusteion was a public square until at least the sixth century when Prokopios referred to it as an "agora."[58] In the later Byzantine period, however, a portion of it appears to have been closed off to create an open-air imperial vestibule to the church. The physical incorporation of at least part of the forum into the Hagia Sophia's ritual space may have led to the association of the forum with the church.[59]

The surviving record indicates that the area was rich in statuary. Late antique emperors and officials stood together with antiquities; however, only the ancient statues are named: Aphrodite, Arcturus, the emperor Carus, the philosopher Hero, a priestess of Athena, two figures described as "Persian statues," which probably were telamones, Selene, the South Pole, Zeus, and the Zodiac (cat. nos. 7–15).

The variety of figures in the group doubtless reflects the addition of sculpture over time to an initial core group of monuments. What such a core group might have been remains unclear; however, on the grounds of iconographical consistency it is likely to have included the statues of Zeus, the Zodiac, Selene, Aphrodite, Arcturus, the telamones, and the South Pole. These figures, all of them either specifically or potentially astrological in nature, suggest that the original ensemble was in fact the visual expression of a horoscope.[60]

Whose horoscope remains, however, unknown. It is possible that the gathering gave substance to the divinations made at the foundation ceremonies. More probable, and in direct keeping with Roman tradition, is the possibility that any such horoscope would have been connected with the emperor or a member of his family. In the Greco-Roman world, horoscopes were associated with monarchies and their legitimation from as early as the Hellenistic age. In the Roman imperial period, forecasts frequently were cast in conjunction with imperial accessions or other significant events in the course of a reign. They were a means to legitimate an emperor's rule, his decisions, and his actions by presenting events as fated. Originally adopted by Augustus, this habit persisted into the fifth century, although there was increasing equivocation about the practice as Christianity gained the upper hand.[61] A set of coronation horoscopes[62] for ill-fated usurper emperors that survives from the period of the emperor Zeno (476–91) preserve not only the forecasts themselves, but also the appended explanations of why these upstarts' claims were not realized: They were based on faulty astrological interpretation. Ignorance of the signs led to false conclusions.

Although it is reasonable to imagine that some of the statues in the Augusteion formed group that visualized an imperial horoscope, the actual subject matter of such a forecast remains unknown. Its general sense can, however, be imagined. Like all such enterprises, the Augusteion horoscope would have projected future success for the emperor and his reign, legitimating the imperial person and the events associated with him by presenting his ascendancy as predestined. In this respect the gathering was not unlike collections elsewhere in the city. Like them, the Augusteion ensemble sought to shore up Constantine and his rule. In this instance, however, it did so not by reaching into the past to create a legitimating history, but by looking to the future.

## THE CONSTANTINIAN AGENDA

Viewed collectively, the evidence for the Constantinopolitan displays reveals a consistent approach to the display of the material. By and large individual collections were shaped according to traditional ideas about how sculpture should be deployed. Thus, statuary was selected and organized around themes appropriate to place. In the Zeuxippos the choice of statuary conformed to the traditional thermal themes, while the gathering in the Hippodrome was of a piece with ancient circus imagery. Across the city in spaces large and small this sense of continuity with established decorative tradition prevailed.

Throughout these collections, thematic consistency resounded. In each and every setting, sculpture worked to describe a Constantinopolitan history. The individual gatherings developed a set number of themes that worked collectively to construct the vision of the Constantinopolitan past. First and foremost was the subject of urban ancestry. Each one of the city's significant public spaces displayed sculpture with an eye to constructing an urban history, and that urban history itself was conceived largely in terms of origins. Throughout the city the theme of continuity with the past was articulated by emphasizing the portentous moments surrounding the rise and fall of Constantinople's own great predecessors, Troy and Rome. In the Forum of Constantine, it was the Judgment of Paris, that fateful no-win decision that led ultimately to the destruction of Troy and through it to the foundation of Rome, that claimed public attention. In the Baths of Zeuxippos, the chain of events continued with the visualization of the Trojan epic and the apparent emphasis within the cycle on the *Ilioupersis* itself. Finally, in the Hippodrome, it was the creation of Rome embodied in the inclusion of the wolf with Romulus and Remus that once again called moments of urban origins to mind.

This focus on urban ancestry was an end in itself. The imagination that went into the visualization of a Constantinopolitan history was not interested in constructing the bridge between these epic origins and the here and now of the fourth century. The intervening events that were associated with Byzantium itself and its Constantinian successor city together with the personalities that shaped them were in a sense superfluous: Quite simply, they clouded the historiographic issue by introducing unnecessary and distracting detail. What mattered in the long run to the Roman imagination was the legitimating force of hoary, epic antiquity, and this is the bond that was claimed for Constantinople in the great Constantinian collections.

This etiological conception of civic history reflected the desire to establish an identity for the city that would establish Constantinople's place within the Empire's urban hierarchy. As such it was perfectly consistent with the aims and methods of Greco-Roman historiographical and rhetorical tradition.[63] Both the description of mythic origins and the accompanying construct of the urban kinships that were so defining a feature of Constantinopolitan identity were a commonplace among local historiographers in the Hellenistic and Roman ages. In his great oration, the *Antiochikos,* the late Roman orator Libanios describes just such an identity for his native city, Antioch-on-the-Orontes, associating its foundation with the Argive search for Inachus's daughter, Io.[64] In the case of both Constantinople and Antioch, the historical record confirmed the Roman penchant for self-identification through comparison to the past. In the urban scheme of things, links to a heroic past guaranteed an almost unrivaled status derived from the sense of age itself. No city had greater prestige than one founded by a god or hero from the heroic age. Origins such as these were synonymous with honor and eternal glory. As Menander Rhetor advised the would-be urban encomiast, "Thus, if a city is very ancient you will say that oldest means honorable, and the city is eternal like the gods."[65] At work in the construct of Constantinopolitan history was the desire to grasp eternity.

In the case of Constantinople, it was as much the selection of stories as the emphasis on antiquity that ensured that eternity was within reach. In complete contrast to Antioch, a city's whose foundation myth was relatively obscure and reserved for local consumption, Constantinople was possessed of a past with a truly catholic appeal. The tales that went into the city's historiographic mix – the Judgment of Paris, the Fall of Troy, the Flight of Aeneas, and the legend of Romulus and Remus – were universally familiar. These were the stories that informed Greco-Roman imagination from first youth up to extreme old age. As such they created a history and through it an urban identity that was as familiar as it was venerable. The myth and history that went into the shaping of the city's identity was in effect that of everyman.

Whereas Libanios's tales of the Antiochene past were unflinchingly local in reference, the history conjured for Constantinople, based as it was on every educated man's knowledge of mythology, was far more universal in tone. In an age when the city of Rome still held sway in the collective imagination as the capital, and other centers such as Milan and Trier vied for imperial standing, this unequivocal proclamation of Constantinopolitan universality through the appropriation of the Greco-Roman world's best-loved and time-honored stories as the city's own was a shrewd and necessary step. The draw of these epic tales not only equipped the city with a venerable past, but also allowed it to transcend the limitations of the parochial to claim a place in the hearts and minds of citizens across the Empire.

The vision of primacy engineered through the manipulation of this subject matter was underscored by the phenomenon of reuse. Antiquities, with their hegemonic implications, walked hand in hand with the new city's historical claims, all of which suggests that it was Jerome with his emphasis on civic primacy, rather than the fiercely Christian Eusebios, who better understood the aims and aspirations that informed the Constantinian project. Indeed, while there was doubtless a sector of the population that responded to the installation of antiquities in a manner similar to that of Eusebios, the whole tenor of the Constantinian scheme is of a piece with the architectural aggrandizement of the city. Just as the great armature of streets and public gathering places that Constantine polished was designed to project an all-encompassing vision of *romanitas*, the city's sculptured installations were intended to shore up that vision by fleshing out the details of an urban history that would legitimate the initial architectural claims and ensure Constantinople pride of place among the already distinguished cities of the Roman world.

## ❧ FOUR ❧

# THEODOSIAN CONSTANTINOPLE

T HE SUCCESS OF CONSTANTINOPLE AS AN URBAN CENTER WAS UNQUALIFIED. At the city's founding, the population of Byzantium is estimated to have been approximately 20,000. One hundred years later, by the middle of the fifth century, it housed somewhere between 300,000 and 400,000 people.[1] This staggering growth at once reflected the city's success as a government center and gave life to the notion of the ongoing need for the development of its public spaces. Nevertheless, the intense and very deliberate development of Constantinople that took place under the Constantinian mandate virtually ceased during the reigns of Julian, Jovian, and Valens. Although the city was not neglected, construction and the embellishment of an urban image in any far-reaching or consistent manner was not at the forefront of imperial policy. Building activity was limited, and evidence for the installation and adornment of public monuments is thin, with the known dedications being limited to imperial portraits.[2] The imaginative and compelling use of antiquities that so characterized the Constantinian efforts with respect to urban decor was entirely absent.

## THEODOSIAN DEVELOPMENT

This situation changed with the accession of Theodosios I in 379 and the rise of his family dynasty in the late fourth and fifth centuries. During the reign of Theodosios and those of his Constantinopolitan successors, his son, Arkadios, and grandson, Theodosios II, development of the city once again became an aspect of imperial concern. Public areas within the old Severan walls were restored and newly decorated, while the territory west of the Forum of Constantine saw the construction and aggrandizement of a new series of monumental civic spaces. Finally, during the reign of Theodosios II, the city itself was enlarged with the construction of a new defensive wall nearly a mile and a half to the west of the Constantinian circuit.[3] In part, these developments were a response to the practical necessity of accommodating a growing population. At the same time, however, the monumental quality of these undertakings reflected the time-honored awareness of building as an imperial right and responsibility that was itself an expression of dynastic greatness. (See Figures 1 and 9.)

That the Theodosians were aware of the expressive potential and power of architecture and urban development is clear from the document known as the *Notitia Urbis Constantinopolitanae*.[4] Written sometime between 423 and 427, during the reign of Theodosios II, the *Notitia* catalogues the buildings, monuments, public spaces, and thoroughfares in each of the city's fourteen administrative regions. Various types of construction are included. Utilitarian projects such as ports and cisterns are listed together with such public trophy works as bath buildings and forums. Palaces and churches are included, as is an enumeration of streets and magistrates for individual regions. Many of the buildings referred to, such as the "ecclesia magna" and the "thermas Zeuxippi," clearly pertain to the Constantinian development of the city; however, it also is evident that a large number of the references apply to specifically Theodosian projects and that this enumeration of the city's architectural treasures represented a dynastic promotional effort.[5]

The development reflected in the *Notitia* took place in the last decades of the fourth and first decades of the fifth century. In the almost thirty years between Theodosios's accession in 379 and Arkadios's death in 308, these emperors oversaw the addition of a series of building projects in the old city center as well as the construction of a series of monumental public spaces in the city's western territories. This penchant for western expansion carried on into the reign of Theodosios II with the construction of a new defensive wall.

As in the Constantinian age, statuary, ancient and modern, was erected as part of the ongoing process of urban development. In both the old city and the new, sculpture was supplied to the capital's forums, streets, and public gathering places. In the old city, antiquities were added to the collections in the Hippodrome and the Augusteion. Ancient statuary was also a feature of the design and decoration of the western territories' new forums, as well as at the Golden Gate, a portal that was eventually incorporated into the Theodosian landwall as the city's major ceremonial entryway.

Together with the building campaigns that characterized the Theodosian revitalization of the capital, the reuse of antiquities in the city's urban decoration represented

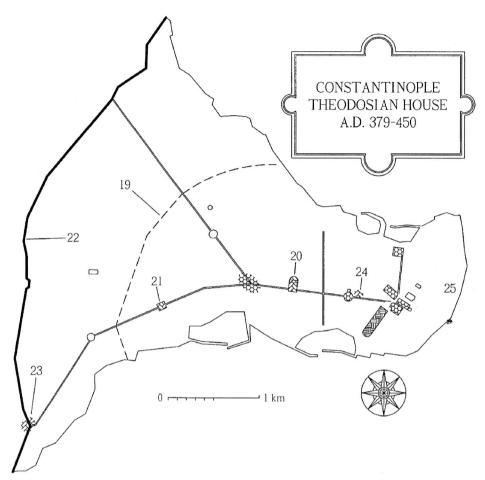

CONSTANTINOPLE
THEODOSIAN HOUSE
A.D. 379-450

FIGURE 9: Constantinople under the Theodosian House (Courtesy of Brian Madigan)

a revival of the Constantinian tradition of monumental public works projects on an encompassing scale. To a certain extent these developments were practical, but as in the earliest phase of the city's development, many of these projects, whether architectural or sculptural, had as their ultimate goal the aggrandizement of the city in the overarching terms of *romanitas*. Thus architectural development conformed to the familiar standards of late Roman urban design set in place under Constantine, while the sculptured installations that gave life to these monumental settings worked to flesh out the details of an appropriate urban iconography as conceived by the Theodosians. It was in the nature of that iconography that the Theodosian projects differed from the Constantinian. Whereas Constantine set out to create a distinct urban history with his sculptured installations, the motivating force behind the Theodosian installations appears to have been one of dynastic aggrandizement. As such, the Theodosian project was more in accord with the standard Roman practice of imperial glorification and, in keeping with such projects, encompassed architectural development as much as sculptural installation.

Architectural additions to the city's Severan core during the reigns of Theodosios I and Arkadios appear to have been few. Development of the monumental streets and spaces at the city center had been achieved effectively under the Constantinian mandate with the result that additions to the urban fabric were largely piecemeal, consisting primarily of the addition of individual buildings. Various members of the dynasty sponsored imperial baths, and service buildings such as ports and cisterns characterized the ongoing development of the old city.[6] Although the exact location of these buildings and their appearance is not known, it is clear that these foundations represented a substantial investment in the monumental civic core. Perfectly in keeping with the established traditions of imperial benefaction, these buildings had the effect not only of equipping the city's burgeoning population with enough public facilities, but also of placing a specific and doubtless very visible Theodosian stamp on the city's antique core that gave testimony to imperial largesse and generosity.

It was in the territories to the west of the Severan wall that the real Theodosian bent for urban planning was engaged in the construction of two monumental public forums along the western extension of the Mese. The first, the Forum of Theodosios, or Forum Tauri, straddled the Mese at a point about a mile west of the Forum of Constantine. Constantine is alleged to have been the first to regularize the terrain, establishing a large plaza on the site, and Valens is said to have added a nymphaeum; however, it was only under Theodosios I that systematic manipulation of the space took place. In the late 380s and early 390s, the emperor oversaw the construction of a large architectural development that included a grand pair of entrance arches over the Mese that gave on to the plaza on its east and west sides, a basilica on its south side, and a historiated column commemorating the emperor's military successes on its north. As the erection of the historiated column suggests, the Forum appears to have been conceived on the model of the Forum of Trajan in Rome. At the same time, given the fact that the elements in the Constantinopolitan forum were combined in a manner that was different from that of the Roman space, it is possible that the likeness was evoked as much by scale as by form.[7]

The second great development in the western territories, the Forum of Arkadios, or Xerolophon, stood further west along the Mese dominating the crest of a hill. Arkadios initiated the organization of this space with the dedication in 402 of a historiated column on the model of the Forum Tauri's Column of Theodosios. The real systematic development of the place did not take place until sometime around 435, however, when the area was regularized with the addition of all the requisite elements: arcades, porticoes, apses, and statuary. The exact distribution of these elements is not known and the forum's plan and appearance remain a cipher.[8]

With the creation of these great forums, Theodosios and Arkadios responded to, accommodated, and spurred on the city's westward expansion by creating a set of monumental public gathering spaces for the new territories that were the rival of the old city's great civic centers. Like those spaces, both the Forum of Theodosios and the Forum of Arkadios were areas in and around which urban life coalesced. Further, the way in which those spaces were developed was consistent with the image projected by the architecture of the old city. Lavishly carved marbles bracketed and shaped monumental spaces in the traditional architectural language of the Greco-Roman world, extending the image of *romanitas* to the newer areas of the city.

At the same time, however, the overall ordering of that space was different from that of the old city. The conscious topographical division into discrete areas that accommodated different religious practices and the juxtaposition of those areas not only to one another but also to more overtly imperial precincts appears not to have been carried out in the expansion of the city. In contrast to a space such as the Augusteion, the new forums themselves appear to have supported a wide range of commercial, legal, and ceremonial activity, much in the manner of traditional Roman civic spaces.[9] Further, the evidence of the *Notitia* suggests that churches were built throughout the area bounded by the Severan and Constantinian walls. No less than eight foundations are mentioned in the western territory, all interspersed with commercial and residential buildings as well as public works projects.[10] This change in the organization of public space may well reflect the growing consensus for Christianity that developed during the reign of Theodosios I. Under his mandate, Christianity became the Empire's official religion,[11] and the need sensed by Constantine to accommodate the diverse religious practice of the later Roman world in his city scheme may no longer have been felt. Certainly no temples were added to the new city, and it is likely that any awareness of or desire for pagan accommodation slipped from urban consciousness.

The integration of ecclesiastical foundations into the fabric of the western territories seen under Theodosios I and Arkadios did not feature in the ongoing Theodosian development of the old Severan center where the Constantinian distinctions between discrete spaces and their functions persisted well into the fifth century. During the reign of Theodosios II a substantial group of important public works projects sprang up within the Severan walls. The dedication of no less than three public baths to various members of the imperial house took place together with the construction of rather more prosaic but no less necessary warehouse and cistern projects.[12] The rebuilding of Hagia Sophia between 405 and 415 was also a feature in this development.[13] The first church, which had been dedicated by Constantius (337–361), was destroyed in 404 by fires started during the riots attendant on the expulsion of the city's controversial bishop, John Chrysostom. Although, with the exception of Hagia Sophia, the exact location of these various projects is not known, their general distribution across the city's regions suggests strongly that the strict Constantinian delineation of a Christian religious precinct at the city center was respected.

No less significant for the development of the old city in the second Theodosian age than these public works projects was the large amount of imperial residential building. At least three palace complexes were built in the old center either within the confines or at the edges of the Great Palace: the Palace of Placidia, the House of Placidia Augusta, and the Palace of Marina.[14] Each residence was built for a female member of the Theodosian house, and the effect of this lavish residential development was to expand the claims made on the city's monumental core by the imperial house. At the same time, however, and in keeping with the strictures observed in the construction of public projects elsewhere in the city center, the established Constantinian zones appear to have been respected. Thus, the new palace construction, although extending the limits of the Great Palace, was contained within the imperial precinct established under Constantine.

Expansion to the west balanced the activity at the city center. Beginning in 413, construction of a new defensive wall established a new western boundary about a mile and a half west of the old Constantinian circuit.[15] At the same time, however, the land claimed for Constantinople remained undeveloped in any real monumental sense, the territory being given over largely to the construction of cisterns for water provisioning, monastic institutions, and farming.[16] The major civic spaces that punctuated the city within the Constantinian walls were entirely absent and remained so throughout the capital's history. Thus, it was in the context of the established, Constantinian limit and the norms of Constantinian development that the Theodosians made their most substantial contributions to the renewed growth and development of the capital.

## THE REUSE OF ANTIQUITIES

A renewed interest in the use of antiquities paralleled the attention paid to the architectural development of the Theodosian capital. Precious little evidence survives for reuse in the two decades separating the death of Constantius from the accession of Theodosios I. The few extant references are isolated, but it is clear that, as with architectural development, there was none of the systematic deployment of ancient statuary seen during the first wave of the city's development (cat. no. 25). Beginning with Theodosios I, however, this trend reversed itself as antiquities once again were sought out and introduced to the public, either as additions to extant collections or in newly formed gatherings.

## THE HIPPODROME

As with Constantine, the Hippodrome was one of the premier venues for Theodosian collecting. Four major additions to an already crowded *euripus* were made during the course of Theodosian rule: an obelisk, a figure of the sea-monster Skylla, a quadriga, and a statue of Herakles. Of these donations, the obelisk (cat. no. 138) was the first. The second, made during the reign of Arkadios, was a figure of the sea-monster Skylla (cat. no. 142). Also brought to the Hippodrome during the Theodosian age was a gilt bronze quadriga (cat. no. 139) that stood not on the *euripus* but above the *carceres*. Reported to have been brought from the island of Chios during the reign of Theodosios II, the statue may have been part of a donation made by the emperor in the aftermath of an earthquake in 447. The last in the series of statues to be settled by the Theodosians on the Hippodrome was the Lysippan Herakles (cat. no. 21). First installed at the Basilika during the Constantinian elaboration of the city, the statue was removed eventually to the circus where it was displayed along the *euripus*.

Although few, the Theodosian additions to the Hippodrome collection were important donations that built on and enhanced the circus's extant image by con-forming to the categories of representation that had been established during the Constantinian elaboration of the circus. This was certainly the case with the raising of the Theodosian obelisk, a project that quite literally completed an initiative un-dertaken by Constantine, and that was an essential ingredient in fostering the desired Constantinian comparison between the Old Rome and the New.

Since Augustus's erection in 10 B.C. of an obelisk from Heliopolis in Egypt at the Circus Maximus, obelisks had become a characteristic element in circus decor. They were not a feature in every circus, because, unlike other prominent monuments, such as the *metae*, or turning posts, they were not essential to the mechanics of the race. Their function was purely visual. Nonetheless they were a popular option, especially in early fourth-century Tetrarchic circuses, because they called to mind the image of the prototypical and ideal racetrack, the Circus Maximus and with it an image of Rome and power. As in the tetrarchic circuses that were its immediate predecessors, the inclusion of an obelisk in the Hippodrome was doubtless meant to signal the comparison to Rome.[17]

In the case of the Hippodrome, however, the evocation of Rome was made uniquely explicit by the presence of not one, but two obelisks (Figure 4). Although other circuses may have had a single obelisk, only Rome was distinguished by two: the Heliopolitan Obelisk donated by Augustus and the Theban Obelisk erected under Constantine.[18] Planners at Constantinople set out to imitate this model first with the erection of the Theodosian obelisk and second with the construction of an imitation obelisk, the Built Obelisk.[19]

Unlike the Theodosian monument, the Built Obelisk (Figure 10) is not a true obelisk, but an imitation constructed out of ashlar masonry. Whereas its history is obscure, its purpose is not. Presumably it would have been planned for installation at the same time as the erection of the true obelisk, thus allowing the Hippodrome to conform visually to the precedent set by the pair of obelisks in the Circus Maximus.[20]

Further, the Constantinopolitan obelisks recall the precedent of Rome not only in number, but also in placement. In the Circus Maximus, the Heliopolitan Obelisk rises on the center of the *euripus* while the obelisk from Thebes stands toward the barrier's southeast end. The Hippodrome repeats this arrangement: The Theodosian Obelisk occupies the central position of the Heliopolitan monument, the Built Obelisk the southeast placement of the Theban monolith. This disposition of monuments confirms the observation of the seventh-century *Chronicon Paschale* that the racetrack was built in imitation of the Circus Maximus.[21]

With the erection of the Theban obelisk, Theodosios did far more than complete the imitation of the Circus Maximus initiated by Constantine. In the realization of what was initially a Constantinian endeavor, the emperor set himself up for comparison with the city's founder, implicitly demonstrating not only continuity of purpose, but also superiority by being able to achieve what his predecessor had not. Further, by placing his own dedication, the Theban Obelisk, in the position enjoyed by the

FIGURE 10: The Built Obelisk, Istanbul (photo: W. Schiele, Deutsches Archäologisches Institut, Istanbul, Institute Negative No. 68/150)

Augustan dedication at Rome, Theodosios likened himself to the first and greatest of all Roman emperors, Augustus, relegating Constantine to a secondary position both literally and figuratively.

Theodosian continuity with Constantinian planning also is evident in the inclusion of the Skylla, Herakles, and Quadriga statues. All three of these monuments picked up on ideas explicit in the Constantinian circus's development. The Lysippan Herakles would have dovetailed with the Hippodrome's imagery on two levels. On the one hand, the statue would have been consistent with the imagery of the Labors elaborated in the inclusion of other Herakles statues (cat. nos. 134, 135). As such it would have functioned as an exemplar for circus competitors. On the other hand, because of its unique Roman associations the statue also could have elaborated the theme of Roman continuity spelled out in the inclusion of such monuments as the wolf with Romulus and Remus (cat. no. 147) and the obelisks, authentic (cat. no. 138) and faux.

The Skylla group would have worked to similar effect. Like the figures of the Dioscuri (cat. no. 128) introduced by Constantine, the Skylla (cat. no. 142) served as an exemplar for competitors in the races. The monster was associated with struggle and combat. In her traditional setting across the straits from Charybdis, she posed a constant menace to travelers, their lives, and fortunes. Those heroes such as Herakles, Odysseus, and Aeneas who traversed the straits with their lives intact represented those who struggled against and conquered death and destruction. They were victors over the ancient forces of darkness and evil who gained, through their efforts, immortal fame. In the setting of the Hippodrome, these iconographical associations were important for two reasons. The presence of the Skylla first called to mind the heroes of the past, and their heroism and glory could be understood as somehow transferable to the athletic heroes of the present: The race through the circus was analogous to the passage through the straits.

Theodosian continuity with Constantinian planning also is evident in the inclusion of the quadriga group (cat. no. 139), a monument that picked up on the notion of victory explicit in so many of the Hippodrome's images. Like the Delphic tripods (cat. no. 145) that had been brought by Constantine from the Sanctuary of Apollo, the quadriga was a kind of generic victory monument that was generally useful for commemorating military triumphs. Typically quadrigae were dedicated in sanctuaries or placed atop triumphal arches. Although these dedications would have had associations with particular people and events, these types of images also had the power to transcend the specific details of time and place to conjure a general image of victory.

Although the original dedication of the Hippodrome quadriga is not known, the monument probably functioned in much the same manner. On the one hand it would have called to mind a very specific event in Chian history. On the other hand it would have stood generally for victory. The transformation from a specific to a generic monument is suggested by the placement over the *carceres*. In this position it would have stood high above the track without base or inscription, a monument not to a particular person or event, but rather to the horses and drivers ready to spring from the gates below in search of their own, fresh victory.

The Hippodrome's Theodosian dedications were major donations that picked up on and underscored the established themes of the circus's decoration. For all their integrity with the aims and sentiment of the earlier Constantinian projects, however, these installations also were different. Unlike Constantine, whose agenda was one of urban affirmation, that of the Theodosians was largely one of dynastic promotion and legitimation. Nowhere is this more clearly demonstrated than by the case of the Theodosian obelisk. As we have seen, the raising of the obelisk at Constantinople completed the Constantinian image of New Rome. At the same time, however, Theodosios co-opted the monument for his own purposes. The series of relief carvings on each of the monument's four sides[22] coupled with the inscriptions add a specifically Theodosian gloss to its presentation. The reliefs together with the inscriptions emphasizing not the occasion for which the monument was raised, but rather the failed attempts by other rulers, the difficulty with which it was erected, and the fact that the project was, ultimately, a Theodosian success story transformed a monument initially selected for its ability to describe a Constantinopolitan history into a paean to dynastic triumph that, by underscoring Theodosian authority, strength, and ingenuity, validated Theodosian rule.

What was true for the obelisk was true for each and every one of the monuments added to the Hippodrome, albeit on a lesser scale. Although hardly so explicit as in the case of the obelisk, the addition of antiquities, itself an imitation of a Constantinian initiative, forced the comparison between Theodosios, his successors, and their great predecessor, Constantine, thus underscoring the new dynasty's continuity with the old, not to mention the shared virtues that legitimated this claim. In this sense, the Theodosian enterprise was more of a piece with standard Roman practice of imperial glorification.

## THE AUGUSTEION

This essentially conservative bent was followed by the display of antiquities at the Senate House in the Augusteion. Constantinople was equipped with two senate houses. The first, built by Constantine, stood in the Forum of Constantine, while the second, of uncertain date, rose at the eastern end of the Augusteion. This second building burned in 404 during the fires that broke out in the riots associated with the expulsion of the controversial bishop John Chrysostom. It was subsequently rebuilt in the fifth century, only to be destroyed again in the Nika rebellion of 532.[23]

Although there is some evidence that the Augusteion Senate was built as early as the reign of Constantine, construction by Julian seems more likely. Zosimos reports that the emperor, upon returning to Constantinople in 362 after campaigns against Constantius in the west, "allowed the city to have a senate just as at Rome."[24] This reference must refer to the Julian expansion of the Senate as Constantine established the first Constantinopolitan curia.[25] Construction of a senate building in the Augusteion may have been a way to acknowledge this expansion. Whether the building was complete at his death in 363 is unclear but seems unlikely given the tumult surrounding his reign. At best, the actual structure would have been complete. Its decoration, accomplished with a combination of ancient statuary and contemporary portraits, is more likely to have been undertaken during the reign of Theodosios.

The building was the setting for several important antiquities. Two major statues, a Zeus from the sanctuary at Dodona in Epiros (cat. no. 19) and an Athena from Lindos on Rhodes (cat. no. 17), flanked the entrance, and a series of the Muses (cat. no. 18) adorned the interior. The destruction of the Senate House in 404 provides a *terminus ante quem* for the sculptures' importation. Given Julian's own desire to reinstate Hellenic cult, it is unlikely that the Zeus and Athena statues, derived as they were from two of the great ancient sanctuaries, were installed under his aegis. Evidence suggests instead a later, Theodosian date of importation. Both the sanctuaries at Dodona and the Lindian sanctuary were closed definitively in the late fourth century, casualties of Theodosios I's systematic suppression of Hellenic cult and religious culture and the continuation of this policy under his heirs.[26] Legislation preserved in the *Theodosian Code* that was enacted in large part as a response to Julian's efforts at reviving pagan tradition, calls, among other things, for the closure of temples as sites of worship.[27] In some instances it also issues directives for the outright destruction of temple buildings.[28] Dodona, where there is evidence of a final phase of destruction in the late fourth century, may well have been the victim of this mandate.[29] At Lindos the evidence is less conclusive. A dramatic decline in Lindian inscriptions in the late third and fourth centuries suggests not a single act of destruction but rather a slow withering of the cult.[30]

Whether by force or attrition, the closing of the sanctuaries made the whole range of images that had been created and maintained in the service of Hellenic cult available for reuse, as not only the temples themselves but also their contents reverted to the imperial fisc.[31] Once under state control, it could be directed to Constantinople for reuse in appropriate settings. Indeed, it is in the Theodosian age that the first consistent use of temple statues occurs. Although Eusebios mentions statuary from sanctuaries, most of the images to which he refers may well have been secondary, votive offerings rather than temple statues per se.

The Muses (cat. no. 18), which were bronze, numbered the canonical nine and ringed the interior of the Senate chamber where they stood in niches against the wall and may have been the same group referred to by Eusebios as having been brought by Constantine from Mt. Helikon. It is possible that this group, which was set up in the palace in the early fourth century, was moved to the Senate at a later date. Alternatively, a second Muse group, also from Helikon, may have been imported for use in the Senate at the time. Two groups of muses were known from the sanctuary, and it is conceivable that the second group was brought to Constantinople in the later fourth century. Whatever the case, reference to the statues in a series of orations by Themistios dated to 384 indicates that the statues were already in place at that time.

As elsewhere in Constantinople, the gathering of antiquities at the Senate House was intended to articulate an identity for the place. In this instance the display of statuary turned on ideas about and ideals of ethics. Referring to the Muse statues in no less than three of his orations (cat. no. 18) Themistios describes the figures as exemplars of philosophical inquiry and virtuous conduct, and exhorts his colleagues to follow their example. As practitioners of a way of life, the Muses were meant to be seen as inspiration for virtuous conduct for those who led the Empire. Seated with the Muses, the emperor and his senate, inspired by their example, were one with their ideals.

Zeus too was a model for the wise and the powerful together with his pendant companion Athena: "those who honor Ares search out what is warlike and appropriate to Ares, the followers of Apollo that which is harmonious and appropriate to this god, and only the lettered are the companions of Zeus." Themistios, the author of these lines, continues the analogy, drawing Athena into the fold by observing that the good of the state derives from the wisdom of the prince in the same way that Athena, the goddess of wisdom, sprang from the head of Zeus, the seat of intellect (cat. no. 18).

The statues at the Senate House both responded to and informed a vision of just rule. Together with the figures of the Muses, Zeus and Athena gave visual life to the sentiments expressed not only by Themistios, but also by contemporaries such as Libanios, who described Zeus as transforming "public life to an administration based on reasoning,"[32] or the Muses as inspiration to "true ideals" that should be held in the highest esteem.[33] These ideals, guarantors of virtue, ensured the happiness and success of the state.

Further, the construction and decoration of this second curia may have been intended to recall Roman precedent. The Roman Senate had been established from time immemorial in the Roman Forum. Under Hadrian, a building known as the Athenaeum was constructed. Described in the sources as a lecture hall in the service of the arts, the building also functioned as a subsidiary meeting place for the Senate.[34] It may well be that Julian had this building, the brainchild of his own model emperor, Hadrian, in mind when he undertook the building of the Augusteion Senate. Certainly, the function of the second Constantinopolitan building, a place associated with the great orations of Themistios among other things, would support such a hypothesis. Later decoration with the Muses and the stress on the values of knowledge and wisdom associated with the statues of Athena and Zeus also would have underscored such a purpose.

## THE WESTERN TERRITORIES

Like the reuse of antiquities in the Hippodrome, the display of ancient statuary at the Augusteion Senate conformed to ideas that had already been expressed in the Constantinian decorative schemes. In this instance, the emphasis on knowledge and wisdom was of a piece with the exploration of the values of the paideia laid out in the Baths of Zeuxippos. As in the bath, statuary served as a reminder that the moral underpinning of the state lay not in military force, but in the qualities of the mind. Where these programs differed from their Constantinian predecessors, however, was in their intended reference. Thus, although the Constantinian installations worked overwhelmingly to describe a specific urban identity by plugging into ideas about and attitudes toward history, the Theodosians manipulated that same history to describe themselves and their dynasty.

The reuse of antiquities in the Hippodrome and the Senate also was consistent with the Theodosian architectural development of the old city. As with the monumental building campaigns, the initiatives for reuse, although substantial, were largely piecemeal, inserted into the extant fabric of the city. The effect was to elaborate on and underscore existing themes. The imaginative conjuring of an urban identity that so characterized the Constantinian efforts at urban decoration was unknown. To some extent these habits of reuse must reflect the fact that the city, already resplendent with sculpture and, as such, possessed of a well-defined identity, was not such a ready candidate for imported goods. At the same time, however, development of public settings in the new territories to the west of the Constantinian wall, places such as the

Forum of Theodosios, the Forum of Arkadios, and the Golden Gate, three areas ripe for sculptural development, made equally spare use of antiquities, suggesting that, even allowing for lacunary records, the overall Theodosian reliance on ancient statuary, at least in terms of numbers, was far less than that of Constantine. This certainly was the case in the Forum of Theodosios, where only two ancient works, a portrait of Hadrian (cat. no. 118) and a silvered bronze equestrian statue of Theodosios I (cat. no. 117), are reported. Although presumably a work of second-century manufacture, details of the Hadrianic portrait remain unknown. The equestrian statue is, however, thoroughly documented, and details of provenance, style, and iconography combine to suggest that the statue was a reused figure of a Hellenistic ruler, possibly even Alexander himself, or a Roman emperor, retooled to fit the Theodosian image. The horses' lively stance is characteristic of late classical or Hellenistic horses, as is the absence of tack. Surviving examples of Theodosian imperial sculpture tend to be much more rigidly and frontally composed as do known statues of horses from the late Roman age. Precedent for this kind of monumental retooling is known from the great bronze statue in the Forum of Constantine (cat. no. 109).

Although limited to two, the statuary selected for reuse in the Theodosian forum appears to articulate themes of kingship in ways well established. In a manner analogous to the reuse of statues of the emperors Hadrian and Trajan at the Milion (cat. no. 158) the reuse of imperial portraits in the Hippodrome, and, ultimately, the reuse of imperial reliefs on the Arch of Constantine in Rome, the Hadrianic portrait set up the comparison between Theodosios and his great imperial predecessor. Similarly, apart from the intrinsic imagery of imperial might that any equestrian statue conveyed, the Theodosian figure invited comparison between the emperor and Constantine by virtue of the nature of its reuse. In assimilating his own portrait into an image of an earlier, Hellenistic or Roman ruler, whoever that ruler might have been, Theodosios not only subsumed the ethos of that ruler into his own identity and in so doing established his right to participate in the traditions of Greco-Roman kingship, but also, and more specifically, called attention to the link between his own rule and that of Constantine by imitating the type of reuse favored by the earlier emperor.

The architectural setting would doubtless have enhanced these comparisons, which itself was intended to evoke the past. With its porticoes, basilica, and towering historiated column, the Forum of Theodosios was itself conceived on the model of the Roman Forum of Trajan.[35] This design strategy, which invited comparison between Theodosios and Trajan as Roman emperors, also was intended to elicit a response on the deeper level of shared ancestry by reminding visitors of Theodosios's alleged descent from Trajan himself, a claim that legitimated his rule and his dynasty in obvious ways.

Although there is a great deal about the reuse of antiquities in the Forum of Theodosios that recalls the precedent of Constantine, the scant deployment of ancient materials represents a departure from the earlier emperor's example and remains noteworthy. In part, this change may be the result of the setting and its components. Specifically, the great historiated column that rose on the north side of the plaza was a visually demanding monument that brooked no visual competition.[36] The combined scale and complexity of the column's spiraling reliefs may have militated against any further display of statuary on the grounds that it offered too great a distraction from the unfolding history of the Theodosian reign. Working as a kind of iconic summation of the facts presented in the full narrative of the column, the equestrian statue, itself dedicated to the defeat of the would-be usurper Maximus, would have been admissible as an image consistent with the theme of the place.

With only four known antiquities, an Egyptian sphinx, a statue of Artemis, a portrait of Septimius Severus, and a tripod (cat. nos. 102–105), the sculptured population of the Forum of Arkadios was equally thin. These slim offerings may be of a piece with the spare reuse of ancient statuary in the Theodosian forum, for as in his father's forum, a towering historiated column dominated that of Arkadios. At the same time, however, the monuments reported to have existed in the space are curious in that, unlike any other space in Constantinople, they demonstrate no trace of iconographic consistency. With the exception of the Septimius Severus portrait that would have picked up on the by now familiar Theodosian penchant for emphasis of historical links to great rulers and with it the attendant emphasis on kingship and rule, none of the other statues seems to have a particular iconographic role to play either in terms of the forum itself or in conjunction with the other known figures. The tripod, a nonfigural monument, was probably of preclassical manufacture as was the Artemis. So too was the sphinx, a work of Egyptian manufacture. It is possible that some emphasis on pre- or nonclassical imagery was intended; however, it is not clear why. More probable, given the mix of figures, the lack of continuity among them, and the relatively late, tenth-century date of their first mention, is the suggestion that the figures were moved to the Forum of Arkadios from elsewhere in the city at some later date. This theory could explain the grab bag–like quality of the gathering as it is described and would be consistent with the removal of statuary from other settings that took place under Justinian as early as the sixth century.[37] Given the abbreviated nature of the sources, however, emphasis must be placed on the speculative quality of this suggestion.

The Golden Gate, the major ceremonial land entrance to Constantinople, was the last major recipient of sculptured dedications under the Theodosians. Set in the southern stretch of the landwall built by Theodosios II, the gate consisted of two separate stages, an inner portal and an outer, or propylon gate. The inner gate was a triple-arched marble entry recessed between two marble-faced pylons. Across the city and the country sides of its central arch ran the inscription that gave the place its name: "Haec loca Theudosius [sic] decorat post fata tyranni/Aurea saecla gerit qui portam construit auro." The outer, or propylon, gate was a single arched entrance that is likely to have been unadorned.[38]

Sculpture completed the basic construction. An elephant quadriga (cat. no. 119) was the centerpiece of an installation on the upper cornice of the inner gate that also included a figure of Theodosios himself accompanied by a Nike and the Tyche of Constantinople.[39] Although there is no direct evidence, it is likely by analogy to similar imperial ensembles that Theodosios rode in the quadriga, flanked by the Nike and the Tyche.

Although it is possible that all of the statuary was ancient, it is more likely that the Gate represents a combination of purpose-made and reused monuments. In addition to the new iconography, the prevalence of Constantinopolitan tyches in installations across the city suggests that these statues were of contemporary manufacture. By contrast, the elephant quadriga, which may also have included the rider identified as Theodosios, is likely to have been a work of pre-fourth-century production. Texts describe the work as an import from the Temple of Ares, Athens (cat. no. 119). Although there is reason to question the details of provenance, the claim, which was made in the tenth century, doubtless reflects awareness of the statue's actual antiquity.

When this installation was created depends on the date of the gate, which is the subject of controversy. Sources identify the gate with both the younger and the elder Theodosios. Although the presence of the gate in the landwall implies that the entrance is the work of Theodosios II, autopsy of the gate itself and its relationship to the surrounding walls supports an association with Theodosios I. In spite of claims to the effect that the gate and the surrounding wall are bonded, there is no evidence that this is the case. Repeated inspection of the site from the nineteenth century to the present day has produced no compelling or consistent evidence of structural integrity between the gate and its surrounding walls that suggests that the gate initially was built not as a monumental entrance through the wall, but as a freestanding ceremonial entrance. Because there is no evidence that Theodosios II ever presided over a triumph, the occasion for the construction of this monument could only have been Theodosios I's triumph of November 380 celebrating the defeat of the would-be usurper Maximus.[40]

The splendor of the installation and the nature of its imagery further support an association with the elder Theodosios. The statuary poised on the upper cornice of the gate was designed to complement the dedicatory verse and its invocation of a golden age. All of the components of the ensemble, the imperial quadriga, the victory, and the tyche, were the standard stuff of such official displays. Use of an elephant quadriga represented a particularly dazzling aggrandizement of such imperial imagery, and may also have been intended to call to mind the similar display on the Roman Porta Triumphalis.[41] Although elephant imagery was known from the early Empire, it became popular only in the late imperial context, where elephant quadrigae began to encroach on the domain of horse-drawn vehicles in such contexts as imperial triumphs. The use of elephants in place of horses was a tactic designed to impress: The scale of even the smallest elephant dwarfed that of even the mightiest horse, thereby lending greater honor to the imperial person. Unsurprisingly, it was Caracalla who was the first to deploy elephant quadriga, hoping through the act to equate himself with those earlier elephant-conveyed gods and heroes, Dionysios and Alexander. Constantine, and Diocletian before him, used the elephant quadriga on coins and medallions, and there is some evidence that Theodosios I himself used elephants in his own Constantinopolitan triumph. Drawings of the Column of Arkadios depicting the event show elephants in the imperial procession.[42] Contemporary poetry further documents the appeal of elephant imagery:

> No longer does the mighty-tusked elephant, with turreted back and ready to fight phalanxes, charge unchecked into the battle; but in fear he hath yielded his thick neck to the yoke, and draws the car of divine Caesar. The wild beast knows the delight of peace; discarding the accoutrements of war, he conducts instead the father of good order.[43]

Harnessed in the quadriga and under control of the imperial hand, the savage elephant offers visible proof of imperial power and with it the magnanimity shown in subduing the ferocious in the service of peace.

This grandiose imagery proclaiming peace and prosperity at the hand of the monarch is consistent with the kind of imagery seen in other works undertaken by Theodosios I. The emphasis on victory, the focus on kingship, and the implied legitimacy of imperial rule explicit in the gathering at the gate shares in the sentiments of the obelisk project and the design of the Theodosian forum. At the same time, the emphasis on peace, prosperity, and the ensuing advent of a golden age is at one with the image of Zeus, Athena, and the attendant Muses proclaimed in the Augusteion Senate.

The city that developed under the Theodosian mandate continued to be the repository of classical sculpture, not only that imported by Constantine and Constantius, but also that introduced by the Theodosians themselves. As in the Constantinian age, antiquities were deployed throughout the city in various public contexts around the ideologies and themes appropriate to public settings. In a departure from the habits of Constantinian reuse, however, Theodosios and his heirs worked with a very different set of aims. Thus, whereas the Constantinian agenda was one of urban affirmation that of the Theodosians turned on issues of dynastic promotion and legitimation. Repeatedly and with the heavy-handed insistence of all authoritarian projects, the installations of Theodosios I underscored the theme of legitimate imperial rule in its specifically Theodosian guise. Some, such as the obelisk project, did so overtly using contemporary relief sculpture and inscriptions in combination with antiquities to hammer home the impact of a specifically Theodosian act of consolidation. Others, such as the Senate house installation, used more subtle tactics, relying less on subsidiary glosses and more on the monuments themselves to achieve their purpose. Whatever the approach, there was a logic at the root of this mind-numbing agenda. Theodosios came to the throne in a period of relative political uncertainty. His challenge was not, therefore, to establish a new capital, but rather to insert himself and his dynasty in the already well-defined political space of Constantinople. With antiquities he rose to the occasion.

This reuse of ancient images to legitimate imperial rule reflected the same mind-set as other aspects of Theodosian public imagery. Almost all of the capital's purpose-built works of contemporary manufacture shared the same goal of dynastic legitimation.[44] This was certainly the case with the great honorific columns erected in the forums of Theodosios and Arkadios. In each, a monumental narrative frieze spiraled around the column shaft documenting imperial achievements and by extension the right to rule. That right was further aggrandized in the individual column's base reliefs, which showed members of the imperial court enthroned in all their hieratic majesty.[45] Thus antiquities expressed the same concerns as contemporary works of official art. At the same time, however, they went one step further. By drawing the past into the present, they claimed past history for present purposes, documenting imperial power and legitimating it with a force that no modern narrative documentation could hope to marshal.

# FIVE

# THE LAUSOS COLLECTION

Together with the building campaigns that characterized the revitalization of the capital in the late fourth century, the reuse of antiquities in the city's urban decoration represented a revival of the Constantinian tradition of monumental public works projects on an encompassing scale. Crucial to this sense of renewal was not only the extent of the activity, but also the consistency of the imagery deployed. From the Hippodrome, the Milion, and the Senate at the heart of the city's monumental core to the capital's farthest outpost, the Golden Gate, the reuse of statuary articulated themes appropriate to kingship and dynastic legitimacy. Although later members of the Theodosian dynasty participated in similar projects, this renewed interest in the expressive potential of antiquities appears largely to have been the work of Theodosios I and his urban planners. Most of the later projects for reuse were initiated under his mandate during the 380s, and the unrelenting focus of their dynastic vision confirms the emperor's hand.

The great exception to this rule is a gathering formed sometime during the first decades of the fifth century at the behest of the Constantinopolitan aristocrat Lausos (Figure 9). The collection, which was displayed prior to its destruction by fire in 475 in a portico along the north side of the Mese immediately to the east of the Forum of Constantine, was unlike any of the other city ensembles. Although publicly displayed in the manner of the great imperial collections, the gathering appears, as the identification with Lausos suggests, to have been a work of private initiative. This private patronage notwithstanding, the collection is reported to have included some of the most famous works of Hellenic antiquity, the Zeus by Pheidias from the sanctuary at Olympia and Praxiteles' Aphrodite of Knidos among them. As the presence of these noteworthy statues suggests, the Lausos collection was a marvel in a city filled with marvels. Remarkable for its holdings even in the context of imperial Constantinople, this rich collection took advantage of its holdings, manipulating them to invite speculation on new ideas pertinent to contemporary experience. Rejecting the standard themes of urban hegemony or dynastic legitimacy that informed the official Constantinian and Theodosian collections, the Lausos ensemble instead took up the new and difficult question of religion. With the display of antiquities, Lausos and his designers invited viewers to speculate on the means by which the two great and potentially antithetical driving forces of late-fourth-century society, Hellenic culture and Christian spirituality, might achieve détente.[1]

Like all of the great Constantinopolitan collections, the Lausos gathering is known exclusively from literary testimonia. Two Byzantine sources provide the basic documentation for the gathering, a late-eleventh-century chronicle known as the *Synoposis historion* by the chronicler George Kedrenos and a twelfth-century work, by John Zonaras, the *Epitome historion*. Kedrenos and Zonaras were compilers of a type of historical compendium known as the universal chronicle. As with most surviving examples of this genre, both the *Synopsis* and the *Epitome* aim to describe a comprehensive world history. Accordingly, each begins with an account of the creation and biblical history before turning to an elaboration of the Greco-Roman past, which in turn merges with the history of Byzantium. Kedrenos tracked world history to the year 1057, while Zonaras continued the record into the twelfth century, concluding with the year 1118. In both authors' works materials were compiled, and, in a manner consistent with Byzantine historiographical practice, taken over wholesale from earlier sources.[2]

Kedrenos mentions the Lausos collection in two separate passages. The first, Kedrenos A, appears as an insertion in the text after a description of the death of Theodosios I in 395 and mentions eight statues of gods and personifications together with a group of animals and half-human creatures. The second passage, Kedrenos B, refers to the collection as part of the description of a chain of events following the inauguration of the usurper emperor Basiliskos in 475. It is not so detailed as Kedrenos A, as it lists only three of the eight statues mentioned in the first passages and omits any reference to the animals and half-human creatures. Finally, Zonaras refers to the Lausos collection in a single passage reminiscent of Kedrenos B.[3]

Working from this evidence it is possible to reconstruct the contents and appearance of the Lausos collection. At least thirteen statues formed the ensemble: an Athena from the Rhodian sanctuary at Lindos by the sixth century B.C. sculptors Skyllis and Dipoinos (cat. no. 152); a statue described as a Samian Hera by another early sculptor, Bupalos of Chios (cat. no. 155); the great chryselephantine Zeus created in the fifth century B.C. by Pheidias for the temple at Olympia (cat. no. 157); Praxiteles' fourth century B.C. Aphrodite of Knidos (cat. no. 151); two other fourth-century statues by Lysippos, an Eros from Myndos (cat. no. 154) and the personification of Kairos (cat. no. 156); and, finally, a series of statues of wild animals and half-human creatures such as pans and centaurs that were probably of Hellenistic or Roman manufacture (cat. nos. 150, 153). What, if anything, was a fifth-century Constantinopolitan viewer to make of such a gathering?

An approach to the answer to this question lies in the understanding of the identity of the patron, Lausos. While Kedrenos and Zonaras are silent on the subject of the fifth-century reception of the collection, they do open the door to speculation by naming Lausos as its patron. Of this historical figure little is known. He is described as *praepositus sacri cubiculi*, or grand chamberlain, at the court of Theodosios II, a post he appears to have held first around 420. By 422 he was replaced, but there is evidence to suggest that he was again chamberlain on two later occasions, in 431 and 436.[4]

In addition to his court service, Lausos is known from his patronage of an inspirational religious history, the *Lausiac History*. Written by Palladios (ca. 365–425) and dedicated to Lausos in the period when he first held office as chamberlain, the book is a collection of stories about holy men and women of the Egyptian desert.[5]

Although these references are elliptical, they do allow certain inferences. First, association with the Theodosian court in general and the high rank of chamberlain in particular describe Lausos as a person of power and influence, an observation seconded by Palladios's description of him as "guardian of our holy and revered empire."[6] Second, it is clear from the history that bears his name that Lausos was a devout Christian. He was the project's patron, and in his dedication Palladios characterized his patron as a "Noble and Christ-beloved servant of God."[7]

Identification of Lausos as a high-ranking Christian aristocrat at the Theodosian court creates a specific context for the interpretation of the collection. Among other things, it establishes a date for the gathering's installation, which probably took place around 420 during Lausos's first stint as chamberlain.[8] Given the prestigious nature of the statuary amassed and the fact that, in the wake of the temple closings of the late fourth century, it would have been considered property of the imperial fisc, Lausos must have held public office at the time of the collection's creation. Without such authority it is difficult to imagine him having access to or control over this material.

In addition to pinpointing a moment for the collection's creation, identification with Lausos provides an intellectual milieu for the gathering's formation. Specifically, it is likely that Lausos and his fellow courtiers were members of a social elite, which, though Christian, defined itself in terms of the long-standing traditions of the Greco-Roman educational tradition of the paideia. This educational package, founded in the literary and rhetorical traditions of the classical world, is likely to have formed the imaginative bedrock on which the Lausos collection stood. At the same time, however, the developing interaction between that classical culture and the new exigencies of Christian spirituality that were increasingly a part of the Roman aristocratic sensibility brought about the seismic transformation of that bedrock in the late fourth and early fifth centuries.[9] It is in this hybrid context that the Lausos collection is best understood.

In the absence of the collection itself, Kedrenos A provides a starting point for understanding. Analysis of the structure and detailing of the inventory reveals not only the contents of the collection but also a sense of some of the attitudes brought to bear on different types of statuary. At least thirteen images are noted. Of these images, six are described in very specific terms, while the remaining seven are mentioned only cursorily. The extent to which individual figures are detailed appears to correspond to subject matter: temple statues are observed with great precision, while animal statues are given only brief mention. The duality is one between cultic and non-cultic images.

In this division it is striking that each of the cult images is identified in terms of a specific history that emphasizes provenance and attribution: the Lindian Athena by Skyllis and Dipoinos, the Knidian Aphrodite by Praxiteles, the Samian Hera by Bupalos, the Myndian Eros by Lysippos, and the Olympian Zeus by Pheidias. Moreover, because each statue was attributed to a particular artist, it was also linked to a particular historic moment. In complete contrast to this careful and consistent documentation is the virtually anonymous presentation of the animal statues. This list is tacked on to the end of the sculpture inventory without any elaboration. References to individual animals are made in both the singular and the plural, but there is no precise or consistent numerical specification. A complete lack of historical information underscores this vagueness; although several ancient artists were famous for their renditions of animals, not one statue in the Lausos collection is attributed, supplied with provenance, or in any way described in terms of conventional historical detail.

The stark contrast between the treatment of the cult images and the treatment of the animal statues suggests that these two types of images were perceived in very different ways. In the case of the temple statues, the clear and detailed documentation in matters of provenance and attribution appears to have been driven by an antiquarian impulse to set these images within a historical framework. Each of the images derives from one of the great Hellenic sanctuaries in the heartland of the Greek world, and there is a distinct geographic distribution of the figures: the

Lindian Athena and the Knidian Aphrodite originated in the Dorian lands, the Hera and the Eros in Ionia, and the Zeus and Kairos in the Peloponnesos.[10] There is, further, a sense of the chronological flowering of individual religious centers. Samos and Lindos were two of the most important centers to develop in eastern Greece during the seventh and sixth centuries B.C., while Knidos came into its own in the fourth century. Olympia, one of the great pan-Hellenic sanctuaries, was located in the western Greek world and had its floruit in the fifth and fourth centuries.

The association of specific statues with specific places may not have been accidental, for Hellenic cult statues, unlike their Christian counterparts, had no universal or generic religious function but were uniquely linked to the locus of their cult. Thus, the specific statue of a specific god or goddess was associated with a distinct cult, its sanctuary, and a unique set of rituals.[11] The sense of place as a point of access to and focus for the sacred informs Pausanias's description of the Greek world, with its enumeration of cities and sanctuaries, their sacred shrines and associated rituals. That this sense remained a component in the mapping of the sacred into Late Antiquity is suggested by the itinerary of Egeria. Written in the fifth century, her travel diary describes the author's journey to the holy places of the Christian east. Like Pausanias before her, Egeria is interested in documenting places, monuments, and the rituals associated with them as points of access to the sacred. Emphasis on typology and provenance in the Lausos collection may be of a piece with this approach. If so, it is possible that it reflects a general understanding of the cult origins of the collection's holdings and, with it, an awareness of both the religious history and sacred geography of the Hellenic world.[12]

In a like manner, attribution may have situated these images in terms of artistic tradition. For the reader, identification of a statue with a particular artist may also have linked the image to a discrete historical moment. For the actual viewer of the collection, that same history could have been expressed in the visual language of style. The statues included in the collection had been created over a span of three hundred years: the Athena and the Hera were made in the sixth century B.C., the Zeus in the fifth century, and the Aphrodite and the Eros in the fourth century. This chronology would have been given life by the formal and material differences between the figures. The still abstraction of Bupalos's sixth-century Hera would have stood in marked contrast to the contrapposto poise of Praxiteles' fourth-century Aphrodite or the dazzling torsion of Lysippos's Eros. Contrasts in scale and medium such as that between the Lindian Athena and the Olympian Zeus also would have contributed to this sense. In these instances the contrasts were great and obvious, but the display could not have been conceived exclusively in such grandiose terms.

Juxtaposition of similar works such as the Athena and the Hera or the Aphrodite and the Eros could have invited more subtle observations of formal similarities and differences.

Taken together, the cult images created what may be described as a visual epitome not only of Hellenic religion but also of the history of sculptural form. It is an epitome familiar from such ancient writings as Pliny's *Natural History*. Pliny's art-historical discussions describe first the invention of individual arts and then their inexorable move toward technical perfection as demonstrated in the accomplishments of individual artists. In the discussion of sculpture, each of the artists included in the Lausos ensemble holds a place in Pliny's developmental outline of history. He characterizes Skyllis and Dipoinos as the first sculptors to achieve fame by sculpturing in marble[13] and notes that Bupalos followed in their wake.[14] He extols Pheidias as an artist who revealed possibilities in the sculptural medium, which were then taken up and elaborated by sculptors such as Praxiteles[15] and perfected with the innovations of Lysippos.[16] Underpinning these observations is the sense of the history of the development of style, a belief in the universality of naturalism as a stylistic point of reference, and a notion of artistic perfectibility.[17]

Implicit, too, in Pliny's approach to sculpture is the understanding of these works in terms of antiquarian retrospection, an emphasis that was perhaps highlighted in the Lausos collection itself by the inclusion of sculpture of recognizable Greek manufacture. Statues of this early date were a rarity in the Constantinopolitan world of the fourth and fifth centuries where it was far more common to see works of Hellenistic and Roman manufacture. Display of statuary of bona fide ancient manufacture in this particular collection therefore would have confirmed an element of antiquarian interest that dovetailed with the sense of religious history outlined in the elaboration of provenance.

It is impossible to say whether the Lausos collection was assembled as a direct response to Pliny, a work that still had wide currency in Late Antiquity. Although the prominent display of works by artists championed in the *Natural History* certainly suggests as much, there is no direct evidence to connect the book with Lausos or members of his circle. It is, however, clear that the *Natural History* was read into the fourth and fifth centuries. Well-known readers included the historian Ammianus Marcellinus, the Roman senator Symmachus, who is reported to have sent a copy to Ausonius, the author Macrobius, and the pharmaceutical writer Sextus Placitus. Eusebios, Jerome, and Augustine also mention Pliny.[18] These readers and others like them would have known and studied the book both in the original form and, more frequently, through excerpted compilations of thematically related passages. It is also possible that Pliny's own Greek sources, specifically Xenocrates and Antigonus, were still in circulation.[19]

It is also possible that a direct connection to a specific source is not necessary and that the collection may be understood as a gathering that reflects an approach to the appreciation of ancient sculpture of which Pliny and his sources are simply the best-known exponents. Evidence from pagan and Christian sources indicates that many of the points of view espoused in the *Natural History* were held into the Late Antique period.

Consider, for example, the issue of artistic perfectibility, so much at the center of Pliny's interpretation of the arts in general and sculpture in particular. The notion of a progressive development of art is a common one that was argued in a variety of ways. Antiquarian authors of the second century like Plutarch and Pausanias described an age before art in which primitive peoples worshiped unformed, aniconic images such as rocks and planks. To their way of thinking, this simple age preceded a subsequent "age of art," a period in which worship was transformed by the introduction of images created with aesthetic sense and skill.[20] The distinction made here is a broad one between two different categories of representation, the aniconic and the figural.

The notion of progress implicit in this before-and-after argument was also a driving force behind more focused discussions of painting and sculpture in the "age of art." Pliny is the primary exponent of this point of view, largely because his text survives. As we have seen, his observations about painting and sculpture focus on the individual works of individual artists that somehow can be seen to have advanced the cause of better – that is, more convincing – illusionistic representation.[21] A very similar approach to viewing in general and to the understanding of individual images in the context of a visual history is documented by the second-century Christian apologist Athenagoras, who writes:

> Statues, while yet there was no art of modeling or painting or sculpturing, were not even dreamt of. Then came the time of Saurius of Samos and Crato of Sicyon and Cleanthes of Corinth and the Corinthian maid. The art of tracing out shadows was discovered by Saurius, who traced the outline of a horse as it stood in the sunlight, and the art of painting by Crato, who painted the outline of a man and a woman on a whitened tablet. The art of relief modeling was discovered by the maid, for being enamoured of a youth, she drew the outline of his form on the wall as he slept, and then her father, a potter, delighted with the marvelous likeness, cut out a mould along this outline and filled it with clay. This mould of his is still preserved at Corinth. After these, Daedalos, Theodoros, and Smilis discovered the additional arts of statuary and modeling.[22]

Here the author upholds the distinction between an age before and after art and then, like Pliny, goes on to describe the stages by which the arts were first discovered and then perfected by the innovations of certain individuals.

That similar approaches were familiar from Late Antiquity is evident from the testimony of Themistios, who wrote, "Before Daidalos, not only were herms worked in rectangular form, but also all the rest of *andriantes* [statues]. Daidalos, because he was the first to separate the two feet of *agalmata* [statues] was thought to make living things."[23] Like Athenagoras in the second century and Pliny in the first, Themistios believed in a primitive age before art that was left behind with the invention of figural representation by Daidalos. As well, he is able to point to certain inventions, specifically, the separation of feet, that put representation on the road to the conquest of naturalistic illusion, which allows artists to create "living things." Thus, from the first century through the fourth century, there appears a sustained tendency to understand the history of representational art in terms of a development toward mimetic perfection that is propelled by the inventive force of individual artists and their techniques.

What of the animal statues? If the detail lavished on the account of the cult images can be said to have shaped an interpretation of this group within the framework of a human history that was defined in terms of sacred geography and aesthetic chronology, then the corresponding absence of such description in the treatment of the animal statues could well have set these images outside that particular construct. Without the identifying flags of sacred provenance or artistic attribution, the animal statues took their place within a different order, that of the animal kingdom and, by extension, the natural world.[24] The nature of this natural context is suggested by the actual choice of animals. Wild beasts and mythological creatures predominate at the expense of domestic animals, and there is an emphasis on origins that are mysterious or alien. Pedestrian European and Mediterranean wildlife such as the bear or stag is rejected in favor of animals such as tigers with origins in the alien turf of Asia and sub-Saharan Africa. Other creatures, such as the vulture,[25] cannot be traced to any known place according to contemporary writings on natural history, which emphasize their air of mystery. The strange and savage behavior attributed to these animals by the ancient naturalists underscores these alien origins.[26]

Association with the alien and the savage also characterize contemporary attitudes toward the mythical creatures. The unicorn was described as terrible and invincible in battle, and pans and centaurs were similarly understood.[27] In ancient lore these half-human creatures were representative of wildlife, animal desire, and barbarism. Pan had the power to induce "panic" terrors among men when roused, while centaurs were known for their wild and lustful natures, as evidenced in stories like that of the battle between the Lapiths and the Centaurs or the tale of Herakles and Nessos.[28] Thus, although describable, these animals and half-human creatures are essentially unknowable, mysterious, unpredictable. As such they point to a world operating beyond the confines of human reason.

How that world might have been perceived is suggested by the one context in which such creatures would have been familiar to the Roman viewer, the staged animals shows, or *venationes*, that were so prominent a part of amphitheater and circus entertainment.[29] Here all manner of wild and exotic creatures, tigresses, giraffes, and wild birds among them, were sent out for slaughter in combats and artificial hunts. Although first and foremost a crowd-pleaser, the *venationes* also had a didactic intent: There was a lesson to be learned in the display and slaughter of wild beasts. In their wild and alien nature, these animals were the embodiment of all that was uncivilized and, therefore, of barbarian irrationality and evil.[30] The ability to marshal the resources for the capture of these dangerous creatures and to control their presentation in the amphitheater was a way to give tangible expression to the wealth, prowess, and far-reaching moral authority of the imperial house.[31] In a very real sense the *venationes* were the quintessential metaphor for the balance between order and chaos.

That this particular image had broad appeal is apparent from its use in contexts far removed from the amphitheater. The appearance of hunt scenes and representations of animal combats in domestic floor mosaics from settings as geographically remote and chronologically separated as the second-century House of Dionysos at Paphos on Cyprus and the unnamed fourth-century villa at Piazza Armerina in Sicily suggests not only the enduring popularity of the theme, but also the extent to which this subject was an expression of the civilizing force of Rome with which the prosperous upper classes identified.[32]

A similar appreciation of animal imagery was carried over into the period of the late Empire, as demonstrated by the sixth-century peristyle mosaic from the Great Palace at Constantinople. In a vast mosaic covering approximately 20,000 square feet (1,872 square meters), scenes of bucolic harmony and sylvan bliss are punctuated by violent episodes in which all manner of wild animals are shown attacking domestic animals, each other, and men. Leopards attack antelope in one section. In another a griffin devours a lizard. Next to this grizzly pair, in complete antithesis, a young boy plays with a puppy. Elsewhere an eagle attacks a snake, while goats lounge to one side, deer wander, and a hunter brandishes his spear. As in other contexts, the presence of wild animals in this mosaic suggests the menace of alien, uncivilized forces in need of the control offered by the imperial house.[33]

The wild animals also may have been understood in a different, but related, sense as apotropaia. Because of their threatening aspect, representations of these creatures were often used to ward off evil. As we have seen, this was the case in the Hippodrome, where animals such as the hyena, notorious as a trickster and killer of men, were displayed with such equally nefarious half-human creatures as sphinxes, their own dark powers harnessed against the very evil that had spawned them.

The animals, pans, and centaurs in the Lausos collection may have evoked the idea of Nature in its most unruly and threatening aspect. Redolent of the irrational and the uncontrolled, these alien, outright barbarous images stood cheek by jowl with some of the most refined and noble creations of the Hellenic past. Comparison must have been inevitable as art confronted nature and the civilized faced the barbarous.

Given the increasingly Christian tenor of the later Roman Empire and Lausos's own religious persuasion, it is not unreasonable to suppose that one point behind the juxtaposition of these different types of statuary was to make a fundamentally negative statement about cult images. Such a statement had been anticipated by Eusebios's explanation of Constantine's use of temple statues and votive offerings in the city's urban decor as a way to humiliate pagan images.[34] In the context of the Lausos collection, it is possible that a similarly negative impact was sought. In fact, emphasis on provenance and attribution may have contributed to this impulse, for as Christian iconoclastic writing indicates, the ability to recognize sacred images as the works of individual artists undermines their sanctity by making them the outgrowth not of divine creation but of human craft. Consider, again, the comments of Athenagoras:

> The time interval then, since statues and statue making began is so short that I am able to mention the name of the craftsmen of each god. The statue of Artemis at Ephesos and of Athena- or rather of Athela, for the more initiate call her Athela, as this was the ancient name for what came from the olive- . . . and Endoeos, a pupil of Daidalos, produced the Seated Goddess. The Pythian Apollo is the work of Theodoros and Telecles, the Delian Apollo and Artemis are due to the skill of Tectaeos and Angelion. The hands of Smilis produced the Hera of Samos and that of Argos, and Pheidias produced the other idols. The Aphrodite of Knidos is another work of Praxiteles' craft; the Askleipios at Epidauros is the work of Pheidias. To put it briefly, no single one of them has escaped being made by the hands of man. If then they are gods, why did they not exist from the beginning? Why are they younger than their makers? Why did they require men of skill for their coming into existence? Earth, stone, wood, and a misapplied skill, that is what they are.[35]

The comparative display of two ostensibly different classes of images also may have helped to underscore a negative view of the temple statuary. Juxtaposition of great images from the great sanctuaries with anonymous statues of animals may have been intended to draw attention to similarities between the two groups and in so doing to denigrate the temple statues by ascribing to them characteristics of beasts. Early Christian antipagan rhetoric is heavily iconoclastic in slant, and in it images are condemned for two reasons: an inherently inanimate nature that in no way corresponds to or captures the sense of the divine and the potential for these lifeless objects to become harmful by housing demons that might take up residence in their dead cores.[36] It was this inanimate quality that was particularly troubling to the Christian apologists. As lifeless objects devoid of soul or sense, temple statues were condemned on the grounds that they could neither feel nor see nor hear. The inability to speak completed the lack of sensation. This lack of language was perhaps the most damning element of all. In the Greco-Roman world the refined mastery of speech and rhetoric was a sure index of cultivation and civility.[37] Conversely, failure to achieve such rhetorical proficiency was an index of barbarism and, by extension, primitivism, a characteristic shared by children, foreigners, and animals.[38] Classed with the mute, cult statues, which were often described in the same category as animals, were thus open to ridicule and derision.

Built into this polemical comparison was the safety valve of the apotropaia. The same beasts that invited comparison with the temple statues also might defend the city and its inhabitants against the demons that, given half a chance, were sure to take up residence in these discredited statues.

Although the bald-faced denigration of idols may well have been a factor in the organization of the collection, it is also possible that much more was intended in this careful selection and display of statuary, an idea supported by the inclusion of the last statue in the group, the Lysippan Kairos. Kairos is the only statue in the Lausos collection that is iconographically distinct from either of the two major sculpture groups. Although documented in detail with the cult images, the statue, properly speaking, is not a devotional image but a personification. As such it is also distinct from the animal group. In this capacity the figure serves as an ideal mediator between the collection's two major sculpture groups,[39] a role implicit in the definition of *kairos* itself.

As noted above, the general meaning of *kairos* is bound up with the definition of time and the sense of the moment. An aspect of this definition was the notion of opportunity, a connection expressed in the figure's unique coiffure, whose particular combination of long forelock and rear baldness suggested the need to seize the moment as it arrives, not after it passes. This sense of the moment also lends the word a secondary meaning, which can be defined as congruence, the essential element in the creation and definition of beauty. Plutarch described this aspect of *kairos* in the following passage of the *Moralia*: "Now in every piece of work beauty is achieved through many numbers coming into a congruence (*kairos*) under some system of proportion and harmony, whereas ugliness is immediately ready to spring into being if only one chance element be omitted or added out of place."[40] *Kairos* is therefore the state in which all of the elements that form a work of art are perfectly balanced to create beauty.

Lysippos's personification is thought to have been created to give visual life to this concept and with it the sculptor's own ideas about artistic excellence. The statue's unique form demonstrated the role of and the relationship among the elements of proportion, movement, and accuracy of detail in successful artistic creation. Because these issues were so fundamental to the Lysippan aesthetic achievement, the statue is thought to have stood outside the sculptor's workshop as an advertisement for his own artistic concerns.[41]

The inclusion of the statue Kairos in the Lausos collection may well have been intended to recall and highlight the particular meaning of the word *kairos* as congruence. However, instead of illustrating the particular achievement of a particular artist, it seems likely that the statue stood as the embodiment of a more general application of the idea of congruence to a range of visual experience.

In conjunction with the temple statues, the display of Kairos may have called attention to the formal history outlined in that series of images. Individually, each statue was representative of a different kind of aesthetic congruence, some more successful than others, according to the standards indicated by authors such as Pliny and his followers. Collectively, the group thus may have demonstrated the changing nature of the idea of congruence over time and the move on the part of the Greek artists toward an imitation of nature that described physical form and the intangible energies that enlivened it in a perfected state.

The emphasis on aesthetic issues contingent on the presence of Kairos may also have been intended to transform the sense of what these images were. Kairos made the great images of Hellenic cult the subject not of religious veneration but of aesthetic contemplation, thereby denying their cult nature and affirming their status as works of art.

The emphasis on formal issues created by the interaction between Kairos and the temple statues also may have colored the viewing of the animal ensemble. In this group, where no formal aesthetic history was described, the aim, as has been suggested, was to describe an untamed state of nature. The brute energy of this natural world was the antithesis of refined *kairos*. Seen in conjunction with the animal statues, the statue Kairos thus may have underscored the very absence of congruence and the aesthetic mediation that produces it in the natural world. This absence stood in contrast to its overwhelming presence in the temple statue group, with the result that the animal statues took their place in the aesthetic order. Untouched by the refining force of *kairos*, wild nature and its savage denizens were shown in their original, unperfected state. In a society for which the principle of idealized naturalism was an acknowledged aesthetic category, this emphasis may well have described nature as the source for artistic invention.

The Kairos statue thus pulled the raw stuff of animal imagery into league with the perfected artistry of the cult statues by making both statue groups the subject of aesthetic meditation. This emphasis on problems of art and artistic creation forced the contemplation of the relationship, at once contradictory and complementary, between the natural and the manmade, the imperfect and the perfect object.

These issues may have been emphasized in the actual disposition of the statuary. Evidence for display is, however, negligible. Although it may be possible that Kedrenos A reflects a display order, comparison of this passage with Kedrenos B, which mentions only three of the cult images, and these in a different sequence, suggests that no hard and fast order should be understood.

That the Lausos collection was at all bound up with issues of art and artistic creation should come as no surprise. In the sense that Roman collectors had long since demonstrated an interest in and sensitivity to the formal issues inherent in the creation and exhibition of works of art, the collection's formal and thematic emphasis falls well within the established norms of artistic appreciation. The invited comparison between images of early and late date or the juxtaposition of natural images with those manmade creatures of pure artifice recalls the kind of tactics used by collectors from as early as the second century. This was the case, for example, in the display of four statues, two each from the Claudian and Hadrianic periods, in a second-century house in Rome. The statues, which include a heroically nude male, a replica of Praxiteles' *Resting Satyr*, and two representations of Skopas's rendition of the personification of Desire, the *Pothos*, one of first-century, the other of second-century date, were set up in pairs to either side of two doorways along the central axis of the house. This exhibit of iconographically unrelated subjects aimed to highlight the formal similarities and differences between the individual figures and encouraged the aesthetic study and appreciation of the series as a whole.[42]

At first glance, the emphasis on art and aesthetics in the Lausos collection and the religious images to which it is applied seems an anomaly in a city where statuary was used to define urban identity. The appeals to history that were so characteristic a feature of the imperial ideology at the base of the development of the Constantinian and Theodosian public collections seem at odds with the Lausos collection's interest in art and aesthetics. Contemporary sources confirm, however, that by the end of the fourth century these seemingly anomalous issues were at the heart of public debate about the relationship between traditional Hellenic religion and the new faith, Christianity.

The formation of the Lausos collection occurred against a backdrop of increasing religious authoritarianism on the part of the Theodosian house. Although Constantine had been the first emperor to accord Christianity legal status, it was not until 380, during the reign of Theodosios I, that the new faith was proclaimed the official state religion.[43] This declaration was part of an ongoing legislative and administrative campaign designed to put the last match to Hellenic religion.[44] The systematic suppression of pagan cult and religious culture is documented in the Theodosian Code. First published in 438 during the reign of Theodosios II, this corpus of Roman law preserves a series of fourth- and fifth-century edicts that curb pagan religious practice. Although they attempt to regulate everything from sacrifice to cult administration, these laws are particularly interesting for their legislation regarding temples and sanctuaries. Five laws issued between 382 and 435 are preserved in the code. Each confirms the illegality of sacrifice and calls for the closing of the temples as sites of worship. Provisions for the fate of temple buildings and their contents also are made. Solutions vary in the case of buildings. In some instances, the edicts enjoin the preservation of the temples.[45] In others, they insist on their destruction.[46] No such ambivalence occurs, however, with respect to sculpture. Although cult images are recognized as the *fons et origo* of superstition and error in a manner consistent with the iconoclastic discussion outlined above, the legislation is unequivocal about saving them. Theodosian Code 16.10.15 stipulates the general preservation of the "ornaments of public works," and 16.10.18 decrees the supervised removal of images from temples by qualified "office staff."

Given the belief in their corrupting potential, it is not immediately clear why or how these images could be reconciled to a new Christian order that simultaneously feared and derided sculpture. That there was any effort at all to preserve cult statues bespeaks the status of sculpture in the later Roman world. As the great medium of public expression in the cities and sanctuaries of the Roman Empire, sculpture was as we have seen the descriptive vehicle that gave life to and documented the history of a place. Accomplishments were commemorated, allegiances expressed, and piety demonstrated with the dedication and maintenance of a vast range of public monuments, an attitude expressed in the adornment of Constantinople itself. This public display of statuary shaped the image of a city and gave visual life to its own claims to importance and prestige. In addition, this distinctive use of sculpture meant that statuary itself was emblematic as a medium of Hellenic tradition.

In a culture that defined itself so completely through the expressive medium of sculpture, the problem thus became one of reconciling the claims of Greco-Roman tradition with the exigencies of Christian piety. An approach to this problem of reconciliation is indicated in Theodosian Code 16.10.8. Issued at Constantinople in December 382, the edict provides for the fate of a temple in the eastern city of Edessa as follows:

> By the authority of the public council we decree that the temple shall be continually open that was formerly dedicated to the assemblage of throngs of people and now also is for the common use of the people, and in which images are reported to have been placed which must be measured by the value of their art rather than by their divinity; We do not permit any divine imperial response that was surreptitiously obtained to prejudice this situation. In order that this temple may be seen by the assemblages of the city and by frequent crowds, Your Experience shall preserve all celebrations of festivities, and by the authority of Our divine imperial response, you shall permit the temple to be open, but in such a way that the performance of sacrifices forbidden therein may not be supposed to be permitted under the pretext of such access to the temple.[47]

What is interesting in the decree is the insistence that the temple images be "measured by the value of their art rather than by their divinity." In other words, viewers are exhorted to see and understand these ancient statues not as religious images but as works of art.

The emphasis on art and aesthetics in the Lausos collection and the religious images to which it is applied is of a piece with this legislative approach to the Christianization of the Empire. In a display that was a visual corollary to the legal language of the law code, the collection sought a way around the impasse between the revered institution of Greco-Roman tradition and the upstart demands of the new religion by exhorting the viewer to reject the claims of religious history and consider statuary as art.[48] As public policy this exhortation was shrewd, for the recommendation could be directed to Christian and pagan alike. Emphasis on the aesthetic appeal of cult images neutralized their sacred qualities and in so doing made them legitimate objects of profane aesthetic contemplation for the Christian viewer. For the pagan traditionalist this same recommendation offered the chance to rethink attitudes toward statuary, and, with it, the very nature of religious belief.

Consider, for example, the words of the fifth-century Christian author Prudentius to a predominately pagan Roman Senate:

> You should give up you childish festivals,
> your laughable rites, your
> shrines unworthy of so great an empire.
> Oh noble Romans, wash your marble statues wet
> with dripping splatters of gore –
> let these statues, the works of great
> craftsmen, stand undefiled;
> let them become the most beautiful adornments
> of our native city – may no
> depraved purpose taint these works of art, no
> longer in the service of evil.[49]

Written at the same time as the formation of the Lausos display, this passage captures the spirit of the Constantinopolitan collection. In language that draws on the same associations between childishness, ignorance, and barbarism that were at work in the Lausos ensemble, Prudentius urges the great senatorial families of pagan Rome to abandon their "childish festivals" and appreciate statues not for their sacred but for their aesthetic qualities. Underpinning this appeal to the beautiful is the unstated belief that this approach is the only correct one for those who would be seen as civilized and refined. It is a dazzling apology, and in it Prudentius walks a fine line. On the one hand, he is unstinting in his criticism of pagan religion. On the other hand, himself a member of a power elite that defined itself and all that it considered worthy in terms of the standards of classical culture, he is eager to reconcile the old with the new. He does so in the realm of the aesthetic, guided by the same sentiments that contributed to the formation of the Lausos collection.

The official nature of the collection's message must have been underscored by its location. In its setting in one of the porticoes flanking the premier Constantinopolitan thoroughfare, the Lausos collection was linked to a long tradition of portico display that had its origins in the late Republican and early Imperial age.[50]

The great Roman porticoes derived their luster from the fame of the statuary they displayed.[51] The earliest and perhaps the best known of these gatherings was the Porticus Metelli, later the Porticus Octaviae. Donated to the city of Rome in about 146 B.C. by Quintus Caecilius Metellus, the portico was outfitted with no less splendid a piece than Lysippos's multifigured equestrian tribute to Alexander the Great and his cavalrymen, the Granikos Monument, a work brought by Metellus to the capital as plunder in the wake of his eastern campaigns. Other famous works of Greek sculpture subsequently joined the Lysippan group, among them figures of Artemis and Askleipios by Kephisodotos and the Eros by Praxiteles from Thespiae.[52] Prized for their status as original autograph works of Greek art, these images stood as witnesses to the civilizing power of Rome.

Because the Lausos collection continued this tradition, the question inevitably arises as to whether the images displayed in Constantinople were originals or copies. The culture of copying that was so defining a feature of Roman artistic experience might suggest that the Constantinopolitan images were replicas, as would questions about the feasibility of transporting such fragile and delicate works as the Olympian Zeus from Greece to Constantinople. At the same time, however, several factors point to the likelihood of originals. First of all, the account in Kedrenos A makes it clear that these statues were prized for the same star quality as the statuary in Rome, a star quality that in large part derived from and depended on their status as originals. Given the interest in particular statues, any difficulty surrounding the transport and subsequent display of individual works could have been overcome. In addition, evidence indicates that copies of cult images proved the exception rather than the rule.[53] The language of the texts also argues for the collection of originals. References are specific and particular, describing details of pose and medium in ways that ring true. Finally, the historical moment of the collection's formation makes it very possible that it contained originals. The early fifth century was an optimum time for assembling such a collection. With the closure of the temples, sacred property reverted to the imperial fisc, providing a man like Lausos with seemingly limitless resources.[54]

The reuse of statuary in the Lausos collection drew on the same ideas about collecting and public display that informed the initial Constantinian gatherings in the city and that had themselves been established in the expansionist age of the Roman Republic. The Roman porticoes displayed statuary that had been brought from the cities of the Greek east in the wake of the military campaigns that had drawn the Hellenic world into the political and administrative orbit of Rome. Thus, the statuary amassed at Rome was as much plunder as it was art, with the difference that statuary was not war booty in the conventional sense of captured arms, but rather spoils whose real value lay in their symbolic importance.

Like the statuary in the great Roman porticoes, the images in the Lausos collection could be understood as spoils. As we have seen, the Lindian Athena, the Samian Hera, the Knidian Aphrodite, the Olympian Zeus, and the Myndian Eros were all images plundered from the great sanctuaries of the Hellenic world. Just as the removal of a statue like the Herakles from Tarentum to Republican Rome described the capture and submission of Tarentum and its population, so these uprooted images embodied the notion of pagan religious defeat. The humiliation embodied in this defeat must have been compounded by the fact of public exposure. Most cult images were never meant to be seen in the open, being displayed instead in the inner sancta of temples where limited viewing access was a defining feature of their sanctity.[55] Contemporary Christian writings confirm this sense of degradation by noting that the removal of a statue from its sanctuary resulted in automatic deconsacration.[56] Ripped from their sanctuaries, deprived of their altars, and paraded openly as art, these spoils were indeed "excellent offerings," great cultural treasures that gave ample evidence of the Christian triumph over Hellenic superstition, and thus stood as witnesses to the success of Theodosian religious policy.

It is the theme of Christian victory that is overwhelmingly at play in the last and greatest of the Theodosian era gatherings of antiquities, the Lausos collection. Like the Constantinian displays in the Hippodrome and the Baths of Zeuxippos before it or the Theodosian offerings to the city, the Lausos ensemble used ancient statuary for the pragmatic end of describing an imperial ideology. Unlike these collections, however, that ideology had little to do with a specifically urban or dynastic identity. Instead, the collection played on the notion of reuse to express the nuts and bolts of imperial policy regarding some of the most potent symbols of Hellenic civilization, cult statues.

At the same time, this collection also charted new ground. Whereas the earlier Constantinian and Theodosian collections used plundered antiquities with a sure hand to describe cultural continuity with the Greco-Roman past, the Lausos collection expressed both the discomfort of rupture and the longing for reconciliation. With the display of cult images as spoils, the Lausos collection gave visual life to the imperial house's intent to wipe out pagan cult and, with it, some of the Greco-Roman world's longest-lived and most prestigious cultural institutions. At the same time, however, the proposed aesthetic interpretation of these images expressed an antiquarian regard for the past and a profound desire to preserve it, if only in a denatured state. Writ large in these contradictory impulses is the conundrum of the later Roman world: A society that defined the civilized in purely philhellenic terms had embraced a religion at odds with many, if not all, of the fundamental precepts of Greco-Roman tradition. The problem was thus one of reconciling these two opposing cultures.

The Lausos collection could have achieved this reconciliation in two ways. First, the emphasis on the selection and display of truly ancient monuments of bona fide Greek pedigree was unique in the Theodosian scheme and may well have established an antiquarian context for this religious and potentially volatile discussion that established a break between the pagan past and the Christian present. Not one of the named cult statues on display was less than seven hundred years old, and some of them, such as the Samian Hera, must have approached one thousand. All of them were famous, but in the context of contemporary religious practice it is clear that, for all their venerability, cult statues other than these would have evoked far more powerful devotional responses on the part of contemporary pagan worshippers.[57] Thus, this religious policy statement could have been interpreted in a context removed from the pricklier issues of contemporary religious piety to a stage in the recognizable but distant past.

Second, to the distance established between past and present by the actual antiquity of the sculpture, the collection added the emphasis on aesthetic issues. This appeal for aesthetic appreciation is interesting in that it implies an awareness of and sensitivity to form that is not usually associated with late antiquity and the early middle ages.[58] In all likelihood intended to defuse any sense or experience of the holy, this emphasis proposed a way of looking at and thinking about statuary that implicitly acknowledged and explicitly built on an idea of art as mimetic illusionism. This realist canon was familiar to contemporaries from all manner of literary contexts. It was not, however, a mode of representation that was in the vanguard with respect to contemporary official production, be it sacred or secular. The Theodosian obelisk base offers a much better sense of what this late-fourth- and early-fifth-century official art was about. Carved on four sides with reliefs depicting members of the imperial house in attendance at the circus games, the base embodies the abstract, hierarchical form that had become the norm in official works of art by the end of the fourth century. Each relief is conceived as a symmetrically arranged composition in two registers. The south side of the base (Figure 11) shows the emperor Theodosios I at the center of the upper register with his sons Arkadios and Honorius beside him and courtiers behind. Theodosios is the largest figure in the group. An architectural enframement designed to suggest the setting of the imperial box sets this central group off from a double rank of courtiers left and right. In the lower register two rows of smaller spectators stare out from the composition, while still smaller figures of dancers and musicians cavort at the feet of the spectators behind a low balustrade. Here, symmetry and frontality in the composition, together with the manipulation of proportion to describe the social hierarchies, have become the norm. Given the gap between the aesthetic values espoused in late imperial official art and the Lausos gathering's emphasis on naturalism, what might a contemporary viewer have been expected to take away from an experience of this collection? It is unlikely that the

FIGURE II: Relief on the base of the Obelisk of Theodosios I (south side) (photo: Sarah Bassett)

gathering was ever intended as a lesson touting the virtues of mimetic form. Instead, it is more probable that the sense of illusionistic development outlined in the selection of sculpture was intended to encourage a distinction between the abstract forms contemporaries used to express the official and the sacred and the mimetic forms used to achieve the same goals in earlier centuries. Linked to the actual antiquity of the statues, this emphasis on different formal values could further have underscored the break between past and present, and in so doing encouraged an understanding of these images as art.

The emphasis on illusionism also might have had significance in terms of meaning. Christian iconoclastic writing rails mercilessly against the idea of sacred images, noting that for all their illusionistic qualities they remain nothing other than "earth, stone, wood and a misapplied skill."[59] Fundamental to this objection was the belief that art could and should express a kind of truth and that naturalistic imitation was at odds with this notion of truth telling.[60] Thus, an emphasis on illusionistic tradition in the cult images of pagan antiquity may have been a way to underscore the philosophically hollow, indeed, false, premises by which pagan worshippers were introduced to the divine.

That such a distinction could have been made is suggested by the fact that the subject matter and style of pagan antiquity's visual traditions survived in the late fourth and fifth centuries not so much in the official and sacred spheres for which they were evolved, but rather in the realm of the private. The late-fourth-century Parabiago plate (Figure 12) is but one example of this phenomenon. In a tondo composition, the figures of Kybele and Attis ride in triumphal procession, drawn by a quadriga of surging lions and accompanied by the twirling figures of ecstatic revelers. Figures of plenty recline in the exergue below, while divine chariots and torch-bearing victories traverse the sky above.

Evidence of the Palace of Marina[61] indicates that the survival of such imagery was not confined to the context of small-scale luxury goods, but that the forms and subject matter of pagan antiquity survived in monumental domestic settings as well. Marina, the unmarried daughter of Arkadios, is known for the bath complex that was built in her Constantinopolitan residence. That palace, located in Region I at the edge of the Great Palace, was built around 420 and included a richly decorated bath described in an ekphrasis written after its tenth-century restoration under Leo VI the Wise. The bath included mosaic scenes of a marine and mythological nature, statues of Herakles, river gods, and a relief representing the struggle of the gods and the giants. In terms of subject matter and media, this choice of decoration was perfectly in keeping with established modes of Late Antique domestic decor, and it is likely that Marina, a woman known for her Christian piety and acts of public charity, saw no contradiction between her own faith and the selection and appreciation of classical subjects in the sensuous environment of the bath. Further, as the Christian patronage of Marina suggests, the notion that pagan traditions be legitimated through the veil of art appears to have been taken to heart.

Finally, and perhaps most importantly, the Lausos collection is interesting precisely because of the status it accords the idea of art. In this ensemble some of the most venerable images of the pagan past were legitimated and redeemed for no other reason than that of artistic merit. At the root of this proposal is a sense of art as a mediating force. In the Lausos collection and for the court of Theodosios II art became a balm that offered a way around the impasse between the iconoclastic demands of Christianity and the high regard with which the empire's ruling elite held the traditions of classical culture. Here in the healing realm of the aesthetic, pagan and Christian were invited to meet and to set aside their most fundamental differences in the joint appreciation of beauty.

The implications for Constantinople itself were important. The Lausos collection came into being nearly four decades after the first Theodosian projects involving

FIGURE 12: Silver plate with Kybele and Attis (Parabiagio Plate), Soprintendenza Antichita', Milan (photo: Scala/Art Resource, NY)

reuse, and, although it could not be known at the time, was the last of the great publicly displayed gatherings of antiquities to be created in the capital. In the years between the erection of the Theodosian obelisk and the installation of the Lausos collection, the breach between pagan and Christian culture had hardened, and the battle lines had been more firmly drawn. Throughout the Greco-Roman world, there was increasing evidence of violence toward statuary. In 391 angry mobs attacked and destroyed the Serapaion at Alexandria.[62] At Gaza, in 402, the Christian bishop Porphyry with the aid of imperial troops and the local Christian populace set about the destruction of the city's pagan shrines, pulling down a statue of Aphrodite and burning the temple of Zeus Marneios.[63] These attacks had the effect not only of destroying religious centers, but also of wreaking havoc on the cities that housed them. Rich as it was in ancient statuary, Constantinople may well have been considered a potential flash point for such destructive activity. Were this the case, the Lausos collection, prominent in its position at the very heart of the city, may well have offered a forceful argument that legitimated and so defended the city's antique holdings.

## ᖆᖆ SIX ᖆᖆ

# JUSTINIAN AND ANTIQUITY

THE THEODOSIAN DYNASTY'S USE OF ANTIQUITIES IN SCULPTURAL INSTALLATIONS
across the city represented the last wholesale reuse of ancient statuary in the
development of Constantinopolitan public space. With the creation of the Lausos
collection, the systematic gathering and presentation of antiquities reached a high
point in terms of consistency and quality. Subsequent examples of reuse as they are
known are sporadic and inconclusive. No references to the installation of new works
survive, and the only evidence for any interest in the display of antiquities in the
later fifth century is a restoration of the Baths of Zeuxippos.[1] Thus, although the
preservation of public sculpture appears to have been a mandate, there seems to have
been little real interest in the expansion or development of the collection beyond
the early years of the fifth century.

In a sense, this development was long heralded. Although the Theodosian reuse of
ancient statuary represented a revival of earlier fourth-century practice, it was limited
from the start. Thus, whereas the list of antiquities known to have been brought by
Constantine in the period immediately preceding the dedication ceremonies of 330
tops 100, no more than 30 ancient monuments are mentioned for the whole of
the Theodosian age. In the Hippodrome, for example, the *euripus* bristled with no
less than twenty statues at the time of Constantius's death in 360. Only four more
antiquities were reported to have been introduced to the circus in the period between
380 and 450. Admittedly the sources that describe these additions are themselves
spottily preserved; however, even allowing for the incomplete nature of the record
and its potential selectivity, the sharp drop in the number of references to antiquities
from the Constantinian age to the Theodosian is startling and likely to reflect the
larger reality.

Further, by the end of the fourth century and throughout the fifth century, fires
and earthquakes began to take their toll on the collections, destroying individual

pieces and whole ensembles within the city. Thus the Muses were destroyed in 404 when the Augusteion Senate burned in the wake of the Chrysostom riot fires,[2] and in 476 the Chalkoprateia fire laid waste not only to the Lausos collection, but also to the temples and their statuary in the Basilika.[3] These losses were not and really could not be replaced, with the result that the collection began to atrophy.

A similar approach to reuse prevailed in the sixth century, a time when Constantinople underwent one of its most important phases of urban development. During the reign of Justinian, the city's urban face was transformed with the addition of a series of major new buildings (Figures 1 and 13).[4] The impetus to this development came in January 532. At that time public opposition to the emperor's rule led to open rebellion. The uprising, known as the Nika revolt from the slogan shouted by the rebels, was quelled, but not before the destruction of the city's monumental core. In the four days between the start of the uprising on January 14 and its containment on the 18, fires started by the rioters burned out of control, destroying the Hagia Sophia and its neighbor Hagia Eirene, as well as the Augusteion, the Senate House, the Chalke Gate, and the Baths of Zeuxippos. The great porticoes leading from the Severan core to the Forum of Constantine and a large swath of buildings to either side of the Mese also went up in smoke.[5] With the capital's monumental center reduced to ash, Justinian undertook its rebuilding, restoring buildings where necessary and possible, constructing new ones when not.

Prokopios reports on the emperor's renewal of the capital, recounting first the project for the reconstruction of the Hagia Sophia. After lingering over the reconstruction, he then lists the large number of churches and shrines erected throughout the city and suburbs before turning to a comparatively cursory account of civic building activity. The most important of these imperial projects was the rebuilding of the Great Palace and with it the Chalke Gate. The Augusteion and its Senate also appear to have been reconstructed, along with the Baths of Zeuxippos and the porticoes along the Mese as far as the Forum of Constantine. An enormous cistern, the Yerebatan Sarayi, was constructed under the Basilika. Elsewhere in the city, along the Marmora shore, a courtyard was added to the Baths of Arkadios. No fewer than six hostels were constructed, as well as a series of suburban palaces.[6]

Although it was the destruction of the city center that provided the impetus to the emperor's prolific building activity, the Justinianic revitalization of Constantinople was comprehensive in that it extended to all of the areas within the walls as well as to the suburbs beyond. Prokopios's account ranges widely and includes not only the city and its immediate suburbs, but also the nearby islands and territories up the Bosporos. For all of its extent, however, there was nothing in the project to transform

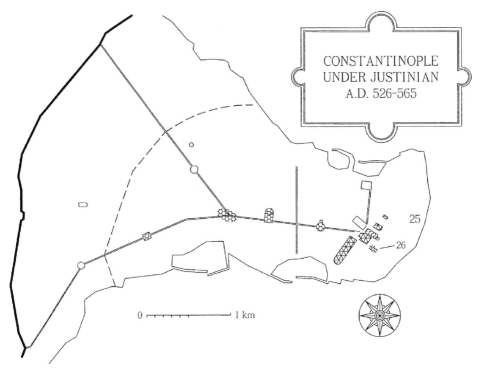

FIGURE 13: Constantinople during the reign of Justinian (Courtesy of Brian Madigan)

the city's basic structure. There were none of the great civic projects for forums and streets that characterized the Constantinian and Theodosian development of the city, and the Severan armature elaborated by Constantine in the 320s and 330s remained the organizing matrix around which the Justinianic projects grew up. Further, these undertakings, although often grand in scale, were largely piecemeal. Individual buildings were restored or rebuilt in their existing positions preserving the essential integrity of the city plan.

Where the Justinianic building effort differed markedly from either the Constantinian or Theodosian campaigns was in the overt emphasis on religious foundations. Apart from the reconstruction of the Augusteion and its Senate together with the Zeuxippos, Prokopios barely mentions civic construction, recording instead the prodigious number of religious institutions constructed by the emperor. This represents a radical reversal of previous imperial campaigns, where the greatest efforts had been directed toward the development of civic spaces and the institutions they housed. The religious foundations in the Constantinian city numbered six and were divided equally between pagan and Christian. The two temples in the Basilika and the Capitolium served pagan civic cult, while the churches of Hosios Eirene and Hosios Mokios met the initial needs of the Christian community under Constantine himself.[7] By the time of the Theodosian *Notitia* there is no evidence for the survival of the temples, which were likely to have been suppressed in the late-fourth-century purges of Hellenic cult, and the number of churches had increased citywide to fourteen.[8] Over a century later, when Prokopios sat down to write *The Buildings*, that number had mushroomed to over fifty.[9] Thus, although the shape of the city remained consistent, its ethos had changed. Once the embodiment of *romanitas* in all of its civic splendor, Constantinople had become the Christian city par excellence.

In all of this activity antiquities, though hardly present, do put in an appearance. Justinian's addition of an open, colonnaded court to the Baths of Arkadios was a case in point. Built of the richest, most lavish marbles, the place also was flush with statuary:

> Columns and marbles of surpassing beauty cover the whole of it, both the pavement and the parts above. And from these gleams an intensely brilliant white light as the rays of the sun are flashed back almost undimmed. Nay more, it is adorned with great numbers of statues, some of bronze, some of polished stone, a sight worthy of a long description. One might surmise that they were the work of Pheidias the Athenian, or of the Sicyonian Lysippos or of Praxiteles.[10]

As the account makes clear, the statuary was Hellenic in style and sentiment. Although it may not actually have been work from the hands of Pheidias, Lysippos, or Praxiteles, it was of a spirit in keeping with the city's major collections.

The origin of this sculpture is unknown. It is possible that monuments also unspecified were transferred to the court from other areas of the city. Clean up in the aftermath of the Nika rebellion resulted in the displacement of statuary from the Augusteion,[11] and statuary from the Zeuxippos, if it survived at all, may have been salvaged and set up anew in the Arkadianae. Importation of monuments is also a possibility. That Justinian engaged in such transport also is evident from Prokopios's account of the fate of sanctuaries in the Egyptian town of Philae:

> These sanctuaries in Philae were kept by these barbarians even up to my time, but the Emperor Justinian decided to tear them down. Accordingly, Narses, a Persarmenian by birth, whom I have mentioned before as having deserted to the Romans, being commander of the troops there, tore down the sanctuaries at the emperor's order, and put the priests under guard and sent the statues to Byzantium.[12]

Where these particular statues were sent and how they may have been used is any-body's guess. No evidence suggests, however, that there was anything like the deliberate, wholesale importation of antiquities that took place under Constantine or even the more modest collecting habits that supplied the Theodosian initiatives. By comparison, the Justinianic undertakings were sporadic and unsystematic. Further, the spirit in which they occurred was altogether different. Although Constantine worked with a peaceful agenda, using the administrative resources of the Empire to manipulate the concept of war booty and carefully harvest the sculptured resources of the great cities and sanctuaries with the purposeful hand of a collector, Justinian's act of importation was the result of an antipagan military intervention. Collecting the sculptured marvels of empire was never a feature on his agenda. Instead, as Prokopios notes and where sculpture was concerned, destruction was the guiding principle, and, ironically, the larger symbolic value of the statuary he gathered appears to have been of little interest to him.[13]

Apart from the example of the Arkadian Baths, the only other known venue for the Justinianic display of antiquities was at the main entrance vestibule to the Great Palace, the Chalke, or Bronze, Gate.[14] Construction of the vestibule, which took its name either from the gilded bronze tiles that covered its roof, or, as is more likely, from its great bronze doors, is attributed to Constantine.[15] Inasmuch as Constantine established the location of the palace and its entrance, this statement is probably true; however, the earliest monumental development of the vestibule appears to have taken place only at the end of the fifth century when the architect Aitherios designed a gateway for Anastasios I.[16] This building burned during the fires attendant on the 532 riots and rebuilding was begun shortly thereafter.[17]

In its Justinianic form the Chalke stood as a rectangular structure with four engaged piers supporting a raised central dome. Mosaics representing the emperor and his court adorned the dome. Scenes from military campaigns covered the lower vaults.[18] The exterior of the rebuilt sixth-century gate is not specifically described; however, hypothetical reconstruction of the entry façade shows a single entryway surmounted by a lunette at street level in which there was a standing image of Christ. Above this doorway ran a series of arcaded niches.[19]

As the main entrance to the imperial palace, the Chalke was an obvious venue for sculptural display,[20] and the new gateway's designers appear to have taken advantage of this fact. A series of eighth-century descriptions records a group of imperial portraits at the gate. Included in the ranks were images of Maximian, Theodosios and all the members of his dynasty, the emperor Zeno and his wife Ariadne, and Justin I. Two statues of philosophers, a figure described as Belisarius, four gorgoneia, and two horses accompanied the imperial portraits (cat. nos. 98–101). This last group of statues was probably antique, a fact suggested by the combined evidence of provenance, pose, and attribute.

Said to have come from Athens, the philosopher statues (cat. no. 101) were described as standing "with hands outstretched." Although the description allows no specific identification, the described pose suggests a type of engagement with space that is characteristic not of the more frontally constructed figures of Late Antiquity but of those of the Late Classical, Hellenistic or earlier imperial periods. The alleged provenance underscores this interpretation. Whether real or imagined, association with Athens suggests an awareness of the figures' antiquity.

The "Belisarius" (cat. no. 99) statue is also likely to have been a work of ancient manufacture. The statue was gilded bronze and, as identification with the military figure of Belisarius suggests, is likely to have worn military dress. It also wore the *corona radiata*, an attribute that suggests the reused figure of a Hellenistic king or a Roman emperor of the later imperial age. That the figure actually represented Belisarius seems unlikely: there is no evidence that any imperial general, however exalted, was ever given such honorific treatment. The *corona radiata* suggests a figure similar to that in the Forum of Constantine and, thus, possible identification with the palace founder, Constantine. Constantine is the last emperor to be depicted wearing the *corona radiata*: All later emperors present themselves with the diadem. Further, portraits of the emperor showing him in military dress with the *corona radiata* survive.[21] At the same time, however, rebuilding by Justinian and the inclusion of a figure of Justin point to a desire for dynastic legitimation that would suggest identification with Justinian himself, in which case the presence of the *corona radiata* would suggest an act of imitation in the selection of statuary that invited the viewer to compare Justinian with Constantine.

The remaining statues, four gorgoneia (cat. no. 98) and a pair of bronze horses (cat. no. 100), shared a provenance in the Temple of Artemis at Ephesos. Reported to have been donated by Justinian, the statues may have been found and removed to Constantinople during construction of the church of St. John.

The display of these figures is not clear. Statues of Maximian and the members of the Theodosian house are said to have stood "in the area of the Chalke," a location that suggests that the figures stood on bases and columns in the vicinity of the entrance, but not actually on it.[22] Also placed on honorific columns were the statues of Zeno and Ariadne. The only figures to adorn the actual façade, probably in the arcade above the main entrance, were those of Justin, Justinian, and the philosophers. The gorgons and the horses appear to have stood inside the vestibule itself. Here the gorgons were displayed on the wall opposite the entrance. The two horses are said to have stood above the gorgons, probably flanking the interior doorway that led into the palace proper from a perch on the upper cornice.

Like so many of the sculptured installations in Constantinople, the display of statuary at the Chalke Gate both responded to and shaped an image of kingship. On the facade itself, the central image is likely to have been imperial. Placed above the entrance, the statue stood juxtaposed to the lunette portrait of Christ,[23] itself a full-length standing image. This arrangement established a relationship between the earthly and heavenly king reminiscent of that outlined in Eusebios's *Praise of Constantine* in which the earthly ruler reigns in imitation of the heavenly: "the One who is over all, through all, and in all, visible and invisible, the all-pervasive Logos of God, from whom and through whom bearing the image of the Higher Kingdom, the sovereign dear to God, in imitation of the Higher Power, directs the helm and sets straight all things on earth."[24] This juxtaposition, very much in keeping with the Justinianic imagery of Christian kingship in the church of San Vitale, Ravenna, in which an enthroned image of Christ sits astride the central apse while images of Justinian and Theodora adorn the walls below, summoned a vision of Christian victory and in so doing proclaimed the imperial agency that made such triumph possible.

Although the notion of Christian kingship was applicable equally to Justinian or Constantine, individual elements invited a more specific identification of the statue with Constantine. The nature of the reuse, so similar to that in the Forum of Constantine (cat. no. 109), suggests an equation between the two images that may have been made even more explicit by virtue of iconography and setting. The military dress in which the figure is likely to have been shown may have called to mind not only known sculptured representations of the emperor, but also and more specifically an earlier representation of Constantine at the Chalke, an encaustic panel placed in the same spot that showed the emperor similarly garbed, his foot crushing a snake.[25] In placement and iconography it is possible that the sculptured image was intended to recall the painted one.

Other statues shored up the theme of Christian rule. To either side of the imperial figure, the philosophers called to mind the qualities of wisdom and justice that were part of the standard repertoire of imperial virtues.[26] Inclusion on the façade of a statue of Justin, Justinian's uncle and predecessor, suggests a desire to emphasize dynastic continuity, and certainly the line-up of imperial images that created a historic imperial court in the area immediately in front of the actual entrance once again implied coherence between contemporary and past rules.

This external vision would have resonated with the imagery on the gate's interior. By articulating the general themes of legitimate rule and Christian victory, the exterior statuary would have prepared the viewer for a more precise documentation of events that took place on the vestibule's interior. Stepping across the threshold and into the Chalke's domed interior, a visitor would have seen the grand theme of victory upheld in the display of the Ephesian horses above the second entrance. With them, and, in a nod to the time-honored traditions of Hellenic visual culture, the gorgoneia mounted the apotropaic defense of the palace. Mosaics on the lower rising walls and in the dome formed the backdrop for these images. In the half-light of the interior, these monumental narratives documented the specifically Justinianic military campaigns that had restored the Roman Empire to its fullest glory and the emperor, triumphant, with his court.[27] With these visual histories, the theoretical proclamation of victory was documented as practice.

The date of the Chalke's decoration is not certain.[28] Reconstruction of the actual building is likely to have been undertaken soon after its 532 destruction; however, the subject matter of the mosaics suggests a date of completion as late as the 550s. Although the subjugation of Vandal North Africa was complete by 535, victory over the Goths in Italy was hard won with the final defeat of the enemy coming only in the 550s.

The displays of antiquities at the Arkadian Baths and the Chalke Gate represent the last systematic installations of antiquities in Constantinople. The remaining evidence for the treatment of the city's collections suggests that Justinian and his contemporaries eventually turned their backs on this tradition of urban display, rejecting antiquities as a vehicle for ideological expression not only by refusing to gather and install them, but also by dismantling extant gatherings when necessary. Dismantling of the city's collections appears to have begun as early as the 530s. During the reconstruction of the Hagia Sophia, a large number of pagan statues is reported to have been removed from the Augusteion, among them the figures associated with the Constantinian horoscope (cat. nos. 7–15). These images were not destroyed but redistributed around the city to other public spaces. The display in the Arkadian Baths may have been the result of this procedure, and the phenomenon of redistribution may account for some of the iconographic inconsistencies observed in some of the city's collections.[29]

The rationale behind the removal of statuary from the Augusteion is not known. Although it may have reflected nothing more pressing than the practical need for access and space associated with the rebuilding of the Hagia Sophia, in retrospect it presages a more deliberately hostile response to antiquities that occurred during the last years of Justinian's reign. In 562 Justinian undertook his last persecution of the pagan religious, arresting offenders and destroying their cultural property.[30] John Malalas recorded the events: "In the month of June in that indiction [A.D. 562], Hellenes were arrested and paraded around. Their books were burnt in the kynegion, together with pictures and statues of their loathsome gods."[31] As this unsavory record makes clear, the Theodosian invitation to view ancient images of the gods as art was only partially successful, as more zealous members of the now majority Christian population considered ancient images as one element in a larger cultural package that was linked to the more perfidious aspects of Hellenic tradition.

Although the events that Malalas recorded took place in Constantinople, the hostility toward images that he observed seems to have had little overt effect on the collection itself. There is no evidence that any of the Constantinopolitan antiquities were destroyed outright. At the same time, however, it is also clear that there was no overriding mandate to replace statues or restore collections once they were damaged. Thus, as early as 532, after the burning in the Nika fires, the Baths of Zeuxippos was restored without sculpture, its statue bases serving as paving stones for the new complex.[32]

The response to the destruction of the Zeuxippos suggests a kind of indifference that is evident both in the nature of the Chalke gathering and in the phenomenon of redistribution. The reuse of antiquities at the Chalke is remarkable not only for the fact that it represents the last major installation of ancient statuary in the city, but also because of the selection of sculpture and the iconographic use to which it was put. To begin with, although there was a large amount of sculpture associated with the Chalke, the actual number of ancient monuments was comparatively small. Between fifteen and twenty freestanding statues stood on or at the Gate, the majority outside. Within this group only five figures were works of ancient manufacture, the two figures of the philosophers, the ruler portrait, and the horses. On the one hand, the display is remarkable for the pride of place given to ancient statuary: Each and every documented antiquity stood on the Gate itself rather than in a secondary position nearby. On the other hand, in comparison to other Constantinopolitan displays, the selection of ancient monuments was lackluster. The diminished numbers contrasted with earlier displays throughout the city where antiquities made up the lion's share of the installations. As well, the wide and subtle range of subject matter seen in these same gatherings was missing, as the prize pieces that characterized both the Constantinian and the Theodosian selections were exchanged for a comparatively limited and undistinguished set of portraits. Gone is the interest in the acquisition of such historically evocative statuary as the Helikonian Muses or the Lysippan Herakles.

In part, this choice of images must have reflected the reality of numbers: by the sixth century, time would have taken its toll, making access to renowned antiquities of high quality limited. Even so, the willingness to settle for such a relatively undistinguished group of figures suggests that the evocative power of ancient statuary was on the wane, except in its most residual sense, as a nod to visual decorum. It was of course unthinkable that the Chalke would stand unadorned. As the main entrance to the imperial palace, the Gate required attention. How that requirement would be met was altogether another matter. Statuary was, by tradition, the requisite medium for such undertakings. Thus, incorporation of sculpture into the Gate's design assumed the necessity of the medium. Further, that some of the pieces were ancient indicates a belief that antiquities were likewise appropriate to the project. At the same time, however, the comparatively banal selection of antiquities for what was arguably one of the most important of the city's imperial venues suggests a real lack of interest in the expressive possibilities of the medium, a notion borne out by the relatively one-dimensional character of the Gate's display. The bold and provocative selection of images that shaped the Constantinian collections and, to a lesser extent, those of the Theodosians, self-consciously tapped into history by making an individual monument's material history an aspect of its subject matter. Thus the Lysippan Herakles was important not only as an image of Herakles *qua* Herakles, but also as a statue with a particular history that was itself evocative of specific events, associations, and ideas pertinent to Roman and by extension Constantinopolitan identity. The evidence for Justinianic reuse suggests that none of this subtle manipulation of the past through the physical appropriation of monuments was at play. Moreover, in cases such as the Belisarius-Constantine-Justinian statue where references were made, they drew less on knowledge of antiquity and more on the experience of the Christian empire and its capital city. Constantinople's own history was now the main point of reference. Thus, recognizable in terms of typologies alone, images such as the philosophers and the ruler portrait stood as deracinated antiquities, half-hearted witnesses to the devaluation of ancient statuary as strong visual currency.

The phenomenon of redistribution is of a piece with the Chalke enterprise. The willingness to not only dismantle the Augusteion ensemble, a collection that had been built up over two hundred years, but also insert its holdings into other urban ensembles without regard to iconographic consistency confirms a sense of diminished power. In dismembering collections, gatherings once carefully constructed were undone and thus lost their meaning as individual statues were separated both from one another and from their larger context. Detached from their environment they no longer held meaning in the same way. Specific associations gave way to generic understandings, and images designed to work in concert with one another found themselves deracinated, displayed either singly or in gatherings with other types of statuary with whose identity they may or may not have resonated. In a very real way, this was an action that undermined and scrambled the historical image of Constantinople that had been so carefully built up over the past two hundred years.

Several factors lie at the root of this indifference. To begin with, the retreat from the reuse of antiquities paralleled a general decline in the contemporary production and installation of monumental sculpture. The fourth and fifth centuries saw a sharp drop in the number of commissions for public monuments. Dedicatory inscriptions measure the decline, which was an empirewide phenomenon that began in the early part of the third century A.D. Consider the case of Aphrodisias in Caria: although there are approximately 1,500 surviving inscriptions from the period between 20 B.C. and A.D. 250, only about 250 remain from the period between 250 and 550. Of these inscriptions, 31 were associated with statues while the remaining 219 were architectural. Thus there was a real decline, not only in the epigraphical evidence itself, but also in the freestanding sculpture that accompanied it.[33]

Constriction of subject matter went hand in glove with the reduced numbers of actual sculptured monuments as the wide range of images familiar from the cities and sanctuaries of the Greco-Roman world declined precipitously. Although portrait statues of emperors and, to a lesser extent, civic figures remained popular, the production of mythological subjects, tripods, and statues of Greco-Roman culture heroes did not. Further, manufacture of the large-scale, multifigure groups, such as the Hippodrome Skylla, that were produced to great fanfare in the early imperial period died out, replaced by works of smaller scale and diminished complexity.[34]

The main images of Late Antiquity were imperial. Portraits, either of emperors or their representatives, take pride of place among the images of the later Roman world. Again the evidence of Aphrodisias: almost all fourth-century inscriptions from the site are concerned with imperial officials with the exception of a pair of private inscriptions accompanying figures by two sculptors as advertisements for their work. Later-fifth-century dedications show more local involvement; however, the numbers are still scant.[35]

Evidence for Aphrodisias parallels that of Constantinople. Apart from the antiquities themselves, most of the city's sculpture was imperial in nature. Imperial portraits were the most common images by far, accompanying almost all of the ancient sculptured installations either as contemporary or later additions.[36]

The falling off in the number of sculptured dedications and the increased emphasis on imperial dedications reflected the changed interests of society and its patrons in the Mediterranean world of the fourth, fifth, and sixth centuries. To begin with, the habits of public patronage that had fired the dedication of public monuments in the early Empire began to decline. Evidence regarding public works projects from late-fourth-century Antioch indicates a significant change in the concept of public duty. Where once city councilors had considered it an obligation to sponsor public works projects such as stoas and baths, this was no longer the case, and the breach was filled in some instances by the imperial administration out of government funds.[37] The practical effect for sculpture and its production must have been to reduce the need for commemorative monuments honoring local citizens and shift the emphasis to emperors and their imperial representatives.

In part, this downturn in local patronage may be the result of the aristocracy's declining financial fortunes. At the same time, however, it reflects a changed sense of where money ought to be spent. Where once funding went into public works it was now increasingly invested in religious buildings or charitable activity.[38] This change in emphasis, in motion since the fourth century and increasingly evident in the fifth, brought with it not only a change in the nature of urban institutions but also a revised sense of what constituted urban beauty, particularly in the cities of the east. Thus, while the fourth century opened with the conviction that *kallos* was vested in the nature of public buildings such as forums, stoas, baths, and circuses, and with them the appropriate sculptured decor, the sixth century stepped back from the nurturing of these formidable civic institutions to place ecclesiastical building with its relics and icons at the center of its aesthetic universe.[39] As Prokopios's list for Constantinople makes clear, churches, not circuses, had become the heart and soul of any city.

As the institutions that had once required and sponsored sculptural commemorations died out so too did the need for sculpture. Thus, although sculpture did continue to be produced for specific contexts such as the Hippodrome,[40] the transformations that overtook city life by the end of the sixth century made it an ever less necessary phenomenon, suggesting that sculpture had essentially outlived its usefulness.

The decline in the reuse of ancient statuary is of a piece with the overall decline in the production of statuary. In keeping with that general trend there is an increasingly imperial emphasis to the deployment of antiquities with the passage of time. Thus, although the whole of the Constantinian project ultimately reflected on the emperor, the aura of the enterprise was above all historical. By the time of the Theodosians, however, antiquities were marshaled for the more overtly imperial purposes of establishing dynastic legitimacy, a trend that dovetailed with the general manner of sculptural production and presentation. At the Justinianic Chalke, that work appears to have been complete.

As with contemporary monuments, the empire's religious culture also affected the reuse of antiquities. It did so wittingly and unwittingly. The appreciation and desire for antiquities fell prey to the same social and institutional changes that cut off the lifeblood of contemporary sculptural production. Thus, in terms of religious culture, as the church came to play a more prominent social and administrative role at Constantinople the impetus to reuse lost its force as energy was channeled into projects such as church-building and decoration. At the same time, however, the increasing success of Christianity over the course of the fourth and the fifth centuries brought about and permitted overt hostility toward those ancient monuments that could be associated with pagan cult. As we have seen, it did so on two grounds: the Mosaic prohibition against idolatry established in the second commandment and the Platonic suspicion that the stuff of this world could not hope to be crafted into something representative of the divine. The materials of stone and metal that created an image of a god were dead matter that no amount of craftsmanship or skill could invest with life. That the pagan religious could ignore this fact by perpetuating the veneration of lifeless images was a source of ridicule and scorn for Christian thinkers and their flocks.[41]

This lack of sympathy with the Hellenic propensity to embody the divine in sculptured form was accompanied by a second conviction, the belief that sculpture could be and often was inhabited by demons. Thus, although it was impossible for the dumb matter that was sculpture to capture the essence of the divine, it could play host to beings of lesser rank, troublemakers who provoked all manner of mischief. Eusebios acknowledged that such dark powers lurked in images and described their modus operandi:

> These then being certain demons who dwell about the earth and underground, and haunt the heavy and cloudy atmosphere over the earth, and have been condemned, for causes which we shall afterwards allege, to inhabit this dark and earthly abode, love to dwell in graves and monuments of the dead and in all loathsome and impure matter, and delight in bloodshed and gore and the bodies of animals of all kinds, and in the exhalation from the fumes of incense and of vapors rising out of the earth. These and their rulers, who are certain powers of the air, or of the nether world, having observed that the human race was groveling low about the deification of dead men, and spending its labor very zealously upon sacrifices and savors which

were to them most grateful, were ready at hand as supporters and helpers of this delusion; and gloating over the miseries of mankind, they easily deceived silly souls by certain movements of the carved images, which had been consecrated by them of old in honor of the departed, and by the illusions produced by oracles, and by the cures of bodies, which these same demons were secretly ravaging by their own operation, and then again releasing the men and letting them go free from suffering.

Hereby they drove the superstitious headlong into supposing sometimes that they were heavenly powers and certain real gods, and at other times that they were the souls of the deified heroes.

From this cause the belief in the polytheistic error began now to be regarded by the multitude as something greater and more venerable, as their thought passed from what was visible to the invisible nature of those who were hidden in the statues, and so confirmed the delusion more strongly. . . . For the shapes of the consecrated images in the various cities were thought to wear the semblance of dead men's bodies, but of their souls and their divine and incorporeal powers the evil demons made counterfeit presentations by abundance of fictitious miracles; until at length their consecrated ministers themselves used continually to exaggerate the folly of the illusion, and prepare most of their contrivances by evil arts of jugglery, while the evil demons again took the lead themselves in teaching these tricks to their ministers.[42]

These demons, unsavory tricksters who hoodwinked mortals into the error of false belief through their actions as divine imposters, were the true cause of human misery. One way to neutralize their threat was to prohibit the practices of sacrifice through which these creatures nourished their being.[43] Far more efficient, as John Malalas's Christian hard-liners knew, was the outright destruction of images. In an atmosphere such as this, small wonder that antiquities ceased to have any expressive appeal, except to invite negative assessment.

Yet for all their potential menace, the fact remains that the Constantinopolitan collections remained largely intact throughout the whole crucial period of the sixth century. What was it that allowed their survival? As Malalas indicated in his report on the burning of pagan books and images during the 562 purge, antiquities in general and ancient temple images in particular were part of a larger cultural package that included not only religious practice but also the literary and rhetorical traditions of the paideia. Thus, the association that was at once their undoing was also their salvation. Although antiquities might be associated with false religion, they could also stand as the sign of tradition and civilization. Thus, for the Romans, a people that defined itself in terms of the past, antiquity had an important dual function. It was both a model for correct behavior and an image that conveyed moral and political legitimacy. In the legal and administrative sphere the sway of the past was evident in the language of law and the structure of the administrative hierarchy.[44] In the visual realm, antiquities gave testimony to the link between past and present that was so crucial to Roman self-definition thereby allowing their continuing presence within the urban landscape.

For all of the respect accorded to classical tradition, however, it was evident by the end of the sixth century that the past and the ways in which it legitimated people and places was being redefined. The general decline in the use of public sculpture, ancient or contemporary, together with the willingness to dismantle collections like the Augusteion gathering indicate that antiquities, the defining heart and soul of the Constantinian and Theodosian capital, were no longer the dominant visual currency.

What kinds of images were deployed in their stead and what kind of legitimacy did they convey? The most lasting and tangible evidence for the Justinianic reconstruction of Constantinople is the great church, Hagia Sophia.[45] Built in the immediate aftermath of the fires and dedicated, as were its predecessors, to the Wisdom of Jesus Christ, the church was the jewel in the crown of the city's redevelopment. Then, as now, the complex dominated the city center, its domed mass rising above the avenues and stoas of the old city. Inside, a series of monumental vaulted spaces sheathed in marbles that were themselves a reflection of the Empire and its marvels in a way analogous to the city's statuary shaped an image of the Christian microcosm, which, like its neighbor the Hippodrome, was intended as a backdrop for imperial ceremonial.[46]

When Justinian stepped over the threshold of this new imperial space on the day of its inauguration he is reported to have cried out, "Solomon, I have outdone thee."[47] Whether apocryphal or not, the response suggests a new type of urban definition. Gone are the references to Troy, Rome, and the overarching traditions of the paideia, their place taken by images that tapped into a new, even more ancient history, that of the Bible. For the reference to Solomon was, of course, one that played on the dedication of the church, drawing the threads of Old and New Testament history – the wisdom of Solomon and the wisdom of Christ – into a definition of the Constantinopolitan present that saw the city less as the embodiment of the New Rome and more as the realization of the New Jerusalem.

This shift in reference is borne out by the development of the city as a whole. The wealth of churches described by Prokopios claimed and sacralized the urban territory for Christianity as they became home to a different type of antiquity: the relic and its relative, the icon. Beginning in the fourth century with the translation under Constantius in 356 and 357 of the mortal remains of saints Timothy, Luke, and Andrew from their original burial sites in the Holy Land to a new resting place in the capital at the Holy Apostles, relics were established as a part of the urban landscape.[48] Thus, in a development that ran parallel to the gathering of antiquities, Constantinople became a repository for relics from the fourth century. The collection and translation of primary relics such as body parts and secondary relics such as clothing became increasingly frequent in the later fourth and fifth centuries as objects such as the Virgin's cincture were brought to the city's churches.[49] In the fifth and sixth centuries, icons came to be included in the mix.[50] Over time, these new antiquities came to dominate the image of the city, so that by 1204 the city's sacred holdings, which included not only the relics of Christ's passion but also some of Christendom's most ancient portraits, were the envy of the Christian world.

The introduction of these sacred objects was of a piece with the reuse of antiquities. The gathering of relics took place concurrently with the collection of antiquities, and like the transport of ancient statuary, itself resonant with the numinous, the deployment of these sacred objects was designed to fill a void in the capital's history. Unlike Jerusalem and the territories of the Holy Land that preserved the legacy of Christian history in the geography and monuments of the place, or Rome with its rich horde of martyr's bones lying at sacred rest, Constantinople had no particular or documentable Christian history. The translation of images, be they relics or icons, to churches and monasteries in and around the capital was a way to overcome this deficit by establishing in residence the great protagonists of Christian history. The physical remains of the saints and their representations in holy images brought with them their sanctity. They also served as testament to the events of the Christian past, a testament that brought that past into the city, sanctifying it as a holy territory of its own.[51] Like the Palladion, the Serpent Column, or the great Lysippan Herakles, antiquities that were themselves relics of a sort and whose very presence endowed the city with the force of the whole system of Greco-Roman belief and with which they initially jostled for recognition, these Christian images referred to and created a new visual culture that eventually shaped the later history of Constantinople, transforming it from the worldly city of the Greco-Roman paideia into the Christian city of God.

# ∽ THE CATALOGUE ∽

# INTRODUCTION TO THE CATALOGUE

T HE CATALOGUE PRESENTS THE EVIDENCE FOR THE RECONSTRUCTION OF THE
Constantinopolitan collection of antiquities. It draws on literary, and, to a lesser
extent, graphic and archaeological materials to do so. In marshaling this evidence,
the principal aim is to create a census of antiquities known to have been in the
capital. This census, in turn, forms the basis for observations about the history and
development of the collection as a whole.

## ORGANIZATION AND MECHANICS

The overall arrangement is alphabetical by topographical location. Within the topographical groupings, monuments are listed alphabetically by subject matter. In most
instances, the designation of subject matter follows that indicated by the sources.
Thus, statues such as the Aphrodite of Knidos or the Zeus from Olympia, two
works mentioned in the tenth-century text of Georgios Kedrenos, appear as such.
In some instances, however, original descriptions either do not identify the figures
they describe or do so in a manner inconsistent with classical typologies. This is
the case, for example, with a statue of Hekate, which the anonymous author of
the eighth-century *Parastaseis syntomoi chronikai* refers to as a statue of Constantine
and his two sons. Because the aim of this project is to reconstruct the range and
number of the city's ancient holdings, monuments treated in this manner are listed
according to classical definitions rather than their later medieval reinterpretations.
Cross-references refer readers familiar with these postclassical identifications to the
classical designations.

The entries themselves present as available the pertinent literary, archaeological, and graphic evidence for individual monuments. Textual sources appear in translation. Translation credits are included parenthetically in abbreviated form at the end of each passage. Full citations appear in the list of abbreviations and in the bibliography of primary sources. Those translations not credited are my own.

In the interests of brevity, the literary sources are reproduced only once. Therefore in instances where a text describes more than one piece of statuary subsequent references to monuments that derive from the source refer the reader to the initial citation.

In the rare instances where there is no literary evidence, archaeological or graphic materials alone are listed. Regrettably, a good deal of the archaeological documentation, most of which came to light in the late 1920s, has not been well published or preserved. As a result, pertinent measurements and museum index numbers are sometimes unavailable.

Where necessary, a commentary designed to assess the information presented in the sources accompanies the documentation. Because the aim of the project is to determine as far as possible the specific classical nature of the Constantinopolitan holdings, each entry examines the sources for information detailing a given monument's appearance (size, medium, pose), presumed date of manufacture, location, and history before and after its importation to the capital. Given that the type of information supplied by the sources is often uneven, these details are not consistently available. Thus, issues of appearance, location, and history are discussed only when information permits, and in instances where the literary evidence does not provide information beyond the identification of subject matter, there is no commentary.

Where possible, associations based on comparisons to ancient sculptural typologies are made. The purpose of these associations is not to provide an absolute definition of type, but rather to suggest a sense of the original monument, its iconographic and aesthetic aspects, with the aim of providing a feel for the larger makeup of the collection.

If extant, a bibliography of secondary sources pertinent to the discussion of a given antiquity in its Constantinopolitan venue completes the entry. Otherwise, detailed discussion of the broad range of archaeological scholarship pertinent to the city's antiquities is beyond the scope of the project. References to these more general sources are indicated parenthetically and are designed to be used with the larger bibliography.

## METHODOLOGICAL CONSIDERATIONS

The ability to envision statuary by analogy to known images is made possible by the nature of ancient sculptural production. In contrast to Renaissance and post-Renaissance notions of creativity with their emphasis on invention, sculptors in the later Greek and Roman world operated from a premise that could eschew the creation of new forms to create statues on the basis of familiar sculptured typologies. As with the manipulation of a musical theme, images such as the Aphrodite of Knidos or the Doryphoros by Polykleitos could be reproduced precisely or as a series of variations on a prototype designed to recall the original that simultaneously posed new questions and offered new insights into the representation of certain subjects. This habit of production and reproduction resulted in the creation of multiple copies of and variations on famous works of art.[1] Thus, the Knidia, which survives in over 200 copies and is arguably the most popular sculpture known from Greco-Roman antiquity, is familiar from a series of replicas that reproduce the statue's features either directly or in mirrored reversal. In addition, a series of figures, the Capitoline Venus and the Medici Venus among them,[2] present variations on this initial theme that both refer to and rethink the initial proposition of Praxiteles' fourth-century creation. According to this creative process, certain iconographic details are associated with given statues and particular moments in time, with the result that references to such details can help to fix an image visually and chronologically.

Because the larger aim of this project has been the reconstruction and analysis of the Constantinopolitan collection in iconographic terms, this study depends on the identification of individual statues in terms of subject matter. Issues of date of manufacture and the related question of style also come into play. Therefore the catalogue discussions draw overtly on the methodological traditions of archaeological reconstruction. At the same time, however, I have relied on the conceptual issues related to problems of perception and reception in the service of textual interpretation. I am well aware that Byzantine authors observed antiquities in a manner different from our own. The issues of typology that drive so many of the modern discussions of Greek and Roman statuary and that also underpin the intellectual structure of this catalogue were certainly foreign to the Byzantine visual imagination. These intellectual constructs represent a modern way of coming to grips with the legacy of the Greco-Roman world. As such they are no less valid than Byzantine points of view. Indeed, they offer modern scholars the means to understand what statuary meant in its initial incarnation, how it was originally perceived, and how, ultimately, Byzantine viewers thought about the classical past. It is therefore my hope that by identifying and understanding the monuments of Constantinople on the basis of classical identities reconstructed from modern methodologies, these methodologies will allow the possibility of looking into questions of typology and identification not as ends in themselves, but as avenues to the understanding of the larger issues of the perception and reception of antiquities across the various phases of Constantinopolitan history.

# AMASTRIANON

## 1. ANIMALS

*Par.* 41:

Spectacle number five. In the neighborhood of the Amastrianon. . . . In this place Zeus Helios on a chariot inlaid with marble, the staffbearer of Zeus, Aristides, the reclining Herakles, a charioteer with the inscription "All powerful Apollo." There was the river . . . the eagle worshipped by a wolf, in it are tortoises full of birds among the eighteen she-serpents, Koukobytios the philosopher, a champion of idols and sacrificer of his wife and two children, his mother Aglaide and his sister Graphentia. In this place the dominion and fall of demons (exemplified) those of the emperors to philosophers, especially if the accursed emperors be fornicators in word or offspring. For this reason let them pay attention to the naked statue and cooking the iron herb with a small spoon and roasting with the nostrils, let them . . . at the friends of the emperor. From these it was known to you how things are likely to happen to them. And much silver, especially denarii was buried below, and also a treasure of gold. It is said that there was a theater and that it was possible for many to watch in the daytime and marvel at sacrifices to Zeus. And there was an earthquake, and people died in the arena in the days of Byzas and Antes before Constantine was revealed as a worshipper of God not in this city but at Rome. And the horses and musical instruments of the dux Galindouch – these can be seen in the building of the Artemision until the present day. Wherefore, Philokalos, though we have gone to a lot of trouble for your honor's sake, we do not grudge it. (Cameron/Herrin)

The description suggests an elaborate, multi-figured fountain group. The river may be actual water or a statue of a river god. Reference to "tortoises full of birds" suggests a series of turtles with birds riding on their backs, while the enumeration of "eighteen she-serpents" calls to mind aquatic figures such as mermaids and hippocamps. This sort of fanciful sculpture was just the type to enliven fountains and gardens. Bronze and marble animals often served as water spigots in fountains, and it is possible to imagine the phalanx of she-serpents functioning in this manner (Jashemski, 1979 and 1993; Kapossy, 1969).

Cameron/Herrin believe that Constantine established and decorated the Amastrianon. In the absence of any direct evidence this statement should remain hypothetical. A date for the removal or destruction of the statuary is also unknown. Janin (1964: 88) believes that Kedrenos wrote his account of the Amastrianon entirely on the basis of secondary sources and that none of the monuments he described had survived to his own day. Cameron/Herrin also believe that *Par.* reproduces a list and posit that the garbled nature of the account derives from a misunderstanding of the inventory. Dagron (1984: 35) suggests that the actual source for this list and others was in the sixth-century writing of Theodore the Lector. Conservative estimate therefore puts the removal of the statuary between the sixth century and the eighth.

*Bibliography:* Du Cange (1680) I, 14, 13; Janin, 1964: 38, 68–69, 70, 95; Guilland, 1969: I, 434; II, 37, 94, 98, 101; Dagron, 1984: 35, 42, 135, 140–41; Cameron/Herrin, 224–28

## 2. ARISTIDES

*Par.* 41: see no. 1.

No statues are recorded in ancient literature and the philosopher's portrait has not been recognized. Cameron/Herrin suggest that identification with the ancient philosopher may not be intended and propose association with contemporary figures of the same name. Although such a reidentification certainly is possible, there is no reason to reject identification with the ancient Aristides. Absence of surviving literary references or sculptures themselves does not in itself indicate that portraits of Aristides were unknown. The very specific identification of this figure may indicate that the statue was inscribed. Whether this was the case, the Aristides statue should probably be envisioned togate in the general manner of a man of letters.

*Bibliography:* Cameron/Herrin, 225

## 3. HELIOS

*Par.* 41: see no. 1.

Kedrenos, 566–67:

The name Amastrianon is explained by the fact that a poor man from Amastris came to the city because he was in need and died there, thus giving the place has a bad name so that the criminals and murderers executed here are called Paphlagonians on account of the vile comportment of those people. There was once here a great temple to Helios and Selene. Seven columns stood to the north of it. In the middle of them there was a conch similar to a rotunda above which rode Helios in a white chariot, followed by the crowned Selene in a biga. Byzas was the patron of the work, with Phidalia his wife. Below in a pavilion by the substructures he sat with a scepter in his lap, exhorting the people to obey the magistrates. Here on the ground was a statue of Zeus in white stone, the work of Pheidias, which appeared to recline as if on a couch.

The sources record a relatively large number of statues in the Amastrianon, and it is likely that there is some overlap between the descriptions. The "Zeus Helios" or the charioteer of *Par.* is likely to be one and the same with Kedrenos's Helios, confirming an identification of one of those figures as Helios. The remaining chariot group should be associated with Kedrenos's Selene.

The description mentions Helios in a white chariot, which suggests a marble group complete with horses. Traditionally Helios's chariot is a quadriga. Helios himself is shown beardless with long hair bound by a fillet. He wears a crown of solar rays and a long, belted chiton. It is impossible to date the statuary precisely; however, several of the described typologies suggest sculpture of fifth-century classical manufacture and later. The text suggests that the statue may

have been part of a pre-Constantinian temple complex.

*Bibliography:* Du Cange (1680) I: 14, 13; Janin, 1964: 68–69, 70, 95; Guilland, 1969: I, 434; II, 37, 94, 98, 101; Dagron, 1984: 35, 42, 135, 140–41; Cameron/Herrin, 224–28

## 4. HERAKLES, RECLINING (PLATE 1)

*Par.* 41: see no. 1.

Kedrenos I, 566–67: see no. 3.

*Par.* refers to the "reclining Herakles." The type is well established. The hero lies back on his lion skin, his torso turned forward, his legs extended and crossed and his weight propped on his left elbow. In surviving examples, Herakles is almost always aged, as indicated by his beard. The type was created in the fourth century B.C. and was copied repeatedly in the Hellenistic and Roman ages (*LIMC*, s.v. "Herakles").

The reclining Herakles may be the same statue described by Kedrenos as a marble Zeus by Pheidias. The figure appears to have reclined as indicated by the reference to the kline, or reclining couch, a description designed to evoke pose rather than furnishing. Reclining statues of Zeus are unknown in antiquity, and although it is possible that the text describes a new typology for Zeus, identification with the reclining Herakles seems more appropriate, especially as the two would have shared certain physical characteristics, specifically their age and the beard. Alternatively, it is conceivable that the statue was that of a river god, a figure that again shares the reclining, pose, and gross physical typology of both Herakles and Zeus.

Attribution to Pheidias should be viewed as an interpretation based on the author's understanding of the sculpture as ancient and his knowledge of Pheidias as an ancient artist. Cameron/Herrin associate the figure with the Herakles by Lysippos (cat. no. 21); however, this association is incorrect as the reclining Herakles was an established type in its own right.

*Bibliography:* Cameron/Herrin, 226

PLATE 1: Reclining Herakles, The British Museum, London (Photo: © Copyright The British Museum)

## 5. HERMES

*Par.* 41: see no. 1.

Description as the "staffbearer of Zeus" identifies the figure as Hermes.

**Zeus:** *see* **Herakles, reclining.**

## ARTOPOLEION

## 6. ANIMALS

*Par.* 40:

Spectacle number four, which is in the buildings of the Bread Market.... A small dog made out of marble, bearing many teats..., as many as twenty, or lumps which they sought to worship, was visible for all who wanted to see from every side. And heads of a peacock and an eagle and a lioness and

rams, and sparrows and crows and one turtle dove and a weasel and five heifers lowing and two Gorgons, one on the right and one on the left, one looking into the face of the other, carved from marble in relief ⟨and⟩ all mixed up together below the same building or Bread Market, as a spectacle, the work of Constantine. There was also an oxherd above an ox plowing, as if intending to dig the earth, a great spectacle for those who saw it. This remained for many years, and the story lasted until the reign of Zeno.... (Cameron/Herrin)

The figures should be considered as a group. The statues included a "dog with teats" and the heads of various birds and animals, specifically a peacock, an eagle, a lioness, rams, sparrows, crows, a turtle dove, a weasel, and five lowing heifers. In addition to animal statues, there was a figure of an "oxherd above an ox plowing." The group is reported to have been erected by Constantine and destroyed in the fifth century during the reign of Zeno (474–91).

With the exception of the rams, Cameron/ Herrin (222) doubt that the figures were actually heads; however, it is possible that the list refers to a series of animal protomes that may well have been waterspouts associated with a fountain (compare cat. no. 1). Alternatively the statues simply may have been arrayed in front of or around a reflecting pool. Lambeck (Preger) proposed that the group be considered as a group of animals surrounding a figure of nature.

*Bibliography:* Du Cange (1680) I: 24, 9; Preger, 1902–07, 44, n. 13; Janin, 1964: 315; Dagron, 1984: 42; Cameron/Herrin, 222–24

## AUGUSTEION

*Par.* 11 (*Patria* II, 96):

At the great church which is now called Holy Wisdom, 427 statues were removed, most of them pagans. Among the many were ones of Zeus, and of Carus, the ancestor of Diocletian, and the Zodiac, and Selene and Aphrodite and the star Arcturus, supported by two Persian statues and the South Pole and a priestess of Athena prophesying to Hero the philosopher, in profile. There were only a few [statues] of Christians, about eighty. Out of the many it is worth mentioning a few: Constantine, Constantius, Constans, Galen the quaestor, (Julian Caesar and another Julian, the eparch), Licinius Augustus, Valentinian and Theodosios and Arkadios and his son, Serapio the governor and three of Helena the mother of Constantine: one of porphyry and [other] marbles, another with silver inlay on a bronze column and the other of ivory, given by Cypros the rhetor. These statues Justinian distributed about the city when he built the Great Church with faith and effort. Those who know the foregoing find a good number of them if they go round the city and look for them. (based on Cameron/Herrin)

A single text from *Par.* documents statuary in the vicinity of the pre-Justinianic church of Hagia Sophia. The list is brief and there is lit-

tle that can be said about the statues themselves. Details of iconography, formal aspects and dates of manufacture are for the most part difficult if not impossible to determine. In the two instances where typology is more evident, the case of the telamones and the zodiac, the statuary is of Hellenistic or Roman manufacture.

It is not clear where the statues stood. Gilles (II.5) placed them to the side of the church following the report in Suidas. Cameron and Herrin (184) place them outside in the vicinity of the church without specifying a precise location. Location near the pre-sixth-century church suggests placement in the Augusteion.

The group has been the subject of some discussion. Maass focused on the number of figures associated with the heavens, specifically those of Arcturus, Selene, and South Pole and suggested that the combined figures represented a horoscope commissioned by Constantine for the church. Preger objected to this interpretation noting, first, that it is not necessarily the case that Constantine founded the church, and, second, that there were so many statues assembled that it was unlikely that the figures were conceived as anything more than decoration. Certainly the variety of figures in the group does not conform to an exclusively astrological schedule.

*Bibliography:* Maass, 1891; Preger, 1902a; Mango, 1963: 57; Cameron/Herrin, 184–86

### 7. APHRODITE

### 8. CARUS

The emperor Marcus Aurelius Carus (A.D. 282).

### 9. HERO THE PHILOSOPHER

The statue represented one of two subjects: an Alexandrian philosopher (fl. A.D. 200) or a fifth-century teacher and student of the Neoplatonist, Proclus. Cameron/Herrin (185) favor identification with the Alexandrian philosopher.

PLATE 2: Telamone, Ny Carlsberg Glyptotek, Copenhagen (Photo: Ny Carlsberg Glyptotek)

*Bibliography:* Cameron/Herrin, 185

**Persian statues,** *see* **Telamones.**

## 10. PRIESTESS OF ATHENA

The statue is likely to have been a portrait statue of a prominent member of a cult of Athena.

## 11. SELENE

## 12. SOUTH POLE

## 13. TELAMONES (PLATE 2)

The reference to "Persian statues" suggests figures of telamones. Pausanias (I.18.8) refers to a similar group at the Olympeion in Athens. The Athenian offering was made by Antiochus IV of Syria and the subject is Hellenistic. Several Roman examples survive, showing consistency in type. Examples from Copenhagen (Poulsen, 1951: nos. 546, 547, 380–81), Naples (Reusch, 1908: no. 579, inv. 6115), and the Vatican (Lippold, 1956: nos. 37, 180–82) confirm a standard iconography and use of materials. The figures, sculptured in exotic marbles, kneel. Each wears the peaked cap, tunic, and long trousers that characterize Persian ethnicity.

## 14. ZEUS

## 15. ZODIAC

Three basic freestanding types characterize zodiac iconography. Type I, the "Himmelsglobe," has two variants (Gundel, 1992: 74–81): the zodiac appears as a flat band with relief representations of individual signs wrapped around a star-spangled sphere or as signs scattered across the surface of the globe. Type II, the Planisphere, shows the signs on the surface of a flat, round disk framing a field showing figural and symbolic representations of stars and planets (Gundel, 1992 cat. 19). Type III, the ring zodiac, depicts the signs in relief on a flat surface surrounding a round, concave niche. A representation of a god, commonly Zeus, may be placed within the niche (Gundel, 1992 cat. 49) supported on the shoulders of Atlas. Date of manufacture is uniform with most surviving freestanding representations dating to the first or second century.

Typology appears to be associated with function (Gundel, 1992 158–59). Type I globe variants were largely decorative. Type II planispheres were used both as decoration and as reference works for astronomers. Type III ring zodiacs were associated with religious functions. It is not possible to determine which of these types appeared in Constantinople.

# AUGUSTEION SENATE

## 16. ASKLEIPIOS

Leo Gramm. 257:

The emperor (Basil I) brought many statues to the senate. Among these decorations there was also a bronze statue in the shape of a bishop, which carried a staff in his hand that was entwined with a snake.

Symeon Magister, 692:

In the eleventh year of the reign of the emperor Basil, Niketas Xylenites etc. The emperor destroyed many bronze vases for use in the New Church. And he brought marbles and mosaics and columns from many other churches. Among these ornaments was a bronze statue of a bishop that was in the senate, holding a staff in his hand around which a serpent coiled.

The statue was bronze. Reference to a snake-entwined staff indicates a statue of Askleipios rather than an actual bishop, a notion first proposed by Mango.

Two Askleipios types exist (*LIMC*, s.v. "Askleipios"): an older, bearded type or a youthful, clean-shaven one. In both instances the god wears the himation and holds the snake-entwined staff in one hand. Both iconographies were established in the fifth century B.C. and remained unvaried chronologically and geographically through the third century A.D. Of the two, the mature, bearded image of the god appears to have been more popular. Description of the Constantinopolitan statue as a bishop suggests a bearded Askleipios.

Information regarding Constantinopolitan history is contradictory. Leo Grammatikos notes that Basil I (867–96) as one of a larger group of statues brought the Askleipios to the Augusteion in the ninth century. In contrast, Pseudo-Symeon states that the statue was taken to the Nea Ekklesia at this time.

*Bibliography:* Mango, 1963: 63

## 17. ATHENA

Zosimos V, 24:

As if this were not enough, Constantinople was faced with a danger beyond all measure from the following cause. John [Chrysostom], having returned after his banishment (as I have said) and agitating the common people against the Empress during his regular church services, when he found himself expelled from his episcopal see and the city as well, took ship and sailed off. His partisans, in their zeal to see to it that no one be appointed to succeed him as bishop, decided that the city must be fired down. Accordingly, during the night they secretly set fire to the church, and towards dawn gathered around outside it, thus escaping detection. By daybreak everybody was aware that the city was already in the utmost peril, for the whole church was burned down and the buildings adjacent to it were being consumed simultaneously, in particular those where a blast of wind started to fan the flame. The fire poured into the house where the Senate customarily assembled, a house which was located in front of the palace and was elegantly, even ostentatiously, fitted out: it was adorned with sculptured works majestic to behold and with colorful marbles which are now no longer mined. It is said that there perished in that fire the very images which had originally been consecrated to the Muses on Mount Helicon and in Constantine's time had been forcibly removed, along with other objects which underwent sacrilege, and dedicated on this site; this calamity portended quite clearly the Muses' aversion from all mankind.

A certain miracle, which happened at this time, it is not fitting to pass over in silence. The Senate house of which I have been speaking had before its doors statues of Zeus and Athena which stood on stone bases, appearing just as they do even today. The former statue is said to have been consecrated long ago at Lindos. Now, when the Senate house had been entirely consumed by the fire and the statues and even the building stones, had they not been fire-resistant by nature, would have been

rolled against them; when, in short, all this beauty had been reduced to rubble, these statues as well (so common opinion holds) crumbled into dust. Yet when the site was cleaned off and made ready for renovation the statues of these gods alone were seen to have survived the general destruction. This event caused all cultured people to conceive better hopes for the city, as if these divinities would always make provision in its behalf. But let all these matters turn out as seems best to divine providence. (Buchanan/Davis)

Hesychios, 17:

. . . And nearby these [buildings] he reconstructed the building of the senatorial Boule, calling it the Senate, in which place he set up a statue of the Dodonaian Zeus, and two statues of the Palladas, and the royal court.

The statue, which stood to one side of the Senate entrance, is said to have come from the sanctuary of Athena at Lindos. Francis (1984) suggests that the statue was of Egyptian manufacture and associates it with a gift made by Amasis of Egypt in the sixth century B.C. As the report of the Chrysostom fire indicates, the Athena was in Constantinople by 404. Date of destruction is uncertain. Zosimos makes it clear that the statue survived the fire, which suggests that it was destroyed by later fires in either 476 or 532.

Hesychios refers to two Palladia; however, this may reflect some confusion resulting from his commentary having been written in the aftermath of the statues' destruction. Reference to the "royal court" may refer to imperial images or possibly to muse statues (see below 18).

*Bibliography:* Gilles (1561 bis): II, 9 and 2, 17; Zucker, 1887; Blinkenberg, 1917–18; Mango, 1959: 42–47, 56–60; Janin, 1964: 59–62, 73–77, 155–56; Guilland, 1969: I, 81–82, 220–26, 230–32, III, 40–54; Francis, 1984; Francis/Vickers, 1984

## 18. MUSES

### Eusebios, *VC* III, 54:

The pompous statues of brass were exposed to view in all the public places of the imperial city: so that here a Pythian, there a Sminthian Apollo excited the contempt of the beholder: while the Delphic tripods were deposited in the Hippodrome and the Muses of Helicon in the palace. In short the city which bore his name was everywhere filled with brazen statues of the most exquisite workmanship, which had been dedicated in every province, and which the deluded victims of superstition had long vainly honored as gods with numberless victims and burnt sacrifices, though now at length they learned to think rightly, when the emperor held up these very playthings to be the ridicule and the sport of all beholders. (Mango)

### Themistios, *Or.* 17: 308:

The present occasion is worthy of celebration no less than any other both for he who bestows the honor and he who receives it: assembled fathers, gather round! To place oneself before others on account of houses, gold or silver is nothing for you to brag about. If instead we achieve fame for having attempted to honor philosophy and value virtue, then we will not have taken the name of our fathers in vain. Instead, our assembly will be truly elected, it will be the temple of the Muses, not simply crowded with bronze statues, but filled with the models themselves.

### Themistios, *Or.* 18: 324:

Oh friends the Muses, who live here together with us in the temple of the Senate, lend me assistance in the song that I intone regarding his recent act of clemency. Know that that man loves you to such an extent as to let you reside with the empress: in honor of this he has erected a statue in this very sanctuary so that in this way, together with the statue of the prince and that of his son, your choir will also become more venerable in such company. The outcome should not be that asked of Homer, because you do not sing of wrath but of the mansuetude and clemency by which the prince has demonstrated to all that there is nothing more than the black vote of condemnation that alienates his soul.

### Themistios, *Or.* 31: 192:

On higher thrones I prefer the words of the divine Theodosios that were read to you a while ago, and if you would like to listen to them and to receive philosophy graciously then no vote on your part could be more appreciated by me. If instead those words harden some of you to prefer those who depend on fate to those who confide in virtue, then I would prefer to not be a part of a choir in which inharmonious song is held in higher regard than singing in harmony with the Muses. Yes, with the Muses, and this is no small thing! You do well to declare the Senate their temple and to display their statues on either side of this room. For you in fact a single line of Muses has not been sufficient, and while Homer speaks of a total of nine Muses residing in the heavens, at least twice that number dwell among you. Helikon has descended to the Bosporos, and this ornament that you find in your Curia is superior to that which was found among the senators of ancient Rome.

Eusebios, Zosimos and Themistios all refer to statues of Muses from the Sanctuary of the Muses on Mt. Helikon in Thessaly. The statues were destroyed in the Chrysostom riots of 404 (Zosimos). Eusebios states that Constantine brought the statues in the fourth century and erected them in the Palace. Zosimos confirms the Constantinian date of importation but locates the statues in the Augusteion Senate House, as does Themistios. Themistios (*Or.* 31) states that the statues numbered the canonical nine. He adds that they were displayed inside in rows on either side of the Senate chamber, and that they were bronze (*Or.* 17).

The information concerning location need not be considered contradictory. If two groups of Muses stood in the Helikonian sanctuary, it is possible that both were brought, either at the same time or in two installments, and set up

PLATE 3: Zeus/Poseidon from Cape Artemision, National Museum, Athens (Photo: H. Wagner, Deutsches Archäologisches Institut, Athens, Institute Negative Number, 1975/605)

in different locations. Alternatively, it is possible that a single group was taken and moved from palace to senate.

The first group, by Kephisodotos, showed the nine muses and stood by the entrance to the Helikonian sanctuary (Paus. IX, 30,1). It is not clear whether the Kephisodotos referred to was the elder or younger sculptor of that name. Picard (1948: 82) favors the elder and dates the statues to the early fourth century B.C. Were the works by the younger, they would date to the late fourth or early third century B.C. The second group (Paus. IX, 30, 1) also showed a complete muse group with three figures each by Kephisodotos, Strongylion, and Olympiosthenes. Again, the reference to Kephisodotos is unclear. Strongylion was active in the late fifth

century B.C. and no dates are known for Olympiosthenes. Date of manufacture is therefore between the end of the fifth century B.C. and the beginning of the third century B.C.

*Bibliography:* Gilles (1561 bis): II, 9 and 2, 17; Du Cange (1680): I 24, 1; Mango, 1959: 42–47, 56–60; Janin, 1964: 59–62, 73–77, 155–56; Guilland, 1969: I: 81–82, 220–26, 230–32, and 3: 40–54

## 19. ZEUS (PLATE 3)

Zosimos V, 24 and Hesychios, 17: see no. 16.

Description of the god as Dodonaeos indicates an image from the sanctuary of Zeus at Dodona near Epiros. A bronze figurine from the sanctuary may reproduce the statue's fifth-century B.C. type: a naked, bearded male stands with legs apart, his arms extended front and back and his right hand holds a thunderbolt (Schiering, 1969). On a monumental scale the statue variously identified as Zeus or Poseidon from Cape Artemision may reflect the statue's appearance. Repeated desecration of the sanctuary by Aitolians, Romans, and Thracians in the third, second, and first centuries B.C. (*PECS*, 280) makes it highly unlikely that the fifth-century image survived to be taken to Constantinople; however, new images or subsidiary dedications in the sanctuary may have copied or preserved the salient features of the classical type (*LIMC*, s.v. "Zeus").

Final destruction of the sanctuary took place by the end of the fourth century (*PECS*, 280), which suggests that the statue was brought to Constantinople during this period. Zosimos's account of the Chrysostom fire indicates that the statue was in place by 404 and that it stood on a base to one side of the entrance. Report of the beams caving in around the sculpture during the fire suggests that the statue stood beneath the entrance porch. The statue ultimately was destroyed in one of two fires in 476 or 532.

## BASILIKA

### 20. ELEPHANT

*Par.* 37:

Spectacle number one. In the Basilika . . . . With these [statues of men] stands a huge elephant; as the exhibitors of animals have assured us, elephants do not come greater in size than this, the big ones being as big as this. This elephant was set up by Severus the son of Carus the pagan as a spectacle, according to tradition. (Cameron/Herrin)

The statue, a life-sized representation of an elephant, is reported to have been erected by Septimius Severus. Elephants most commonly appeared in imperial biga and quadrigae (s.v. Golden Gate); however, single statues are known, such as a figure from the main avenue at Leptis Magna advertising the city's role in the elephant trade (Scullard, plate XIX).

*Bibliography:* Gilles (1561 bis) II: 18–19; Du Cange (1680) II: 9, 13; Mango, 1959: 48–51; Janin, 1964: 156–60; Guilland, 1969: 3–13; Cameron/Herrin, 210–15

### 21. HERAKLES BY LYSIPPOS (PLATE 4)

*Par.* 37:

And there too [in the basilika] Herakles was worshipped, the recipient of many sacrifices. And ⟨the statue⟩ was removed to the Hippodrome to be a great spectacle. But originally it was brought from Rome to Byzantium in the time of Julian the consularis with a chariot and a boat and twelve statues. (Cameron/Herrin)

Suidas, s.v. βασιλική:

Basilika. There a statue of Herakles was worshipped after he received many sacrifices. It was transferred to the Hippodrome. In the consulship of Julianus it came to Byzantion from Rome having been conveyed by ship and wagon, along with ten columns.

Constantine Manasses, *Ek.* I, 21–32:

Many are the works in painting and sculpture from which Pheidiases, Praxiteleses, Lysippoi and Parrhasioi are famous even until now. Hence was wrought the cow of Myron, absolutely alive, so as to deceive even the young calf and entice the bellowing bull into love; hence Herakles, the son of Zeus, was wrought in bronze, noble and great and a hero and mighty, seated on a woven basket with the right hand . . . supporting his head bent in despondency; one would say that he was lamenting his own misfortune, so living is the work in bronze, so truly alive the image. (Johnson)

PLATE 4: Herakles after Lysippos, Bibliothèque nationale de France, Paris (Photo: Cliché Bibliothèque nationale de France, Paris)

Niketas Choniates, 519:

[The Empress Euphrosyne] decided to scourge on the back with many whips the glorious Herakles, the most beautiful of Lysimachos' (sic) works; the work in which the lion-skin is spread over a basket, and the hero rests his head on his hand and grieves over his own misfortunes. Alas, Herakles, for the absurdity; and alas for the outrage against

you, mighty and great-hearted hero. What Eurystheus ever proposed for you such a trial? Or
what Omphale, worn out prey of passions and
vilely artful wench, treated you so arrogantly as
this? (Johnson)

Niketas Choniates, 649–50:

Also overturned was Herakles, mighty in his
mightiness, begotten in a triple night and placed
in a basket for his crib; the lion's skin which
was thrown over him looked terrifying even in
bronze, almost as though it might give out a roar
and frighten the helpless populace standing nearby.
Herakles sat without quiver on his back, or bow
in his hands, or the club before him, but with his
right foot as well as his right hand extended as far
as possible. He rested his left elbow on his left leg
bent at the knee; deeply despondent and bewailing
his misfortunes, he held his inclined head at rest
in his palm, vexed by the labors which Eurystheus
had designated, not out of urgency, but from envy,
puffed up by the excess of fate. He was thick in
the chest and broad in the shoulders, with curly
hair; fat in the buttocks, strong in the arms, he
was an incomparable masterpiece fashioned from
first to last by the hands of Lysimachos and portrayed in the magnitude which the artist must have
attributed to the real Herakles; the statue was so
large that it took a cord the size of a man's belt to
go round the thumb, and the shin was the size of a
man. They who separated manliness from the cor-
respondent virtues and claimed it for themselves
did not allow this magnificent Herakles to remain
intact, and they were responsible for much more
destruction. (Magoulias)

Cameron/Herrin (214) identify this statue
with the Lysippan Herakles that later stood in
the Hippodrome. The Roman origin of the figure combined with the notice of its removal to
the circus and its characterization as a "spectacle" make the suggestion reasonable.

The statue was a colossal bronze. The hero sat
hunched on an upturned basket over which his
lion-skin cloak was thrown, his chin propped
in his left hand, his elbow resting on his bent

left knee. The right leg and the right arm were
extended. Although destroyed during the 1204
sack of the city various visual sources document the Herakles: a bronze statuette (Babelon and Blanchet, 556) and Byzantine ivory
carvings of the eleventh and twelfth centuries
(Floren).

Beyond identification as Herakles, the sources
do not specify subject matter. Modern scholarship generally sees the statue as a representation of the hero at the completion of his
twelfth and final Labor, the cleaning of the
Augean stables; however, Madigan (1975) argues
that the statue is more properly understood as
the induction of Herakles into the Eleusinian
Mysteries.

Originally created for the city of Tarentum
in the fourth century B.C. by Lysippos (Strabo,
VI, 3,1), the statue was taken as booty when
the city fell to Rome in the second century. At
that time it was dedicated on the Capitol by the
victorious general Fabius Maximus (Pliny, *NH*
XXXIV, 40; Plutarch, *Fabius Maximus*, XXII, 6)
and its base survives to this day in the Capitoline
Museum (Helbig, 4; 417). Niketas's attribution
of the Hippodrome statue to Lysimachos must
represent a corruption of Lysippos. *Par.* reports
that it was brought to Constantinople "in the
time of Julian the *consularis*." Cameron/Herrin
(214) connect this figure with Julian cos. 322 and
prefect of the city of Rome 326–29 (*PLRE*, I,
s.v. "Julianus 23"). This date is also consistent
with the recorded history of the Basilika. Zosimos (II, 31) states that Constantine erected the
building. Kedrenos (I, 564), Zonaras (III, 131),
and Suidas (s.v. Malchos) all report that the complex burned in 476. *Chron. Pasch.* (619), Theophanes (176), and Kedrenos (I, 645) note that
in the aftermath of this fire consul Illius reconstructed the complex during the second reign of
Zeno (476–91). This history suggests that Constantine erected the statue in the Basilika and
that it was removed to the Hippodrome sometime prior to the 476 fire.

*Bibliography:* Madigan, 1975; Floren, 1981; Cameron/
Herrin, 210–15

## 22. KYBELE

Zosimos II, 31:

There being in Byzantium a very great forum with four porticoes, at the end of one of these, to which there are not a few steps leading up, he constructed two temples and set therein cult-statues. One was of Rhea, mother of the gods, which Jason's sailing companions had once upon a time placed upon Mount Dindymus overlooking the city of Kyzikos. They say that Constantine, out of indifference to divine objects, treated this despitefully, removing the lions on either side and changing the attitude of the hands; for formerly the goddess appeared to be holding the lions, but now her gesture was changed to that of one praying, as she vigilantly looked out over the Romans. (Buchanan/Davis)

The statue described as Rhea was probably one of Kybele, the Anatolian mother-goddess. During the Hellenistic and Roman periods, Kybele's cult came to be associated with that of Rhea, but her iconography remained distinct. Although Rhea is shown as a draped female in a variety of poses with attributes such as children underscoring her connection with the earth and fertility, Kybele appears enthroned or riding on a lion. The turreted crown, tympanum, cymbals, and lion are her attributes. The Constantinopolitan statue, which originally showed the goddess with a pair of flanking lions, appears to have represented a standard type of Kybele. The enthroned goddess wearing the chiton and mural crown sits upright, facing forward, her arms outstretched toward the pair of lions that flank her throne (*LIMC*, s.v. "Kybele").

The Constantinopolitan statue is reported to have been brought from the Kybele sanctuary at Kyzikos, a claim endorsed by Amelung. Zosimos attributes the importation to Constantine and notes also that the statue, which was set up in one of the Basilika's temples, was substantially remodeled for the installation by removing the lions, thereby creating the impression that the statue was praying. He adds further that the statue was an ancient one dedicated by Jason and his companions. This observation suggests

that the statue may have been one of archaic manufacture.

The Constantinian Basilika burned in 476 (Kedrenos I, 564; Zonaras III, 131, Suidas: s.v. "Malchos") and was reconstructed during the reign of Zeno by consul Illius (*Chron. Pasch.*, 619; Theophanes, 176, Kedrenos I, 564). Zosimos's language does not read like an eyewitness account, which suggests destruction prior to the late fifth or early sixth century when Zosimos wrote. The most likely date for this destruction would be the 476 fire.

*Bibliography:* Amelung, 1899

## 23. PHILOSOPHER

Leo Gramm. 257–58:

And there was a statue of Solomon in the great Basilika, which he [Basil I] ordered melted and reshaped his own image, and which he then offered as a sacrifice to this monument and to God, placing it in the foundation of the New Church.

*Patria* II, 40:

Regarding the Basilika cistern. Constantine the Great built the so-called Basilika cistern. There is a large enthroned statue of Solomon which was erected by Justinian the Great in such a way that, holding his chin, Solomon looks out over Hagia Sophia to demonstrate his [Justinian's] surpassing in size and beauty of the temple raised by Solomon in Jerusalem.

The statue was bronze and showed the sitter with his chin propped on his hand. It cannot be identified with any degree of certainty; however, Mango (1963: 62–63) suggests that the figure was an ancient philosopher given a Christian reinterpretation. It might also have been a statue of a poet or any other classical man of letters. This seated contemplative type is an invention of the third century B.C. (Zanker, 1995: 90), the period that saw the most creative developments in the portrait of the intellectual. The seated pose was intended to convey a notion of abstraction and introspection that differs substantially from the upright portraits of poets and philosophers that were the fifth- and fourth-century standards (Zanker, 1995: 92). Reinterpretation of this type as the figure of Solomon would be consistent with the Christian understanding of Solomon as the embodiment of wisdom.

Details of Constantinopolitan history can only be inferred. Zosimos (II, 31) states that the construction and decoration of the Basilika was Constantinian. The statue may therefore have been in place as early as the fourth century, although it is more likely that it was put in place when the Basilika was remodeled in the late fifth century after a fire in 476 (Kedrenos I, 564; Zonaras III, 131; Suidas, s.v. "Malchos"). *Patria* attributes the installation to Justinian. Leo Gramm. dates the destruction to the reign of Basil I (867–86).

*Bibliography:* Du Cange (1680) II, 9, 13; Cameron/ Herrin, 210–15; Guilland, 1969: 3–13; Gilles (1561 bis) II, 18–19; Janin, 1964: 156–60; Mango, 1993: 62– 63; Mango, 1959: 48–51

## 24. TYCHE/FORTUNA (PLATES 5 AND 6)

Zosimos II, 31: see no. 21.

Socrates III, 11:

Moreover, he [Julian] favored the pagan superstitions with the whole weight of his authority: and the temples of the heathen were opened, as we have before stated; but he himself also publicly offered sacrifices to Tyche, the goddess of Constantinople, in the basilika, where her image was erected. (modified from Schaff/Wace)

Tyche (Fortuna) is invariably shown as a female figure wearing a long belted tunic and mantel. She is veiled and often wears a mural crown to indicate her status as a protectress of cities. Her left arm cradles a cornucopia. The right hand carries a scepter. Individual cities may show variations.

Zosimos describes the statue as the Roman Tyche. Like all Tyches, Roma (Plate 5) wears a belted tunic and mantel; however, she exchanges the traditional attributes of Tyche, the cornucopia, scepter, and mural crown, for shield, lance, and helmet. Sometimes she carries a victory on her outstretched palm.

Socrates identifies the statue as the Tyche of Constantinople. This figure (Plate 6), also known as Anthousa, followed the standard Tyche iconography more closely. The goddess wore the belted tunic and mantle and carried the cornucopia and scepter. Constantinian coin issues show her seated with the mural crown and a ship's prow beneath her feet. Later fourth-century representations show her wearing a double-crested helmet.

The extent to which the Tyche in the Basilika conformed to any of these types is unclear. Equally uncertain is the date of manufacture. Were the Tyche a true representation of Constantinopolis, then the statue would have been made in the fourth century. A figure of Roma or a more generic statue of Tyche could have been reused from an earlier period.

*Bibliography:* Toynbee, 1947; *LIMC* s.v. "Fortuna Romana"

## BATHS OF CONSTANTINE

### 25. PERSEUS AND ANDROMEDA

*Par.* 85 (*Patria* II, 85):

From the above-mentioned Ikonion comes a statue of Perseus and Andromeda, who was the daughter of Basiliskos; as the myths and one of the historians say, she was given as a sacrifice to the dragon that lived there. For this was an ancient custom, for a young maiden to be offered to the beast. In accordance with it Andromeda was bound, undeserving of death, and was about to be given to the beast. And the aforementioned Perseus, passing that way, asked the weeping Andromeda why she was bound and lamenting. She

PLATE 5: Tyche of Rome, British Museum, London (Photo: © Copyright The British Museum)

told him what had happened. But as he took up his position the beast came up. Turning away and facing backwards, Perseus showed the gorgon's head he was carrying in his satchel to the beast, which expired on seeing it. So the city was called Ikonion by Philodorus the *logistes* because Perseus came and saved Andromeda, a bright stroke of luck for the city from the coming of Perseus. The name of the city from its foundation was Doria. Then it was called Threnodia, but by (according to?) Philodorus the *logistes* it was called Ikonion from the coming of Perseus. Then the same Perseus was commemorated in a statue with Andromeda above the city gate. Many sacrifices took place there by order of Decius and Diocletian and Maximian, and many saints were martyred there. The statues of Perseus and Andromeda came, so we are told, in the reign of Constantius, after the completion of the church of Antioch, to the bath of Constantinianae. (Cameron/Herrin)

Representations of Perseus and Andromeda are plentiful (*LIMC* s.v. "Andromeda"). They may show the couple as a single sculptured pair or as individual statues. Surviving sculpture favors two moments: the dramatic scene in which Perseus rescues a chained Andromeda or the calmer aftermath of the dragon's slaughter in which the hero helps Andromeda down from her rocky perch. Perseus appears as a naked youth with his chlamys tossed nonchalantly over one shoulder, the Medusa's head hanging from his hand. In these scenes Andromeda is shown both nude and draped.

Secure identification of the Constantinianae group is not possible; however, the lengthy account of the Perseus and Andromeda tale led Cameron and Herrin (274) to posit that the account was based on an unnamed written source. It is possible that this source was a lost ekphrasis by Helladios to which Suidas (s.v. "Helladios") refers. If the ekphrasis were the inspiration for the story, then emphasis on dramatic action suggests that the group would have shown the rescue scene.

Surviving examples of Perseus and Andromeda all date to the Hellenistic or Roman period. The statue's Constantinopolitan history can only be inferred. The baths lay to the west of the city center in the area around Holy Apostles. They were referred to variously as the Constantinianae or the Constantianai (Prinzing/Speck, 1973: 179). Named for Constantine the Great, they appear to have been part of a series of buildings and institutions that the emperor projected for the area around the church (Eusebios: *VC*, IV, 59; *Par.*, 73). It is unlikely, however, that Constantine completed the baths. *Chron. Pasch.* (I, 580–81) reports that construction began only in April 345 and that the building was completed in October 427 during the reign of Theodosios II. At that time it was inaugurated as the "Constantinian now Theodosian" baths. Janin (1964: 220) believes that Constantine was somehow involved with the initial project and that Constantius substantially completed them. A remark by Themistios (*Or.* 4) supports this idea: speaking in praise of Constantius he observes that the bath that was given Constantine's name is not yet finished, but that he hopes its beauty will one day equal its grandeur. Socrates (VI, 18) and Sozomen (VIII, 21) note that the followers of John Chrysostom celebrated Easter services in the complex in 404, which suggests that the baths were open and functioning by that time. Sozomen states that the complex was built by Constantius (337–61), a date consistent with *Par.'s* claim for the importation of the statue group. At the same time, however, the Theodosian dedication in 427 may have celebrated the completion of the building's decoration, rather than its actual public opening. Date of installation thus ranges between the mid-fourth and the early fifth century. The Constantinianae are mentioned in the eighth century (*Par.* 73) in a manner that suggests that they were still standing. By the tenth century, the bath appears to have been in ruins (Berger, 1982: 152, after *De cer*, 532, 16–18). The probable remains of the Constantinianae were excavated in 1955–56 and then quickly filled in (Müller-Wiener, 1977: 48).

*Bibliography:* Cameron/Herrin, 274–76

PLATE 6: Tyche of Constantinople, British Museum, London (Photo: © Copyright The British Museum)

## BATHS OF ZEUXIPPOS

The Baths of Zeuxippos stood in the center of Constantinople on a slice of land between the northeastern corner of the Hippodrome, the Great Palace, and the Augusteion. Sources record the complex as an inheritance from the pre-Constantinian era of the city's history that had been founded and built by the emperor Septimius Severus in the last years of the second century (Malalas, 321; *Chron. Pasch.*, 494; Preger, 15–16, 132, 168). Taken over by Constantine, who made it a showpiece by dowering it with freestanding sculpture in bronze and marble, the Zeuxippos burned in the Nika riots of 532. Sculpture was thus in place from the early years of the fourth century through the early years of the sixth century.

### 26. ACHILLES (PLATE 7)

*Ek.* 292–96:

Divine Achilles was beardless and not clothed in armor, but the artist had given him the gesture of brandishing a spear in his right hand and of holding a shield in his left. Whetted by daring courage he seemed to be scattering the threatening cloud of battle, for his eyes shone with the genuine light of a son of Aeacus. (Paton)

A nude, beardless youth carried a spear in his right hand, a shield in his left. Secure association of the figure with known statue types is not possible; however, the description suggests a possible association with the fifth-century B.C. Doryphoros of Polykleitos, a figure sometimes identified as Achilles on the basis of Pliny's (*HN* XXXIV, 18) description of statues of nude, spearbearing youths as "Achillean" (Lorenz, 1966: 10–13; 1972: 4–17). Arguing against such an identification is the use of the verb "ἑλίσσειν." Paton translates the word as "to brandish" and in so doing suggests an altogether more active stance than that of the more contained figure of the Doryphoros.

### 27. AENEAS AND CREUSA

*Ek.* 143–54:

Hail! Warrior son of Troy, glittering counselor of the Trojans, Aeneas! For wise modesty redolent of beauty is shed on thy eyes, proclaiming thee the divine son of golden Aphrodite. And I wondered looking on Creusa, the wife of Aeneas, overshadowed in mourning raiment. She had drawn her veil over both her cheeks, her form was draped in a long gown, as if she were lamenting, and her bronze tears signified that Troy, her nurse, was captive after its siege by Greek warriors. (Paton)

### 28. AGLAOS

*Ek.* 263–65:

The prophet Aglaos stood there, who, they say, was the father of the inspired seer Polyidos: he was crowned with leafy laurel. (Paton)

Sculptural representations of Aglaos are unknown, and identification is problematic. Christodoros describes Aglaos as a prophet, doubtless on the basis of his laurel crown, a feature that he deems essential to the iconography of the visionary. This identification is, however, open to question as none of the known Aglaoi were prophets. In myth and literature, Aglaos is known variously as a son of Thyestes and Laodameia (*Schol. Eur. Or.* 5; Tzetzes, *Chil.* I, 449), a son of Hermione (*Schol. Eur. Androm.* 32), and the poorest man in Arcadia (Pliny, *NH*, VII, 151; *Val.Max.* VII 1, 2; Paus 8, 24). As well, the described genealogical relationship between Aglaos and Polyidos is incorrect: Koiranos, not Aglaos, was the father of Polyidos. Stupperich favors identification as Koiranos, but because statues in the Zeuxippos were identified by inscription (cat. nos. 31, 75), the original identification with Aglaos should probably stand. In this case, the figure in question is likely to have been Aglaos, son of Thyestes, because of his connection with the Trojan epic, one of the themes favored in the bath.

*Bibliography:* Stupperich, 1982: 223–25; Guberti Bassett, 1996: 502

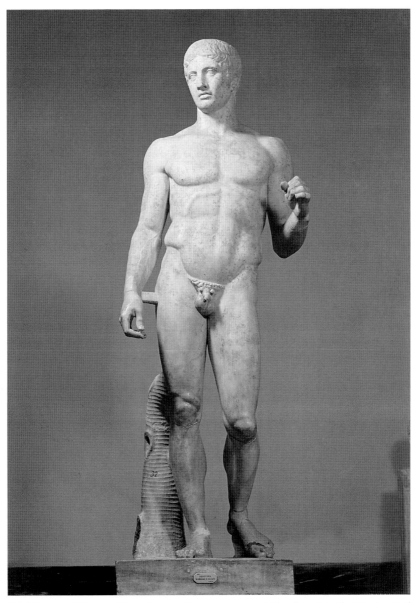

PLATE 7: Polykleitos of Argos, Doryphoros, Roman copy of Greek original, Museo Archeologico Nazionale, Naples (Scala/Art Resource, NY)

## 29. AIAX, LOCRIAN

*Ek.* 209–214:

And at Aiax I marveled, whom valorous Oileos begat, the huge bulwark of the Locrian land. He seemed in the flower of youth, for the surface of his chin was not yet marked with the bloom of hair. His whole well-knit body was naked, but weighty with valor he wielded the goad of war. (Paton)

PLATE 8: Aischines Base from the Baths of Zeuxippos, Istanbul Archaeological Museum (after Casson, 1929, fig. 11)

## 30. AIAX, TELAMONIAN

*Ek.* 271–76:

All naked was stout-hearted Telamonian Aiax, beardless as yet, the bloom of his native beauty all his ornament: his hair was bound with a diadem, for he wore not his helmet, and wielded no sword, nor was his seven-hide shield on his shoulders, but he exhibited the dauntless valor of his father Telamon. (Paton)

PLATE 9: Aischines, Museo Nazionale, Naples (Photo: Schwanke, Deutsches Archäologisches Institut, Rome, Institute Negative Number, 85.486)

## 31. AISCHINES (PLATES 8 AND 9)

*Ek.* 13–16:

And there shone Athenian Aischines, the flower of wise persuasion, his bearded face gathered as if he were engaged in struggle with the tumultuous crowd, looking sore beset by anxiety. (Paton)

Statue Base

Istanbul Archaeological Museum (Plate 8), Circular, marble base with molded flanges top and bottom. 1.35 × 0.67 m. Inscribed: AICXHNHC (Aischines).

The statue represented the Athenian orator Aischines (c. 390 – after 330 B.C.). An inscribed

163

base unearthed during the 1928–29 Zeuxippos excavations confirms the literary testimony. The size of the base indicates that the figure was approximately life-size. Dowel marks in the upper supporting surface show further that the statue was bronze, an observation that conforms to Christodoros's use of ἔστραπτο (to shine).

Created in the fourth century B.C., the Aischines portrait (Plate 9) shows the orator standing, wearing chiton, himation, and sandals. Beneath his robes his right arm bends across his chest, while his left is propped behind on his hip in a classic declamatory stance. His head inclines slightly to the left. Long curling locks cover a furrowed, receding brow and the face is bearded. The speaker's lips part slightly and his open eyes gaze straight ahead.

*Bibliography:* Casson 1929; Casson, 1930: 235; Mango, 1963: 58; Stupperich, 1982: 210–35; Guberti Bassett, 1996: 18–19, 491–506

### 32. ALKIBIADES

*Ek.* 82–85:

And I marveled at the son of Kleinias, seeing him glistening with glory, for he had interwoven with the bronze the rays of his beauty. Such was he as when in Attika, the mother of the story, he awoke wise counsel. (Paton)

The statue was bronze. The Alkibiades (450?– 404 B.C.) portrait was a fifth-century B.C. creation (Richter/Smith, 1984: 82).

### 33. ALKMAION/ALKMAN

*Ek.* 393–97:

There stood one named Alkmaion the prophet; but he was not the famous prophet, nor wore the laurel berries on his hair. I conjecture he was Alkman, who formerly practiced the lyric art, weaving the Doric song on his sweet-toned strings. (Paton)

Identification is problematic as the figure is described first as Alkmaion and then as Alkman. Christodoros calls the figure a seer, but is unhappy with the identification on iconographic

grounds, noting that the statue was without the laurel crown, the soothsayer's necessary attribute. He therefore suggests an alternative identification as Alkman, the seventh-century B.C. Spartan poet. Stupperich favors this choice; however, because statues were identified by inscription (cat. nos. 31, 75), the identification as Alkmaion is probably correct. It is possible though that a different Alkmaion was intended. The statue may have represented Alkmaion, the son of Amphiaraos, a character in the Theban mythical cycle or Alkmaion of Croton (c. 500 B.C.), a younger contemporary of Pythagoras known for his writings on science.

*Bibliography:* Stupperich, 1982: 225–26; Guberti Bassett, 1996: 502

### 34. AMPHIARAOS

*Ek.* 259–62:

Amphiaraos, his fiery hair crowned with laurel, was sighing, musing on a secret sorrow, foreseeing that Thebes, founded where lay the heifer, shall be the death of the Argives' home-coming. (Paton)

Statues and marble reliefs of the mythical seer Amphiaraos, one of the seven who went against Thebes, show Amphiaraos as an Askleipios type (*LIMC*, s.v. "Amphiaraos"). The type was developed in the fourth century B.C., and consistency among the extant representations suggests that the Zeuxippos figure would have conformed to this standard. A standing male figure leans on a staff. Drapery falls across the lower half of his torso, leaving his chest bare. Full curling locks and a beard characterize the face and head.

### 35. AMPHITRYON

*Ek.* 367–71:

Amphitryon glittered there, his hair crowned with virginal laurel. In all he looked like a clear-seeing prophet; yet he was no prophet, but being the martial spouse of Alkmene, mother of a great son, he had set the crown on his pleated tresses to signify his victory over the Taphians. (Paton)

Use of the verb to glitter (ἀστράπτω) suggests that the statue was gilded bronze.

## 36. ANAXIMENES

*Ek.* 50–51:

Anaximenes the wise philosopher was there, and in deep absorption he was revolving the subtle thought of his divine intellect. (Paton)

## 37. ANDROMACHE

*Ek.* 160–64:

And Andromache, the rosy-ankled daughter of Eetion, stood there not weeping or lamenting, for not yet, I deem, had Hector with the glancing helm fallen in the war, nor had the exultant sons of the shield-bearing Greeks laid waste entirely her Dardan nurse. (Paton)

## 38. APHRODITE

*Ek.* 78–81:

And near shone Cypris, shedding drops of beauty on the bright bronze. Her bust was naked, but her dress was gathered around her rounded thighs and she had bound her hair with a golden kerchief. (Paton)

The description suggests a figure in the tradition of any one of a number of half-draped fourth-century B.C. Aphrodites, such as the Aphrodite of Arles (Louvre, MA439).

## 39. APHRODITE

*Ek.* 99–101:

And another high-born Aphrodite I saw all of gold, naked, all glittering; and on the breast of the goddess, hanging from her neck, fell in coils the flowing cestus. (Paton)

Use of "glittering" (παμφανόωσαν) suggests that the statue was gilded bronze. The figure was nude, a fact that indicates a figure type of the fourth century B.C. or later.

## 40. APHRODITE

*Ek.* 288–90:

And here was a third Aphrodite to marvel at, her bosom draped: on her breasts rested the twisted cestus, and in it beauty rested. (Paton)

## 41. APOLLO

*Ek.* 72–77:

There stood Phoibos who speaketh from the tripod. He had bound up behind his loosely flowing hair. In the bronze he was naked, because Apollo knoweth how to make naked to them who enquire of him the true decrees of Fate, or because he appeareth to all alike, for King Phoibos is the Sun and his pure brilliancy is seen from far. (Paton)

The statue was bronze and depicted the nude Apollo with long, bound hair, attributes that suggest a late classical or Hellenistic type.

## 42. APOLLO

*Ek.* 266–70:

There I saw the far-shooter with unshorn hair, I saw the lord of song, his head adorned with locks that bloomed in freedom: for a naturally curling tress hung on each shoulder. He rolled his prophetic eyes as if he were freeing men from trouble by his oracular power. (Paton)

## 43. APOLLO

*Ek.* 283–87:

Next was a third Apollo the fair-haired speaker from the tripod, beautiful to see; for his curls fell over both his shoulders, and the lovely beauty of a god was manifest in him, adorning the bronze; his eyes were intent, as if he were gazing from his seat on the mantic tripod. (Paton)

Reference to the god appearing to speak as if from the tripod (ἐπὶ τριπόδεσσι δοκεύων) may indicate a statue type similar to relief representations such as the Xenokrates relief that show the god seated on his tripod. See Ridgway (1981: fig. 97).

## 44. APULEIUS

*Ek.* 303–05:

Apuleius was seated considering the unuttered secrets of the Latin intellectual Muse. Him the Italian siren nourished, a devotee of ineffable wisdom. (Paton)

## 45. ARISTOTLE

*Ek.* 17–22:

And near him was Aristotle, the prince of Wisdom: he stood with clasped hands, and not even in the voiceless bronze was his mind idle, but he was like one deliberating; his puckered face indicated that he was solving some doubtful problem, while his mobile eyes revealed his collected mind. (Paton)

Portraits of Aristotle (384–22 B.C.) show a bearded, middle-aged man with hair falling forward from the crown of the head in loose, waving strands. The face has a long nose, thin lips, deeply set eyes, and strong bones (Richter, 1965; Richter/Smith, 1984). No full-length sculptural representations survive; however, Christodoros's description of the statue as standing with clasped hands suggests an image similar to that of Demosthenes (cat. no. 53).

## 46. ARTEMIS

*Ek.* 306–10:

There stood maiden Artemis, sister of Phoebos, who haunteth the mountains: but she carried no bow, no quiver on her back. She had girt up to her knees her maiden tunic with its rich border, and her unsnooded hair flowed loose in the wind. (Paton)

The described details of dress and coiffeur, specifically the chiton that appears to have been hiked up around her waist to shorten it and the loose hair, identify the goddess with post-fifth-

century B.C. representations of the goddess in her guise as huntress.

## 47. BASE (PLATE 10)

Istanbul Archaeological Museum, measurements: H: 1,40 m; D: 1,08 m

Excavation yielded a circular, marble base. Carved with the image of a small vase on one side, it is otherwise uninscribed. Identical in scale and shape to the Hekube base (cat. no. 75), this base may have supported Hekube's partner, Odysseus. Dowel holes in the top indicate that the statue it carried was bronze. The base is worn on one side, suggesting reuse in a later age, possibly as a step or paving stone.

*Bibliography:* Casson, 1928: 28

## 48. JULIUS CAESAR

*Ek.* 92–96:

Near him shone forth Julius, who once adorned Rome with innumerable shields of her foes. He wore on his shoulders a grisly-faced aegis, and carried exulting in his right hand a thunder-bolt, as one bearing in Italy the title of a second Zeus. (Paton)

Use of the verb to shine (λάμπω) suggests bronze as the medium. The figure is likely to have been a work of first-century B.C. manufacture. Reference to the aegis and the thunderbolt indicates that Caesar (100–44 B.C.) appeared carrying the attributes of Aegiochus Zeus (Bernoulli: I, 147). Therefore the figure would have been nude or partially draped (Petsas).

## 49. CHRYSES

*Ek.* 86–91:

Near him stood the priest Chryses, holding in his right hand the scepter of Phoebus and wearing on his head a fillet. Of surpassing stature was he, as being one of the holy race of heroes. Methinks he was imploring Agamemnon. His thick beard

PLATE 10: Statue base from the Baths of Zeuxippos, Istanbul Archaeological Museum (Photo: Sarah Bassett)

bloomed in abundance, and down his back trailed the clusters of his unplaited hair. (Paton)

## 50. DARES AND ENTELLUS

*Ek.* 222–27:

Dares was fastening on his hands his leather boxing-straps and arming himself with wrath, the herald of the fight; with mobile eyes he breathed the hot breath of valor. Entellus opposite gazed at him in fury, handling too the cestus that pierceth the flesh, his spirit big with blood-thirsty menace. (Paton)

## 51. DEIPHOBOS

*Ek.* 1–12:

First Deiphobus stood on a well-carved pedestal, daring all, in armor, a valiant hero, even as he was when he met the on rush of Menelaos before his house that they were pillaging. He stood even as one who was advancing, side-ways, in right fighting attitude. Crouching in fury with bent back, he was collecting all his fierce strength, while he turned his eyes hither and thither as if on his guard against an attack of the enemy. In his left hand he held before him a broad shield and in his right his uplifted sword, and his furious hand was even on the point of transpiercing his adversary, but the nature of the brass would not let it serve his rage. (Paton)

Representations of Deiphobos in vase painting date only to the fourth century B.C. and there are no known freestanding statues. Heyne associated this figure with the Borghese Warrior type.

*Bibliography:* Heyne; Angel de Elvira, 1984

## 52. DEMOKRITOS

*Ek.* 131–35:

Hail, Demokritos, glory of the land of Abdera; for thou didst explore the laws of Nature, the mother of the beautiful children, discerning the subtle mysteries of the Muse of Science: and ever didst thou laugh at the slippery paths of life, well aware that ancient Time outstrippeth all. (Paton)

## 53. DEMOSTHENES (PLATE 11)

*Ek.* 23–31:

And the trumpet-speaker of the Paeanians stood there conspicuous, the sage father of well-sounding eloquence, who erst in Athens set alight the wise torch of entrancing Persuasion. He did not seem to be resting, but his mind was in action and he seemed to be revolving some subtle plan, even as when he had sharpened his wit against the warlike Macedonians. Fain would he have let escape in his anger the torrent of his speech, endowing his dumb statue with voice, but Art kept him fettered under the seal of her brazen silence. (Paton)

The statue appears to conform to the established Demosthenes (383–22 B.C.) typology. Created by the sculptor Polyeuktos in 280 B.C., this portrait shows the middle-aged orator standing and draped, his hands clasped loosely before him at hip level (Richter, 1965; Richter/Smith, 1984).

## 54. ERINNA

*Ek.* 108–10:

The clear-voiced maiden Erinna sat there, not plying the involved thread, but in silence distilling drops of Pierian honey. (Paton)

Portraits of the poet Erinna (fourth century B.C.) are unknown.

## 55. EURIPIDES

*Ek.* 32–35:

There stood he who bears the name of the Euripus, and methought he was conversing secretly in his heart with the Tragic muses, reflecting on the virtue of chastity; for he looked even as if he were shaking the thyrsus on the Attic stage. (Paton)

PLATE 11: Demosthenes, Ny Carlsberg Glyptotek, Copenhagen (Photo: Ny Carlsberg Glyptotek)

A drawing of a lost statuette (Richter, 1965: 138) shows Euripides (485–06 B.C.) standing, barefooted, and draped with outstretched arms. Though missing, his head doubtless conformed to the stock Euripides type: bearded, with flowing locks, thin lips, and deeply set eyes. The portrait type was created in the fourth century B.C.

## 56. KALCHAS

*Ek.* 52–55:

And Kalchas, son of Thestor, stood there, clear-sighted prophet, as if prophesying, and he seemed to be concealing his message, either pitying the Greek host or still dreading the king of golden Mycene. (Paton)

## 57. HEAD OF A GODDESS (PLATE 12)

Casson described the fragment, which is now lost, as a work of fifth-century B.C. manufacture in Pentelic marble and identified it as a representation of Hera or Athena.

*Bibliography:* Casson, 1930: 236

Hekube: *see* Odysseus and Hekube.

## 58. HELEN

*Ek.* 165–70:

There one might see Menelaos warlike, but rejoicing in victory, for his heart was warmed with great joy as he saw near him rosy-armed Helen reconciled. I marveled at her lovely image that gave the bronze a grace most desirable, for her beauty even in that soulless work breathed warm love. (Paton)

The statue, which was bronze, was one of a pair showing Helen with her estranged husband, Menelaos. Although no sculptured representations are known, a rich iconographic tradition develops around her story in classical, Hellenistic and Roman vases and reliefs (*LIMC*, s.v. "Helen").

## 59. HELENOS

*Ek.* 155–59:

Nor did Helenos cease from wrath, but seemed pitiless to his country, still stirring his wrath. In his right hand he raised a cup for libations, and I deem he was foretelling good to the Greeks and praying to the gods to bring his nurse to the extremity of woe. (Paton)

## 60. HERAKLEITOS

*Ek.* 354–56:

And Herakleitos the sage was there, a god-like man, the inspired glory of ancient Ephesos, who once alone wept for the works of weak humanity. (Paton)

Representations of Herakleitos (535 B.C.–c. 475 B.C.) are few. A seated statue survives from the Serapeion in Memphis (Lauer/Picard, 1955: 137–43). Although badly damaged, enough remains to reconstruct the philosopher's dress. He wears the himation wrapped around his body and his torso is bare. Propped next to him against the throne is his identifying attribute, the notched stick or club. A standing statue from the agora in Gortyn also has been identified as Herakleitos (Richter, 1965). The statue is complete and shows the philosopher with the notched stick and dress of the Serapeion figure. Further, it preserves its head to show a middle-aged man with long unkempt hair and beard. Lauer and Picard (1955: 143) suggested that this physiognomy would have been applicable to the Memphis statue. More recently, Zanker (1995: 264–65) has rejected the identification with Herakleitos, proposing instead that the figure is that of an unidentified charismatic philosopher. Richter (1965) believes the portrait to have been an invented one of the later fifth or fourth century B.C.

PLATE 12: Head of a goddess from the Baths of Zeuxippos (from Casson, 1929: fig. 48)

## 61. HERAKLES AND AUGE

*Ek.* 136–43:

Herakles, no down yet visible on the circle of his chin, was holding in the hand that had slain the lion the golden apples, rich fruit of the Libyan land, and by him stood the priestess of Pallas, the maiden Auge, her mantle thrown over her head and shoulders, for her hair was not done up with a kerchief. Her hands were uplifted as if she were calling on the grey-eyed daughter of Zeus under the hill of Tegea. (Paton)

The description suggests that two freestanding statues were combined to create the group. A young, beardless Herakles stood, the golden apples of the Hesperides sisters in his hand. Stupperich (1982: 220) believes that the apples indicate that the statue was reused from a group showing the Hesperides sisters. The figure of Auge stood, her hands raised in an orant gesture. Auge was seduced by Herakles and bore

his son Telephus. The infant was taken from her at birth. Later Herakles helped her to recognize the child. The group probably was meant to show Auge imploring Herakles's aid in the search for her son.

*Bibliography:* Stupperich, 1982: 220

## 62. HERMAPHRODITOS

*Ek.* 102–07:

There stood lovely Hermaphroditos, nor wholly a man, nor wholly a woman, for the statue was of mixed form: readily couldst thou tell him to be the son of fair-bosomed Aphrodite and of Hermes. His breasts were swelling like a girl's but he plainly had the procreative organs of a man, and he showed features of the beauty of both sexes. (Paton)

Hermaphroditos first appears in literary sources in the fourth century B.C. The pedigree

PLATE 13: Hermes (Sandalbinder), Ny Carlsberg Glyptotek, Copenhagen (Photo: Ny Carlsberg Glyptotek)

as the offspring of Hermes and Aphrodite dates to the first century B.C. Only Roman examples of Hermaphroditos survive. These show a variety of frontal-standing compositions in which Hermaphroditos appears nude and seminude with a pose and iconography similar to that of Aphrodite.

### 63. HERMES (PLATE 13)

*Ek. 297–302:*

There too was Hermes with his rod of gold. He was standing, but tying with his right hand the lace of his winged shoes, eager to start on his way. His right leg was already bent, over it was extended his left hand and his face was upturned to the sky as if he were listening to orders of his father. (Paton)

The statue, which showed the god leaning over to tie his sandal, has long been associated with the famous image of Hermes known as the Sandalbinder, a figure known from numerous replicas, fragmentary and restored (Ridgway, 1964). There are variations among them, generally in the position of the arms and hands, but all show essentially the same form. The statue portrays a nude male, his left leg straight and stiff, his right bent with his foot raised on a support. The upper torso is bent over the right leg and his arms reach down either to fasten or unfasten his sandal. The statue is dated variously to the fourth, third, and second centuries B.C. Lippold (1939: 280–81), Bieber (1961: 74), and Inan (1975: 94) consider the work Lysippan on the basis of its proportions and place that statue in the fourth century B.C. Others, among them Johnson (1927: 175–77) and Dörig (1957, 55), claim the Hermes for Lysippos's third-century school, saying that the anatomy is too advanced for Lysippos himself. Finally, Ridgway (1964: 128) suggests that the figure was produced in the eclectic milieu of the second century B.C. Although the range of date and attribution is wide, the statue conforms to the general trend in Constantinopolitan reuse in that it is essentially a product of the late classical age.

## 64. HERODOTOS

*Ek.* 377–81:

Nor did I fail to notice the divine nightingale of Halikarnassos, learned Herodotos, who dedicated to the nine Muses, intermingling in his eloquence the flowers of Ionic speech, all the exploits of men of old that two continents produced, all that creeping time witnessed. (Paton)

Surviving portraits of Herodotos (484–before 420 B.C.) show the historian as a middle-aged man with deeply set eyes, a furrowed brow, and a full lower lip set off by a flowing beard and receding hairline. All copies are thought to derive from an original of the first half of the fourth century B.C. (Richter, 1965).

## 65. HESIOD

*Ek.* 38–40:

Hesiod of Ascra seemed to be calling to the mountain Muses, and in his divine fury he did violence to the bronze by his longing to utter his inspired verse. (Paton)

The figure was bronze. Surviving representations of Hesiod (c. 700 B.C.) share a consistent iconography, showing an older, balding man with flowing beard and deeply set eyes. The type is based on an imaginary portrait of the fourth century B.C. The Psuedo-Seneca type also may portray Hesiod (Richter, 1965).

## 66. HOMER (PLATE 14)

*Ek.* 311–50:

Homer's statue seemed alive, not lacking thought and intellect, but only it would seem his ambrosial voice; the poetic frenzy was revealed in him. Verily some god cast the bronze and wrought this portrait; for I do not believe that any man seated by the forge was its smith, but that wise Athena herself wrought it with her hands, knowing the form which she once inhabited; for she herself dwelt in Homer and uttered his skilled song. The companion of Apollo, my father, the godlike being, divine Homer stood there in the semblance of an old man, but his old age was sweet, and shed more grace on him. He was endued with a reverend and kind bearing, and majesty shone forth from his form. His clustering grey hair, tossed back, trailed over his bent neck, and wandered loose about his ears, and he wore a broad beard, soft and round; for it was not pointed, but hung down in all its breadth, weaving an ornament for his naked bosom and his loveable face. His forehead was bare, and on it sat Temperance, the nurse of Youth. The discerning artist had made his eyebrows prominent, and not without reason, for his eyes were sightless. Yet to look at he was not like a blind man; for grace

PLATE 14: Homer (Hellenistic Blind Type), The British Museum, London (Photo: © Copyright The British Museum)

dwelt in his empty eyes. As I think, the artist made him so, that it might be evident to all that he bore the inextinguishable light of wisdom in his heart. His two cheeks were somewhat fallen in owing to the action of wrinkling, but on them sat innate Modesty, the fellow of the Graces, and a Pierian bee wandered round his divine mouth, producing a dripping honey-comb. With both his hands he rested on a staff, even as when alive, and had bent his right ear to listen, it seemed, to Apollo or one of the Muses hard by. He looked like one in thought, his mind carried hither and thither from the sanctuary of contemplation, as he wove some martial lay of the Pieran Siren. (Paton)

A bronze statue of Homer (before 700 B.C.) leaned with both hands on a staff. Four basic portrait types are known, all of them invented likenesses. The Epimenides type, from an original of the mid–fifth century B.C., shows the poet with eyes closed, his center-parted hair combed and bound by a fillet. He wears a long beard, rounded at the bottom and a thick moustache. The Modena type depicts Homer as a middle-aged man with open, downcast eyes. He wears the flat taenia, has a moustache and a long beard made up of thick tufts that grow in different directions. His hair is long and tidy. The Modena type is thought to derive from a Greek original of the fourth century B.C. The third or Apollonios of Tyana type dates to c. 300 B.C. and shows the poet with open eyes, long, disorderly hair bound by a fillet, beard, and moustache. Finally, the Hellenistic blind type, an invention of the second century B.C., shows Homer as an old man, with parted lips framed by sunken cheeks and wide, staring eyes. As in all representations, he is bearded and wears a moustache. His hair, which is bound by a fillet, curls on his neck but does not fall to his shoulders.

Richter (1965: 53) identified the Zeuxippos Homer with the Hellenistic blind type because of the wide-staring eyes and sunken cheeks that appear to match Christodoros's description. No full-length portraits of any version of Homer survive, but the manner in which many of the Hellenistic blind-type portraits hold their neck suggests that the bodies to which they were attached might well have leaned on a staff as indicated by Christodoros.

Richter (1965: 46) believes that this Homer was the same statue described by Kedrenos; however, it is likely that that statue, which is described as having closed eyes and a different pose, was of a different type (see cat. no. 67).

*Bibliography:* Richter, 1965

## 67. HOMER (PLATE 15)

Kedrenos, I, 649:

Among the eminent men of outstanding thought was Homer, made exactly as he was, concentrating in thought, his hands clasped in front of his chest. He had a short beard and his hair fell thinly on each side of his forehead. His bearded face was the result of his age and concern for all. His nose was proportionate to the rest of the face. His drooping eyelids resembled a blind man, as he was widely known. He was wearing a worn himation on top of the chiton, and at the base of the statue there was a bronze strap on his feet representing sandals.

The figure was bronze. Richter (1965: 46) thought that this Homer was the same as the figure described by Christodoros; however, differences in physiognomy and pose indicate a different statue. Specifically, this statue is described with closed eyes and hands clasped to his chest, while that mentioned by Christodoros depicted the poet with open eyes leaning on a staff. Reference to closed eyes indicates that the figure recorded by Kedrenos may be identified with the Epimenides Homer type, an invention of the mid-fifth century B.C. (see cat. no. 66).

*Bibliography:* Richter, 1965

## 68. HOMER OF BYZANTIUM

*Ek.* 407–13:

A second Homer stood there, not I think the prince of epic song, the divine son of fair-flowing Meles, but one who by the shore of Thrace was the son of the famous Byzantine Moero, her whom the Muses nurtured and made skillful while yet a child in heroic voice. He himself practiced the tragic art, adorning by his verses his city Byzantium. (Paton)

The statue depicted Homer, son of Moero (third century B.C.), a tragedian in the Alexandrian mode. No sculptural representations are known, but the portrait was obviously one of the Hellenistic age.

PLATE 15: Homer (Epimenides Type), Glyptothek, Munich (Photo: from Richter, 1965, Fig. 1)

## 69. ISOKRATES

*Ek.* 256–58:

Hail, Isokrates, light of rhetoric! For thou adornest the bronze, seeming to be revealing some wise counsels even though thou art wrought of mute brass. (Paton)

The statue was bronze. Several statues of Isokrates (436–338 B.C.) are recorded from

176

antiquity: an equestrian statue on the Athenian Akropolis showing Isokrates as a youth; a bronze statue by Leochares (fl. 372 B.C.) at Eleusis; and an anonymously sculptured bronze in the Olympeion at Athens (Richter, 1965). Surviving portrait representations show a long, bearded face with high forehead, long nose, and small, full lips. Richter (1965) suggests that the likeness is a product of the late fourth century B.C.

## 70. KASSANDRA

*Ek.* 189–91:

There I saw the prophetess Kassandra, who, blaming her father in silence, seemed filled with prescient fury as if prophesying the last woes of her city. (Paton)

**Klitios:** *see* **Panthous.**

## 71. KRATINOS

*Ek.* 357–60:

And there shone the delicate form of gifted Kratinos, who once sharpened the biting shafts of his iambics against the Athenian political leaders, devourers of the people. He brought sprightly comedy to greater perfection. (Paton)

Portraits of Kratinos (fifth century B.C.) are not known.

## 72. MELAMPOS

*Ek.* 243–45:

And thou wouldst marvel looking on Melampos: he bore the holy semblance of a prophet, and with his silent lips he seemed to be breathing intensely the divine breath of inspiration. (Paton)

Two identifications of Melampos are possible. In myth and literature he was a prophet. In history he was a second century B.C. author of two extant works on divination. Christodoros's

description is ambiguous as to which of the two figures are represented; however, given the large number of literary figures at the Baths it seems likely that the statue represented the author.

## 73. MENANDER (PLATE 16)

*Ek.* 361–66:

There stood Menander, at fair-towered Athens, the bright star of the later comedy. Many loves of virgins did he invent, and produced iambics which were servants of the Graces, and furious ravishers of unwedded maidenhoods, mixing as he did with love the graver flower of his honeyed song. (Paton)

The Athenian comic poet Menander (342/1–293/89 B.C.) is among the most well represented of all Greek men of letters in the Roman portrait repertoire. Over seventy portraits survive as herms, busts, and medallions with dates ranging from the first century B.C. to the fifth century A.D. (Richter, 1965). In all representations, Menander is readily identifiable as a clean-shaven, strong-jawed man of indeterminate middle age. Artfully tousled hair frames a slim face characterized by a high, slightly creased brow, deeply set eyes above an aquiline nose, pronounced cheekbones, and a full mouth. Where dress appears, he wears the tunic and himation. The isolated head type preferred by the Romans is thought to derive from an original full-body portrait by Praxiteles' sons, Kephisodotos the Younger and Timarchos, that was set up in the Athenian Theater of Dionysios shortly after the poet's death in 293 B.C. (Fittschen, 1991). That image shows the poet seated in a high-backed chair, sporting the tunic and himation of the Roman versions. His pose is upright, but relaxed, as indicated by the turn of the torso to the right, the curved shoulders, and what would have been the casual placement of the now missing legs with one foot forward and one back between the legs of the chair. The arms are also missing, but the turn of the shoulder and the angles at which the remains of the limbs run

PLATE 16: Reconstruction of the Menander portrait, Göttingen Archäologisches Institut (Photo: from Fittschen, 1991, plate 74)

along the side of the upper torso suggest that the right hand would have rested casually in the poet's lap, while the left hung loosely by his side.

## 74. MENELAOS

*Ek.* 165–70:

There one might see Menelaos warlike, but rejoicing in victory, for his heart was warmed with great joy as he saw near him rosy-armed Helen reconciled. I marveled at her lovely image, that gave the bronze a grace most desirable, for her beauty even in that soulless work breathed warm love. (Paton)

## 75. ODYSSEUS AND HEKUBE (PLATES 17 AND 18)

*Ek.* 171–88:

Goodly Odysseus was rejoicing in his wily mind, for he was not devoid of his versatile wits, but still wore the guise of subtlety. And he was laughing in his heart, for he gloried in having laid Troy low by his cunning. But do thou tell me, mother of Hector, unhappy Hekube, which of the immortals taught thee to shed tears in this thy dumb presentment? Not even the bronze made thee cease from wailing, nor did lifeless Art have pity on thee and stop thee from thy irremediable fury: but still thou standest by weeping, and, as I guess, no longer dost thou lament the death of unhappy Hector or the deep grief of poor Andromache, but the fall of thy deity; for thy cloak drawn over thy face indicates thy sorrow, and thy gown ungirt and descending to the ground announces the mourning thou hast within. Extreme anguish hath bound thy spirit, the tears ran down thy cheeks, but Art hath dried them, proclaiming how searching is the drought of thy incurable woe. (Paton)

Statue Base

Istanbul Archaeological Museum (Plate 17), Circular, marble (?) base with molded flanges top and bottom. 1.40 × 1.08 m. Inscribed: EKABH (Hekube).

Excavation at the Zeuxippos unearthed a marble base inscribed with the name EKABH (Plate 18). The inscription links the base to the figure of Hekube mentioned in Christodoros's description. The scale of the base and the dowel holes in its upper supporting surface indicate that the statue it supported would have been life-size and of bronze.

*Bibliography:* Casson, 1929: 12–19; Casson, 1930: 235; Mango, 1963: 58; Guberti Bassett, 1996: 497–99

## 76. OINONE AND PARIS

*Ek.* 215–21:

Oinone was boiling over with anger – boiling, eating her heart out with bitter jealousy. She was furtively watching Paris with her wild eyes and conveyed to him secret threats, spurning her ill-fated lord with her right hand. The cowherd seemed ashamed, and he was looking the other way, unfortunate lover, for he feared to look on Oinone in tears, his bride of Kebrene. (Paton)

The subject matter was popular with Hellenistic poets and is also taken up by Ovid who explored the psychological aspects of her tale. Popularity with late Greek and Roman authors suggests that the statuary would have been of the same period.

## 77. PALAEPHATOS

*Ek.* 36–37:

Palaephatos the prophet stood forth, his long hair crowned with laurel, and he seemed to be pouring forth the voice of prophecy. (Paton)

## 78. PANTHOUS, THYMOETES, LAMPON, AND KLYTIOS

*Ek.* 246–55:

There was Panthous, the Trojan senator; he had not yet ceased from menacing the safety of the Greeks. And Thymoetes the counselor was thinking of some elaborate plan, plunged in the sea

PLATE 17: Hekube base from the Baths of Zeuxippos, Istanbul Archaeological Museum (Photo: Sarah Bassett)

of silence. Verily he seemed to be yet meditating some design to help the Trojans. Lampon was like one vexed; for his mind had no more the power of giving birth to healing counsel to keep off from the sore-worn Trojans the wave of war that was to overwhelm them. Klytios stood at a loss, his clasped hands heralding hidden trouble. (Paton)

PLATE 18: Detail of the inscription from the Hekube base, Istanbul Archaeological Museum (Photo: Sarah Bassett)

## 79. PERIKLES

*Ek.* 117–20:

I marveled beholding thee, Perikles, that even in the dumb brass thou kindlest the spirit of thy eloquence, as if thou didst still preside over the citizens of Athens, or prepare the Peloponnesian War. (Paton)

The statue was bronze. Portraits of Perikles (495–29 B.C.) survive primarily as busts and herms. Richter (1965) believes that the style of the extant heads points to a single original carved c. 430, probably by Kreisilas. These images show a youthful, bearded face capped with a tall, pointed helmet. Large eyes, a long straight nose, and a full lower lip characterize the face. Because these portraits are bodiless Roman copies, the statesman's full appearance is not known. Plutarch (*Perikles*, 31, 4) claims that Pheidias showed Perikles armed on the shield of the Parthenos, and the Strangford shield (Smith,

1892–1904: 302) gives a general impression of how such an armored representation might have looked. There are also bronze statuettes thought to show a heroically nude Perikles in the stance of the Doryphoros (Richter, 1965, figs. 446–47). Richter suggests that these figurines copy the statue of Perikles that stood on the Athenian Acropolis (Paus. I, 25 and 28).

## 80. PHEREKYDES

*Ek.* 351–53:

Pherekydes of Syra stood there resplendent with holiness. Plying the holy compasses of wisdom, he was gazing at the heavens, his eyes turned upwards. (Paton)

Statues of the Ionian mythographer and cosmographer Pherekydes of Syra (sixth-century B.C.) are not known.

## 81. PINDAR

*Ek.* 382–87:

There stood the Helikonian swan of ancient Thebes, sweet-voiced Pindar, whom silver-bowed Apollo nurtured by the peak of Boeotian Helikon, and taught him music; for at his birth bees settled on his melodious mouth, and made a honey-comb testifying to his skill in song. (Paton)

All portraits of Pindar (518–438 B.C.) are thought to originate in a prototype of the fifth century B.C. A fifth-century A.D. medallion portrait establishes the physiognomy: Pindar is shown with a bearded, square jaw and short hair, his brow creased in the manner of a philosopher. Archaeological evidence indicates that there were two body types, standing and sitting (Richter/Smith, 1984), both of which show the poet wearing the himation and carrying a lyre. It is unclear which type stood in the baths.

## 82. PLATO

*Ek.* 97–98:

There stood god-like Plato, who erst in Athens revealed the secret paths of heaven-taught virtue. (Paton)

Numerous representations of Plato (427–347 B.C.) survive, mostly as portrait heads and herms. All show a bearded, square face with high, broad forehead, small eyes, protruding lower lip, and finely curved nose. Richter (1965) dates the original to the mid-fourth century B.C. The body type is less firmly identified. A seated draped figure now known only from plaster casts offers one possibility (Richter, 1965); another is an over-life-size standing male from the Serapeion in Memphis (Picard/Lauer, 1955). Said to be a Hellenistic original, this figure shows Plato barefoot and draped in a voluminous robe. It is not clear which type was used in the baths.

## 83. POLYIDOS

*Ek.* 40–42:

And near him stood another prophet, Polyidos, crowned with the laurel of Phoibos, eager to break into prophetic song, but restrained by the gagging fetter of the artist. (Paton)

The exact identity of Polyidos is unclear, but the statue probably showed the mythical Corinthian seer who was a member of the prophetic clan of the Melampodidae. No sculptured representations of Polyidos are known, and the iconography is rare (LIMC, s.v. "Polyidos"). It does not appear before the fifth century in vase painting. In the Roman period the figure is especially popular in the aftermath of the *Aeneid*, which suggests an early imperial (first century) date.

## 84. POMPEY

*Ek.* 398–406:

Pompey, the leader of the successful Romans in their campaign against the Isaurians, was treading under foot the Isaurian swords, signifying that he had imposed on the neck of Taurus the yoke of bondage, and bound it with the strong chains of victory. He was the man who was a light to all and the father of the noble race of the Emperor Anastasius. This my excellent Emperor showed to all, himself vanquishing by his arms the inhabitants of Isauria. (Paton)

Stupperich (1982: 226) believes that the statue represented the Republican general Pompey the Great; however, the statue is more properly identified as that of the late-fourth, early-fifth-century general Pompeius (*PRLE*, II, 898 s.v. "Pompeius 2"). The statue would most likely have been put in place in the later fourth century.

*Bibliography:* Stupperich, 1982; Guberti Bassett, 1996

## 85. POSEIDON AND AMYMONE

*Ek.* 61–68:

There sat rosy-fingered Amymone. She was gathering up her unfilleted hair behind, while her face was unveiled, and with upturned glance she was gazing at her black-haired lord the sea-king. For near her stood Poseidon, naked, with flowing hair holding out to her a dripping dolphin, bringing a suitor's gifts for the hand of the much-sought maiden. (Paton)

Amymone was the daughter of Danaos, who bore a son, Nauplios, by Poseidon. Three separate versions of her story exist: Apollodoros (II, I, 4, 10), Hyginus (*Fab.* 169), and Lucian (*Di-all. deor. marin*, 6). Freestanding representations are unknown, and the iconography of the couple appears first in the fifth century B.C. in vase painting. Two interpretations of the story are popular: one showing Amymone fleeing, the other showing her seated beside Poseidon. Because the story of Poseidon and Amymone unfolds in the territories of Argos, the pair is also popular on Argive coin issues where the seated iconography appears. The group followed the seated iconography formula, a choice that appears to have been preferred in the Hellenistic and Roman age. Numismatic evidence suggests further that the group was from Argos (*LIMC*, s.v. "Amymone").

## 86. PYRRHOS

*Ek.* 56–60:

Look on the cub of Aeacidae, Pyrrhos the son of Achilles the sacker of cities, how he longed to handle the bronze weapons that the artist did not give him; for he had wrought him naked: he seemed to be gazing up, as if directing his eyes to windswept Ilion. (Paton)

The iconography of Pyrrhos is well established in vase painting and relief sculpture where he is depicted as a warrior (*LIMC*, s.v. "Pyrrhos I"). The Zeuxippos statue is therefore unusual in its treatment of the subject, because it shows him nude and unarmed as a young, inspired hero. The upturned head and gaze suggest a work of post–fourth-century B.C. manufacture.

## 87. PYRRHOS AND POLYXENE

*Ek.* 192–208:

Here was another Pyrrhos, sacker of cities, not wearing on his locks a plumed helmet or shaking a spear, but naked he glittered, his face beardless, and raising his right hand in testimony of victory he looked askance on weeping Polyxene. Tell me, Polyxene, unhappy virgin, what forces thee to shed hidden tears now thou art of mute bronze, why dost thou draw thy veil over thy face, and stand like one ashamed, but sorry at heart? Is it for fear lest Pyrrhos of Phthia won thee for his spoil after destroying thy city? Nor did the arrows of thy beauty save thee – thy beauty which one entrapped his father, leading him of his own will into the net of unexpected death. Yea, by thy brazen image I swear had Prince Pyrrhos seen thee as thou here art, he would have taken thee to wife and abandoned the memory of his father's fate. (Paton)

## 88. PYTHAGORAS

*Ek.* 120–24:

There stood too Pythagoras, the Samian sage, but he seemed to dwell in Olympos, and did violence to the nature of the bronze, overflowing with intellectual thought, for methinks with his pure eyes he was measuring heaven alone. (Paton)

No sculptured representations of Pythagoras (sixth to fifth century B.C.) are known; however, Samian coins of the Roman imperial period and contorniates show a draped, bearded male, an image consistent with Christodoros's emphasis on the philosopher as intellectual. The Pythagoras portrait was invented no earlier than the fifth century and more probably in the fourth century B.C. (Richter, 1965).

## 89. SAPPHO

*Ek.* 69–71:

And the clear-toned Pierian bee sat there at rest, Sappho of Lesbos. She seemed to be weaving some lovely melody, with her mind devoted to the silent Muses. (Paton)

Richter believes that a statue of Sappho (b. 612 B.C.), a native daughter, appears as a seated female figure on coin issues from Mytilene. It is possible that the statue was brought from Lesbos.

*Bibliography:* Richter, 1965

## 90. SARPEDON

*Ek.* 277–82:

There stood Sarpedon, the Lycian leader; terrible was he in his might; his chin was just marked with tender down at the point. Over his hair he wore a helmet. He was nude, but his beauty indicated the parentage of Zeus, for from his eyes shone the light of a noble sire. (Paton)

The figure was beardless and nude save for a helmet. No freestanding sculptured representations are known, and it is not possible to determine date of manufacture; however, surviving representations in vase painting generally show him as dead and often in the presence of Hypnos and Thanatos who carry him away for burial (*LIMC*, s.v. "Sarpedon"). The Zeuxippos statue thus presents an unusual iconography.

## 91. SIMONIDES

*Ek.* 38–49:

Nor hadst thou, Simonides, laid to rest thy tender love, but still dost yearn for the strings; yet hast though no sacred lyre to touch. He who made thee, Simonides, should have mixed sweet music with the bronze, and the dumb bronze had reverenced thee, and responded to the strains of thy lyre. (Paton)

The figure of Simonides (556–468 B.C.) was bronze, and stood with representations of Hes-

iod (cat. no. 65) and Polyidos (cat. no. 83). No sculptural representations are known and Christodoros's mention of his statue is the only known literary reference to a sculptured portrait. Like all such representations of early historical figures, the portrait was probably an imaginary likeness of the late classical period or later.

## 92. STESICHOROS

*Ek.* 125–30:

There saw I clear voiced Stesichoros, whom of old the Sicilian land nurtured, to whom Apollo taught the harmony of the lyre while he was yet in his mother's womb. For but just after his birth a creature of the air, a nightingale from somewhere, settled secretly on his lips and struck up its clear song. (Paton)

No freestanding sculptured representations of Stesichoros of Himera (640–555 B.C.) survive; however, Cicero (*Verr.* 2, 2, 35) describes a statue at Himera noting that Stesichoros was shown as an old man, bent forward, and carrying a book. Coin issues from Himera may reproduce this figure (Richter, 1965: fig. 268). The early date of Stesichoros means that his portrait was an invention of the later period. Emphasis on the poet's age suggests similarity to the described numismatic iconography and with it a late classical or Hellenistic date for the type.

## 93. TERPANDER

*Ek.* 111–16:

Pass not over sweet-voiced Terpander, whose image thou wouldst say was alive, not dumb; for, as it seemed to me he was composing, with deeply stirred spirit, the mystic song; even as once by the eddying Eurotas he soothed, singing to his consecrated lyre, the evil spite of Sparta's neighbor-foes of Amyclae. (Paton)

Statues of Terpander (fl. 647 B.C.) are not known.

## 94. THUKYDIDES

*Ek.* 372–76:

Thukydides was wielding his intellect, weaving as it seemed, one of the speeches of his history. His right hand was raised to signify that he once sang the bitter struggle of Sparta and Athens, that cut down so many of the sons of populous Greece. (Paton)

The statue stood with his right arm raised, as if in speech. Approximately fifty portrait busts of Thukydides (460/55–400 B.C.) are known from the Roman period. These images show a middle-aged man with closely cropped hair and beard. Thukydides has a high forehead incised with three horizontal furrows, narrow eyes, and a small mouth. Richter (1965) believes the Roman portraits to derive from a single fourth century B.C. original. No full-length representations survive and literary references to statues are unclear. Christodoros's description is the only secure mention of a statue. Richter (1965) believes that the statue was bronze, although there is no mention of medium in the verse. She also associates the statue with a bust from Holkum Hall, suggesting, albeit tentatively, that the slightly turned head and hint of a raised arm in the bust conform to Christodoros's description.

*Bibliography:* Richter, 1965

## 95. VIRGIL

*Ek.* 414–16:

And he stood forth – the clear-voiced swan dear to the Romans, Virgil breathing eloquence, whom his native Echo of Tiber nourished to be another Homer. (Paton)

## 96. WRESTLER

*Ek.* 228–40:

And there was a strong man skilled in wrestling, Apollo knows if his name were Philo or Philamon, or Milo, the bulwark of Sicily; for I could not learn it to tell you, the famous name of this man of might; but in any case he was full of valor. He had a shaggy trailing beard, and his face proclaimed him one to be feared in the arena. His locks were fretful, and the hard stretched muscles of his sturdy limbs projected, and when his fists were clenched his two thick arms were as firm as stone. And his robust back stood out a powerful muscle running up on each side of the hollow of his flexible neck. (Paton)

Statues of pugilists were made and used throughout antiquity as decoration for stadia and gymnasia (Pliny, *NH*, XXXIV, 91). Christodoros identifies the statue with one of three fighters: Philo, Philammon, or Milo of Croton in south Italy. Stupperich (1982) believes the figure was that of Herakles.

*Bibliography:* Stupperich, 1982: 223

## 97. XENOPHON

*Ek.* 388–92:

Xenophon stood there shining bright, the citizen of Athena who wields the shield, he who once proclaiming the might of Cyrus the Achaemenid, followed the sonorous genius of Plato's Muse, mixing the fruit rich in exploits of History, mother of noble deeds, with the drops of the industrious bee. (Paton)

Reference to the statue as "shining bright" suggests that the image was bronze. Images of the Athenian statesman and general Xenophon (428/7–354 B.C.) are uncommon. No full-length representations are known; although Pausanias (5.6.6) states that there was a statue of Xenophon on his tomb in Athens. An inscribed marble herm from Alexandria allows identification of the portrait type. Xenophon appears as a middle-aged man, bearded and with tousled hair. He has deeply set eyes and high cheekbones. The portrait was probably a posthumous creation of the later fourth century B.C. (Richter, 1965).

## CHALKE GATE

Belisarios: *see* Hellenistic ruler

### 98. GORGONEIA

*Par.* 44a:

As this Papias also explained in his writings that the gorgon-like heads on the Chalke gate – which are on the left as the spectator approaches and on the right if he is walking away from it – came from the Ephesian temple of the goddess Artemis. There were ⟨eight⟩. Four of these are in the area of the Forum Tauri, fixed on the ancient palace of Constantine, where the statues of Julian and his wife, and also of Constantine the Great and his sons and Gallus can be seen. The other four are on the left of the above-mentioned gate. In the same place is also a cross put up in the time of the earlier Justinian; restored ⟨statues⟩ of Belisarius ⟨and others⟩ were also set up. And on the gate Belisarius is to be seen gilded, with a crown of rays; and Tiberius the Thracian, with a hunched back, and Justin I, slender in appearance, and very close to his real likeness; and seven relatives, some in marble and some in bronze, who can be accurately recognized by passersby from their dress.

*Par.* 78:

The four so-called Gorgons came from Ephesos from the temple of Artemis. They surround the vestibule of the Chalke and the sign of the cross stands above them. (Cameron/Herrin)

*Patria* II, 28:

Opposite the Chalke, in an apse, there were gorgoneia, two gilded females. And there were two horses which stood together with the gorgons in the apse, and they say that these horses were brought from the temple of Artemis at Ephesos by Justinian the builder of Hagia Sophia, and that they were placed there in such a way to protect against the agitation of other horses.

Justinian brought gorgons' heads from the Temple of Artemis, Ephesos, in the sixth century. Reference to gilding suggests that they were bronze. Date of manufacture cannot be determined. Number and placement are unclear. *Par.* describes four, while the *Patria* places only two in an apse opposite the entrance. The apparent contradiction might be because of an error in transmission, for example, the dropping of "one another" from the *Patria*, which would mean that the four gorgons were disposed as pendants in an architectural setting. Janin (1964) places the gorgons under the vault opposite the doorway. It is also possible that there was a gorgon on each of the four supporting piers around the central space.

*Bibliography:* Cameron/Herrin, 233–34, 271; Janin, 1964: 111

### 99. HELLENISTIC RULER

*Par.* 44a: see no. 98.

The statue, which was gilded bronze, wore the *corona radiata*. Mango (1959) thinks an image of Belisarios with a *corona radiata* unlikely and identifies the figure as a Hellenistic king or a pre-Constantinian Roman emperor. There is no specific mention of Constantinopolitan history; however, reference to Justinian together with the identification as Belisarios suggest that the statue is likely to have been set up in the sixth century as part of the Justinianic restoration of the gate.

*Bibliography:* Cameron/Herrin, 233–34, 271; Mango, 1959: 101, n. 122

### 100. HORSES

*Patria* II, 28: see no. 98.

The horses are said to have been brought from the Ephesian sanctuary of Artemis by Justinian. This association is not unreasonable. Votive offerings from the site include bronze and ivory statuettes of horses (OAI, 1906), gifts to the goddess in her guise as protectress of horses. Large sculptural dedications also may have been made.

The association with Justinian is also reasonable. He rebuilt the Chalke after the Nika rebellion. Moreover, the building of St. John, Ephesos, was accomplished under his patronage, and it may well be that the horses were found during that building campaign and claimed for the Chalke. Mango (1963: 58) suspects that the Chalke horses are the last imperial gift of antiquities to have been brought to Constantinople.

*Bibliography:* Mango, 1963

## 101. PHILOSOPHERS

*Par. 5b (Patria* II, 89):

About the statues at the Chalke. The two statues whose hands are outstretched towards each other came from the land of the Athenians; they say they are of philosophers, as Ligurius the pagan says. (Cameron/Herrin)

Said to have been brought from Athens, the statues were probably representations of men of letters, either poets or philosophers. The text records the figures "with hands outstretched," a description that suggests any one of a number of rhetorical gestures. Reference to extended arms suggests the type of engagement with space characteristic of late classical, Hellenistic or Roman style.

## FORUM OF ARKADIOS

## 102. ARTEMIS

*Par. 20 (Patria* II, 19):

Formerly some people used to call the Xerolophos a spectacle. For in it were sixteen spiral columns, and Artemis, a composite statue, and one of the builder, Septimius Severus, and a monument – a tripod. And there too many prophecies were given in the same place, at which a virgin was also sac-

rificed, and an astronomical position prevailed for thirty-six years. (Cameron/Herrin)

Cameron/Herrin (196) believe that the description of the statue as "composite" indicates a multifigured group and suggest that it may have depicted Artemis of Ephesos surrounded by animals. The Ephesian typology is not, however, a multifigured one. Artemis stands facing forward, her feet close together. She wears her hair pulled back beneath the polos crown. An elaborate chest plate adorned with signs of the zodiac falls across her shoulders and sternum. Below it, multiple breasts descend to the goddess's waist. She wears a straight skirt from which animal protomes project in ordered tiers to the ground. Although complex, the image, which is a Hellenistic or Roman creation, is essentially one of a single figure.

True multifigured representations of Artemis do exist. The Artemis-Potnia type of the archaic period depicts the goddess with wings and surrounded by animals (*LIMC*, s.v. "Artemis"), and classical and postclassical representations show her accompanied by her hounds (*LIMC*, s.v. "Artemis"). It is likewise possible that the Artemis was a composite statue in the modern sense: a figure sculptured from a variety of materials. It is not clear whether "composite" can be understood in this sense in *Par.*, but if it can, then the statue may well be one of the Ephesian goddess who is often created as a composite figure (*LIMC*, s.v. "Artemis").

*Bibliography:* Millet, 1948; Cameron/Herrin, 196

## 103. SEPTIMIUS SEVERUS

*Par. 20 (Patria* II, 19): see no. 102.

## 104. SPHINX

Istanbul Archaeological Museum, no. 1136 (Mendel)

A male sphinx (0.62 m × 0.55 m × 1.47 m) in synite crouches with legs tucked close to the body and tail wrapped around the right rear flank. The head, which faced forward, is missing, but remains of the stiff Egyptian headdress fall across the shoulder. Iconography and the hardstone medium indicate Egyptian manufacture. The statue is not dated; however, by analogy to the bulk of Egyptian statuary in imperial Rome, it is likely to be of late Roman period manufacture (Roullet, 13). The sphinx may have been brought from Egypt at the same time as the Theodosian obelisk (Mendel). If so, there is no indication of where it may have been prior to installation in the Forum of Arkadios.

*Bibliography:* S. Reinach, 1895, 1896; Mendel, 1912

## 105. TRIPOD

*Par.* 20 (*Patria* II, 19): see no. 102.

The ancient tripod was normally a kettle with ring handles resting on a three-legged support. Profiles of the kettle varied, as did the physical relationship between the kettle and its support. In some instances the kettle was attached to the legs, while in others it had its own separate three-legged stand. Tripods are known as votive offerings as early as the eighth century B.C. Bronze was the most common material for such dedications, although wood, stone, and ceramic tripods also are known, as well as rare gold and silver offerings. These votive dedications had a wide range in size, from no more than a few centimeters in height to two to three meters tall. The common practice was to award a tripod as the prize for victory in a contest. The recipient of the prize then dedicated the tripod to Apollo in his own name, thereby achieving a modicum of immortality. Tripods were given for athletic games and dramatic contests. Their use in the dramatic milieu seems to have stopped in the second century. It is not known when they ceased to be awarded for athletic contests. It also is known that the Pythia at Delphi sat on the oracular tripod to prophesy. Thus the tripod was considered a symbol of Apollo's oracular powers.

## 106. APHRODITE

*Par.* 8:

In the Senate there were placed charioteers in their chariots, and they were put at the place of astronomical calculations, where stand the statues of Artemis and Aphrodite. This is where Arkadios the archdeacon of S. Irene was beheaded with clubs by the Arians. They say that the statues there shook for three days after his death. The chariots were buried beneath the arch in the time of the Emperor Theodosios (presumably Theodosios I, 379–95). (Cameron/Herrin)

Use of the present tense to refer to the figure, one of a pair with Artemis, suggests that it was still extant in the eighth century. Janin (1964) thought that the statues stood by the Senate in the Augusteion. Because of the reference to an execution, Cameron/Herrin propose that the Forum of Constantine is a more likely spot given its proximity to the Praetorium. They suggest further that the statue be identified with two figures of Athena mentioned by Hesychios; however, those statues are more properly associated with the Augusteion.

*Bibliography:* Janin, 1964, 156; Cameron/Herrin, 184

## 107. ATHENA

Arethas, *Schol. Arist. Or.* 50t. III:

I believe this (viz. the Athena) is the one set up in the Forum of Constantine at the porch of the council chamber, or senate, as they call it now; facing it on the right hand side of the porch as you go in is Thetis the [mother] of Achilles with a crown of crabs. The common file of today call the Athena "Earth" and Thetis "Sea" being misled by the marine monsters on her head. (Jenkins)

Constantine the Rhodian, 150–63:

But the powerful and wise Constantine brought them [statues] here to be a source of amusement for citizens and delight for children and laughter for men. And this same charming female copper statue which stands on a high column raising one hand high resembles the Pallas Athena coming from the deceit of the Lindians, the first inhabitants of the plain of poor Rhodes who were brought up in impiety. This is revealed by the helmet and the monstrous gorgoneion and the snakes, which twine about her neck. Thus, they, who in the old days were insane, used to represent in vain the image of Athena.

## Kedrenos I, 565:

On the open plaza of the Forum stand two statues: to the west that of Athena of Lindos wearing a helmet and the monstrous gorgon's head and snakes entwined about her neck (for so the ancients used to represent her image); and to the East, Amphitrite, with crab claws on her temples, which were also brought from Rhodes.

## Niketas Choniates, 559–60:

The wine-bibing portion of the vulgar masses smashed the statue of Athena that stood on a pedestal in the Forum of Constantine, for it appeared to the foolish rabble that she was beckoning on the Western armies. She rose to a standing height of thirty feet and wore a garment made of bronze, as was the entire figure. The robe reached down to her feet and fell into folds in many places so that no part of the body which Nature has ordained to be clothed should be exposed. A military girdle tightly cinctured her waist. Covering her prominent breasts and shoulders was an upper garment of goatskin embellished with the Gorgon's head. Her long bare neck was an irresistible delight to behold. The bronze was so transformed by its convincing portrayal of the goddess in all her parts that her lips gave the appearance that, should one stop to listen, one would hear a gentle voice. The veins were represented dilated as though fluid were flowing through their twisted ways to wherever needed throughout the whole body, which, though lifeless, appeared to partake of the full bloom of life. And the eyes were filled with deep yearning. On her head was set a helmet

with horsehair crest, and terribly did it nod from above. Her braided hair tied in the back was a feast for the eyes, while the locks, falling loosely over the forehead, set off the braided tresses. Her left hand tucked up the folds of her dress, while she pointed her right hand toward the south; her head was also gently turned southward, and her eyes also gazed in the same direction. Whence they who were wholly ignorant of the orientation of the points of the compass contended that the statue was looking toward the west and with her hand was beckoning the Western armies, thus erring in their judgment and misapprehending what they beheld.

As the result of such misconceptions, they shattered the statue of Athena, or, rather, guilty of ever-worsening conduct and taking up arms against themselves, they discarded the patroness of manliness and wisdom even though she was but a symbol of these. (Magoulias)

Several sources describe a statue of Athena in the Forum. The earliest, that of Arethas (ninth to tenth century), is a scholion based on the following remark by Aelius Aristides:

Not to mention physical beauty, in modeling and sculpture by what is the spectator most overcome? Is it not by the fairest and most magnificent statues, the ones which have achieved the limits of perfection in these matters? The Olympian Zeus, the Athena at Athens – I mean the ivory one, and also, if you wish, the Lemnian Athena –, all these statues embody the unsurpassable skill of the craftsman and offer unsurpassable pleasure to the spectator. (Jenkins)

In response to Aristides' reference to the Pheidian statues, the Athena Parthenos, and the Athena Lemnia, Arethas posited identification of a statue in the Forum of Constantine with one of these figures.

Arethas's contemporary, Constantine of Rhodes (ninth to tenth century), also described a statue of Athena, a bronze representation of the goddess in her guise as Pallas Athena that stood on a column. Designation of the statue as Lindian indicates a provenance in the Sanctuary of Athena at Lindos on Rhodes.

Georgios Kedrenos (twelfth century) also referred to an Athena. Like Constantine the Rhodian, Kedrenos described the statue as Lindian, adding that the goddess wore a helmet and the aegis, as indicated by the reference to the gorgon's head and snakes. Kedrenos located the statue in front of the Curia and described it as a pendant to a figure of Amphitrite.

Finally, Niketas Choniates (thirteenth century) documented a bronze Athena that was destroyed in a riot of 1202, noting that the figure, which stood to a height of thirty feet, was shown in a contrapposto pose, with one leg bent and one arm outstretched. She wore a helmet and long peplos over which was draped the gorgon-adorned aegis. Her hair was tied back in a thick braid. There is no mention of placement, nor is there any attribution or reference to provenance.

Taken together the texts describe a monumental bronze image of the armed Pallas Athena at the entrance to the Senate House in the Forum of Constantine. The statue stood ἐπὶ στήλης, that is, on an honorific column or a base. Reference to its great height favors the solution of stylite display. Identification remains problematic, however, because of the conflicting reports about attribution and provenance.

It is precisely the issue of identification that has claimed the attention of scholars since the nineteenth century. The earliest references to the Athena, those of Gilles, Du Cange, and Heyne, worked from Kedrenos's text alone and noted only the statue's location. The factual nature of discussion changed when Jahn (1848) introduced the Arethas text as evidence, doing so with the added suggestion that the statue by the Senate was none other than the chryselephantine figure of Athena Parthenos by Pheidias. Colossal in scale, this statue, which was the temple statue for the Parthenon, showed the goddess standing. She wore the peplos and the aegis and was armed with helmet, lance, and shield. Her right hand was extended and carried a small figure of victory.

Jahn's suggestion of a specific attribution opened the door to a series of exchanges in which the statue was identified with one or another of the various Pheidian Athenas. Führer (1892) rejected the association with the Parthenos, claiming that the statue could not have been in Constantinople as it had been destroyed in a fire sometime between 429 and 485. Gurlitt (1893) then stepped into the attributional fray by introducing the Choniates text as evidence. Choniates' description of a thirty-foot high bronze statue of Athena, coupled with Arethas's attribution to Pheidias, led Gurlitt to conclude that the statue was not that of the Parthenos, but rather the Athena Promachos, the colossal Pheidian bronze that stood outside the Temple of Athena on the Athenian Akropolis. In addition to its colossal scale and medium, this statue fit Choniates' description in terms of dress and attribute: It wore the peplos and was armed with helmet, lance, and shield.

Discovery in 1894 of Constantine the Rhodian's poem and its subsequent publication by Reinach (1896) introduced new evidence. Reinach saw no reason to associate the statue with Pheidias and came down squarely on the side of the Lindian attribution and a Rhodian provenance.

The issue lay dormant until the mid-twentieth century when Jenkins (1947, 1951) supported Gurlitt's claim for the Promachos in a pair of articles that sought evidence for the Constantinopolitan presence of the Promachos in two Byzantine miniatures. The first, a representation of the martyrdom of St. Nikephoros in a now lost eleventh-century manuscript of the *Physiologos* originally published by Stryzgowski (1899), shows an armed female figure atop a column. Jenkins (1947) took this miniature to be a representation of the Constantinopolitan Athena. A second miniature, a representation of Athena in a tenth-century copy of Oppian's *Cynegetica,* was also thought to derive from the statue. Here the image is not understood as a direct copy of the monument itself, but rather as a representation of the goddess that reflects the pose of the Constantinopolitan statue (Jenkins, 1951).

Subsequent study assumed (Thompson, 1959; Cutler, 1968) or at least did not reject (Mango, 1963) the Constantinopolitan presence of the Promachos until Linfert (1982) proposed that the statue in question was neither the Parthenos nor the Promachos, but a third Pheidian Athena referred to by Aristides, the Lemnia. Commissioned by the people of Lemnos for dedication on the Athenian Akropolis, the statue showed the goddess in a contemplative pose. As in the representations of the Parthenos and the Promachos, Athena wears the peplos and the aegis. Unlike these figures, however, she does not wear her helmet. Reconstructions of this statue place the helmet by her side or, alternatively, in her extended left hand. Her right hand carries a lance. Linfert argued that the Constantinopolitan statue must have been the Lemnia, claiming that Kedrenos's description of the statue as Lindian represented a corruption of the original Lemnian provenance.

Franz (1988) rejected Linfert's proposal to return to the association with the Promachos. Finally, Stichel (1988) in a radical departure from previous discussion rejected any association with Pheidias to suggest that the statue was an archaizing work of the Roman imperial age.

Jahn's introduction of Arethas into the Athena discussion forever changed the focus of scholarship. From that point on, the issue became one of precise identification with a great classical masterpiece, yet the available descriptive information either does not support any of the various claims or is inconclusive. Jahn's association with the chryselephantine Parthenos must be discarded on the basis of Choniates' reference to the bronze medium. Similarly identification with the Lemnia may be discounted if Harrison's (1988) suggestion that the statue was acrolithic is correct. Apart from the specific difficulty in reconciling medium, in each reference the pose and attributes mentioned are those of virtually any classical or postclassical representation of Athena. It is therefore impossible to associate the statue with any particular image of the goddess, much less the work of Pheidias. The same is true for the image in the eleventh-century miniature. Here the figure is clearly that of Athena, and it is indeed possible that the miniature shows the statue; however, the treatment of the form is so generic as to make a particular identification impossible.

The willingness to identify a Constantinopolitan Athena with one of the great works by Pheidias in the face of such flimsy documentation represents an interpretation of evidence based on two suppositions: 1) the primacy of Arethas as a text, and 2) the assumption that Byzantine authors looked at and thought about ancient statuary according to the same criteria as modern scholars. These points of view were the natural outgrowth of the nineteenth-century intellectual milieu in which Jahn, Führer, Gurlitt, and their successors first formulated these discussions. This period was a formative one for the study of art history in general and classical art history in particular. Identification of works of art and typological classification was a primary concern as scholars sought to establish a corpus for individual artists and their schools. The nineteenth century was, after all, the age in which the great statues of Athena were first identified and described. It was also an age that saw in fifth-century classical art the perfection of beauty. It is doubtless this sentiment, coupled with a desire for certainty, that led to the preference for Arethas and his clear attribution over the vagaries of Kedrenos's Lindian provenance.

If the Athena cannot be identified as Pheidian, how should Arethas's remark be understood? The attribution to Pheidias, although doubtless made with all due consideration, should be seen less as an assignation based on the understanding of Pheidias as an artist working in a particular style and more as an educated, if incorrect, guess. Based not on the study of ancient statuary but rather on textual information, Arethas's attribution represented the logical equation of a work known to have been of ancient manufacture with the name of an artist renowned for his images of Athena.

Constantine the Rhodian's claim for a Lindian provenance and that of Kedrenos after him are more difficult to interpret. Reinach considered the identification valid and attributed the specification of provenance and the omission of any reference to the pendant statue to the author's own sense of Rhodian pride. Although the designation of the Athena as Lindian in Constantine the Rhodian's poem is unique, it is one of three such assignations of provenance in Kedrenos who observed an additional two Lindian Athenas in the Augusteion (cat. no. 17) and the Lausos collection (cat. no. 152).

The sources do not state when the Forum Athena was added. Reinach assumed the dedication to be Constantinian; however, the Lindian provenance, if correct, suggests a later fourth-century installation date (cf. no. 17 for commentary). It is, however, possible that the association between the statue and Lindos is false, an interpolation based on the knowledge that there were other Lindian Athenas in the city, in which case a Constantinian dedication would make sense. The statue was destroyed in 1203.

*Bibliography:* Gilles (1561 bis) III. 4; Du Cange (1680) 2.9.1 (s.v. Senatus); Jahn, 1848; Zucker, 1887; Führer, 1892; Gurlitt, 1893; Blinkenberg, 1917–18; Jenkins, 1947: 31–33; Jenkins, 1951; Mango, 1959: 42–47, 56–60; Thompson, 1959: 61–72; Mango, 1963; Janin, 1964: 59–62, 73–77, 155–56; Cutler, 1968; Guilland, 1969: I, 81–82, 220–26, 230–32, III, 40–54, 99–121; Linfert, 1982; Linfert, 1989; Francis, 1984; Francis and Vickers, 1984; Franz, 1988: 74–77; Stichel, 1988: 155–64

## 108. ARTEMIS

*Par.* 8: see no. 106.

The statue appears to have been one of a pair with Aphrodite. Use of the present tense in the description suggests that it was still extant in the eighth century. Janin thought that the statues stood by the Senate in the Augusteion. Because of the reference to an execution, Cameron/Herrin propose that the Forum of Constantine is a more likely spot given its proximity to the Praetorium. They suggest further that the statue be identified with two figures of Athena mentioned by Hesychios (18);

however, those statues are more properly associated with the Augusteion (s.v.)

*Bibliography:* Janin, 1964: 156; Cameron/Herrin, 184

## 109. A AND B) COLUMN OF CONSTANTINE AND ITS STATUE (PLATES 19–23)

### Literary Testimonia:

Socrates I, 17:

In this manner then was the genuine cross discovered. The emperor's mother erected over the place of the sepulchre a magnificent church, and named it New Jerusalem, having built it facing that old and deserted city. There she left a portion of the cross, enclosed in a silver case, as a memorial to those who might wish to see it: the other part she sent to the emperor, who, being persuaded that the city would be perfectly secure where that relic should be preserved, privately enclosed it in his own statue which stands on a large column of porphyry in the forum called Constantine's at Constantinople. I have this from report indeed; but almost all of the inhabitants of Constantinople affirm that it is true. Moreover the nails with which Christ's hands were fastened to the cross (for his mother having found these also in the sepulchre had sent them) Constantine took and had made into bridle-bits and a helmet, which he used in his military expeditions. (Schaff and Wace)

Hesychios, 41:

After this [Constantine having assumed power], he built also a water system for the city. He erected two arches in the so-called Forum, and the famous porphyry column on which Constantine himself stands, who shines like the Sun God on the mountains over the citizens.

Malalas, 321:

He [Constantine] also built a large and very beautiful forum, and set up in the middle a marvelous column, all of porphyry. On this column he set up a statue of himself with seven rays on his head. He had this bronze statue brought from where it had

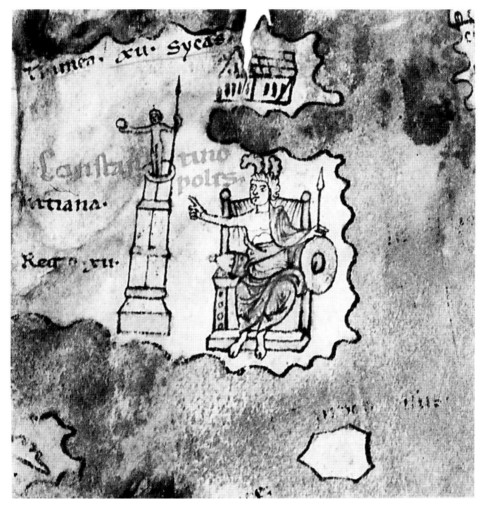

PLATE 19: Constantinopolis and the Column of Constantine from the *Tabula Peutingeriana* (Photo: from Bosio, 1983: fig. 22)

stood in Ilion, a city in Phrygia. Constantine took secretly from Rome the wooden statue known as the Palladion and placed it in the forum he built, beneath the column which supported his statue. Some of the people of Byzantion say that it is still there. (Jeffreys et al.)

*Chron. Pasch.* I, 528:

And he also built a Forum which was large and exceedingly fine; and he set in the middle a great porphyry column of Theban stone, worthy of admiration, and he set on top of the same column a

great statue of himself with rays of light on his head, a work in bronze which he had brought from Phrygia. The same emperor Constantine secretly took away from Rome the Palladion, as it is called and placed it in the Forum built by him, beneath the column of his monument, as certain of the Byzantines say who have heard it by tradition. (Whitby/Whitby)

*Chron. Pasch.* I, 573:

416. Indiction 14, year 8 the 7th consulship of Theodosios II Augustus and that of Palladios. In

PLATE 20: Column of Constantine, *The Freshfield Album*, Trinity College Library, Cambridge, MS 0.17.2, folio 1 (The Master and Fellows of Trinity College Cambridge)

the time of these consuls a great stone tore away during the night from the lower stonework of the porphyry column on which stood Constantine the great emperor in the month Dystrus, on the 5th day before the Kalends of April [28 March], as Tuesday was dawning. And in the same year all the drums of the same column were bound. (Trans. Whitby/Whitby)

PLATE 21: Bronze statuette of Constantine, The National Museum of Denmark, Copenhagen (Photo: The National Museum of Denmark)

Theophanes, 125–26:

[AM 5970, AD 477/8]

Zeno, 4th year – Valas, 2nd year – Simplicius 9th year – Akakios, 7th year – Anastasios, 2nd year – Timothy Salophakialos, bishop of Alexandria again (4 years), 1st year – Stephen, bishop of Antioch (3 years), 1st year. In this year there was a terrifying earthquake in Constantinople

PLATE 22: Cameo showing Constantine with the Roman Palladion (Photo: from Bruns, 1948: fig. 11)

PLATE 23: Column of Constantine, Istanbul (Photo: G. Berggren, Deutsches Archäologisches Institut, Istanbul, Institute Negative Number R 29.046)

on 25 September of the first indiction, and many churches, houses and porticoes collapsed to the ground and countless numbers of people were buried. The globe of the statue in the Forum also fell and so did the statue of Theodosios the elder, the one on the column of the Tauros, and also the inner walls for a considerable distance. The earthquake lasted a long time, so that the city began to stink. (Mango/Scott)

Theophanes, 222:

[AM 6034, AD 541/2]

Justinian, 15th year – Chosroes, 17th year – Vigilius, 4th year – Menas, 5th year – John, 8th year – Paul, 2nd year – Ephraim, 15th year. In this year, in October of the 5th indiction the great plague broke out in Byzantium. In the same period the feast of the Presentation of the Lord was first celebrated in Byzantium on 2 February. On 16 August of the same 5th indiction, a great earthquake occurred in Constantinople, and churches, houses, and the city wall collapsed, especially the part near the Golden Gate. The spear held by the statue which stands in the Forum of the holy Constantine fell down as well as the right arm of the statue of the Xerolophos. Many died and there was great fear. (Mango/Scott)

George Harmatolos, 500:

After he first built the palace and the Hippodrome and the two great ports and the forum in which he placed a monolithic porphyry column, very admirable, that he had brought from Rome, he placed on it a statue which he had carried from the city of Troy in Phrygia. Above its head it has seven rays. Because of its large size and weight it took three years to transport the column by ship. From the sea to the forum it took one year, and the monarch was visiting the place very often and giving away innumerable gold coins to the crowd. After that he placed in the foundations the twelve baskets, blessed by Christ, along with fragments from the Holy Cross and holy relics to support and protect the city. This magnificent man then erected the admirable monolithic column with much care, mastery, strength, and wisdom.

Patria II, 45:

Concerning the porphyry column. The Palladion and many other miracle-working devices were placed beneath the column in the forum. And the circumference of the forum in which that column stood which had been brought from Rome was equal to the circumference of the base of Constantine's crown. The statue of Apollo, called Helios, was placed there by Constantine the Great in his

own name, with nails in its head (as rays). These were said to be from the crucified Christ.

Leo Gramm. 87:

He founded the city of Byzantium in the 21st year before he moved, the 25th year of his reign and the 5837th year from the Creation of Adam. He came to Byzantium leading holy and illustrious fathers, so that the city, which he founded, would be inaugurated. He built a palace, a hippodrome, two porticoes and a forum in which he set up a column made from a single stone and entirely of porphyry. He brought this column from Rome and he furnished it with sculptured bronze bands. He placed on top of this same column a statue of himself with an inscription on the very rays: To Constantine who shines as the equal of the sun. It was a work of Pheidias and it was brought from Athens.

Leo Gramm. 254:

A great earthquake having occurred at the festival of Hagios Polyeuktos, the earth shook for forty days and forty nights, and it was then that the globe of the statue in the forum and the most sacred Theotokos of the Sigma fell, so that all who were chanting died.

Kedrenos I, 564:

The porphyry column stood in the Forum, erected by Constantine himself, and his column stood there and on it four lines were written:

You, O Christ are the lord and ruler of the world
    I your servant dedicate this city to you.
With this scepter and with all the power of Rome.
Guard it, save it from all harm.

Beneath the column lay the twelve baskets.

Anna Komnena, Alexiad, XII, 4:

Nearly in the middle of the Forum of Constantine there was a bronze statue looking towards the East standing on a conspicuous purple pillar and holding a scepter in its right hand, and in its left a sphere fashioned of bronze. This was said to be the statue of Apollo, but the inhabitants of

Constantinople used to call it Anthelios, I believe. But that great one among kings, Constantine, the father and master of the city, changed its name to his own, and called it a statue of the Emperor Constantine. Yet the name given originally to the statue persisted, and everybody called it Anelios or Anthelios. Suddenly a very violent southwest wind arose, blew this statue off its pedestal and hurled it to the ground, the sun was then in the sign of the Bull. (Dawes)

Zonaras III, 17–18:

Thus he built temples and adorned the city with many things, among them the round porphyry column which he, so they say, brought from Rome and set up in the forum, which is paved with stone, for which reason it is known as the Plakoton. And he erected to himself the bronze statue which is a wonder to behold both because of its artistry and its size. This statue was indeed colossal, and again displayed the perfection of a skilled hand which formed it completely by inspiration. It is said that the statue portrayed Apollo and was brought here from Ilion in Phrygia. That divine emperor placed the statue there, giving it his own name, and on its (the statue's) head he placed one of the nails which fastened the body of our Lord to the Holy Cross; and the same statue remained on the column until our time. It fell, however, during the reign of Alexios Komnenos when a violent and dreadful wind blew and lightening struck and it fell from its place destroying it along with several bystanders.

Michael Glykas, 464:

In the same vein he brought the column made from a single piece that stands in the Forum to Constantinople from Rome; and he placed a statue of himself on it, which came from Heliopolis in Phrygia.

Nikephoros Kallistos VII. 49:

In what is today called the Forum of Constantine, he erected the large porphyry column, which he brought from Rome. On this column he placed a

bronze statue of himself of which the Holy Cross was fixed with the following inscription: To you, Christ, O Lord, I dedicate this city. The column stood on four strong arches in the center of the circular forum and beneath the base of the column the 12 baskets, and the seven baskets and seven loaves which Christ blessed and with which he fed the multitude, plus Noah's ax, which he used to build the ark, the emperor placed under his seal. And all of these things appear there still as the undisturbed treasure of the city.

Tzetzes, *Chil.* VIII, 192:

Pheidias was a student of Geladus from Argos, who created the statue of Herakles from Melite in Attica. Pheidias is descended from the Athenians, and makes bronze statues. I can speak at length about his art, about the ivory statue of Athena which is in Athens, about the gold hammered statue of Zeus in Olympia, and about the bronze statue of Athena, similar to that of Hera, about the statue of Apollo, the statue of Herakles who carried the Augean manure, and a myriad of his works; some of which are buried, and others of which have been prey to time. Of course some of them have survived and are in the Hippodrome and the Forum, while the head of Apollo is in the palace.

**Graphic Evidence:**

*Constantinopolis: Detail from the Tabula Peutingeria* (Plate 19)

12th or 13th century after a late 4th- or 5th-century original Vienna, National Library, MS Vindobon. 324

*Bibliography:* Bosio, 1983: 87–88; Hermann, 9 n. 2; Hotz, 215; Levi, 1967: 153–54; Wartena, 1927

*Anonymous drawing, 1574* (Plate 20)

MS 0117.2, Trinity College Library, Cambridge

*Bibliography:* Freshfield

*Melchior Lorichs, drawing of column base, 1561*

Royal Museum of Fine Arts, Copenhagen

*Bibliography:* Becatti, 1960: 86f; Delbreuck, 1932: 141 ff; A. Grabar, 1936: 54, n. 1, p. 271 f; Harbeck, 1910; Klauser, 1944: 144; Mango, 1965

*Two anonymous watercolors, 17th century*

Dresden, Kupferstichkabinett

*Bibliography:* Delbreuk, 1932: 142–43, figs. 58, 59

*Anonymous engraving, late 16th century*

Cod. 8628, National Library, Vienna (fig x)

*Bibliography:* Mango, 1993

## Sculpture:

*Bronze statuette of Constantine* (height 50 cm.) (Plate 21)

Copenhagen, National Museum, no. 8040

*Bibliography:* Mackprang, 1938; L'Orange, 1962: 101–05; Calza, 1972: 3/234–35; L'Orange 1984: 122

*Cameo with Constantine* (Plate 22)

Lost, originally in Cathedral treasury, Cammiz, Poland

*Bibliography:* Bruns, 1948: 16; Calza, 1972: 3/235

## 109 A. THE COLUMN (PLATE 23)

Although greatly altered from its original state, the column still stands on what is now the north side of modern Istanbul's Divan Yolu. Six porphyry drums wreathed with laurel crowns at their joins and braced intermittently with bronze rings rise to a height of 34.80 meters from a bulbous, masonry base to a built capital.

The column probably was erected in 328 (*Chron. Pasch.* 528), although the date may vary by a few years (Mango, 1985: 25). In 416 a piece of one of the lower drums broke off (*Chron. Pasch.* 573), occasioning the addition of the bronze braces. Fires damaged the column in the fifth and sixth centuries (Müller-Wiener, 255).

A statue originally surmounted the column (see below, no. 109b). This figure fell together with the crowning capital, during a wind-storm in 1105 (Glykas, 617 and 694). Manuel I Komnenos (1143–80) restored the column by adding the built masonry capital. This restoration also may have included the addition of four arches around the base (Mango, 1981: 108). Nicephoras Kallistos (VII, 45) describes a set of four arches, one on each side, that frame the base. These arches may have been added as buttresses. None of the drawings of the column records these arches; however, excavations of the area by Mamboury (1936) in the 1920s and early 1930s revealed patterns of wear and tear consistent with their placement. Squared cuttings at the corners of the top steps on all four sides led to the conclusion that the cuttings had been made to accommodate the supporting piers of the arches described by Nicephoras. It is not clear why the drawings do not show the arches. Perhaps they were removed before the sixteenth century. Fires and earthquakes further affected the stability of the column in the sixteenth and seventeenth centuries (Müller-Wiener), and in 1779 (Mango, 1981) when the masonry base visible today was added to prevent the column's collapse.

Sometime before the ninth century when it is referred to during the reign of Leo VI (886–912), a chapel known as the Oratory of Constantine was added to the base. Mango (1993: 110) suggests that it may have been added during the period of Iconoclasm to house relics associated with the column. The exact nature of the chapel is unclear. Mamboury suggested that the four arches demarcated the chapel; however, references to the shrine in the *Book of Ceremonies* mention a doorway and a window. Mango (1981: 107) therefore concludes that the chapel was built into the base on the north side.

Graphic evidence and archaeological research allow the reconstruction of the original column prior to the loss of its capital and the addition of the new base. Three general views show that the shaft was comprised of seven drums that rose above a square column base that was in turn supported on a square sockle rising from a stepped base. Then as now the joins between drums were concealed by a series of rings in the form of laurel wreaths which may have been gilded (Becatti, 86). Although there is a tradition that the column once had as many as eight, nine, or ten drums, Mango (1965: 311–12) has demonstrated that there were never more than seven. Further on the strength of the column base profile as revealed in the surviving drawings, he suggests that the capital would have been one of the Corinthian order (Mango 1965: 313). The colossal scale and late date of the monument also make this suggestion likely.

The base itself was square, sat on a stepped sockle, and appears to have been in white marble. Drawings consistently show four stairs; however, excavation around the base in 1929–30 (Dalleggio D'Alessio) showed that there were actually five. Since the earliest drawing dates to the late sixteenth century (Plate 20), this difference may reflect the raising of the Forum's ground level over time. The stairs were 8.35 meters square at their upper level. The base itself was 3.80 meters square. The top stair thus functioned as a wide platform about 4.55 meters on each side. This proportional relationship is generally not observed in the drawings. Drawings do show, however, that the base was decorated at its lower level with carved moldings. One drawing shows a single band of fleurons along the lower edge of the base where it joins the step platform. Another shows a more complex sequence of moldings. The fleurons occupy the same position. Above them three fascia run below a rinceau frieze. The Freshfield drawing and the Dresden watercolors depict the flat sides of the base as undecorated; however, a drawing by Melchior Lorsch shows an elaborately composed relief in which an imperial bust framed by a laurel wreath floats against the neutral ground between representations of victories and tribute bearers. Pointing to a Turkish engraving that shows a shack built up against the edge of the column, Mango (1981: 1) explains the absence of any depiction of the relief by the fact that it may have been obscured.

The combined evidence suggests that when erected in the fourth century the column had seven drums that rose to support a Corinthian column with a statue on top. Its height was 37 meters. The base was 3.80 meters square and

carved on the north side with the relief composition facing the entrance to the Senate. A stepped sockle made up of five stairs supported the whole.

The column is said to have come from Rome (*Patria*, Leo Grammaticus, Zonaras, Glykas, and Nicephoras Callistus). Delbreuck (1932: 144) and Fowden (1991: 124) agree, and suggest that it was part of a monument to Diocletian that was never realized. Noting the late date of the first reference, Mango (1993, 5–6) finds the tradition suspicious and argues instead that the material could have been ordered directly by Constantine from the quarry at the Mons Porphyreticus, which was still operational. Either scenario is possible, but none is demonstrable in any absolute way. Whatever the case, it is clear that the pieces of the column were designed to go together. Whether ordered from the quarry or brought from Rome it is likely that its erection in Constantinople represented its first use. Thus, the column was neither antique nor reused in the sense of other monuments in the city.

*Bibliography:* Gilles (1561 bis) III, 3; Du Cange 1. 24. 6; Schede, 1929; Dalleggio D'Alessio, 1930; Delbreuck, 1932; Mamboury, 1936; Becatti, 1960: 84–88; Firatli, 1964: 207–08; Janin, 1964: 77–79; Mango, 1965; Müller-Wiener, 1977: 255–56; Mango, 1981; Fowden, 1991; Mango, 1993

## 109 B. THE BRONZE STATUE

The porphyry column was the vehicle for the display of a colossal bronze statue outfitted with a rayed crown, a lance, and a globe (Malalas, *Chron. Pasch.* 528, Anna Comnena, and Zonaras). Early sources agree that the figure represents Constantine. Later texts describe the figure as Apollo Helios (*Patria*) or Apollo (Anna Komnena, Zonaras) and with the exception of the *Patria* reject identification with the emperor. Zonaras and Tzetzes attribute the figure to Pheidias. There is no consensus on provenance: references are to "Ilion in Phrygia" (Malalas, Zonaras), Ilion (*Chron. Pasch.*), and "Heliopolis in Phrygia" (Glykas). The figure was put in place in 328 (*Chron. Pasch.* 528) and was blown down during a storm in 1105 (Anna Komnena) at which point the head may have been salvaged from the mangled body and taken off to the palace (Tzetzes). Prior to its final destruction the statue suffered the loss of its attributes. The globe fell twice as the result of an earthquake (*Chron. Pasch.* 125–26; Leo Gramm.). The lance was likewise affected in an earthquake of 541–42 (*Chron. Pasch.* 222). It appears to have been replaced with a scepter (Kedrenos, Anna Komnena).

This information has made for lively discussion in the secondary literature. Gilles and Du Cange both identify the figure as an Apollo from Troy. Gilles does so unequivocally and in a manner that reflects his acquaintance with the later sources. Du Cange is more even-handed and surveys the full range of evidence before identifying the statue as an image of Apollo that was then given the name of Constantine. Unger (1879) identified the statue as one of Constantine-Sol, and suggested on the basis of Glykas's Heliopolitan provenance that the statue came not from Phrygia, but from the great temple of Sol at Heliopolis in Syria (Baalbek). Preger (1901) confirmed the solar association preferring to call the statue Helios. He rejected the Syrian provenance, however, in favor of Ilion, saying that the statue was not a work by Pheidias, as indicated by Zonaras and Tzetzes, but rather a later work of Hellenistic or Roman manufacture. Lathoud (1929) described the statue as Apollo as part of a larger discussion of the city's foundation in which he argued in favor of a pagan foundation. Karayanoupolis (1956) rejected any association with pagan gods to identify the image as the divine Constantine and confirm the Christian nature of the capital's foundation. Janin (1964) identified the statue as Constantine-Helios, noting, however, that the inscription recorded at the base of the column dedicated the city to Christ and that the two images combined confirm a compromise between pagan and Christian in the foundation of Constantinople. Dagron (1974) felt that there was no trace of doubt about an Apollonian identity, while Barnes (1981) rejected any such notion,

adding further that there was no pagan sculpture in Constantinople. Franz (1988) associated the figure with the only known bronze statue of Apollo by Pheidias, the Apollo Parnopius. Fowden (1991) interpreted the figure as a statue of Constantine–Apollo that incorporated the identity of Helios. Finally, Mango (1993) discussed the statue as an ambiguous figure of a god-emperor that he did not consider reused, but purpose made for Constantinople or another setting.

What was the statue in the Forum? The evidence itself, and particularly the early material, is firm in stating that the statue was an image of Constantine. It should thus be understood as such. Like all imperial statues, however, the figure was a presentation of the emperor. As such it chose to emphasize certain qualities. The question is, which ones and by what means?

The answer to these questions lies in the statue's appearance, an iconography that can be only partially reconstructed. Although there is no direct statement to the effect, the statue appears to have stood. As noted, Constantine wore the *corona radiata*, carried an orb in his left hand, a spear in his right. The latter was probably held upright, its lower end touching the ground. Although the attributes are well documented, there is no other information about the statue. It is not known, for example, if the figure was nude or draped.

Visual evidence offers some possible approaches to reconstruction. L'Orange (1962 and 1984) identifies a fourth-century bronze statuette (National Museum, Copenhagen, inv. 8040) (Calza, 1972) (Plate 21) with the Constantinopolitan image. A small figure with a rayed crown wears a full-length gown with long sleeves belted above the waist. A chlamys falls from the shoulders. A fourth-century cameo also has been associated with the statue (Plate 22). Originally in the treasury at Cammiz in Poland, the gem, which disappeared at the end of World War II, shows Constantine crowned with the *corona radiata* (Bruns, 1948). He wears military dress and carries a lance in one hand, the Palladion in another. Finally, the *Tabula*

*Peutingeria*, a thirteenth-century copy of a late-fourth- or early-fifth-century map, marks the location of Constantinople with two figures: an enthroned image of the city tyche and a depiction of the Column of Constantine (Plate 19). The column is shown in shorthand as a series of three drums in ever-decreasing scale surmounted by a statue that must be that of Constantine. The emperor is nude, and, in conformity with the texts, shows the figure with the globe in one hand, the lance in the other. He is, however, bareheaded, without the *corona radiata*.

The three different images show the emperor in three different guises. The Copenhagen statuette's long belted robe recalls the dress of Apollo Kitharoedos and suggests the solar connection that is so much a feature of modern discussion of the statue. The rayed crown, an attribute familiar from Hellenistic royal portraiture and later imperial portraiture, underscores this connection. In the case of the cameo, the effect of military dress is to evoke the time honored image of the soldier emperor and his qualities of *virtus*, an image with a long life in Roman imperial tradition beginning with Augustus. Here the rayed crown may well refer to Helios and the solar connections stressed periodically in Constantine's dynastic imagery. The long history of the crown's use indicates, however, that it is not exclusively linked to a solar context. It may also be intended to convey a more general notion of radiance and with it the sense of imperial epiphany (Smith, 1988: 33). Finally, the nude figure of the *Tabula Peutingeriana* with its orb and lance recalls Hellenistic ruler portraits and imperial statues of the late second and third centuries in which nudity expressed the above human status of the ruler (Smith). The distancing effect of undress would have been confirmed by the presence of the orb and lance describing the king as an all-powerful ruler. The image of the king with scepter or spear is also one known to go back to Alexander, and it was used regularly after his death to convene the notion of royalty and power (Smith). Although missing in the drawing, the rayed crown would have complemented the picture by once again evoking the solar dynastic connections and the sense of imperial radiance and revelation.

Although each of these figures might reasonably claim to reproduce the general characteristics of the Constantinian statue, the *Tabula Peutingeria* image has the best claim to do so. Absence of the rayed crown should not be seen as suspicious as it doubtless represents the kind of shorthand rendering that was so much a feature of medieval copying. In addition, the *Tabula Peutingeriana* figure also is consistent with Constantinian iconography. Although no freestanding nude sculptures of the emperor survive, he appears half-draped in the colossal statue from the Basilica Nova and coin issues imply his nudity in some of the profile portraits by showing his neck and shoulder bare (Kantorowicz). Further, even though the armed cameo image is consistent with Constantinian imagery and Mango (1993) proposed that the statue wore the cuirass, the iconography of nudity is more appropriate to a civic dedication such as this than is armor (Smith). The least well equipped of the representations to reproduce the Forum statue is probably the Copenhagen statuette. Although the figure may well represent Constantine, the image is something of an anomaly in the Apollonian cast of its dress. No other images of Constantine are known in this guise, nor is it the kind of imagery that has any real tradition in the public imperial sphere.

All other authors assume that the statue was a reused antiquity, save for Mango (1993) who believes that it was made purposely for the Forum or another similar project. Given the fact that several of the known monumental portraits of the emperor in marble have been recut from earlier images, the possibility that the statue was reused is distinct. It is, however, less likely, as has been claimed (Unger, Preger, Fowden), that the figure was a reused statue of Apollo or Helios. It is far more likely that the statue was a reshaped imperial image or, as is more likely, a Hellenistic ruler portrait. These statues are known to have come equipped with attributes similar to that of the Constantinian statue, including the rayed crown (Smith). The bronze medium claimed for the statue suggests further that it was an honorific dedication rather than any kind of cult figure, as the latter were generally made in marble (Smith).

*Bibliography:* Gilles (1561 bis) III, 3; Du Cange (1680): I.24.6; Unger, 1879; Preger, 1901; Lathoud, 1929; Bruns, 1948: 16; Karayannoupolis, 1956; Becatti, 1960: 84–88; L'Orange, 1962: 101–05; Janin, 1964: 78–97; Mango, 1965; Calza, 1972: 3/235; Dagron, 1974: 38; Barnes, 1981: 222; L'Orange, 1984: 122; Franz, 1988; Fowden, 1991; Mango, 1993

## 110. DOLPHIN

Istanbul Archaeological Museum, no. 5554

The fragmentary remains of a marble dolphin were found in the area of the Forum during a recovery excavation in 1963. The head and body of the dolphin are preserved to the tail, which is broken. Barsanti (1990) associates the figure with the "gilded sirens" mentioned in *Patria* II 45 (see no. 112, Hippocamps). Although it is possible that the statues were part of the group with the sirens, it is not likely that the figures were the same as there are distinct differences in iconography.

*Bibliography:* Firatli, 1964; Barsanti, 1990: 34

## 111. ELEPHANT

*Par.* 17 (*Patria* II, 102a):

In the same forum also stood an awe-inspiring statue of an elephant, in the area on the left near the great statue. This manifested a strange spectacle. For once there was an earthquake and the elephant fell over and broke one back foot. The soldiers of the Prefect (for the forum falls under their sphere of duty) shouted to each other and came running up to reerect it, and found inside the same elephant all the bones of a complete human body, and a small tablet, which had written at the top, "Not even in death am I separated from the holy maiden Aphrodite." The Prefect added this to the public treasury for coins, in addition to the above cases. (Cameron/Herrin)

The elephant stood near the "great statue," that is, the stylite figure of Constantine. Cameron/Herrin believe the figure to have been made of stone. *Patria* II, 103 attributes the installation of the elephant and other statues to Constantine the Great.

*Bibliography:* Cameron/Herrin, 193

## 112. HIPPOCAMPS

*Par.* 15:

⟨In⟩ the Forum on the right part of the eastern side, he received twelve statues of porphyry and other marbles and twelve sirens which most people call gilded sea horses. The Emperor in our day moved three of them into the region of St. Mamas, but the other four are preserved in place up to the present day. (Cameron/Herrin)

The statues are said to have numbered twelve at their initial installation during the reign of Constantine I. Reference to gilding suggests that the statues were bronze. Only seven of the original twelve survived into the eighth century. Of these, three are reported to have been moved to the region of San Mamas during the reign of a Constantine. Cameron and Herrin (191) take this to be a reference to Constantine V (741–75).

Although the text refers to the figures first and foremost as sirens, the alternative identification of the figures with sea horses suggests that the statues actually represented a type of marine creature known as the hippocamp. In ancient iconography the siren is a creature with a female head and torso, bird legs and wings. Hippocamps, by contrast, were sea creatures with the head and forelegs of a horse and the finny, spiraling tail of a marine snake, a typology that is consistent with identification as a sea horse.

Hippocamps appear regularly in Greek and Roman art as part of the larger composition of the marine thiasos, a group depicting Poseidon, Thetis, and often Achilles with attendant sea creatures (Lattimore, 1976: plates XVIII, XIX). The statues may have been part of a similar display as there was a large nymphaeum on the south side of the Forum (Kedrenos: see earlier), which could easily have served as the setting.

## 113. JUDGMENT OF PARIS

Niketas Choniates, 648:

Because they were in want of money (for barbarians are unable to sate their love of riches), they covetously eyed the bronze statues and consigned these to the flames. The brazen Hera standing in the Forum of Constantine was cast into a smelting furnace and minted into coins; her head could barely be carted off to the Great Palace by four yokes of oxen. Paris Alexander, standing with Aphrodite and handing to her the golden apple of Discord, was thrown down from his pedestal and cast on top of Hera. (Magoulias)

Although described as three ostensibly independent figures, the statues of Hera, Paris, and Aphrodite together with the reference to the Apple of Discord indicate that the group's intended subject was the Judgment of Paris. This iconography was introduced in the fifth century B.C. and remained popular into Late Antiquity. It showed Paris as a young man among the goddesses rather than fleeing from them or in procession as had been the case in pre-fifth-century representations (*LIMC*, s.v. "Paris").

The group was bronze, as indicated by the fact that the statues were tossed into a cart to be hauled away to the smelting furnace in 1204. That at least one of the statues, the Hera, was of monumental, even colossal scale is indicated by the reference to the difficulty incurred in carting the head away.

*Bibliography:* Mango, 1963: 68

## 114. PALLADION

### Literary testimonia:

Prokop. *De Bello Goth* I, 15:

The city (Beneventum) was built in antiquity by Diomedes, the son of Tideos, when, after the fall of Troy, he was exiled from Argos. He had left to the city, as an emblem, the teeth of the Kalydonian boar, which his uncle Meleager had won as

a hunting trophy, and these are still there, very interesting to see, because they are not smaller than three palms in circumference and curved like a half moon. It is further said that Diomedes met Aeneas, the son of Anchises, there when he was coming from Troy and, in obedience to an oracle, gave him the statue of Athena, which he himself had taken away as a spoil, together with Odysseus when the two of them had gone to spy inside of Troy before the city was conquered by the Greeks. It is in fact said that after that undertaking, Diomedes, having fallen ill, wanted to know in what way it was possible to get well and the oracle responded that he would not be freed from his sickness until he had restored the statue to a citizen of Troy. In what part of the world the statue is now, the Romans say that they do not know. But still in our times these show a copy of it, sculptured in marble, which is at the Temple of Fortune, in front of the bronze statue of Athena, which is, however, outside the temple under the open sky. The marble copy represents a warrior who holds in her hand the lance as if to fight, but at the same time has a long tunic to her feet. The face does not look like those of Greek statues of Athena, but it is rather similar to the figures that the ancient Egyptians created. The Byzantines thus say that this statue was brought by the emperor Constantine to the Forum which bears his name and set up there. But now enough about this subject. (Dewing)

Malalas, 320: see no. 109.

*Chron. Pasch.* 528: see no. 109.

*Patria* II, 45: see no. 109.

### Visual evidence:

Cameo with Constantine: see no. 109 (Plate 22).

Malalas and *Chron. Pasch.* report that Constantine placed the Roman Palladion in the Forum. Although many cities claimed the Palladion, the Roman image was considered to be *the* Palladion, an ancient wooden guardian statue of the armed Athena that was associated first with Troy and its fortunes and later with Rome and its destiny.

The Palladion was an image of divine origin. Said to have fallen to Troy from heaven, it was kept in the citadel as a guarantee of the city's safety. Odysseus and Diomedes carried the statue away, thus creating the conditions for the city's sack (Ovid, *Fasti* 6, 419–60, Dion. Hal., 1, 68–9). Roman tradition states that Aeneas rescued the Palladion and brought it to Lavinium. From there it was taken to Rome (Dion. Hal.) where it was kept in the inner sanctum of the Temple of Vesta (Livy 26.27.14). The cult of Vesta expressed the permanence of Rome, a notion bound up with the presence of the Palladion. Augustus is thought to have underscored this notion by placing the Palladion itself or its copy on the Palatine where he had built a small shrine. Herodian (1.14.4) reports that it was still in the Temple of Vesta in A.D. 191, having been saved from numerous fires. Epigraphical evidence (*CIL* X, 6441) suggests that the Palladion or its copy was still in situ on the Palatine hill in the fourth century (*EAA*, s.v. "Palladio"). The Temple of Vesta was closed by Theodosios in 394 (*NTDAR*, 412).

The Palladion or its copy is shown on the coinage of Galba (*RIC* 1.206) and reflected generally in the appearance of several bronze statuettes. It is also described by Apollodoros (*Biblio.* 3, 12, 3). Athena stands in a rigid frontal pose, her feet together. Her dress falls in stiff pleats to the ground. She wears a helmet and her raised right arm carries a lance or spear. Although the designation Palladion originally refers to a particular image of Athena, it eventually can refer to any image conceived in this rigid, Archaic mode (*EAA*, s.v. "Palladio").

Three sources claim the Palladion for Constantinople. Its Constantinopolitan history is attested first by Malalas, who also reports that the statue was wood and then, by the *Chron. Pasch.* Both authors state that the statue was brought from Rome by Constantine and placed in the Forum beneath his column. *Patria* confirms this claim, adding that it was placed there with other miracle-working objects.

If the inscription referring to the Palladion records its continued fourth-century presence in Rome, then it is certainly possible that Constantine brought the statue. It is not clear, however, where the statue would have been placed. All sources agree that it was beneath the column; however, it is not clear what this means. The statue might have been in the ground beneath the column or somewhere inside the column base.

The historiography of the statue is complex. Gilles (III, 3) and Du Cange (I, 24, 6) discussed the Palladion, identifying it with a statue that they claimed was still visible by the temple of the Roman Tyche. This passage is, however, completely derived from Prokopios, and neither the statue nor the temple, which these authors describe as visible, was extant at their time. Their assessment of the Palladion is, however, interesting because it is based on the later, more generic definition of the statue.

Later scholarship breaks with the tradition of Gilles and Du Cange to presume a more specific identification with the Roman Palladion. Preger (1901) and Janin (1964) both believe that the statue was brought to Constantinople, and that it had been placed beneath the column in an attempt to mollify pagan members of the aristocracy. Failure to find any evidence of the Palladion during the course of the few cursory excavations that took place at the site has led, however, to skepticism regarding its presence. Given the relatively late date of the early sources, Alan Cameron (1983) believes that references to the image represent a misinterpretation of Malalas that is in turn an effort at later mythmaking on the part of the Constantinopolitan clergy.

Although it is true that the first references to the statue are relatively late, the figure is consistent with other aspects of Constantinian iconography. The fourth-century Cammiz cameo (see earlier) showed the emperor with the Palladion in his hand, thus demonstrating the emperor's interest in Rome and its sacred talisman well before Malalas and *Chron. Pasch.* refer to its presence in Constantinople.

*Bibliography:* Gilles (1561 bis) III, 3; Du Cange, 1680: I 24.6; Preger, 1901: 17; Janin, 1964: 78; Cameron, 1983

PLATE 24: Tiberius, Istanbul Archaeological Museum (Photo: W. Schiele, Deutsches Archäologisches Institut, Istanbul, Institute Negative Number 78/5)

**Sirens:** *see* **Dolphin and Hippocamps**

### 115. THETIS/AMPHITRITE

Arethas, *Schol. Arist. Or.* 50t. III:

I believe this (viz. the Athena) is the one set up in the Forum of Constantine at the porch of the council chamber, or senate, as they call it now; facing it on the right hand side of the porch as you go in is Thetis the [mother] of Achilles with a crown of crabs. The common file of to-day call the Athena "Earth" and Thetis "Sea" being misled by the marine monsters on her head. (Jenkins)

Kedrenos I, 565:

On the open square in front of the Forum stand two statues: to the west that of Athena of Lindos wearing a helmet and the monstrous gorgon's head and snakes entwined about her neck (for so the ancients used to represent her image); and to the East, Amphitrite, with crab claws on her temples, which were also brought from Rhodes.

Kedrenos reports that the statue came from Rhodes. Identification is problematic. Arethas calls the figure Thetis, while Kedrenos identifies it as Amphitrite. Both identifications are made on the basis of the figure's crustacean crown, and both may be correct. On the basis of attribute, it is likely that the statue was originally one of Amphitrite. Context suggests, however, that this figure was intended to depict Thetis.

The crustacean crown suggests identification with Amphitrite, as known representations of Thetis show her without the crown. By contrast, several two-dimensional representations of Amphitrite are consistent with the described iconography. Third-century mosaic representations from North Africa (*LIMC*, s.v. "Amphitrite") show the nereid with a crustacean crown in the manner described by both Arethas and Kedrenos, as do third-century B.C. coin types (*LIMC*, s.v. "Amphitrite"). The crustacean crown also suggests a date of manufacture for the figure in the later Hellenistic or Roman period when the marine aspect of Amphitrite's history was emphasized and she even became a personification of the sea (*LIMC*, s.v. "Amphitrite").

Although identification with Amphitrite is consistent with the statue's described iconography, context suggests that the figure was actually intended to represent Thetis. In favor of this identification is the fact that the other figures in the Forum with which the statue was displayed depicted the Judgment of Paris (cat. no. 113), an event that took place at the wedding of Peleus and Thetis. If this identification as Thetis is correct, then the statue affords a particularly interesting example of reuse in that it demonstrates how extant figures could be appropriated and

reinterpreted to suit the iconographic needs of the collection.

## 116. TIBERIUS (PLATE 24)

Istanbul Archaeological Museum, no. 5555

The head (0.263 m × 0.230 m × 0.199 m) is of white marble. It is broken off at the neck, and looks to the left. The features are those of Tiberius: a square head and jaw with thin lips and a sharp, high-ridged nose. A cap of hair frames the face. It is summarily worked with sharp, broad strokes in the area around the brow. The back of the head has been worked with a chisel to obliterate any details.

The head was found during a recovery excavation in the area of the Forum in 1963. It is not clear from the initial report whether it was found at the level of the pre-Constantinian necropolis or above the paving of the fourth-century Forum. Barsanti believes that it was recarved in the fourth century, which would therefore indicate Constantinian reuse.

*Bibliography:* Firatli, 1964: 11–12; Inan/Alföldi-Rosenbaum, 1979: 68; Barsanti, 1990: 35

# FORUM OF THEODOSIOS/FORUM TAURI

## 117. EQUESTRIAN STATUE

*Anth. Gr.* XVI, 65:

On a statue of the Emperor Theodosios:

Thou didst spring from the East to mid heaven, gentle-hearted Theodosios, a second sun, giver of light to mortals, with Ocean at they feet as well as the boundless land, resplendent on all sides, helmeted, reining in easily, O great-hearted King, thy magnificent horse, though he strives to break away. (Paton)

*Chron. Pasch.* I, 565:

In the time of these consuls was set up a great statue of Theodosios Augustus in the Theodosian

Forum in the month of Lous, on Kalends of August. (Whitby/Whitby)

## Patria II, 47:

Concerning the area of the Tauros. In the Tauros there is a statue of Theodosios the Great. Initially it was made of silver. There they received visitors from other states. In the very place known as Alonitzi there were palaces from antiquity and a Roman guesthouse. A statue of Theodosios stood on top of the large column. Statues of his sons were also set up; to the west, the statue of his son Honorios stood on a stone arch and to the east a statue of Arkadios stood on a stone arch above large, prominent square columns. In the center of the forum there is a huge equestrian statue. Some claim that it is that of Joshua the son of Navi. Others say that it is Bellerophon. It was brought from Antioch the Great. The square base of the equestrian statue is of carved stone and bears engraved scenes of the last minutes just before the Russian raid, which aimed to conquer the city. The giant hoof of the horse is above a bronze representation of a very small man, bound and kneeling. This to denote what is depicted here. Likewise there is a giant, hollow column both there and in the Xerolophos [Forum of Arkadios] telling tales of historical moments and the fall of the city.

## Constantine the Rhodian, 219–40:

A life-like statue of Theodosios, this brave knight, was erected again by him [Arkadios] to honor his father for his achievements and rare labors, as if he were returning victorious from battle at the time when he removed Maximus from power and expelled all the Scythians from Thrace. The observer loves the pride of the statue, which is made with fine copper craftsmanship showing movement of mane and hide. The horse bites the bit with urgency, its neck raised as a tower with sobriety and pride. Its hoof appears ready to move and it neighs and is alive as if bearing the victorious ruler. The rider is depicted with proud glance, stretching out his right hand and pointing in the direction of the achievements, that is the killing of the Scythians

and the slaughter of the barbarians, depicted on the large column, which he had erected.

## Kedrenos I, 566:

The statue of the rider that stands in the above district is Theodosios the Great, pointing his right hand towards the city and indicating the achievements carved on the column.

## Niketas Choniates, 643:

The Latins resolved to overturn the celebrated ancient palladia of the City stationed along the wall and moat to ward off the enemy who arrayed phalanxes and set up ambushes against her, especially those which had been set up against their race. Among the statuary made in the image of men and fashioned of bronze, which had earlier been removed from their pedestals and cast into the flames, they carefully examined the front left hoof of the brazen horse which stood on a four-sided white marble base in the Forum of the Bull; on its back it carried a hero of great strength and whose comeliness was well worth seeing. The horse was no less a wonder because of the perfection of its art; it was depicted without trappings, snorting and leaping with its ears pricked up as though at the sound of the war trumpet. Some claimed that the horse was Pegasos and its rider Bellerophontes; others contend that it was Joshua, the son of Nave [Nun], mounted on the horse, and that this was evident from the composition of the figure which extended his right hand in the direction of the chariot-driving sun and the moon's course to stay them in their procession and held a bronze globe in the palm of his left hand. Overturning the sole of the horse's hoof with hammers, they found lying underneath the image of a man pierced through with a nail and wholly covered by led, whom the majority conjectured to be of the Bulgar race or to represent a Lain, as it was broadcasted by all in the past. And this too was cast into the smelting furnace of the assayers of silver. (Magoulias)

## Niketas Choniates, 649:

Nonetheless, they gave over this most beautiful work to the smelters as well as an equestrian statue of heroic form and admirable size that stood on the trapezium shaped base in the Forum of the Bull. Some maintained that it was of Joshua, son of Nove, conjecturing that his hand was pointed towards the sun as it sank in the west, commanding it to stand still upon Gabaon. The majority were of the opinion that it was Bellerophontes, born and bred in the Peloponnesos, mounted on Pegasos; the horse was unbridled, as was Pegasos, who, according to tradition ran freely over the plains, spurning every rider, for he could both fly through the air and race over the land. But there was an ancient tradition which came down to us and which was in the mouths of all, that under this horse's front left hoof there was buried the image of a man which, as it had been handed down to some, was of a certain Venetian; others claimed that it was of a member of some other Western nation not allied with the Romans, or that it was of a Bulgarian. As the attempt was often made to secure the hoof, the statue beneath was completely covered over and hidden from sight. When the horse was broken into pieces and committed to the flames, together with the rider, the statue was found buried beneath the horse's hoof; it was dressed in the kind of cloak that is woven from sheep's wool. Showing little concern over what was said about it, the Latins cast it also into the fire. (Magoulias)

A statue of Theodosios I was erected in the Forum Tauri on August 1, 394 (*Chron. Pasch.* I, 565). Set up to commemorate the emperor's victory over the usurper Maximos in 388, it is thought to be one and the same as the equestrian figure of the emperor described in the sources above (Janin, Guilland, Mango, Müller-Wiener).

The statue, which was of silvered bronze (*Patria*), stood on a square base of white marble and faced east, towards the monumental center of Constantinople (Choniates). The rider sat astride a horse with his right hand extended towards the city (*Patria*, Choniates). The dedicatory epigram from the statue base (*Anth. Gr.*) reports that the emperor wore a helmet, and according to Choniates the horse, which was without tack, appeared to snort and leap, a description that suggests that it was rearing. References in the *Patria* and in the two passages by Choniates to figures beneath the horse's hooves suggest that one or more personifications may have figured in the composition at one point. By the thirteenth century, however, they were no longer visible, having been covered over with lead (Choniates), presumably in an attempt to stabilize the statue, which eventually was destroyed in 1204.

*Anth. Gr., Patria*, Constantine the Rhodian, and Kedrenos all identify the statue as one of Theodosios, with Kedrenos specifying Theodosios I. Choniates does not appear to be aware of the imperial identification. Instead, he repeats the information offered in the *Patria* that the statue was identified by some as Joshua, by others as Bellerophon on Pegasos. *Patria* states that the statue came from Antioch.

Modern discussion begins with Du Cange who mentions the statue and the various sources. Unger (1879) thought that the figure was the same as that on top of the forum's historiated column. Noting that the texts specify the existence of the rider long after the statue atop the column is reported to have fallen and that the statue stood on a square marble base, Reinach established the distinct identity of the equestrian figure.

Occasional commentary speculates on the absence or presence of personifications and their location. Kollwitz (1941: 9) took the reference to Earth and Ocean in *Anth. Gr.* to indicate relief carvings on the base. Janin (1964: 65) thought that the reference was to statues beneath the horse's hooves. Becatti (1960: 96) agreed that there may once have been a sculptured figure that was removed at an unspecified date; however, he preferred to see it as one of a trampled victor.

The equestrian statue has also been identified with the stylite representation of Justinian in the Augusteion. Lehmann (1959) proposed that a sixteenth-century drawing now in Budapest and that generally is thought to depict the statue of Justinian reflects the appearance of the Theodosian statue. She argued that the drawing copied a lost Theodosian medallion, which in turn reproduced the statue. Mango (1959 bis) and Becatti (1960) both rejected this suggestion, and confirmed the identification of the drawing with the destroyed statue of Justinian.

What was this statue of Theodosios? It is perfectly possible that it was a work of contemporary manufacture; however, noting the Antiochene provenance offered by the *Patria*, Becatti (1960: 97) suggested that the figure could have been a reused piece of sculpture brought from the east. The suggestion that the statue shows the horse rearing and tossing its head supports this claim. Surviving examples of Theodosian imperial sculpture tend to be much more stable in their aspect as do known statues of horses from the late Roman age. A rearing attitude is more characteristic of a late-classical or Hellenistic sculpture.

If the statue were reused, the identity of the original piece might be suggested by the identifications as Joshua or Bellerophon. It is, however, unlikely that either of these figures was intended to be the subject of the forum's equestrian monument, which would have been intended from the start as Theodosios. As an Old Testament figure, Joshua would have been an unlikely candidate for heroic representation in monumental sculpture. Moreover, the identification is based on identification of the statue's outstretched right arm with the Old Testament figure's attempt to stop the sun rising (Joshua 10.12–13). Mango (1963: 68) viewed this type of identification as an allegorical interpretation. Identification with Bellerophon indicates, however, that there was a range of possibility. Interestingly, the description has much in common with the iconography of Bellerophon and Pegasos as it survives. Two monumental sculptures are known and show great iconographic consistency: Bellerophon, clad in a flowing chlamys, sits astride a winged and rearing Pegasos while the Chimera crouches below (*LIMC*, s.v. "Bellerophon"). The type is of late classical or Hellenistic invention and is in many respects consistent with the elements in the Constantinian statue. The rearing pose and the figure

beneath the horse's hoof recall descriptions of the Forum Tauri statue. There is, however, a major difference: All representations of Pegasos show the horse with wings. None of the Byzantine descriptions make reference to wings. In fact the association with Pegasos is made not because of the distinctive physical features of the horse, but because of the animal's lack of riding tackle.

If the statue was not an image of Joshua or Bellerophon, it is possible that it was a reused image of a Hellenistic ruler, possibly even of Alexander himself, or a Roman emperor. Such a tactic would have found precedent in the Forum of Constantine's focal image, and may well have been intended as a way to make an equation between Constantine and Theodosios.

*Bibliography:* Du Cange (1680): II. 24. 7; Unger, 1879; Reinach, 1896; Kollwitz, 1941: 8–16; Mango, 1959 bis; Lehmann, 1959; Becatti, 1960: 88–112; Mango, 1963: 68; Janin, 1964: 64–68; Cutler, 1968: 118; Guilland, 1969: II, 56–59; Mango, 1985: 43–45

## 118. HADRIAN

*Patria* II, 38:

Equestrian statues of Arkadios and of his son Theodosios and of Hadrian stand near the statue of Theodosios the Great at the placed called the Tauros near the column.

Presumably the statue was a reused image from the second century. Details of Constantinopolitan history are not provided, but can be inferred on the basis of the Forum's own history. The Forum of Theodosios stood on the south branch of the Mese on the area that had once been the center of Byzantium's necropolis. Constantine is alleged to have first regularized the terrain, establishing a large plaza on the site (Preger, 176, 216; Müller-Wiener, 1977: 258). It was only under Theodosios I, however, that systematic development took place. This began in 386 with the erection of an historiated column commemorating the emperor's military campaigns and victories (Theophanes, 70). As the erection of a large spiral column suggests, the Forum appears to have been conceived on the model of the Forum of Trajan in Rome (Kollwitz). Like the Roman forum, the Constantinopolitan space included not only an historiated column, but also a large basilica. An official dedication took place in 393, and a year later, on 1 August 394, the equestrian statue was added (*Chron. Pasch.* 565) and this together with other imperial images stood in the Forum until 1204. The statue of Hadrian stood alongside of other imperial images and may have survived into the thirteenth century.

## GOLDEN GATE

### 119. ELEPHANTS

*Patria* II, 58:

About the elephants. The statues of elephants at the Golden Gate were brought from the Temple of Ares in Athens, by Theodosios the Younger, the builder of the land walls that extended to the Blachernae.

Kedrenos I, 567:

And the elephants which are on the Golden Gate are similar to those with which Theodosios once entered the city.

Robert de Clari:

Elsewhere in the city there is another gate which is called the Golden Gate. On this gate there were two elephants made of copper which were so large that it was a fair marvel. (Mc Neal)

A group of bronze elephants stood atop the Golden Gate. Robert de Clari put their number at two, noting also that the figures were bronze. Date of installation is not known, but presumably they were contemporary with the erection of the gate. They remained in situ until at least 1204. It is not known if they survived the crusader sack. Beyond these general remarks nothing is known of the particular details of their appearance and it is difficult to draw conclu-

sions about their date of manufacture; however, in general, monumental imagery of this type is of Roman imperial date. An Augustan coin issue of 18 B.C. depicts the emperor in an elephant biga, and a Tiberian coin shows divus Augustus riding in an elephant quadriga. Both coins are thought to reflect the monumental sculpture (Scullard, 1974: 255), placed in architectural settings such as triumphal arches. With respect to the Constantinopolitan gate, there is no direct mention of how the elephants were displayed. Schneider and Meyer-Plath (II, 41) refer to the elephants in their discussion of sources pertinent to the gate; however, they do not include the elephants in their reconstruction drawing (I, plate 19). By analogy to other Roman examples, it is likely that they were part of a larger biga or quadriga composition that would have been placed above the gate's central passageway.

The Golden Gate elephants are said to have come from the Temple of Ares in Athens. The provenance is not impossible, but at the same time it might simply be the result of the perceived antiquity of the sculpture. Franz (1988) believes the provenance unlikely as the temple was destroyed in the Herulian invasion of Athens (A.D. 267) and thereafter lay in ruins. She argues that the temple's identity may well have been forgotten. Further, it seems unlikely that statues so large and precious as the elephants would simply have been left to lie unused. Such sculpture is far more likely to have been taken and melted for coin or weapons.

*Bibliography:* Franz, 1988: 75

## HIPPODROME

### 120. ALEXANDER THE GREAT

*Anth. Gr.* XVI, 345:

Thou standest near victory and King Alexander, Thou who hast gathered the glory of both. (Paton)

An epigram in honor of the sixth-century charioteer Porphyrios refers to a nearby statue of Alexander. The Porphyrios statue is known to have stood on the *euripus*, and it is likely that the Alexander statue stood there as well. Several portrait types were created for Alexander during his life time, and these in turn were copied and modified in the Hellenisitc and Roman periods (Smith, 1988; Stewart, 1993). Although the hippodrome statue is likely to have been a work of Hellenistic or Roman manufacture, it is not possible to determine to which of the various Alexander types it conformed.

## 121. ANIMALS

Robert de Clari:

Upon this wall (*euripus*) there were figures of men and women, and of horses and oxen and camels and bears and lions and many other kinds of animals, all made of copper, and all so well made and formed so naturally that there is no master workman in heathendom or in Christendom, so skillful as to be able to make figures as good as these. (McNeal)

The statues, which stood on the *euripus*, were bronze. They were probably works of Hellenistic and Roman manufacture. Although not specifically stated, it is likely that the figures were destroyed in the Crusader sack of 1204.

## 122. ASS AND KEEPER

*Par. 64 (Patria II, 82):*

The riddle of Kranos is as follows: he asked the emperor if he could inspect the statues in the Hippodrome, and at the emperor's command he immediately chose one. The statue is shaped like a man with a helmet on its head, completely naked, but with its private parts covered. The philosopher asked, "Who set it up?" and a lector replied, "Valentinian put it here." And the philosopher said, "When did he add the donkey?" And when the other said, "At the same time," he said, "One day a donkey will be like a man, what a fate for a man to follow a donkey! May the works of the seer not come to pass!..."(Cameron/Herrin)

Niketas Choniates, 650:

Together with Herakles they pulled down the ass, heavy-laden and braying as it moved along, and the ass driver following behind. These figures had been set up by Caesar Augustus at Actium (which is Nikopolis in Hellas) because when going out at night to reconnoiter Antony's troops, he met up with a man driving an ass, and on inquiring who he was and where he was going, he was told, "I am Nikon and my ass in Nikandros, and I am proceeding to the camp of Caesar." (Magoulias)

A bronze statue depicted an ass being driven by its keeper. It was brought from Nikopolis in Greece and stood on the *euripus*. It was destroyed in 1204.

This statue appears to have been one and the same as a figure set up by Augustus in the aftermath of his victory at Actium. Suetonius (*Augustus*, 96) described the events commemorated by this unique subject:

At Actium, as he was going down to begin the battle, he met an ass with his driver, the man having the name Eutychus (Prosper) and the beast that of Nikon (Victory); and after the victory he set up bronze images of the two in the sacred enclosure into which he converted the site of his camp. (Rolfe)

*Bibliography:* Cameron and Herrin, 258; Guberti Bassett, 1991: 90

## 123. ATHENA (?)

*Par. 61 (Patria II, 78):*

In the ⟨area⟩ of the Kathisma, Justinian the Great rode ... on a bronze horse, after the victory over the Medes. The woman seated on a bronze chair in the Hippodrome – she too is above ⟨the imperial seat⟩ as we mentioned before – Herodian told me she is Verina ⟨the wife⟩ of Leo the Great. But as I have myself heard from many people, it is instead the statue of Athena from Hellas, and this I believed. (Cameron/Herrin)

A seated female bronze identified as the empress Verina or Athena stood above the *kathisma*.

### 124. AUGUSTUS

*Par.* 60 (*Patria* II, 73):

In the Hippodrome statues were set up which came from Rome, as many as 60, among which was a statue of Augustus as is told, but not written down. (Cameron/Herrin)

The figure was probably an imperial portrait made during Augustus's lifetime. The statue is reported to have come from Rome, but there is no mention of a specific date of importation. Use of the past tense and the reference to an oral tradition reporting the figure's existence suggests that the Augustus was no longer standing in the eighth century.

### 125. BOAR, KALYDONIAN

*Anth. Gr.* XV, 51:

Archias, On the Caledonian Boar.
It is of bronze, but see what strength he contrived to show, the sculptor of the boar, molding a living beast with the bristles standing up on its neck, with sharpened tusks, grunting and darting terrible light from its eyes, all its lips wet with foam. No longer do we marvel that it destroyed a chosen host of demi-gods. (Paton)

Niketas Choniates, 519:

He [Alexios Angelos] found his wife Euphrosyne in no way content with keeping within doors, but playing the man against the seditionists and demagogues and unraveling the machinations woven by a certain Konstostephanos like the threads of Penelope. These things would not have been held in contempt, nor would they have excited wonderment from afar, had they been bound by limitations, but the empress's mad delusions and excessive zeal led her to believe that by inquiring diligently into the future, she could vitiate and dispel impending misfortunes even as the sun dissolves black clouds. In her predictions of things to come, she devoted herself to unspeakable rituals and divinations and practiced many abominable rites. She went so far as to cut off the snout of the

bronze Kalydonian boar which stands in the Hippodrome with its back bristling and advances with projecting tusks against a lion, and she conceived of having the back of the gloriously triumphant Herakles, Lysimmachos's [sic] most beautiful work, in which the hero holds his head in his hand and bewails his fate while a lion's skin is spread out over a basket, lacerated by repeated flogging. (Magoulias)

The statue, which was bronze, was destroyed in 1204. Specific identification of the boar as Kalydonian links the statue to the myth of Menander; however, given that the labors of Herakles figure prominently in the Hippodrome, it is possible that this statue was originally part of a group showing the hero in combat with the Erymanthean boar.

### 126. JULIUS CAESAR (?)

*Patria* II, 81:

Appian, Dion, and other Roman historians say that when Caesar was crossing from Nicopolis to Durrachium, a great wave rose up and the pilot was at a total loss and was also ignorant that he was transporting Caesar, for Caesar was veiled so that he might not be recognized. Uncovering himself, Caesar said to the pilot, "Go against the wave! You bear Caesar and Caesar's fate!"

Although the text makes no reference to an actual statue it is possible that an image of Julius Caesar inspired the anecdote as the passage, which describes an event in Caesar's life (100–44 B.C.), occurs in the midst of a sequence of a series of descriptions of the Hippodrome and its monuments.

### 127. DIOCLETIAN

*Par.* 76 (*Patria* II, 73):

From the place called Nicomedia many statues came to Constantinople, including that of Diocletian which is preserved up to the present day in the Hippodrome, stooping in the middle of the so-called Kathisma. (Cameron/Herrin)

The reference is too generic to permit identification with a specific imperial typology; however, the figure would have been created in the late third century. Although the statue is reported to have come from Nicomedia, Cameron and Herrin (270) are skeptical about the claimed provenance, which they think may be a supposition derived from knowledge that that city served as Diocletian's capital.

The statue is said to have stood "in the middle" of the *kathisma*. Cameron and Herrin (270) reject the idea that the portrait would have stood inside the imperial box and suggest instead that it stood on the *euripus* opposite the box. There is no real reason to imagine why the figure of Diocletian could not have stood in the box itself. In this way the "living statue" that was the emperor himself could have mingled with representations of his righteous forebears. Alternatively, reference to placement "in the middle" might mean that the statue stood in the middle of the roof above the box.

*Bibliography:* Cameron/Herrin, 270

## 128. DIOSCURI

Zosimos II, 31:

In addition he decked out with every finery a hippodrome, a part of which he made a shrine to the Dioscuri; their statues even now may be seen standing in the porticoes of the hippodrome. (Buchanan/Davis)

Comparanda from sites in Italy and North Africa suggest several possible types for the Hippodrome works. Two colossal statues of the twins on the Quirinal (*LIMC*, s.v. "Dioskouroi/Castores" no. 77) in Rome exemplify the most common image of the Dioscuri in the Roman age. Said to be Roman copies of a fifth-century B.C. prototype, each statue shows one of the twins, heroically nude, in vigorous stance, with arms open, head flung back and eyes wide. Armor is cast at their feet, while a windswept chlamys curls over one arm and horses rear at their sides. Figures flanking the entrance to the Roman Capitol (Helbig 4, no. 1164; *LIMC*, s.v. "Dioskouroi/Castores" no. 57) represent a second type. Thought to be Roman classicizing creations of the first century A.D., these statues shows the twins in a calm, sober stance, their horses quiet by their sides. Like the Quirinal statues, the Capitoline twins stand in heroic nudity, chlamydes thrown over their shoulders. Unlike the Quirinal figures, however, the Capitoline Dioscuri sport the conical pilos cap. Dioscuri from Carthage and Baia (Ruesch, 1908: n 136bis) show a third type. Nude save for the chlamys and cap, these statues share the quiet, stately pose of the Capitoline figures, but exchange the full horses present in both Roman types for protomes at the divinities' feet.

Shrines to the Dioscuri were common in circus décor. There was no established location or typology for such shrines. An open-air altar was dedicated to them at the start of the race course in Olympia (Paus. V, 15, 5) as was the lap counter in the Roman Circus Maximus (Tertullian, *De Spect.* VIII). The Constantinopolitan shrine is reported to have stood in the porticoes, but the exact location of the porticoes themselves is not specified. There is, however, precedent for shrines to and images of the twins in similar locations at Sparta and Olympia (Paus. V, 15, 5 and II, 14, 7). The statues were brought by Constantine in the fourth century and could still be seen in the sixth when Zosimus wrote his history.

## 129. DRAGON

*Par. 62:*

Philip the dynast expounded many things in the course of which he passed this on: that while the dragon statue is an erection of Arcadius, it is a display of his brother Honorius, reigning in Rome. There not a few oracles have taken place, both before our time and up to the present day. (Cameron/Herrin)

Cameron and Herrin suggest that the passage may refer to the Serpent Column (see later); however, the association with Arkadios makes this unlikely. An alternative identification may be as Skylla (cat. no. 142) or a sphinx (cat. no. 143).

*Bibliography:* Cameron/Herrin, 252

### 130. EAGLE

Niketas Choniates, 651:

There was set up in the Hippodrome a bronze eagle, the novel device of Apollonios of Tyana, a brilliant instrument of his magic. Once, while visiting among the Byzantines, he was entreated to bring them relief from the snakebites that plagued them. Resorting to those lewd rituals whose celebrants are the demons and all those who pay special honor to their secret rites, he set up on a column an eagle, the sight of which gave pleasure to onlookers and persuaded any who delighted in its aspect to stay on like those held spellbound by the sound of the Sirens' song. His wings were aflap as though attempting flight, while a coiled snake clutched in his claws prevented its being carried aloft by striking out at the winged extremities of his body. But the venomous creature accomplished nothing, for, transfixed by the sharp claws, its attack was smothered, and it appeared to be drowsy rather than ready to give battle to the bird by clinging to his wings. While the snake breathed its last and expired with its venom unspent, the eagle exulted and, all but screeching out his victory song, hastened to lift up the serpent and bore it aloft to leave no doubt as to the outcome by the flashing of his eyes and the serpent's mortification. It was said that the very sight of the snake uncoiled and incapable of delivering a deadly bite frightened away, by its example, the remaining serpents in Byzantion, convincing them to curl up and fill their holes. This eagle's likeness was remarkable, not only because of what we have said but also because the twelve segments marked off in lines along the wings most clearly showed the hour of the day to those who looked upon it with understanding when the sun's rays were not obscured by clouds. (Magoulias)

A bronze statue of an eagle stood on top of a column, its wings outstretched, a coiled snake

in its claws. Said to have been erected in the pre-Constantinian era of the city's history, the statue is described as a gift of the Neopythagorian sage, Apollonius of Tyana. The history can only be a fantastic one, as Apollonius of Tyana lived in the first century and the Hippodrome was built at the end of the third century. This record of the statue's past is, however, interesting as it suggests the kinds of attitudes and interpretations that viewers brought to bear on such works in the later middle ages. With its focus on nature and violence, the subject matter, together with a formal interpretation that appears to emphasize movement in space, suggests a Hellenistic or Roman date of manufacture. The statue was destroyed in 1204.

### 131. ELEPHANT

Niketas Choniates, 650–51: see no. 135.

The elephant was bronze and appears to have been waving its trunk. It was destroyed in 1204.

### 132. GOOSE (PLATE 25)

London, British Museum, GRA1859.6-1.1

Said to have been found in the Hippodrome during the construction of a house. The figure stands 415 mm high and is 565 mm long. It is bronze and cast in three separate pieces: the body, neck and head, and right leg. The neck and head are designed to be removed, and there are orifices in the beak and beneath the tail. The statue may have been part of a fountain, or a burner, and has been identified tentatively as a Capitoline Goose (Buckton).

*Bibliography:* Walters, 1899: n. 1887; Keller, 1909: 223; Buckton, 1994: 44; Maguire, 2000: 287

### 133. HELEN

Niketas Choniates, 652:

What of the white-armed, beautiful-ankled and long-necked Helen, who mustered the entire host

PLATE 25: Bronze goose from the Hippodrome, British Museum, London (Photo: © The British Museum)

of the Hellenes and overthrew Troy, whence she sailed to the Nile, and, after a long absence returned to the abodes of the Laconians? Was she able to placate the implacable? Was she able to soften those men whose hearts were made of iron? On the contrary! She who had enslaved every onlooker with her beauty was wholly unable to achieve this, even though she was appareled ornately; though fashioned of bronze, she appeared as fresh as the morning dew, anointed with the moistness of erotic love on her garment, veil, diadem, and braid

of hair. Her vesture was finer than spider webs, and the veil was cunningly wrought in its place; the diadem of gold and precious stones which bound the forehead was radiant, and the braid of hair that extended down to her knees, flowing down and blowing in the breeze was bound tightly in the back with a hair band. The lips were like flower cups, slightly parted as though she were about to speak; the graceful smile, at once greeting the spectator, filled him with delight; her flashing eyes, her arched eyebrows, and the shapeliness of the rest of her body were such that they cannot be described in words and depicted for future generations. (Magoulias)

A bronze statue of Helen was vandalized during the Crusader sack of 1204. No freestanding figures of Helen are known; however, reference to "vesture finer than spider webs" and emphasis on the erotic, form-revealing quality of the statue's drapery suggests a formal tie to late classical and hellenistic art.

## Herakles by Lysippos: for texts and discussion, see cat. no. 21.

## 134. HERAKLES WITH THE HESPERIDES SISTERS

*Par. 5 (Patria* II, 87):

In the place called the Neolaion stood a statue (stele) of a woman and an altar ⟨with a⟩ small calf; with these too were four horses, shining with gold; and in a ⟨chariot with a⟩ charioteer was a ⟨statue of a female⟩ (stele) holding in her right hand a small figure (stelidion) a running image (agalma). About this some say that the group (kataskeve) was erected by Constantine, while ⟨others say⟩ merely the group of horses, while the rest is antique and not made by Constantine. For up to the time of Theodosios the Great there was a spectacle (theama) enacted by the citizens in the Hippodrome, when everyone with candles and white chlamydes came in conveying this same statue (stele) alone on a chariot [or a carriage] up to the stama from the starting gates. They used to perform this each time that the birthday of the city was celebrated. And there were represented in statues (zoda) on columns, Adam and Eve and Euthenia and Limos. (Cameron/ Herrin)

The text mentions four figures of Adam and Eve, Euthenia (Plenty) and Limos (Famine) at the close of a passage describing a quadriga. The figures are said to have stood on columns in the Neolaion, an area thought to be above the *carceres* (Janin, 1964).

Although the statues are identified as biblical characters and personifications, Mango (1963: 63) believes that they should be considered antique, arguing that the decline in the manufacture of monumental statuary in the period of Late Antiquity would have mitigated against the manufacture of figures of this sort. Dagron (1984) is of like mind. What ancient statues may have inspired such a reinterpretation is not clear. It is possible, however, that the reidentification was rooted in the appearance of the group. The names associated with the figures indicate that there were three female and one male figure. Further, the association with Adam and Eve suggests the presence of key attributes such as the apple and the snake, and these attributes in their turn suggest the ancient subject of Herakles with the Hesperides sisters (Guberti Bassett, 1991). In the Roman period, Herakles is often shown with the sisters beside the apple tree around which a snake coils (*LIMC*, s.v. "Herakles VI").

*Bibliography:* Mango, 1963: 63; Janin, 1964: 194; Dagron, 1984: 135; Guberti Bassett, 1991: 91

## 135. HERAKLES AND THE NEMEAN LION

Niketas Choniates, 650–51:

Nor of a truth did they keep their hands off the hyena and the she-wolf which had suckled Romulus and Remos [Remus]; for a few copper coins they delivered over the nation's ancient and venerable monuments and cast these into the smelting furnace. This was also the fate of the man wrestling with a lion, and of the Nile horse whose posterior terminated in a spiniferous and scaly tail, and of the elephant waving its proboscis. They did the same to the Sphinxes that are comely women in the front and horrible beasts in their hind parts, that move on foot in a most bizarre manner and are nimbly borne aloft on their wings, rivaling the great-winged birds; and [the same] to the unbridled, snorting horse with ears erect, playful and docile as it pranced; and to the ancient Skylla depicted leaning forward as she leaped into Odysseus' ships and devoured many of his companions: in female form down to the waist, huge-breasted and full of savagery, and below the waist divided into beasts of prey. (Magoulias)

The figure of a man wrestling with a lion is likely to have been a representation of Herakles and the Nemean Lion. The statue, which was bronze, was destroyed in 1204. The figure was one of several in the Hippodrome to depict the Labors of Herakles (cat. nos. 21, 134). Of all the labors the fight against the Nemean lion was the most popular, and the sculptural typology, thought by some to derive from a Lysippan original, is well known from Roman examples: The bearded Herakles moves left but looks right with the lion in a headlock beneath his left arm (*LIMC*, s.v. "Herakles").

## 136. HORSE

Philip, *Anth. Gr.* IX, 777:

Look how proudly the art of the worker in bronze makes this horse stand. Fierce in his glance as he arches his neck and shakes out his wind-tossed mane for the course. I believe that if a charioteer were to fit the bit to his jaws and prick him with the spur, thy work Lysippos, would surprise us by running away, for Art makes it breathe. (Paton)

Psellos, *Anth. Gr.* XIV, 267:

On the bronze horse with the raised foot in the Hippodrome.

This bronze horse that you see is full of life; verily he is alive and he will soon leap about, and raising this forefoot he will strike and kick you if you go near him. He is starting to run: stay back, do not approach him, but rather flee lest you receive such injury as I mentioned. (Paton)

The attribution to Lysippos may or may not be correct, but the description of the horse's arched neck, raised foreleg, and sense of implied motion are consistent with the late fourth-century B.C. interest in interaction with space that characterize the Lysippan oeuvre.

## 137. HYENA

*Par.* 62 (*Patria* II, 79):

The hyena above the dragon statue came from Antioch, first to Constantinople in the reign of Constantine the Great as the aforementioned Philip told. (Cameron/Herrin)

Niketas Choniates 650–51: see no. 135.

The statue was bronze and is said to have come from Antioch. Association with the "dragon statue" suggests placement near the Skylla on the *euripus*.

*Bibliography:* Cameron/Herrin, 252

## 138. OBELISK OF THEODOSIOS (PLATE 26)

Marc. Com. A.D. 390:

An obelisk was placed in the circus.

Niketas Paphlagonias:

And from the top of the four-sided monolithic column in the Hippodrome, the heavy bronze, pinecone fell the furthest, breaking into pieces.

*Patria* II, 60:

And the monolith which had been there broken was now standing in the Hippodrome, and it came from Athens under the Patriarch Proclus in the time of Theodosios the Younger.

The obelisk is one of the few antiquities to have survived in Istanbul. It stands on a square base of late-fourth-century manufacture toward the southeast end of the *euripus* in what is today the Istanbul Atmeidan. The base is carved on four sides with reliefs showing members of the Theodosian household in stately attendance at the circus games. Inscriptions in Latin and Greek accompany these images. On the south side a verse in Latin:

I was formerly reluctant to obey the serene masters, even when ordered to proclaim the victory after the extinction of tyrants (the victory over the extinction of tyrants), but since all things yield to Theodosios and his everlasting offspring, I was conquered and subdued in three times ten days and raised to high heaven on the advice of Proclus. (Iversen)

Greek appears on the north side:

It was only the Emperor Theodosios who succeeded in raising the four-sided column which had ever lain as a burden to the earth. He committed the task to Proclus, and so a great column stood erect in thirty-two days. (Iversen)

The obelisk itself is a single piece of red granite inscribed on four sides with hieroglyphs. Broken at the bottom, it now stands to what is probably only about two-thirds of its original height. When the damage occurred is not known; however, references in the inscriptions to the difficulty of raising the monument suggest that the breakage happened after arrival in Constantinople. That the monolith was broken at the time of its erection is clear from the relief on the lower part of the fourth-century base. The relief records the raising of the monument, and it shows a sequence of hieroglyphs that terminates in exactly the same place as those on the obelisk as it stands.

Base inscriptions and a notice by Marcellinus Comes establish the date of erection as 390. The inscriptions mention Proclus, the city prefect under Theodosios I between 388 and 392 (*PLRE*, I, 746, s.v. "Proclus 6"). The occasion appears to have been the defeat of the usurper Maximus (Wrede, 1966).

Prior to its raising in the Hippodrome, the obelisk's history is hazy. The monument was originally one of a pair of obelisks erected by Tutmosis III (1490–36 B.C.) in the Temple of Amon at Thebes. Amm. Marc. (XVII, 4: 1–5) reports that one of these monoliths was taken by Constantine for the Circus Maximus in Rome. The likelihood is that Constantine tore not one but two obelisks from their bases, intending one for Rome, the other for Constantinople. Presumably this would have occurred between 324 and 337.

Although the one obelisk was indeed sent to Rome, the second one appears to have remained at Alexandria as indicated by the correspondence of Julian (III 48). Thus, although initially a Constantinian project, the removal of the obelisk took place only later in the century. Conservative dating places the move sometime between 363 and 390.

Epigraphical and textual evidence suggest that after its arrival in Constantinople there were unsuccessful attempts at raising the monument, perhaps at sites other than the Hippodrome. Reference in the base inscriptions to the obelisk's lengthy rest as "a burden to the earth" and its reluctance to "obey the masters . . . even when ordered to proclaim victory," as well as the assertion that it was "only the Emperor Theodosius who succeeded in raising the four-sided column" hint at failed attempts to raise the monument.

Because the fifth-century *Notitia Urbis Constantinopolitanae* (Seeck, 1876: 223) does not refer to the obelisk in the Hippodrome, but does mention a "Theban" obelisk in the Strategeion (s.v.), Gilles (II, 11) proposed that the Theodosian obelisk had originally been raised on the parade ground where it stood until shaken and broken in an earthquake of unspecified date. In the aftermath of this event, Gilles suggests that the fallen upper portion of the obelisk was brought to the Hippodrome. Guilland (1969: 56) adopts this position. Although it is clear that the Hippodrome obelisk was erected after it was broken, and the designation of the Strategeion obelisk as "Theban" conforms to the known provenance of the Hippodrome monument, Iversen (1972: 32) rejects this view, stating that there is no factual evidence in support of the hypothesis that he believes was propounded by Gilles as an explanation for the *Notitia's* silence on the subject of the Hippodrome obelisk. Indeed, the existing evidence flatly contradicts this proposition. The erection of the Hippodrome obelisk took place in 390, twenty to twenty-five years before the writing of the *Notitia*. Further, it seems unlikely that a broken obelisk would be considered an appropriate decor for an area

PLATE 26: Obelisk, Hippodrome, Istanbul (Photo: W. Schiele, Deutsches Archäologisches Institut, Istanbul, Institute Negative Number R 29.421)

as important as the Strategeion. Furthermore, other obelisks, also destroyed, are known to have been in the city. It is therefore possible that the Strategeion obelisk was yet another import from Thebes in Egypt.

*Bibliography:* Gilles 1561 bis II. 11; Bruns, 1935; Wrede, 1966; Guilland, 1969: 56; Iversen, 1972: II: 9–35; Kiilerich, 1998

### 139. QUADRIGA (HORSES OF SAN MARCO) (PLATE 27)

*Par. 84 (Patria II, 75):*

The four gilt horses that stand above the Hippodrome came from the island of Chios under Theodosios II. (Cameron/Herrin)

Niketas Choniates, 119:

The sultan sojourned with the emperor for some time and feasted his eyes on the horse races. Now, in the Hippodrome there was a tower which stood opposite the spectators; beneath it were the starting posts which opened into the racecourse through parallel arches and above were fixed four gilt bronze horses, their necks somewhat curved as if they eyed each other as they raced round the last lap. (Magoulias)

Four gilt bronze horses said to have been brought from Chios in the reign of Theodosios II (408–50) stood above the Hippodrome *carceres*. Cameron and Herrin posit that they were part of a donation made by that emperor following an earthquake in 447. How long the animals stood in place is not known. The likelihood is that the horses were either removed or destroyed in 1204. In fact, scholarship has long associated the group with the bronze horses on the façade of the Venetian basilica of San Marco.

The four horses placed above the entrance to the Venetian basilica were brought to the Serinissima in 1204 as part of the booty gathered during the Fourth Crusade (Demus, 1960). Each of the horses is 2.33 meters high and 2.534

meters long. They are thus somewhat over life-size (Crome, 1963: 210). Stylistically they form a homogenous group. All four animals have large, barrel-like bodies, relatively small heads, closely clipped manes, and long tails that are bound at the end in a knot. Each horse also wears the studded harness of the quadriga around its neck. Style and harness typology indicate that the San Marco horses originally formed part of a single composition, most probably a quadriga. Technical information supports this assertion. Each horse was cast in ten separate pieces after the lost wax technique. The pieces are the four legs, the rump, head and neck, tail, tail loop, harness, and forelock (Crome, 1963: 2; Metropolitan Museum of Art, 1979). Gilding took place after assembly.

Although similar in these general respects, no two horses are exactly alike. Each animal stands with three feet firmly on the ground and raises one forefoot: two horses lift their right forefeet, two their left. Similarly two horses turn their heads to the right, two to the left. As they stand today, the animals are arranged symmetrically according to the position of their heads and legs. The horses raising their right forefeet stand on the proper right of the composition, those raising their left forefeet to the proper left. Those on the ends turn their heads inward and those in the center turn their heads out. This arrangement probably repeats their original disposition, for given the variations from horse to horse, it is the most unified and logical compositional solution. It is also a common arrangement for Late Antique quadrigae (Weitzmann, 1979, nos. 16 and 98).

It has been argued that the horses are Greek in origin; however, autopsy has confirmed a date between the second and fourth centuries A.D. (Metropolitan Museum of Art, 1979). The solid bodies and stately poses contrast with the wild, rearing images of delicate animals popular in the fifth and fourth centuries B.C., and their compatibility with an arrangement in a symmetrical, static pose that only hints of action is consistent with the preference for formalized composition that occurs in Late Antique art. The stately,

PLATE 27: Horses of San Marco, Venice (Photo: Erich Lessing/Art Resource, NY)

isocephalic symmetry and essentially frontal nature of the group seem a translation into the third dimension of the compositional principles seen in such works as the silver Meleager hunt plate in Leningrad (Weitzmann, 1979: no. 141) and the Missorium of Theodosios I (Weitzmann, 1979: no. 64).

Although association of the *carceres* group with the San Marco horses is tempting, no solid evidence either supports or refutes the claim. All that is known archivally about the horses is that they come from Constantinople. No Venetian source contemporary with the Crusade records a hippodrome provenance. This association appears first in the sixteenth century and derives from the observed similarity between Choniates' description and the configuration of the horses; however, the properties attributed the animals by Choniates – curved necks and gilded bodies anxious to race – are too generically those of quadriga horses to allow firm conclusions. There were, moreover, other quadriga in the circus (cat. no. 140) that might easily have furnished the Venetian booty. Nevertheless, the identification has persisted. Cameron and Herrin argue that the description of the quadrigae horses without chariot favors identification of the *carceres* group with the San Marco horses. Harnesses indicate, however, that the horses were once part of a major quadriga group complete with chariot. When they were disassociated from that quadriga cannot be determined; however, Choniates' failure to mention a chariot is no clear index that there was not one associated with the *carceres* group.

*Bibliography:* Demus, 1960; Crome, 1963; Mango, 1963: 68; Metropolitan Museum of Art, 1979; Cameron/Herrin, 273–73; Guberti Bassett, 1991: 89

## 140. QUADRIGA

*Par.* 5 (*Patria* II, 87):

In the place called Neolaia stood a statue of a woman and an altar ⟨with a⟩ small calf, with these too were four horses, shining with gold; and on a ⟨chariot with a⟩ charioteer was a ⟨statue of a female⟩ holding in her right hand a small figure, a running image. About this some say that the group was erected by Constantine, while ⟨others say⟩ merely the group of horses, while the rest is antique and not made by Constantine. For up to the time of Theodosios the Great (379–395) there was a spectacle enacted by the citizens in the Hippodrome, when everyone with candles and white chlamydes came in conveying this same statue alone on a chariot up to the Stama from the starting gates. They used to perform this each time that the birthday of the city was celebrated. And there were represented in statues on columns Adam and Eve and Plenty and Famine. (Cameron/Herrin)

A gilded bronze quadriga driven by a figure described as female with a small statue in its right hand stood in the area of the Hippodrome known as the Neolaia. The location is not clearly known. Janin (1964) and Guilland (1969) believe it to be one and the same as the *carceres*. Cameron and Herrin, following Borelli Vlad and Guidi Toniati (Metropolitan Museum of Art, 1979), associate it with a seating section given over to youths, as suggested by the name. This multifigured group is reported to have been erected at least in part, as early as the reign of Constantine. *Par.* notes disagreement about the monument's history, acknowledging that some believe the entire group to have been made and erected by Constantine, while others insist that the horses were Constantinian in manufacture, the chariot ancient.

The group described was clearly a quadriga. Cameron and Herrin identify the driver as female and the small statue as that of an athlete. Were the statue indeed female it is most likely that it would have been a victory figure. It is also possible that the quadriga group was an ancient one with a driver similar in type to the Delphi Charioteer whose peplos, flowing locks, and generally youthful appearance appeared female to the authors of *Par.* who were familiar with an altogether different type of racing gear, the short tunic and leather cuirass of the late Roman race driver. Whatever the sex of the driver, the smaller statue is likely to have been a victory or a tyche rather than an athlete. The quadriga is reported here to have been used in the birthday celebrations of the city, an event described by the sixth-century historian Malalas (322). Malalas reports that a quadriga with a wooden statue of Constantine carrying the city Tyche at the helm was brought into the Hippodrome where it was paraded amidst columns of white-robbed Constantinopolitans. Malalas is, however, specific that that quadriga was brought from the Milion. The group at the Neolaia should therefore be considered a different one.

*Bibliography:* Janin, 1964: 194; Guilland, 1969: I, 385; Metropolitan Museum of Art, 1979: 127–36; Cameron/Herrin, 171–74

**Romulus and Remus: see Wolf.**

## 141. SERPENT COLUMN OF THE PLATAEAN TRIPOD (PLATES 28–30)

Eusebios, *VC* III, 54: see no. 18.

Ignatius of Smolensk:

When we had finished attending the holy liturgy, we went to Constantine's palace where we saw the imperial building. There, in the imperial playing field called the "hippodrome," stands a bronze column apparently [made of] three twisted strands; there is a serpent head on each end of the divided top. Serpent venom is enclosed in the column. There were many other stone columns there, as well as [other] marvelous things. (Majeska)

The twisted Serpent Column on the Istanbul Atmeidan is one of the few antiquities to survive in Constantinople (Plate 28). The great bronze monument consists of three snakes that twist around one another to form the column's shaft before separating into three outward spreading

PLATE 28: Serpent Column of the Plataean Tripod, Istanbul (Photo: Sèbah-Joaillier, Deutsches Archäologisches Institut, Istanbul, Institute Negative Number R 28.999)

branches at the column's top and stands 5.53 meters high. Originally each branch terminated in a serpent's head (Plate 29), but in 1700 all three were cut off (Ménage, 1964: 172). Two heads have since been lost. The third survives in the Istanbul Archaeological Museum: a wide, flat snake's head with wide eyes and open jaws (Plate 30). Originally the eyes, now empty sockets,

PLATE 29: View of the Hippodrome, *The Freshfield Album*, Trinity College Library, Cambridge MS 0.17.2, folio 20 (Courtesy of Master and Fellows of Trinity College Cambridge)

PLATE 30: Head from the Serpent Column, Istanbul Archaeological Museum, (Photo: Sèbah-Joaillier, Deutsches Archäologisches Institut, Istanbul, Institute Negative Number KB 1144)

would have been filled with glass and a bronze tongue would have darted out between the teeth (Devambez, 1937: 9–12).

The Serpent Column originally was part of the larger victory tripod, which the Greek allies dedicated in the sanctuary of Apollo at Delphi after their victory over the Persians in the Battle of Plataea (479 B.C.). The appearance of this tripod remains a matter of debate, but it is clear from descriptions that the Serpent Column functioned as a support member, holding either the bowl or the feet of the dedicatory tripod. Herodotus (IX, 81) described the donation of the tripod in the fifth century B.C., paying particular attention to the serpents. In the second century A.D., Paus. (X, 13, 9) reported that only the Serpent Column remained. Thus, from at least the second century on the column alone functioned as the emblem for the Plataean victory.

Byzantine references to the column are few. The earliest, by Eusebios of Caesarea, is vague, referring only to Delphic tripods. The next sure mention is that of the fourteenth-century Russian pilgrim, Ignatius of Smolensk. A ninth-century account referring to four snakes biting their tales outside the palace by the Arab commentator Harun ibn Yahya has been rejected as a description of the Serpent Column as the number of heads, pose, and placement are completely at odds with the monument as it is known (Madden, 1992).

The 1927 excavations in the Hippodrome revealed that the Serpent Column rested on a base formed from a trimmed, reused column capital. The base in turn stood on two water conduits, one of which was reported vaguely as "rather late Byzantine," the other "Turkish" (Casson, 1928: 7). These conduits were themselves imbedded in the circus's early Byzantine ground level and served to transform the Column into a fountain. Casson's interpretation of the find is indecisive. The late date of the Byzantine conduit led him to suggest that the column stood in another location before it was brought to the circus. However, because of fourth-century references to the Delphic tripods in the Hippodrome, he made no firm commitment to an earlier siting outside the circus.

The conduits clearly cannot be used as *termini post quem*. One is Turkish, and because the Column was seen in the Hippodrome by Ignatius of Smolensk in the fourteenth century, it must be a later insertion under the foundation. The same could therefore be true of the "late Byzantine" conduit, whatever its date. Madden believes this conduit was added in the fifth century. Further, because the conduits are lodged in the yellow clay of the Hippodrome's fourth-century level it is likely that the column stands on the foundation level of the *euripus*, an observation in support of a fourth-century installation. Corroboration comes from less specific references to the generic group of Delphic tripods (cat. no. 144) in the Hippodrome made by Eusebios, Zosimos, and the *Patria*, which suggest that the monument was described together with these offerings, all of which were Constantinian.

*Bibliography:* Frick, 1859; Casson, 1928; Devambez, 1937; Ménage, 1964; Müller-Wiener, 1973: 71; Guberti Bassett, 1991: 89–90; Madden, 1992; Gauer, 1995; Stichel, 1997

## 142. SKYLLA (PLATE 31)

### Literary Sources:

*Anth. Gr.* IX, 755:

Unless the bronze glistened and betrayed the work to be a product of Hephaestus' cunning art, one looking from afar would think that Skylla herself stood here, transferred from sea to land, so threatening is her gesture, such wrath does she exhibit, as if dashing ships to pieces in the sea. (Paton)

*Anth. Gr.* XI, 271:

Nigh to Skylla they set up cruel Charybdis, this savage ogre Anastasios. Fear in thy heart Skylla, lest he devour thee too, turning a brazen goddess into small change. (Paton)

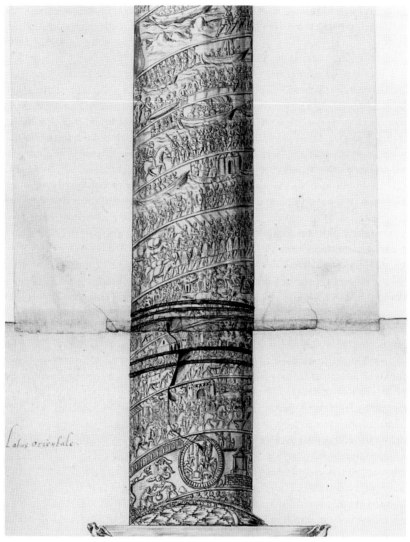

*cotus orientale*

PLATE 31: Column of Arkadios (west side) showing Skylla in the lowest relief spiral, *The Freshfield Album*, Trinity College Library, Cambridge, MS 0.17.2, folio 11 (Courtesy of Master and Fellows of Trinity College Cambridge)

*Par.* 61:

Philip the eparch confirmed many things for us; that the Thessalian statue in the Hippodrome is the work of a certain Pontios – the one that stands above the imperial box. Among the female statues, that near the epigram of the Medes ⟨is of women⟩ giving birth to wild beasts and they devour men. One ⟨of them⟩, Herodian made clear to me, re-

veals the story of the godless Justinian. The other, which is accompanied also by a boat, has not been fulfilled, but remains. (Cameron/Herrin)

*Patria* II, 77:

And some say that there is a Skylla who snatches men from Charybdis. And there is Odysseus whom she holds out in her hand by the head. And others say that this is the earth, the sea, and the seven ages, which were sent forth throughout the deluge.

Niketas Choniates, 651: see no. 135.

## Graphic Sources:

*Freshfield Album*, 1574 (Plate 31)

Trinity College Library Cambridge, MS 0117.2
Column of Arkadios, East Side, center

The Skylla was a bronze statue that formed part of a large, multifigured group on the *euripus*. The group illustrated Odysseus's voyage through the Straits of Messina. Skylla was shown as a furious, half-human monster. Comely and voluptuous from the waist up, she sported a series of man-eating, serpentine tails from the waist down. *Patria* reports that she grasped the head of Odysseus and *Par.* suggests the devastation of a shipwreck.

Sixteenth-century drawings of the Column of Arcadios from the *Freshfield Album* supplement the textual information, providing generally reliable documentation of the Skylla's gross physiognomy and pose (Becatti, 1960: 75). Sketches of the south, west and east sides of the Column depict the Hippodrome (Plate 31). The circus is recognizable by the continuous arcade of seating along one side and by the line of statues placed along the *euripus*, Skylla among them. The creature appears as a human torso with two fantastic legs in the form of spiraling dolphin's tails terminating in animal heads, a depiction generally consistent with the literary sources. The monster's left hand flies out from the body, while the right wields a club or rudder above its head. The statue is shown in isolation, which is perhaps a case of visual synecdoche, that is, the artist chose to represent the whole group by its most characteristic aspect, the sea-monster.

This general picture may be fleshed out through comparison to known ancient representations. The monster appears most frequently in coinage, funerary monuments, and villa sculpture. There are two known Skylla types in ancient literature, the Homeric and the Virgilian. The former is completely fantastic, the latter, anthropomorphic. *Od.* XII, 85–100 creates a grim portrait. The monster is female, with twelve feet and six long necks, each with a gruesome head in which three rows of teeth line up "Thick and close and full of black death." Virgil (*Aen.* III, 420–432) is marginally more benign: His Skylla is a fair young woman to the waist with monstrous form below where an imprecise number of dolphin's tails are joined at the belly to the heads of snarling wolves. This anthropomorphic Skylla was the inspiration for most representations of the monster in antiquity and it is this type which stood in the Hippodrome.

The foremost three-dimensional rendering of the anthropomorphic Skylla type is the statue from the Canopus at Hadrian's Villa (Aurigemma, 1956). Fragments show that the creature had a human, female body from head to waist and a lower body that was part fish, part animal. Although the statue's arms are missing, their remaining stumps together with the depiction of the torso's musculature show that the right arm would have been raised and the left lowered. A strut in the back of the figure at the base of the neck suggests that an implement like an oar could have been held back above the head. Three male torsos grasped by leonine claws, and a number of fragments including three fantastic animal heads, claws, and several scaly chunks show that the monster had man-eating protomes. There is also part of a single dolphin's tail that presumably waved behind Skylla's body.

The known three-dimensional representations of Skylla come from aquatic settings. The Hadrianic Skylla stood in isolation on a base at the middle of the canal known as the Canopus. Other representations, such as the group from the Grotto of Tiberius at Sperlonga, stood in the middle of a pool and showed the monster snatching men from a boat and devouring them (Conticello, 1974; Andreae, 1974). Evidence for the Constantinopolitan Skylla indicates that as in these earlier examples, an anthropomorphic monster was shown presiding over the carnage of a shipwreck. *Par.* refers to a ship and *Patria* interprets the statue as a representation of the earth, the sea, and the seven ages of man, a description that suggests a multifigured group. The Hippodrome Skylla also may have been placed in a reflecting pool along the central spine of the circus. The statue's date of installation is not known; however, the emphasis given to the figure on the Arkadian relief suggests that the figure may have been an Arkadian or Theodosian addition to the circus.

*Bibliography:* Becatti, 1960: 200–09

## 143. Sphinxes

Niketas Choniates, 650–51: see no. 135.

An unspecified number of winged sphinxes stood on the Hippodrome *euripus*. The fact that the statues were melted for coin points to a bronze medium, while the presence of wings indicates that the sphinxes were not true Egyptian or even Egyptianizing monuments but Greco-Roman creations. In this iconographic tradition the sphinx is conceived as a composite creature with a female human head and breasts, a feline body, and wings. The general type is of great antiquity; however, the introduction of human female attributes such as breasts occurs only in the fifth century B.C. and later. The Hippodrome sphinxes conformed therefore to a classical and postclassical iconographic scheme (*LIMC*, s.v. "Sphinx").

## 144. THEOPHANES OF MYTILENE

Inscribed statue base, Istanbul
Archaeological Museum:

Because of his valor and his piety to the divinity, (the people honor) Gnaeus Pompeius Theophanes, son of Hiroitas, who won back from our common benefactors the Romans, the city, its territory, and its ancestral liberty, and who reestablished the sanctuaries, their cults, and honors for the gods. (Robert)

A large circular statue base from the Hippodrome preserves a Greek inscription honoring the historian and statesman Theophanes of Mytilene (80–30 B.C.). Because the inscription is written in the Aeolic dialect, it is clear that the base and its accompanying statue were brought to Constantinople from Lesbos (Robert, 1969: 54). Dowel holes in the base indicate that the statue was bronze. The appearance of the statue is not known; however, Mytilenean coin issues from the time of Tiberius and Septimius Severus show Theophanes as a clean-shaven man with short hair in the Republican portrait tradition (Richter, 1965: 165).

*Bibliography:* Robert, 1969

## 145. TRIPODS, DELPHIC

Eusebios of Caesarea, *VC*, III, 54: see no. 18.

Socrates I, 16:

Nor did he only improve the affairs of the Christians as I have just said, but he also destroyed the superstitions of the heathens; for he brought forth their images into public view to ornament the city of Constantinople and set up the Delphic tripods publicly in the Hippodrome. (Schaff and Wace)

Zosimos II, 31:

Also, in another part of the hippodrome, he set up the tripod of the Delphic Apollo, which had on it the very image of the god. (Buchanan/Davis)

*Patria* II, 79:

And similarly both the tripod of the Delphic cauldron and the equestrian statues speak (i.e., are inscribed) and for this reason they stood and they tell us something.

An unspecified number of tripods, the Serpent Column (no. 141) among them, were brought by Constantine from the Sanctuary of Apollo at Delphi to the Hippodrome. The context of the *Patria* indicates that at least one tripod stood on the *euripus*; all of the tripods may have been gathered there or some may have stood in other areas. There is no mention of size or medium. Zosimos and the *Patria* author refer to decorations and inscriptions, which reproduce the image of Apollo.

## 146. VICTORY

*Anth. Gr.* XVI, 345:

Thou standest near victory and King Alexander,
Thou who hast gathered the glory of both. (Paton)

Niketas Choniates, 653:

The following should also be recounted. There was set up on a pedestal a woman youthful in form and appearance and in the prime of life, her hair bound in the back and curled along both sides of the forehead; she was not raised up out of reach but could be touched by those who put out their hands. The right hand of this figure, with no underlying support, held in its palm a man mounted on a horse which was poised on one leg more easily than another would have clasped a wine cup. The rider was robust in body and encased in a coat of mail, with greaves on both legs and he fiercely breathed out war; while the horse pricked up its ears as though in response to the war trumpet. With neck held high, it was fierce in countenance, the eyes betraying its eagerness to charge forth; the legs were raised high in the air, exhibiting warlike agitation. (Magoulias)

A standing female figure carried a rearing horse with armed rider in the palm of her outstretched right hand, an iconography that suggests that the figure was a personification of Victory. The fact that the statue was felled in 1204 indicates, however, that it was bronze. Heyne thought the figure was allegorical: the woman represented the city and the rider the competitors in the Hippodrome.

*Bibliography:* Heyne, 1790–91: 28

## 147. WOLF

Niketas Choniates, 650–51: see no. 135.

A bronze statue of a wolf, identified as the animal that suckled the Roman twins Romulus and Remus, referred to the legend of Rome's foundation. The fact that the statue is reported to have been melted for coin indicates a bronze medium. Because of the specifically Roman imagery it is likely that the statue would have been brought from Rome.

It is not clear from the description whether the wolf actually was accompanied by the twins or whether they were mentioned by way of identification. By analogy with other representations of the wolf, it seems likely that the twins were present. Cicero (*Cat.* III, 9; *de div.* I.19; II.47) and Livy (I, 23, 12) mention Roman images of the twins being nursed by the wolf. The so-called Capitoline Wolf in Rome is associated with Cicero's statue (*EAA*, s.v. "Lupa Capitolina"; *LIMC*, s.v. "Lupa Romana") and numismatic examples give further evidence of the animal's appearance. The verso of two Hadrianic aurei from the mint of Rome shows the she-wolf full teated and standing with the twins seated beneath her, their heads raised to drink (Mattingly, 1936: III, pl 55, 6, 7). This image was especially popular in the Augustan, Hadrianic, and Antonine periods.

## 148. ZEUS

*Par.* 83:

A great many statues have come from the place called Iconium to Constantinople, among them one of Zeus that is still in the Hippodrome. (Cameron/Herrin)

The statue is one of many said to have come from Ikonion (Konya) in the fourth century. It still appears to have been standing in the eighth century, as indicated by use of the present tense.

### 149. ZODIAC

*Vita Euthemii:*

For now Alexander, the emperor, hindered of his amorous passion, and remaining impotent therein, addressed himself to sorcerers, being led by them to lawless deeds, putting clothes upon the bronze figures of the zodiac in the hippodrome, incensing them, and having them illuminated with candelabra, he, in the imperial tribune in the hippodrome, was struck down like another Herod by the invisible hand of God and they took him and carried him into the palace, in great and intolerable pain. (Karlin-Hayter)

The statues were bronze. What the actual figures might have been is not clear; however, the reference to clothing them suggests that the individual signs were treated as freestanding personifications, an iconography unknown from antiquity. The text, which dates to c. 920–25 (Karlin-Hayter, 10), documents the life of Euthymios, patriarch of Constantinople (907–12). This means that the statuary was in place in the ninth-century Hippodrome. Preger believes that the statuary was moved there from the Augusteion at the time of the sixth-century rebuilding; however, the iconographic differences between the Hippodrome statues and the Augusteion image (no. 15) suggest otherwise.

*Bibliography:* Preger, 1902 bis

## LAUSOS COLLECTION

### Kedrenos I, 564 (Kedrenos A):

Note that in the quarter of Lausos there used to be various buildings and certain hostels at the place where the [cistern of] Philoxenos provided its water, whence its name ["fond of guests"]. There stood there also a statue of Lindian Athena, four cubits high, of emerald stone, the work of the sculptors Skyllis and Dipoenos, which Sesostris,

tyrant of Egypt, once sent as a gift to Kleoboulos, tyrant of Lindos. Likewise, the Knidian Aphrodite of white stone, naked, shielding with her hand only her pudenda, a work of Praxiteles of Knidos. Also the Samian Hera, a work of Lysippos and the Chian Bupalos: a winged Eros holding a bow, brought from Myndos; the ivory Zeus by Pheidias, whom Perikles dedicated at the temple of the Olympians; the statue representing Chronos, a work of Lysippos, bald at the back and having hair in front; unicorns, tigresses, vultures, giraffes, an ox-elephant, centaurs and pans. (Mango)

### Kedrenos I, 616 (Kedrenos B):

When he [Basiliskos] had been proclaimed, there occurred a conflagration in the city which destroyed its most flourishing part. For it started in the middle of the Chalkoprateia [Copper Market] and consumed both porticoes and everything adjacent to them and the so-called Basilika, in which there was a library that had 120,000 books. Among these books was a dragon's gut 120 feet long upon which Homer's poems, namely the Iliad and the Odyssey, were written in gold letters together with the story of the heroes' deeds. [The fire] also destroyed the porticoes on either side of the street Mese and the excellent offerings of Lausos: for many ancient statues were set up there, namely, the famous one of the Aphrodite of Knidos, that of the Samian Hera, that of Lindian Athena made of a different material which Amasis, king of Egypt, had sent to the wise Kleoboulos, and countless others. The fire extended as far as the Forum of the great Constantine, as it is called. (Mango)

### Zonaras III, 131:

A great consuming conflagration broke out in Constantinople, beginning in the Chalkoprateia and spreading to all the nearby areas and reducing the public portico and adjacent buildings to ashes, including the so-called Basilika where there was library that housed 120,000 books. Among these books was a dragon gut measuring 120 feet with the poetry of Homer, the Iliad and the Odyssey, written in golden letters, which Malchos mentioned in writing of the emperors. The fire utterly destroyed this object and both the splendor in the city's Lausos quarter and the statues set up there, the Samian Hera, the Lindian Athena and the Knidian Aphrodite, famous works of art.

## 150. ANIMALS

An inventory of a collection amassed by Theodosios II's court chamberlain, Lausos, concludes with a list of animals and half-human creatures. Excluding the unicorn and the taurelephant or ox-elephant, most of these animals are familiar from the natural world. Mango (Mango/Vickers/Francis, 1992) identifies the ox-elephant as a wild buffalo. What these various figures were or where they came from is not immediately clear, as the account makes no effort to provide any sort of descriptive or historical information. It is therefore impossible to visualize the animals in any but the most generic manner. Absence of any viable sculptural comparanda makes the task even more difficult. Although animal statuary certainly was known and many famous works existed, no statues corresponding to any of the Lausos figures survive or are mentioned in the literary sources. Evidence of extant animal sculpture suggests, however, that the Lausos statues probably would have been of Hellenistic or Roman manufacture. The statues were probably assembled in the late fourth century. They were destroyed by fire in 476.

*Bibliography:* Mango, 1963: 58; Mango/Vickers/ Francis, 1992: 91; Guberti Bassett, 2000: 10–11, 15–17

## 151. APHRODITE OF KNIDOS (PLATE 32)

The texts refer to a statue of the fourth-century B.C. statue of Aphrodite made by Praxiteles for the goddess's sanctuary at Knidos. Among the most famous statues in the ancient world, its appearance is well known from coin issues and later copies. The goddess stands naked in a contrapposto pose, her weight carried on her straight right leg, her left leg slightly bent. Her right hand shields her pubic area, while her left arm is raised at the elbow and her left hand holds a piece of drapery that falls onto an amphora. Her head turns toward the right. The Knidia was probably brought to the capital in the latter years of the fourth century by Theodosios II's court chamberlain, Lausos. It was destroyed by fire in 476.

*Bibliography:* Blinkenberg, 1933: 32–34; Mango, 1963: 58; Corso, 1991: 3/131–32; Mango/Vickers/ Francis, 1992: 93–96; Havelock, 1995; Guberti Bassett, 2000: 8–9, 13–14

## 152. ATHENA OF LINDOS

The statue is said to have come from the sanctuary of Athena at Lindos on Rhodes. It stood to four cubits, that is, between one and two meters, and was made of "emerald stone." This reference probably indicates color rather than medium, and both Zucker (1887) and Francis and Vickers (1984) suggest green basalt, granite, porphyry, or serpentine as the medium.

Attribution is to Skyllis and Dipoinos, two Cretan sculptors born between 580 and 577 B.C. (Pliny, *NH*, 36.9). The statue is also said to have been a gift made by an Egyptian ruler to Kleoboulos of Rhodes. Kedrenos A credits Sesostris of Egypt with the donation, while Kedrenos B claims the gift for Amasis. In broad outline this information accords well with what is known about the Lindian sanctuary. Located on the acropolis at Lindos, the shrine is alleged to have been founded by the mythical king Danaos. Kleoboulos, ruler of Lindos in the mid–sixth century B.C. is said to have refurbished the sanctuary by outfitting it with a new temple. Reference to Kleoboulos is consistent with attribution to Skyllis and Dipoinos.

The only misshapen chronological piece in this puzzle is the conflicting report about patronage; however, the issue is easily resolved in favor of Amasis. Although all Egyptian rulers named Sesostris predate Kleoboulos by centuries, Amasis, who ruled during the sixth

PLATE 32: Praxiteles, Aphrodite of Knidos, Roman copy after Greek original, Vatican Museums (Photo: Alinari/Art Resource, NY)

century B.C., was the Lindian tyrant's contemporary. Moreover, he is known to have made donations in Hellenic sanctuaries, Lindos included. Among the gifts recorded are "two stone images and a marvelous linen breastplate" at the sanctuary of Athena (Herodotus I, 30).

What was this green statue of Athena? It is clear that it was not the sanctuary's main cult image. That statue, a jewel-encrusted wooden image of the enthroned goddess, not only was different in medium but also appears to have been destroyed when the temple burned in the fourth century B.C. (Blinkenberg, 1917–18). Kedrenos's Lindian Athena therefore must have been a votive offering, as reference to the foreign source of the gift suggests.

Attribution to Skyllis and Dipoinos coupled with references to Amasis and Kleoboulos confirm the Lindian Athena as a work of sixth-century B.C. dedication. Egyptian patronage suggests further that the figure may well have been one of Egyptian manufacture, a notion supported by the characteristically hard stone medium. Although seemingly at odds with the artistic attribution, such a picture is not out of keeping with the archaeological evidence for the period. Excavation of the Greek settlement at Naukratis, the first autonomous foreign settlement permitted in Egypt under pharaonic rule, yielded a series of sixth-century B.C. Greek votive images created in an Egyptianizing style (Flinders Petrie, 1886: 13, pl. I, 1). Nor were such dedications restricted to Egypt proper. As fragmentary remains of a black basalt statue carved in the Egyptian manner and inscribed with Greek from Kameiros on Rhodes indicate, such offerings were exported to the Greek sanctuaries as early as the seventh century (Trolle, 1978). The Lindian Athena is likely to have belonged to this tradition; however, beyond a general association with the formal conventions of late Egyptian and early Archaic sculpture, the appearance of the statue cannot be reconstructed.

*Bibliography:* Gilles 1561 bis II, 9 and II, 17; Du Cange 1680 I. 24; Zucker, 1887: 785–91; Blinkenberg, 1917–18; Mango, 1959: 42–47, 56–60; Janin, 1964: 59–62, 73–77, 155–56; Guilland, 1969: I, 81–82, 220–26, 230–32, III, 40–54; Francis, 1984: 68–69; Francis/Vickers, 1984: 119–30; Corso, 1991: III, 128–42; Mango/Vickers/Francis, 1992: 89–98; Guberti Bassett, 2000: 6–25

## 153. CENTAURS AND PANS

Although there is nothing in Kedrenos's report to connect the statues with any particular historical period, the increasing popularity of such subject matter in the Hellenistic and Roman age suggests a reasonable chronological frame of reference.

*Bibliography:* Guberti Bassett, 2000: 11, 13–14

## 154. EROS (PLATE 33)

The statue, which is said to have come from Myndos, is mentioned without attribution. Because such an omission is uncharacteristic of this text, Frickenhaus (1915) emended the passage to identify the artist as Lysippos. If, as seems likely, Lysippos was the sculptor of the Eros it is possible to suggest its general appearance. An Eros attributed to Lysippos on stylistic grounds is known in several copies, of which the best preserved is a replica in the British Museum. Dating from the last quarter of the fourth century B.C. the statue shows a prepubescent youth with tousled hair and wings sprouting from his back. As in Kedrenos's description, the little god holds a large bow out to his right side, which he attempts to string or unstring. A statue of Eros attributed to Lysippos in the British Museum may reflect the statue's appearance (Johnson, 1927).

*Bibliography:* Frickenhaus, 1915; Johnson, 1927: 115; Corso, 1991: 3/131; Guberti Bassett, 2000: 9, 13–14

## 155. HERA OF SAMOS

Kedrenos I, 564 describes the figure as the work of two sculptors, Lysippos and Bupalos of Chios. This joint attribution is curious. Lysippos lived in the fourth century B.C. and Bupalos in the latter half of the sixth century, so the image could not have been the product of these two hands unless Lysippos somehow completed or restored a statue made initially by Bupalos. Alternatively, the joint attribution may be explained as the result of an error in textual transmission. Arguing that the name of Lysippos should be connected with a statue more properly associated with his name, the next statue in the sequence, an Eros, Frickenhaus (1915) assigns the Hera to

PLATE 33: Eros after Lysippos, The British Museum, London (Photo: © Copyright The British Museum)

PLATE 34: Kairos after Lysippos, Museo di Antichità, Turin (Photo: Koppermann, Deutsches Archäologisches Institut, Rome, Institute Negative 74.1609)

Bupalos alone. Although he is known to have created several temple statues, no other source credits him with the carving of the Samian Hera. Manufacture of that image, which was of ivory and gold (Paus. IV.30.6), is generally given to another early sculptor, Smilis (Paus. V, 17). Moreover, Smilis's statue replaced an aniconic wooden image that was still in existence in the second century (Paus. VII, 4, 5). Attribution to Bupalos therefore suggests that, as in the case of the Lindian Athena, a votive statue other than the main cult image was brought to Constantinople. Whatever the case, the image of Hera should be understood as a sacred representation of sixth-century B.C. manufacture. No specific description is possible. The statue is likely to have been brought to Constantinople sometime in the wake of the Theodosian closing of the temples in 480. It stood in a portico along the Mese and was destroyed by fire in 476.

*Bibliography:* Frickenhaus, 1915; Corso, 1991: 3/131; Guberti Bassett, 2000: 9

## 156. KAIROS (PLATE 34)

Kedrenos refers to a statue by Lysippos, which he describes as being bald at the back of the head with a shock of hair in front. He identifies the figure as Chronos. Although the reference is to Chronos, the explicit description of the figure's coiffeur and the Lysippan attribution relate the sculpture to that artist's image of Kairos, a freestanding bronze statue created sometime in the later fourth century B.C. No freestanding versions of this figure survive; however, literary sources and relief representations document its appearance. Descriptions characterize the statue as a running figure with winged feet that moves forward on tiptoe while carrying a razor. The distinctive coiffeur remarked by Kedrenos also is noted. Images corresponding to this description are known from reliefs and gems, among them a relief in Turin showing a winged youth running along on tiptoe. In his left hand he carries a razor on top of which a scale balances. His right hand tips these scales as if to test them. As in the descriptions, the youth is bald in back with flowing locks in front.

Identification of this figure as Chronos may be explained in the definition of kairos itself. In its most straightforward interpretation kairos expresses the idea of a moment within the longer passage of time. Time itself, conceived of as a series of linked but fleeting moments merging with one another over a sustained period, is expressed as chronos. At times, however, the words are used interchangeably, and sometime in the late Hellenistic period there is a shift in meaning as chronos takes on the meaning of kairos in certain contexts (Levi, 1923, 1924).

*Bibliography:* Johnson, 1924: 163–65, 280–87; Stewart, 1978; Corso, 1991: 3/131; Mango/Vickers/Francis, 1992: 96; Guberti Bassett, 2000: 9–10, 12, 17

### 157. ZEUS OF OLYMPIA (PLATE 35)

The ivory Zeus by Pheidias was the main temple statue in the Temple of Zeus at Olympia. Created in the fifth century B.C., it is well known from numismatic and literary evidence. A chryselephantine figure of Zeus sat on a jewel-encrusted throne carrying a small figure of Nike in his left hand, a scepter in his right. Visitors remarked that the statue was enormous and would have broken through the temple ceiling had the god chosen to stand, an observation confirmed by the analysis of an epode by Kallimachos that puts the height of the statue at fourteen meters. Kedrenos's description makes no mention of any of these details except to state that the statue was ivory, an observation that has led to

the suggestion that the gold had been removed from the statue, possibly in the time of Constantine.

*Bibliography:* Becatti, 1951: 125–40; Corso, 1991: 3/131; Mango/Francis/Vickers, 1992: 95; Guberti Bassett, 2000: 9

## MILION

### 158. EQUESTRIAN STATUES

*Patria* II, 37:

Near the Milion arch there was an equestrian statue of Trajan, and close to him an equestrian statue of Theodosios the Younger.

Kedrenos I, 564:

Above the arch of the Milion there are two statues, Constantine the Great and his mother, and between them there is a cross. Behind this there was an equestrian statue of Trajan, and next to him there was a statue of the knight Aelius Hadrian.

Suidas, s.v. Theodosios, Basileus of the Romans, the younger:

And in the Milion Theodosios erected a statue of a bronze horse. Upon completion a food distribution was provided for the city.

Three equestrian statues are mentioned in conjunction with the Milion: one each of Trajan, Hadrian, and Theodosios II. It is not clear whether there actually were three statues, or if the identity of one was conflated with the other. Both *Patria* and Kedrenos mention a statue of Trajan, which suggests that this image was certainly there. *Patria* refers to a figure of Theodosios, while Kedrenos claims that there was a statue of Hadrian. Although there is no proof, it seems likely that there were only two equestrian statues at the Milion. Because the marker was a Constantinian foundation, it seems more likely that the second statue was one of Hadrian, a

PLATE 35: Pheidias. Zeus, Temple of Zeus, Olympia (Reconstruction by H. Berve and G. Gruben, *Griechische Tempel und Heiligtumer* [Munich, Hirmer Verlag, 1961], 123)

perennial Constantinian favorite and ideal pendant for Trajan.

*Bibliography:* Mango, 1959: 47–48; Janin, 1964: 103–04; N. Firtali/T. Ergil, 1969; Guilland, 1969: II, 28–30; Müller-Wiener, 216–18; Cameron and Herrin, 215–18

## 159. HEKATE

*Par. 43:*

⟨*Spectacle number*⟩ *seven. From the + Milion a spectacle of the? official Dioscorus; from the things to be seen in the reign of the Emperor Maurice. . . . And the porphyry statue there of three stones with three stone heads, which some said was Constantine the Great in the middle, Constantius on the left, and Constans on the right with two feet but six hands – a strange spectacle for those who saw it, each one looking in a different direction – and one head.* (Cameron/Herrin)

The description of a porphyry statue with three stone heads points to an identification of the image with the goddess Hekate. Although Hekate may be represented in a variety of ways, she is most popularly depicted as having three joined bodies standing back to back around a central column or triangular stele. The pose of each statue is stiff and frontal. Hekate stands feet together facing forward, her arms at her sides. She wears the chiton and peplos of the sixth-century B.C. and with it the polos crown. She may also carry lighted torches held close to her side (*LIMC*, s.v. "Hekate"). As the polos crown and antiquated garments suggest, these representations were largely archaizing in style (Harrison, 1965; Fullerton, 1986). Pausanias (II.30.2) credits the invention of this statue type to Alkamenes in the fifth century B.C. Known as the Hekate Epipyrgidia, it became the most popular way of representing the

239

goddess in the Greek and Roman world (Harrison, 1965: 87; Edwards, 1986: 318).

Although the three-bodied Hekate type was invented in the fifth century B.C., the statement that the statue was porphyry suggests a Roman copy. Because later porphyry statuary appears to be limited to the representation of imperial figures, this statue may well be of an earlier date in the second or early third centuries when porphyry was much in vogue (Delbrueck, 1932).

The text is difficult and corrupt (Cameron/Herrin). The title, which mentions the Milion and its statues at the time of Marcian, seems at odds with the text, which makes no reference to the Milion, talks only of Theodosios, and places the statue near the "Senate in the Forum." The iconography of the statue may be of use in resolving this contradiction. Hekate is traditionally the goddess of the crossroads and of entrances. It would be logical therefore to see her statue at the Milion, the crossroads of the Empire. The Milion faced the entrance to the Augusteion. It is therefore possible that the statue stood near this entrance.

*Bibliography:* Cameron/Herrin, 230–32

## 160. ZEUS HELIOS

*Par.* 38 (*Patria II*, 42):

Spectacle number two. On the Helios at the golden Milion. At the golden Milion a chariot of Zeus Helios with four fiery horses driven headlong (?) beside two statues, has existed since ancient times. There Constantine the Great was acclaimed after defeating Azotios and Byzas and Antes, the Blue faction shouting,

"you have taken up the whip again,
and as though young again you race madly in the
    stadium,"

but the Green faction said, "We don't need you, miserable wretch; the gods above have taken him." And the chariot of Helios was brought down into the Hippodrome, and a new little statue of the Tyche of the city was escorted in procession carried

by Helios. Escorted by many officials, it came to the Stama and received prizes from the Emperor Constantine, and after being crowned it went out and was placed in the Senate until the next birthday of the city. But because of the cross engraved on it, it was consigned by Julian to a ditch where there were many other spectacles. And if anyone researches accurately the inscriptions of the Forum he would be still more amazed. (Cameron/Herrin)

No images of Zeus-Helios are known and there is no evidence for a solar cult in connection with his name (Cook, 1914: I, 186–87). Literary descriptions indicate, however, that there is a tradition of depicting Zeus in a quadriga: A monumental bronze stood on the fastigium of the temple of Capitoline Triad (Pliny, *NH* XXVIII. 16). This iconography is relatively limited, which suggests that the statue may have been one of another god more closely associated with the chariot, Helios or Apollo. The distinction between the different gods would have been made on the basis of physiognomy and attribute. Zeus commonly sported a beard and appeared half-draped, while Apollo and Helios were clean shaven and more fully covered. Unfortunately, *Par.* makes no mention of these details, and the exact identity of the driver remains a conundrum. What the author of *Par.* understood in the identification with Zeus-Helios is likewise unclear. Cameron and Herrin (216) suggest that this identification gives life to the claims that the statue in the Forum of Constantine (see cat. no. 109b) was one of Helios; however, examination of the evidence for that statue indicates that it was probably the reused figure of a Hellenistic or Roman ruler rather than a statue of Helios himself. It is also possible that the chariot group was not one of a god at all, but rather a reused imperial ensemble that was designed to be identified with the emperor himself.

*Par.* associates this quadriga group with the annual celebrations held in honor of the anniversary of Constantinople's foundation. Without actually referring to a quadriga at the Milion, Malalas, 322, and *Chron. Pasch.*, 530, describe these celebrations, noting that a statue of Constantine carrying a figure of the city Tyche, Anthousa, was paraded in a chariot in the Hippodrome. *Par.* states that the Milion chariot was one and the same as that used in the anniversary celebrations. Cameron and Herrin (216) rightly disagree. Sculptured chariot groups were not made for practical use, and so they would have had no moving parts. Moreover, the mechanics of removing such a statue from display would have been formidable. The two chariots must therefore be considered different.

*Bibliography:* Cameron/Herrin, 215–18

## PALACE OF MARINA

*Leo Choirosphaktes*:

The music of instruments resounds throughout the city. Why? Let him who has recognized say, and if he knows let him speak. The emperor Leo in his works has surpassed the imagination of Daidalos. I shall strike the shrill lyre in a pounding dance rhythm. Joyful citizens, come to the sight, behold these bath-houses, strike up the music of instruments. The edifice is aglow like the vault of heaven. All around you will see gilded stones sprouting at the tips, with statues now too.

He who has drawn glory by wit and wisdom now finishes off his heroic arduous toils.

As you go towards the doors, a long entrance-hall will envelop you, from which charm shines forth, the wonder of sculpture. There as you look you will behold the shapes of venerable old men, the raging fury and slaughter of wrath-raising war. As you see the gilded work of dome and conch in the delightful colonnaded corridors, you will have to screen the rays of your eyes to safeguard them.

Streams of heat-radiating water pour forth, pure and rich. O city, be here with me.

See especially the sight of the earth-ruler on the proconch, wearing a rosy appearance, and holding a sword in his hands. From there the empress in turn throws out the beauty of petals, in her sweet face wearing a rosy appearance. Words cannot describe the beauty. O sisterly one, who has painted

you and set you up to be gazed at like a luxuriant shoot? After this scene, he has drawn the forms of rivers, with fiercely-tuned faces, and inscribed metrical encomia.

Write divine doctrines, o youths; rain precipitates from godlike mouths.

You will see the catching of fish with rod, net, and reel; on every island you will behold a delightful spread. Another strange and delightful wonder is that the beauties of the flowing springs take on many forms in their appearance, and wear the grace of young girls. The noise of the doors with artful contrivance sends out a musical song. The song says, "Glory of rulers, o Basileus, King." At the lord's feet, among green fronds, bathes a sweet warbling bird, murmuring lyrical songs. Reject all babble of false words; Leo has now gathered all rhetorical eloquence.

The flow of countless waters sends forth the melody of instruments, imperceptibly, without any players weaving the emperor's praise. The serpent creeps up in his wisdom, the lion roars "great," the sapphire-colored sapling bears a melodious crop, gracefully tinkling among golden leaves. Under the center glitters a hot, hot swelling current of waters in an octaconch, no small cure for the sick.

Let the revolving axis of heaven rejoice that Leo perceives the unalterable threads of the bearers of light.

O friends, it is an awesome sight. A griffin projects a jet of blazing breath, terrifying the mortal nature of those present. The manifold beauty of the bath has the grace of healing; it takes away men's sickness and grants strength. The vitality of the limbs, drawing from hot liquid drops, has found vigor returning, and is youthful for years to come.

The guardian of rhetoric has excelled himself; begone, o forgers of artless words. (Magdalino)

### 161. GIGANTOMACHY

Magdalino (1984: 230) suggests that the reference to a relief showing "...the raging fury and slaughter of wrath-raising wars..." describes a gigantomachy.

## 162. HERAKLES

The figure "who has drawn glory by wit and wisdom" and "now finishes off his heroic arduous toils" must be that of Herakles; however, the passage, suitably vague, does not specify a typology.

## 163. PROTOMES

Protomes of various sorts served as water spouts. Some appear to have been zoomorphic, as indicated by references to the heads of various animals and birds. Others, as suggested by the reference "rain precipitates from godlike mouths," may have been anthropomorphic.

## 164. RIVER GODS

Magdalino (1984: 230) believes that the verse "shapes of venerable old men" refers to river gods, reclining male figures with long, flowing beards.

*Bibliography:* Magdalino, 1984, 1988; Mango, 1991; Guberti Bassett, 2000

## PHILADELPHION

## 165. TETRARCHS (PLATE 36)

Basilica of San Marco, Venice

The four porphyry military figures in the southwest corner of the exterior wall of the Basilica of San Marco were brought to Venice as spoils of the Fourth Crusade. The statues, which now stand to a height of 1.30 m, originally derive from monumental porphyry columns that flanked the western entrance to the Philadelphion (Verzone, 1958). The four figures are shown as two pairs. All are the same height. Each wears late Roman military dress and clasps an eagle-headed sword in his left hand. In each group the left figure turns slightly to the right in receipt of the embrace of the right figure's right arm. In each of the two groups one figure is bearded. This attribute represents a later addition (Cagiano de Azevedo, 1962), and initially all of the figures would have

been clean shaven. Carving is sharp and the figures are abstract. The overall composition is compact and contained within a single plain, volumes are geometric and without muscular definition, and the details of facial features and dress, which are treated in terms of linear pattern and surface design, are standardized from figure to figure. A highly polished surface enhances these qualities.

The figures are generally well preserved. Apart from a breakage of the nose common to all four figures and the removal of metal fixtures from their caps, the only real damage appears in the southwest pair where the feet and lower legs are missing. One of the feet was recovered in the excavation of the nearby Bodrum Cami (Myrelaion Church) in 1965 (Naumann, 1966), confirming a Constantinopolitan origin for the group.

Identification of the figures has varied. Although there is widespread agreement that the group represents a fourth-century imperial ensemble, suggestions as to iconography are by no means consistent and have included Diocletian and the members of the first tetrarchy (Delbreuck, 1932; L'Orange, 1932, 1965; Bauer, 2001) and Valentinian and Valens (Cagiano de Azevedo, 1962). The style of the images and the emphasis on similarity between them suggests identification with Diocletian and the first Tetrarchy.

*Bibliography:* Cicgogna, 1844; Strzygowski, 1902; Michon, 1903; Delbreuck, 1932: 84–91, 94–96; L'Orange, 1932; Verzone, 1958; Cagiano de Azevedo, 1962; Ragogna, 1963; L'Orange, 1965; Naumann, 1966; Cagiano de Azevedo, 1966/67; Firatli, 1990: 1; Bauer, 2001:30–31

## STRATEGEION

## 166. ALEXANDER THE GREAT

*Patria* II, 59:

Concerning the Strategeion. In the so-called Strategeion there was set up a statue of Alexander the Great, which stood to a great height. This

PLATE 36: Tetrarchs, San Marco, Venice (Photo: Sarah Bassett)

statue stood first in Chrysopolis because the army of Alexander broke through two lines at one time in that place. And because of this act, Chrysopolis was so named by the Macedonian. And from the army came the name Strategeion. And the statue stood in Chrysopolis just as the soldiers had erected it. And Constantine the Great brought the statue to the city.

243

Kedrenos I, 563:

In the Strategeion there is the tripod of Hekate and an equestrian statue of Constantine the Great holding a cross.

*Patria* and Kedrenos report on equestrian statues in the Strategeion. It is possible that they refer to the same image and that Kedrenos has re-identified a statue of Alexander as Constantine.

The report that the statue, which is said to have been brought by Constantine from Chrysopolis, stood "to a great height" suggests display on a high base or honorific column. Identification with any of the known Alexander types (cf. cat. no. 120) is impossible.

### 167. OBELISK

Notitia urbis Constantinopolitanae, 223 (Seeck):

Strategeion, in which there is a Theodosian forum and a square Theban obelisk.

Mordtmann (1892) and Guilland (1969) identified this obelisk with one that Gilles (II. 9) saw in the Seraglio; however, Gilles, who was aware that there once had been an obelisk in the Strategeion, considers the Seraglio obelisk, which was no longer extant when he was writing, to have been different. Iversen (1972) is of the same opinion. Because the fifth-century *Notitia Urbis Constantinopolitanae* does not refer to the obelisk in the Hippodrome, but does mention a "Theban" obelisk in the Strategeion, a provenance identical to that of the Hippodrome monument, Gilles (II. 11) proposed that the monolith now in Istanbul had originally been raised on the parade ground where it stood until shaken and broken in an earthquake of unspecified date. In the aftermath of this event, Gilles suggests that the fallen upper portion of the obelisk was brought to the Hippodrome. Guilland (1969) adopts this position. Although it is clear that the Hippodrome obelisk was erected after it was broken, and the designation of the Strategeion obelisk as "Theban" conforms to the known provenance of the Hip-

podrome monument, Iversen (1972) rejects this view stating that there is no factual evidence in support of the hypothesis, which he believes was propounded by Gilles as an explanation for the *Notitia's* silence on the subject of the Hippodrome obelisk. Indeed, the existing evidence flatly contradicts this proposition. The erection of the Hippodrome obelisk took place in 390, twenty to twenty-five years before the writing of the *Notitia*. Further, it seems highly unlikely that a broken obelisk would be considered an appropriate decor for an area as important as the Strategeion. Furthermore, other obelisks, also destroyed, are known to have been in the city. It is therefore possible that the Strategeion obelisk was yet another import from Thebes in Egypt.

*Bibliography:* Gilles 1561 bis II. 9 and II. 11; Mordtmann, 1892: 5; Guilland, 1969: 56; Iversen, 1972: II: 9–35

### 168. APHRODITE

*Patria* II, 65:

Concerning the guest house of Theophilos. At the place called the Zeugma on the hill, the large building, which appears to be a hospital, was turned into a brothel by Constantine the Great. [It also had been used as Isidore the patrician's house, and then later as a convent: it was Theodore who made it into a hospice.] A statue of Aphrodite also stood there on an elaborate column of stone. The aforementioned building was a place for fornicators who went there to have intercourse with the prostitutes who lived in it. There was an order that neither another brothel nor any such prostitutes could exist outside this house.

### 169. APOLLO KITHAROEDOS

*Patria* II, 4:

Concerning the statue carrying a kithara. The sculptors have Apollo holding a kithara in his hand, as if the sun were the harmony of all things.

Generating light for the rest of the stars it creates the conditions for the birth and animation of all living things.

The statue appears to have been a variant of the Apollo Kitharoedos type created by the fourth-century B.C. sculptor Euphranor (*LMIC*, s.v. "Apollo"). The standing god wears a floor-length peplos belted above the waist and a long chlamys flows from his shoulders. He carries a kithara in one hand, while taking a step forward. Hair falls in long, curling locks around his shoulders and a laurel wreath crowns his head (Helbig 4, n. 82).

## 170. APOLLO, PYTHIAN

Eusebios, *VC* III, 54:

The pompous statues of brass were exposed to view in all the public places of the imperial city: so that here a Pythian, there a Sminthian Apollo excited the contempt of the beholder: while the Delphic tripods were deposited in the Hippodrome and the Muses of Helikon in the palace. In short, the city which bore his name was everywhere filled with brazen statues of the most exquisite workmanship, which had been dedicated in every province, and which the deluded victims of superstition had long vainly honored as gods with numberless victims and burnt sacrifices, though now at length they learned to think rightly, when the emperor held up these very playthings to be the ridicule and the sport of all beholders. (Mango)

A specific Pythian Apollo typology is unknown, even though statues dedicated to this aspect of the god's nature are referred to at various shrines throughout the Hellenic world. The major Pythian cult center was the sanctuary at Delphi. Shrines and cult centers also existed at Argos, Megara, and Athens. In describing the statue as Pythian, Eusebios could be referring either to a specific cult image, or to another statue taken from one of the titular sanctuaries. It also is possible that he is simply using the term to refer generally to statues of Apollo scattered

about the city, without meaning to identify or imply a specific image.

## 171. APOLLO, SMINTHIAN

Eusebios, *VC* III, 54: see no. 170.

The statue is said to have been brought by Constantine. Designation as Sminthian indicates a provenance at Chryse in the Troad, the site of the cult of the Sminthian or Mouse Apollo. The cult took its name from the fact that a mouse (σμίνθος) appeared with the god in his image. In describing the Constantinopolitan statue as Sminthian Eusebios could be referring to the temple statue itself, or to another figure of Apollo taken from the sanctuary. Several Sminthian Apollos appear to have existed and the reference might easily refer to more than one statue. It is also possible that Eusebios may have used the epithet in a general way to conjure a vision of a variety of ancient images in the city.

The appearance of the Sminthian Apollo is the subject of controversy. Strabo described the statue as a figure with a mouse beneath its foot and attributes the work to the fourth-century B.C. sculptor Skopas of Paros. Although the description is fairly straightforward, the issue is clouded by numismatic evidence. Coins from Alexandria Troad, the administrative center of the cult, clearly depict the temple statue but in a style alien to that of Skopas (Grace, 1932: figs. 1–4). The coins show a stiff, archaic or archaizing image, while the style of Skopas partakes of the lively naturalistic style of the late fourth century B.C. The discrepancy between word and image has led to various suggestions: that Skopas did indeed create the statue, but in a deliberately archaizing manner under the pressure of religious conservatism (Grace, 1932: 229; Lehmann, 1982: 258–61), or that the sculptor made only the mouse, leaving the original, archaic image in place (Grace, 1932: 230).

Numismatic evidence from the Roman period has generated yet another set of ideas. Two bronze coins issued under Commodus (Arias, 1952: 110–11) show a far more naturalistic image of the god that fits well with what is understood as Skopas's style. Apollo stands on his straight left leg, his torso bent over a bent right leg that is raised on a support. The figure is naked and carries a bow. Coin legends describe the image as a representation of the Sminthian Apollo. Objections to this identification have been raised on the grounds that this particular iconography does not appear before the Roman period and then on coins other than those of Alexandria Troas (Grace, 1932: 229).

The iconography and date of manufacture for the Sminthian Apollo remains problematic (Stewart, 1977: 128); however, if "Sminthian" is taken as a designation of provenance, it is possible for the various images to be accommodated to the epithet. Both types may have come from the sanctuary where they served different functions. For example, one may have been the main temple image, while the other may have been erected elsewhere in the sanctuary.

## 172. ATHENA

*Patria* II, 3:

Concerning the statue carrying a spear. The statue of Athena carried a spear and a shield in accordance with strength and gallantry and on account of her repulsion of all evil through wisdom. For so she is in her own mind. And she wore a helmet to draw attention to her head as the apex of wisdom. And (she had) a wild olive as if she were the essence of purity. For the olive is the light of the forest. And she wore a gorgoneion on her breast to indicate the quickness of her mind.

Reference to the attributes of spear and shield suggest identification with any one of a number of images derived from the fifth-century Promachos type by Pheidias or its variant the Parthenos.

## 173. BACCHANTE (PLATE 37)

Paulus Silentiarius, *Anth. Gr.* XVI, 57:

On a Bacchant in Byzantium

Not Nature, but Art, made the Baccant frenzied, mixing madness with the stone. (Paton)

Anonymous, *Anth. Gr.* XVI, 58:

Hold the Baccant, lest, though she be stone she leap over the threshold and escape from the temple. (Paton)

Agathias Scholasticus, *Anth. Gr.* XVI, 59:

The sculptor set up a stone of a Bacchant, yet ignorant of how to beat the swift cymbals with her hands and ashamed. For so does she bend forward, and looks as if she were crying, "Go ye out, and I will strike them with none standing by." (Paton)

Simonides, *Anth. Gr.* XVI, 60:

A. Who is this? B. A Bacchant. A. And who carved her? B. Skopas. A. And who made her frenzied, Bacchus or Skopas? B. Skopas. (Paton)

The statue was of stone, probably marble. Attribution is to Skopas of Paros (fourth century B.C.). The general description indicates a frenzied pose, an observation consistent with a statue of a maenad (Dresden, inv. 133) identified as a copy of a Skopasian original executed around 360 B.C. (Stewart, 1977: 91–93; 140–41). Broken off below the knees and without its once-raised arms, the maenad writhes in Bacchic ecstasy, her torso arched and twisted and her head thrown back. Loose hair streams down her back and a disheveled garment open at the side only partially covers her nude body. Kallistratos (Stewart, 1977: 140–41) described the figure as stone and it is entirely possible that the statue was taken to Constantinople from an unknown provenance.

## 174. HERAKLES

*Patria* II, 8a:

On the statue of Herakles carrying three apples . . . these three apples show that he possesses the whole harmonious universe as if it were a sphere divided into three parts.

PLATE 37: Skopas, Bacchante (Dancing Maenad), Staatliche Kunstsammlungen, Dresden (Photo: © Staatliche Kunstsammlungen)

Herakles stands with apples in his hand. Reference to the apples specifies the subject as the twelfth Labor, the capture of the golden apples of the Hesperides sisters. Numerous representations of this subject exist. The earliest is a freestanding youthful depiction in which the hero stands with his hand behind his back, concealing the apples. Although reconstructed by analogy to the Herakles Farnese, the invention of the general type has been attributed to Polykleitos in the fifth century B.C. (*LIMC*, s.v. "Herakles"). A second representation shows Herakles seated with club and apples in an outstretched hand (*LIMC*, s.v. "Herakles"). Like the standing Herakles, this statue is of fifth- or fourth-century B.C. origin. It is impossible to tell which Herakles type stood in Constantinople. Given the popularity of the Herakles as a subject it is likely that the figure was a work of later Roman manufacture.

### 175. HERMES

*Patria* II, 10:

Concerning the statue of Hermes carrying a bag. They say that Hermes is the agent of wealth and business. Because of this, the Hermes carries a purse. But the Phoenicians made images of the same god carrying a purse of gold, which is symbol of power. And the Greeks made statues of him bearing arms as if he were a hoplite subjugating men.

Although the passage is too vague in terms of descriptive detail to allow specific association with any known ancient statue, mention of the purse as an attribute identifies the figure as one of several Roman Hermes types originally associated with commerce (*RE*, XV, 1, 100, s.v. "Hermes"; *LIMC*, s.v. "Hermes"; Babelon/Blanchet, 1895: 149–50).

### 176. HERMES (?)

*Patria* II, 2:

Concerning the statue of Januarius. They represent the statue of Januarius as a tetramorph because of the four seasons. Some modeled the statue holding out keys in its right hand as if it were the origin of time, the opener of the year, a guard. Others [modeled it] holding three hundred small pebbles in its right hand, sixty-five in its left, as if [symbolic of] the year. Hence Longinus is compelled to interpret Eonarius [i.e. eternity] incorrectly [as Januarius] as the father of time.

Janus, the Roman god of Beginnings, was associated with Januarius, god of the first month. Representations of Januarius are not known, and it is possible that Janus was intended; however, the described iconography, that of a four-

headed figure, or tetramorph, does not correspond to that of Janus who was shown as a double-headed herm. An alternative identification is as the four-headed Hermes, an invention of the Roman imperial age (*RE*, XV, 1, 997–1000; Babelon/Blanchet, 1895: n. 362).

Januarius: see Hermes (no. 176).

### 177. PAN

*Sozomen* II, 5:

The brazen images which were skillfully wrought were carried to the city, named after the emperor, and placed there as objects of embellishment, where they may still be seen in public places, as in the streets, the hippodrome and the palaces. Amongst them was the statue of Apollo which was in the seat of the oracle of the Pythoness, and likewise the statues of the Muses from Helicon, the tripods from Delphos, and the much extolled Pan, which Pausanias the Lacedaemonian and the Grecian cities had devoted, – after the war against the Medes. (Schaff and Wace)

### 178. PRIAPUS

*Patria* II, 12:

Concerning the statue of Priapos. They made the statue of Priapus-Horus that was given human form by the Egyptians, holding a scepter in its right hand pointing to the dry land and the sea. And in his left hand he holds his erect penis, as if to reveal the hidden seeds of the earth. He bears wings for swiftness of movement; and a round-edged mirror symbolizing universal worship, for they believe this thing itself to be the sun. As noted, the statue has human form and holds a scepter in its right hand, his erect penis in his left; there are wings on it and in the middle of the wings a round mirror.

Priapos is a divinity associated with fecundity and the generative forces of nature, a role recognized in the text. In certain instances his image also functioned as an apotropaion, his erect phallus warding off evil, along with various other attributes such as the mirror. Throughout antiquity Priapos maintained a lively and close association with other divinities, Hellenic and alien. Among others, he was linked to the Egyptian god Horus, as also noted in the *Patria*. Another Egyptian deity with whom he was associated was Serapis, an association apparent in the mirror slung across his back.

## 179. SELEUKOS

*Patria* II, 14:

Concerning the statue having horns on its head. The statue was of Seleukos, the son of Antiochos, who was called Nikander throughout his manhood. This very man fell in love with the woman Stratonike and because of the proximity of his lover he was weakened and enslaved. They were joined by the priest Erasistratos. It is said that when Seleukos was with Alexander of Macedon a sacrificial bull escaped and Seleukos alone prevailed, placing horns upon his own head. And on account of this event, he bestowed upon the statue of himself horns around the head.

The reference is to Seleukos I Nikator (358–281 B.C.), founder of Antioch-on-the-Orontes (301 B.C.) and the Seleucid Kingdom of Syria. Numismatic evidence shows two portrait types (Richter, 1965). In the first Seleukos appears in profile with short, tousled hair bound by a fillet, the typical image of a Hellenistic ruler. The second type shows him wearing the horned helmet of a Syrian king. A large horn, indicating divinity, rises from above the earpiece of the helmet. Similarity between this numismatic type and the *Patria* description suggests that this portrait type existed in sculpture and stood in Constantinople.

# NOTES

## INTRODUCTION

1. This book derives from subject matter first presented in my dissertation. See Bassett, 1985. It also incorporates ideas from my previously published work on particular aspects of the Constantinopolitan collection: see Guberti Bassett, 1991, 1996, 2000.

2. Janin, 1964: 35–36 lists fires and earthquakes chronologically. For further information on fires see Schneider, 1941. On earthquakes Dück, 1903/04: nr. 6–12, and, more recently, Guidoboni, 1989: 190–94. On the melting of statuary for coin see *Par.* 13, 42, 54.

3. For the Crusader sack, see Niketas Choniates, 647–55; Robert de Clari and Geoffroy de Villehardouin, 11–186. For a discussion of looting with respect to Venice, see Demus, 1960: 22–27 and accompanying notes; Buckton, 1984. For the particular case of the Horses of San Marco, see cat. no. 139.

4. On the events of the Ottoman conquest see Runciman, 1969, in general and page 152 in particular for the Sultan's response.

5. For an overview of the extant archaeological material and excavation history, see Barsanti, 1990.

6. "Insomma, per questa e molte alter cagioni, si vede quanto già fusse al tempo di Gostantino venuta al basso la scultura e con essa insieme l'altre arti migliori. E se alcuna cosa mancava all'ultima rovina lora, venne lora data compiutamente dal partirsi Gostantino di Roma per andare a porre la sede dell'Impero a Bisanzio, perciò che egli condusse in Grecia non solamente tutti i migliori sculptori et altri artefici di quella età, comunche fussero, ma ancora una infinità di statue e d'altre cose di sculptura bellisime" (*Vite* 1: 15).

7. For Vasari's views on the perfectibility of art and the cyclical nature of artistic production, see the introduction to part two of the *Vite* 3: 3–19.

8. On Vasari as a historian, see Boase, 1979, and Rubin, 1995.

9. On the development of Byzantine studies, see Ostrogorsky, 1969: 1–21.

10. Ostrogorsky, 1969: 1–21 and Musto in Gilles, 1729: xvi–xx.

11. Musto in Gilles, 1729: xvi–xx.

12. On Gilles, see Ebersolt, 1918: 72–83; Pascal, 1857; Reulos and Bietenholz, 1985–87: 2/98; Van der Vin, 1980: 276; Musto in Gilles, 1729: xvi–xx.

13. See Gilles, 1533.

14. See Gilles, 1532.

15. See note 12 for pertinent sources.

16. For the *Notitia Urbis Constantinopolis* see Seeck, 1877: 229–43.

17. For examples of earlier texts, see the accounts of Robert de Clari and Geoffroy de Villehardouin (as in note 3), and Majeska, 1984.

18. Ostrogorsky, 1969: 2–21.

19. Du Cange, 1688.

20. In addition to describing the city plan and its architectural components, all modern topographical studies inevitably incorporate references to antiquities as a matter of course. See Janin, 1964; Guilland, 1969; Bauer, 1996.

21. See Heyne, 1790–91: 3–38. On Heyne himself, see "Christian Gottlieb Heyne," *Encyclopedia*

*Britannica*, 11th edition (Cambridge, 1910–11): 13: 438.

22. A bronze statue of Athena in the Forum of Constantine has received the most attention. See two early articles: Jahn, 1848, and Gurlitt, 1893. For a complete bibliography see cat. no. 107.

23. See Dawkins, 1924.

24. See Mango, 1963.

25. The issue is taken up in the following articles: Cutler, 1968; Angel de Elvira, 1984, 1987; James, 1996. For monographic treatment, see Dagron, 1984, and Berger, 1988.

26. Angel de Elvira, 1984, tackles the issues of appearance and typology with respect to statuary in the Baths of Zeuxippos. For consideration of actual collections, their location, display, and meaning, see Stupperich, 1982; Guberti Bassett, 1991; Mango, Vickers, and Francis, 1992; Guberti Bassett, 1996, 2000.

27. In the context of art-historical study, the issue of appropriation touches not only on such issues related to objects and their history as collecting and display, but also on the more ephemeral ideas of adaptation and emulation. The literature is vast. For a summary discussion of appropriation and its intellectual place in the discipline of art history, see Nelson and Schiff, 1996: 116–28.

28. For the text and translation see Christodoros of Thebes. On Christodoros himself, see Baumgarten, 1881; *RE* 3/2: 2450–52 s.v. Christodoros; Viljamaa, 1963: 29–31. On ekphrasis as a genre, see Lehmann-Hartleben, 1941; Downey, 1971: 2/ 32–77; Maguire, 1974; Hunger, 1978: 1/178–88; Maguire, 1981; James and Webb, 1991.

29. For the text and translations, see Niketas Choniates. On Niketas, see Hunger, 1978: I: 430–41; and Cutler, 1968.

30. Most famously, Christian Blinkenberg denied the claims of the tenth-century author Georgios Kedrenos for the presence of the Aphrodite of Knidos and other famous ancient statues in Constantinople. Scornful of the whole notion he characterized Kedrenos's writing as "ein Gewebe von Fabeln" ("a tissue of lies"). See Blinkenberg, 1933: 32–34.

31. For analysis of the text and the reconstruction of Kedrenos's sources, see Mango, Vickers, and Francis, 1992.

32. Crucial to the reassessment of the Byzantine literature are the two landmark studies by Gilbert Dagron (1984) and Albrecht Berger (1988). In their studies of the eighth-century *Parastaseis syntomoi chronikai* and its tenth-century derivative the *Patria Konstantinopoleos*, Dagron and Berger not only observe the medieval imagination but also do so in a way that accepts the changed modes of seeing and understanding that characterize this period as legitimate. For purposes of this study, the implications have been great. Texts once dismissed as fiction can now be understood to have documentary validity, albeit in a way unique to the Middle Ages. Thus, for those inquiring into the sculptured collections of Constantinople, references to statuary can and probably should be considered legitimate. At the same time, however, awareness of changed attitudes toward statuary and other ancient monuments allows for the possibility of stripping away later, accumulated definitions and meanings.

33. The major resources for the study of Constantinopolitan topography are Gilles, (1561bis); Du Cange,(1680); Mango, 1959; Janin, 1964; Guilland, 1969; Müller-Wiener, 1977; Mango, 1985; Magdalino, 1996; Bauer, 1996.

34. On urbanism, see Lynch, 1960; Kostof, 1991, 1992. For the discussion of these issues with respect to Roman antiquity, see MacDonald, 1986.

35. For specific discussion, see Becatti, 1973; Strong, 1973; Pape, 1975; Pollitt, 1978; Ridgway, 1984: 109–11.

36. See Bagnall, 2001: especially 229–30; Empereur, 1998, includes evidence for the large number of pharaonic monuments, among them obelisks and sphinxes of the New Kingdom and Saite periods, that were marshaled for display in the city. Although the date for the importation of these monuments is controversial, with opinion divided between the Ptolomaic and the Roman periods, Bagnall and Empereur both favor the former.

37. On the fortunes of the Tyrannicides, see Pliny, *NH* XXXIV.19.70; Paus. I.8.5. Plutarch *Themistocles*, 31, describes the Athenian general's encounter with plundered statuary from his home city at Sardis.

38. The literature on the history and practice of collecting is immense, embracing, among

others, the disciplines of history, art history, anthropology, and sociology. Although it is neither possible nor desirable to survey that literature completely, it is useful to point out the consensus regarding the purposes and definitions of collecting and collections as argued in the modern literature. Generally scholars agree to the fact that it is impossible to exhibit objects without putting a construction on them, and that such a construction, itself the result of the selection of objects, is in and of itself a statement not only about the objects chosen, but also about the culture from which it comes and those who choose it. For elaboration of these points see the essays collected in Karp and Lavine, 1991, and Elsner and Cardinal, 1994. Also useful are MacPherson, 1962; Clifford, 1988; Baxandall, 1991; Pearce, 1993. For a more complete survey of recent trends, see Berlo et al., 1995.

39. For a discussion of the social role of the paideia, see Kaster, 1988, and Brown, 1992.

40. On the relationship between history and myth, see Veyne, 1988; Le Goff, 1992; and Fentress and Wickham, 1992. On history and historiography in Late Antiquity, see the essays in Clark, 1990, especially Croke, 1990.

41. Jerome, *Chron.* 324.

## CHAPTER ONE

1. The 324 date derives from Themistios *Or* 4: 83, which states that the foundation took place at the same time that Constantine's son Constantius was raised to the rank of Caesar. That date is established as November 8, 324. See Seeck, 1919: 174. For more detailed discussion and bibliography, see Krautheimer, 1983: 134, n. 5.

2. Alternative sites included Ilion, Chalcedon, and Thessaloniki. For Ilion, see Theophanes, 23; Zonaras III, 13–14. For Chalcedon, see Michael Glykas, 462; Constantine Manasses, 101–02; Kedrenos I, 496; Zonaras III, 13–14. For Thessaloniki, see Kedrenos I, 496.

3. On the dedication and the foundation of the city, see Eusebios *VC* III, 48; Philostorgios II, 9; Zosimos II, 30; Hesychios, 41; Malalas 319–20; John Lydus, *De Mens*, 65; *Chron. Pasch.* 528–30; *Par.* 55–56; *Patria* III, 10.

4. On the topography and development of the city, see most recently Janin, 1964; Beck, 1973; Müller-Wiener, 1977: 16–28; Mango, 1985.

5. For sources pertinent to the dedication, see note 3, this chapter.

6. Eusebios *VC* II, 48, on the dedication, which not only states that the city was replete with Christian shrines, but also claims that there were no temples or temple images. For the development of Christian interpretation of the dedication, see Frolow, 1944.

7. On the dedication to Tyche/Anthousa, see Malalas, 321, and *Chron. Pasch.* 277.

8. Debates regarding the extent to which the foundation and dedication were pagan or Christian events dominate the scholarship. In addition to Frolow, 1944, see Strzygowski, 1893; Preger, 1901, 1902; Maurice, 1904, 1911: III, lxxvi–lxxxii; Bréhier, 1915; Lathoud, 1924, 1925; Janin, 1964: 21–31; Dagron, 1974: 29–47; Krautheimer, 1983: 41–67; Mango: 1985: 23–35.

9. On the early history of Byzantium, see Dagron, 1974: 13–19, especially 13, n. 1, which lists primary sources relevant to the pre-Constantinian city; Müller-Wiener, 1977: 16–19; Mango, 1985: 13–21; Jones, 1971: 1–27. See *RE* 3 (1899), 1117–57 (Miller); "Byzanz," *Dictionnaire d'Histoire et de Géographie ecclesiastiques* 10 (1938): 1501–11 (Bréhier).

10. For general remarks on pre-Constantinian topography, see Müller-Wiener, 1977: 16–19; Janin, 1964: 9–20; and Mango, 1985: 13–21. Mango, 1985: 14–17, presents sources for the early wall, arguing for a single wall rather than two early walls as adduced by Janin and Müller-Wiener. He notes that Herodian (III, 17) appears to have seen the city wall around 240 and commented at that time that it was still in ruins; however, because Byzantium was not overrun in the barbarian incursions of the late third century, he supposes that the wall was restored sometime before 260 or 270. On the theater of Byzantium, see Martiny, 1938.

11. The Severan developments are attested in the sources. See *Chron. Pasch.* 494–95; Malalas, 291–92; Kedrenos I, 422; Zosimos II, 33. Archaeological excavation, though sporadic, confirms many of the Severan developments. See especially Casson, 1928 and 1929.

12. *Patria* I, 68, outlines the major streets. For further information, see Müller-Wiener, 1977: 268–70; Schneider, 1950; Berger, 1997.

13. On the Severan Tetrastoon see Zosimos II, 33; Malalas, 291; *Chron. Pasch.* 494. See also Mango, 1959: 42–47; Janin, 1964: 59–62; Müller-Wiener, 1977: 248.

14. On the Basilika, see Zosimos II, 31; Bauer, 1996: 151, n. 19; and Janin, 1964: 157–60.

15. See Malalas, 321; *Chron. Pasch.* 494; Hesychios, 37; *Patria* II, 37; Casson, 1929 and 1996 for excavation of the site and a discussion of the building remains.

16. For a general outline of the circus's history, see Müller-Wiener, 1977: 64–71. On the Severan circus, see Guilland, 1970.

17. Ephesos came under Roman rule in 133 B.C. and in 29 B.C. attained the rank of capital of the Province of Asia. The city's heyday dates to the second century, a time that saw construction of the Library of Celsus, the Serapeion, numerous altars, nymphaea, and gymnasia. See Oster, 1987 for bibliography. For general surveys of the city, see Bammer, 1988; Hogarth, 1980; Alzinger, 1972. Detailed reports on individual buildings may be found in *Ephesos*. For postclassical development of the city, see Foss, 1979, and Bauer, 1996: 269–300.

Miletus shared a similar history to that of its neighbor, Ephesos. Although the provincial capital was nearby, the city maintained an active building program. For an overview, see Kleiner, 1968; Müller-Wiener, 1988. Reports from the ongoing excavations may be found in *Milet*.

Leptis Magna was incorporated into the Roman Empire in 46 B.C. Its architectural development peaked in the second century under the patronage of its native son, Septimius Severus. Ward-Perkins, 1948; Squarciapino, 1966. For specific buildings, see Bartoccini, 1929, 1931, 1960.

18. Roman imperialism and the related phenomenon of romanization are the focus of a large body of contemporary scholarship. Current scholarly focus emphasizes the varieties of response to Roman occupation. See Woolf, 1992, and the collected essays in Mattingly, 1997, especially Whittaker, 1997. For historiographical and methodological considerations, see Freeman, 1997, and Barrett, 1997. On the structural and architectural development of the Roman Empire's cities and the meaning of romanization within the urban context, see Hanfmann, 1975; MacDonald, 1986; Mitchell, 1987; Alcock, 1989; Whittaker, 1997; Yegül, 2000; Zanker, 2000.

19. Philostorgios II, 9, describes the event. On the rites of *limitatio*, see *RE* I: 672–701, s.v. "Limitatio."

20. On the divinations and horoscopes, see John Lydus, *De Mens.* IV.2., which states that the priests Sopater and Praetextatus performed the rites. For Sopater, see *RE* III (ser. 2.5): 1006–7, s.v. "Sopater."

21. Zosimos II. 30 documents the expansion of the city with the addition of the new wall. See also Preger, 1910.

22. On the street system surrounding the Augusteion and the Milion, see Malalas, 321; *Chron. Pasch.* 528; *Patria* I, 68. For modern discussion, see Müller-Wiener, 1977: 216–18; Bauer, 1996: 151; Janin, 1964: 36–37; Mango, 1959: 78–81; and Berger, 2000. Berger's reconstruction does not include a north fork leading to the Strategeion, while Mango's does. This branch of the street is also mentioned in the Byzantine life of St. Photeine. See Talbot, 1994: 112. For the Milion in particular: Janin, 1964: 103–04; Mango, 1959: 47–48.

23. The earliest reference to the space by the name of Augusteion is in the fifth-century *Notitia Dignitatum* (region 4). Hesychios, 17, explains the dedication to Constantine's mother, a notion confirmed by Malalas, 321. Later sources, specifically Kedrenos 1. 657 and George Pachymeres, 917, state that the term Augusteion derives specifically from the statue of Helena set up by Constantine. On the Augusteion in general see: Mango, 1959: 42–47; Janin, 1964: 59–62, 73–77; Guilland, 1969: 40–54; Bauer, 1996: 148–67.

24. A 1933 excavation at the site of the demolished Ottoman Palace of Justice revealed two lengths of wall that have been identified as the southeast corner of the Augusteion. See Mamboury, 1938; Schneider, 1939: 187; Mango, 1959: 42–43. The western wall of the forum came to light in 1934. See Mamboury, 1934 bis. Fragmentary remains of a third wall established the northern limit of the forum. See Mango, 1959: 42–43, who also considers the space enclosed by these

walls to be too vast to constitute the Augusteion and suggests that the latter space was carved out of the Severan forum. He estimates the size at 17.500 square meters. Stichel, 2000, reduces these measurements substantially, arguing that the Justinianic Augusteion of the post-Nika rebellion rebuilding would have measured around 3.500 square meters. It is not clear from his article whether these tailored dimensions derive from those of the earlier Augusteion or whether they represent a further diminution of the Constantinian space.

25. Prokop. *De Aed.* I, 2,1, describes the Augusteion as an agora, indicating the public nature of the space. He makes no reference to commercial activity. By contrast, John Lydus, *De Mens*, 163, refers to the Augusteion as a food market. Berger (1987: 23–28) recognizes the public function of the space, and Bauer, 1996: 148–65 does as well. In the middle Byzantine period the area appears to have been remodeled as a courtyard to the Hagia Sophia. See Mango, 1959: 46, for discussion and bibliography.

26. Zosimos II, 31; Bauer, 1996: 151, n. 19.

27. Zosimos II, 31. On the location of the temples in the Basilika complex, see Mango, 1959: 44. For discussion of the temples and their images see Chapter three of this volume.

28. For a general outline of the circus's history, see Müller-Wiener, 1977: 64–71. On the Severan and Constantinian circus, see Guilland, 1970.

29. Both terms are valid, although the Romans and the Byzantines appear to have preferred *euripus*. See Humphrey, 1986: 175–76; Vickers, 1972: 30; Mango, 1949: 180–93.

30. Archaeological remains of the Great Palace are few and none date to the fourth century. The earliest surviving material from the Palace is a vast sixth-century floor mosaic from the Justinianic age. See Ebersolt, 1910; Bury, 1912: 210–25; Mamboury, 1934; Brett et al. 1947; Talbot Rice, 1958; Mango, 1959; Guilland 1969: 1:3–367; Miranda, 1976; Jobst, 1987; Trilling, 1989.

31. Casson, 1928, 1929, 1930; Janin, 1964: 222–24; Müller-Wiener, 1977: 51.

32. On the bath-gymnasium, see Nielsen, 1990: 105–08; Yegül, 1992: 250–313.

33. Malalas, 321.

34. On the Strategeion, see Mordtmann, 1892: 5; Guilland, 1959: 53–55, 1969: 2: 55–56; Janin,

1964: 13, 17, 41, 94, 431–32; Mango, 1985: 57, 43.

35. See note 7, this chapter.

36. See Socrates, II, 16, which records the Constantinian foundation of H. Eirene and reports that the church was enlarged from a smaller foundation, possibly a *domus ecclesia*. Justinian rebuilt the original church. See Peschlow, 1977.

37. Beck, 1973, takes up the problem of the monumental development of the city in these terms. MacDonald, 1985, and Zanker, 2000, discuss more generally the phenomenon of bestowing *romanitas* through architectural development. On the larger issues of romanization and *romanitas*, see Mattingly, 1997, and Fentress, 2000.

38. On late Roman and Tetrarchic circuses, see Humphrey, 1986: 579–638.

39. On the Roman *miliarum aureum,* see *LTUR 3*, 250–51; *NTDAR* 254; Nash II, 64; and Platner-Ashby, 342.

40. MacDonald, 1985. See especially 189–202 on column displays and their meaning in the urban context: "Column displays in general were certainly suffused with imperial content. This was not only a matter of signaling dominion or authority. Across the empire, column displays conveyed an architectural message of common membership in an urban society under the care of Rome, the steward of received classical culture." For further consideration of the symbolic value of column displays, see Onians, 1988. See especially 41–58 on Roman sensitivity to columns and columnar display, their viewing and aspects of their reception. For a discussion of this reception with respect to reused building materials, see Kinney, 2001.

41. MacDonald, 1985: 32–66; on streets and plazas, Zanker, 2000.

42. Janin, 1964: 328–29; Mango 1985: 30–31; Berger, 1997: 396

43. Janin, 1964: 62–64; Müller-Wiener, 1977: 255–57; Reinach, 1896; Bauer, 1996: 167–86.

44. On the disposition of buildings in the Forum, see most recently Bauer, 1996: 167–86.

45. Rounded public spaces delimited by colonnades began to appear during the period of the high empire in the cities of North Africa, the eastern Mediterranean, and the Balkans. See MacDonald, 1985: 54–55, and Segal, 1997: 55–81;

Bauer, 1996: 184, n. 284 provides an extensive bibliography.

46. Segal, 1997: 70.

47. On Gerasa, see Parapetti, 1983–84.

48. Bauer, 1996: 184–85.

49. Bauer, 1996: 184–85.

50. See Constantine the Rhodian, 90–162; Kedrenos I, 610; Zonaras III, 124. For general remarks, see Berger, 1988: 293; Reinach, 1896: 88; Wulff, 1898: 319; Bauer, 1996: 171.

51. On the Constantinopolitan Senate as an institution see Dagron, 1974: 119–46, who claims that Constantine founded the Senate. Contrast Jones, 1964 III: 546, who believes it was constituted by Constantius II in 357.

52. Contrast Speck, 1995, who proposes that the temple stood on a north-south axis paralleling the course of the Mese's northern fork with stairs fronting both the southern and the northern sides giving access respectively to the main cella and a series of smaller niches.

53. The name Philadelphion is first used to identify the space in the eighth century. See *Par.* 56 and 70. Identification as such derives from the observation of the porphyry figures of the Tetrarchs, now in Venice. Described by the author of the text not as tetrarchs, but as representations of Constantine and his three sons, the group was thought to represent the brotherly love implied in the name. The original name adduced by the *Par.* author is Proteichisma, or walled area. The exact nature of the place is not well understood. To begin with, location is not agreed on. Although mentioned in conjunction with the Capitol, which is known to have stood at the fork in the Mese, the location of the Philadelphion together with its shape is not known. Mango, 1985: 28–30, believes it simply to have been an elaborated stretch of the Mese outfitted with porphyry columns and sculpture. Bauer points out that the outfitting of the area with sculpture and the tenth-century description in *De cer.* suggests a formally defined plaza. Janin, 1964: 410; Unger, 1888: 175; Müller-Wiener, 1977: 267; and Krautheimer, 1983: 55, all favor some sort of regularly defined public space. Berger, 1988: 330, locates it on the wedge of land at the fork in the road immediately in front of the Capitol itself as if it were a kind of vestibule to the Capitol, and Bauer, 1996: 228–33, concurs with this solution.

The early name, Proteichisma, would support this reconstruction, as it suggests an area defined by a wall. On the Constantinian development of the site, see Mango, 1985: 30, n. 46 esp.

54. On the Capitol, see: Bauer, 1996: 230–32; Berger, 1988: 330–37; Mango, 1985: 28–30; Janin, 1964: 174–76.

55. As in all Roman cities, the Capitol took its name from and referred to the Capitol in Rome. See *LTUR* 1: 226–34; *NTDAR*, 68–69; Platner-Ashby, 95–98. Reference to Rome was sealed in the construction of a temple to the deities of the Capitoline temple, the triad of Jupiter, Juno, and Minerva. Temples to the triad, the official divinities of the Roman state, in the outlying cities of the Empire confirmed a link with Rome and the guiding presence of the Roman state in the life and fortunes of a city. See MacDonald, 1985: 119, 129. Mango, 1985: 30, notes the particular importance of the Capitol given its antiquity as an institution.

56. For a description of the mausoleum, see Eusebios *VC* IV. 58–60. As Mango, 1990: 54, points out, the building itself may be envisioned by analogy to other late imperial mausolea, specifically the tombs of Diocletian at Split, of Galerius at Thessaloniki, and, at Rome, of Maxentius on the Via Appia and of Helena on the Via Labicana. On the church of Holy Apostles, see Müller-Wiener, 1977: 405–11, and Johnson, 1986: 80–91, for general history and bibliography. For comparanda, see Spieser, 1984: 127–32, with a critical bibliography on the rotunda; Rasch, 1984; Deichmann and Tschira, 1957.

57. See Johnson, 1986, for a discussion of Late Antique imperial burial.

58. Krautheimer, 1983: 56. See Regions VI through IX in Seeck, 1876: 229–43, for an account of buildings in the newly developed western territories.

59. The residential nature of the area is agreed on. Unclear is the nature of the housing. Were most houses freestanding single-family units as suggested by the term "domus" or apartments, "insulae," in the Roman sense? The answer depends on the interpretation and understanding of the term "domus" as it is used in later sources. The major source for housing statistics is the fifth-century *Notitia*. Here the terms for residence are essentially two, "domus" and "palatium." Palatium

obviously signals an aristocratic residence of some degree of elegance and importance. The meaning of domus is less clear. In earlier Latin texts the term refers to a self-contained single-family dwelling, which by its very nature describes a certain level of elegance. This aspect clearly remains a feature of its definition in later texts; however, by the later Roman period, specifically in the fifth century when the *Notitia* was being compiled, it is possible that the term came to have a more generic meaning that encompassed a wider range of residential typologies. Specifically, the term domus may also have absorbed the term insula (apartment block), which is never used in the *Notitia* and which appears to have died out as a term. As a result, the class distinctions implicit in the earlier distinction between domus and insula are eliminated as well. Greater levels of luxury in housing that appear around A.D. 300 have been used to adduce the all-encompassing nature of the term domus. On the question of terminology see: Kriesis, 1960; Strube, 1973; Berger, 1997: 382.

Krautheimer, 1983: 56, believes that the housing was similar to Antioch villas. On these, see Stilwell, 1961. However, as Wharton 1995: 23–33, has shown, urban housing has decidedly local characteristics and it is therefore prudent to consider a range of possibility with regard to the appearance of Constantinopolitan housing. Given the overall dependence of the city on building types from western Asia Minor, it is possible that the city's villas were more similar to residences such as the Slope Houses at Ephesos. See Strocka, 1977. The definition of housing stock is important in that it determines population estimates. For the relationship between the two see Jacoby, 1961.

60. On the dedication ceremonies see Malalas, 321; *Chron. Pasch.*, 277. Bauer, 2001, comments on the ceremonies described in the sources.

61. Sozomen II, 3.

62. Zanker, 2000: 33–35, notes in particular the relationship between forum and temple that defined Roman urban development at its civic core.

63. On the Roman cult of Fortuna, see Champeaux, 1982. For archaeological documentation of the various aspects of the Fortuna cults, see *LTUR*, 2: 267–87, especially 285–87 on the state cult. On Magna Mater, see Roller, 1999; Ferguson, 1970:

13–31; Vermaseren, 1977. For archaeological evidence see *LTUR* 3: 206–08.

64. Krautheimer, 1983: 7–40, believes that the decentralized placement of Christian building in Rome under Constantine constituted a deliberate avoidance of the center that was meant to downplay the emperor's Christian patronage and the role of Christianity within the city. By contrast, Curran, 2000: 115, argues that the same building activity should be seen as consistent with Tetrarchic traditions and as such a proclamation of Constantine's imperial presence in the city.

65. Eusebios *HE* X, 5, 2–14, and Lactantius *De mort. pers.* XLVIII, 2–12, report that Constantine granted religious toleration in the edict of Milan. Although the authenticity of the text has been called into question and the notion of the edict itself challenged, the fact remains that Constantine was pragmatic in his dealings with the various religious groups within the Empire and that toleration was a lynchpin of his policy. It was more important for the emperor to consolidate his own power, and he did so by accommodating as many groups as possible. This ability to carve out détente between various groups also extended to his dealings with the various factions within the Christian community. On the Edict of Milan, see Seeck, 1891; Anastos, 1967; Christiensen, 1984. On Constantine and his ability to accommodate rival groups, see Drake, 2000.

### CHAPTER TWO

1. See among other references, *Par.* 7, 11, 16, 34.

2. On the use of copies in Roman art and their public display, see Hanfmann, 1975: 54–75; Vermuele, 1977: esp. 91–93; Ridgway, 1984.

3. The appreciation of a wide chronological and stylistic range in sculpture is by no means limited to Constantinople. Private collections throughout the Empire attest to this zest for variety. See Brinkerhoff, 1970, for a collection from Antioch. For collections from the Villa at Chiragan in Gaul, see Bergmann, 1999. For other Western collections see Wrede, 1972, and Stirling, 1996. As Bergmann points out, a good deal of the statuary that supplied this taste was of contemporary

manufacture. Specifically, she traces the material at Chiragan to Aphrodisias and links it to a taste for the classicizing prevalent at Constantinople. For further observations on the question of style in Late Antiquity, see Hannestadt, 1994: 105–49.

4. For example, the surviving description of the Baths of Zeuxippos makes direct and indirect reference to the use of bronze. See *Ek.* For direct reference, see lines 12, 18, 31, 39, 47, 73, 78, 83, 122, 152, 178, 198, 256, and 314. For indirect reference, see the use of αστράπτω (flash), λάμπω (shine), and παμφαίνω (shine brightly) in lines 13, 92, 99–100, 357, and 388. Nearly one-third of the statues were described as bronze, a high proportion for a bath complex where marble was generally the preferred medium.

5. *VC* III, 54. See cat. no. 18 for text and translation.

6. *Chron. Pasch.* 324.

7. Zosimos II, 32.

8. For Antioch, see *Par.* 62/*Patria* II, 79; Iconium (modern Konya), *Par.* 85, *Patria* II, 85; Chrysopolis *Patria* II. 59.

9. *Patria* II, 73.

10. Installations of ancient statuary were especially numerous at Rome where the piecemeal gathering of antiquities over time resulted in the presence of a large number of famous works of ancient art in the city. For a topographical list of Greek statuary and other works of art on display in Rome, see Pollitt, 1978: esp. 170–71; Ridgway, 1984: 109–11. On Roman public collections and their display, see Becatti, 1973: 18–54; Strong, 1973: 247–64.

11. Sozomen II, 3.

12. Malalas, 319–20. Translation Jeffreys: 173–74.

13. On the components and administrative structure of imperial government, see Jones, 1964: I, 321–410. For the civil service in general and the Praetorian Prefecture in particular, see Jones, 1964: II, 563–606. For finance and taxation, see Jones, 1964: I, 411–69; Jones, 1974; Duncan-Jones, 1990: 174–75; MacMullen, 1976: 129–52. In the early imperial age the dividing line between public and private expenditure was unclear as many public works projects were paid for out of private liturgies. The balance changes in the later Empire, with the imperial government stepping in to underwrite public works projects. For the increasing role of imperial administration at the civic level, see Liebeschuetz, 1972: 119–66. On liturgies, see Finley, 1999: 150–04.

14. On tax collection, see Jones, 1974: 10, 26; Liebeschuetz, 1972: 110–14.

15. On regional diversity, see MacMullen, 1976: 143; for taxation in money and taxation in kind, see Duncan-Jones, 1990: 187–98.

16. For text and French translation, see Baillet, no. 1889.

17. Baillet, no. 1265.

18. On this point see, Baillet, no. 1889, and Clinton, 1974: esp. 64 and 65, both of whom champion the idea; and Graindor, 1924.

19. Tacitus *Annals*, VI, 18.

20. See *CTh* XV for legislation regarding public works in general and building maintenance in particular as well as Alchermes, 1994.

21. For discussion of equipment and moving techniques, see Wurch-Koselj, 1988.

22. See Jones, 1974: 36–37, for pricing and price structures regarding transport.

23. On forced labor, see Liebeschuetz, 1972: 133.

24. See *CTh* XIII, 4, for legislation regarding exemption of artisans. XIII, 4, 1 and XIII, 4, 2, are Constantinian edicts dating to 334 and 337, respectively. XIII 4, 3, dates to 344 in the reign of Constantius, and XIII, 4, 4, to 374 during the reign of Valentinian. All postdate the actual years of the initial, intense building activity that must have accompanied the development of the city, but it is fair to assume that the initial Constantinian legislation addresses a problem of which the emperor was aware as a result of his Constantinopolitan labors.

25. See Marvin, 1983: 380–81, and Duncan-Jones, 1982: 78–79, on individual and relative costs associated with the construction and decoration of bath buildings. On the pragmatic aspects of reuse in an architectural context, see Ward-Perkins, 1999.

26. See Hanfmann, 1974: 54–75.

27. Duncan-Jones, 1982: 126, discusses prices of materials and craftsmanship in the manufacture of silver statuary.

28. On the notion of urban beauty, see Saradi, 1995.

29. Hanfmann, 1975: 54–75; Bauer, 1996: 316, who observes the phenomenon, categorizing it as

an effort to create an artificial historicity; Yegül, 2000.

30. For a discussion of these traditions, see Pape, 1975. Also useful is Blank, 1984.

31. On the phenomenon of war plunder and its display in antiquity, see Pape, 1975; Guberti Bassett, 1991, 1996. For the term *spolia*, see Kinney, 1995, 1997. See also Alchermes, 1994.

32. Duncan-Jones, 1982: 126.

33. *VC* III. 54. Translation, Mango 1963: 56–7.

34. Jerome, *Chron.* 324

### CHAPTER THREE

1. Malalas, 321. Translation, Jeffreys, et al. 174.

2. For the text, see *Ek.* On Christodoros, see Baumgarten, 1881; RE III 2: 2450–52, s.v. Christodoros (Baumgarten); Viljamaa, 1963: 29–31, 56–7, 100; Stupperich, 1982: 210–35, esp. 213–14. Christodoros was once referred to as Christodoros of Thebes. Current usage prefers the designation Koptos.

3. *Chron. Pasch.* 595.

4. On the display of thermal statuary in general, see Manderscheid, 1981: 28–46, for thermal iconography.

5. Manderscheid, 1981: 30–40.

6. See Lehmann-Hartleben, 1941: 36–39. The tale of Poseidon and the Argive princess Amymone, for whom the god brought spring water to the drought-stricken Argolid, recalled the relationship between sea and spring, symbolizing as it did so water's continuous capacity for renewal.

7. Paus. X, 10, 4, describes a group of the Epigonoi at Delphi, and II, 20, 5 mentions a monument at Argos.

8. The full roster of Trojan characters included Achilles, the Locrian and Telemonian Aiaxes, Andromache, Calchas, Charidemos, Chryses, Clytios, Creusa, Dares, Deiphobos, Entellus, Hecube, Helen, Helenos, Kassandra, Lampon, Menelaos, Odysseus, Oenone, Paris, Polyxene, Pyrrhos (two statues), Sarpedon, and Thymoetes. Homer mentions most of the figures, but some, such as Dares and Entellos, owe their Trojan origins to Virgil.

9. Characters from the Trojan epic were displayed together with other mythological themes

in the Baths of Caracalla, and the Hadrianic Baths at Aphrodisias. For Caracalla, see Manderscheid, 1981: no. 64. The subject matter is identified as Troilus with Hector or Achilles. Marvin, 1983: 358–63. For Aphrodisias, see Manderscheid, 1981: nos. 250–51. These are statues of Achilles and Penthesileia and Menelaos and Patroklos.

10. For examples, see Weitzmann, 1979: nos. 195–97, 200, 201.

11. Zosimos II, 30.

12. Sozomen II, 3,1–3.

13. *Aeneid I*, 1–7.

14. Rose, 1991: 70–71.

15. Rose, 1991, and Erim, 1986: 118 and 180.

16. On Virgil in the Roman curriculum, see Marrou, 1956: 265–83. On the poet's Late Antique reception, see MacCormack, 1998, and Albrecht, 1997: 664–710.

17. Augustine, *City of God*, I, 4.

18. The idea of a specifically Trojan iconography in the bath is first suggested by Stupperich, 1982, an idea that I initially rejected in a subsequent article about the Zeuxippos collection. See Guberti Bassett, 1996. Although I still have reservations about Stupperich's methods and conclusions, I now see the wisdom of his initial proposal that the Trojan theme is one related to civic identity.

19. See Manderscheid, 1981: 34–38.

20. Manderscheid, 1981: nos. 229–58, see nos. 235–49 for the portraits.

21. The full roster of portraits at the Zeuxippos included Aischines, Alkibiades, Anaximenes, Apuleius, Aristotle, Julius Caesar, Cratinus, Demokritos, Demosthenes, Erinna, Euripedes, Herakleitos, Herodotos, Hesiod, Homer, Homer of Byzantium, Isokrates, Menander, Melampos, Palaephatos, Perikles, Polyeidos, Pompeius, Pythagoras, Pherekydes, Plato, Sappho, Simonides, Stesichoros, Terpander, Thukidides, Virgil, and Xenophon.

22. *Chron. Pasch.* 565.

23. See generally Jaeger, 1936, and Marrou, 1956: 95–100. On the role of the paideia in Late Antiquity, see Kaster, 1988, and Brown, 1992: 35–70.

24. Brown, 1992: 38.

25. See Zosimos, 31; *Chron. Pasch.* 495; Malalas, 292; Kedrenos I, 422. For a general outline of the

circus's history, see Müller-Wiener 1977, 64–71. On the Severan and Constantinian phases specifically see: Guilland, 1970.

26. For statues of emperors and competitors, see *Anth. Gr.* XV, 41–50; XVI, 335–87. The most famous of the Hippodrome charioteers was the sixth-century competitor Porphyrius. See Cameron, 1973.

27. On fires, see Schneider, 1941. On the destruction of statuary in 1204, see the eyewitness account of Niketas Choniates, 647–55, and Cutler, 1968.

28. On the excavation of the Hippodrome, see Casson, 1928 and 1929. For an abbreviated version of the reports, see Casson, 1930.

29. *Par.* 5 and 84 and cat. nos. 129, 139, 140.

30. For comparative material on circuses, see Humphrey, 1986: 40, 176–254, 372, and 474–75. The most plentiful evidence for sculptural display comes from the Circus of Maxentius on the Via Appia. The *euripus* was excavated in 1825 and again in 1960. See Nibby, 1825; Nibby, 1838: 632–44, and Pisani Sartorio and Calza, 1976.

31. The main literary evidence for the Hippodrome may be found in the eighth-century *Par.* and its tenth-century derivative, the *Patria*. See Preger, 1902–07, and Cameron/Herrin, 1984, for texts. Also useful are epigrams from *Anth. Gr.* and Niketas Choniates. Isolated references in works by historians and poets help to complete the record. The most important of these references are Eusebios, *VC* III, 54, Socrates I, 16, and Zosimos II, 31. Other texts are collected in Overbeck, 1868, Unger, 1878, and Mango, *Sources.*

32. Numerous ancient sources attest the evil powers of the hyena, among them Aelian, *De. nat. an.*, VI, 14 and VII, 22. See also Keller, 1887: 156–7; Keller, 1909: II, 89–90.

33. Suetonius, *Augustus*, 96.

34. Pausanias, X, 13, 9.

35. Pindar, *Olymp.* II, 36.

36. Horace, *Carmen* III, 3.

37. Pliny, *NH* XXXIV, 57, reports that there was a temple of Herakles by the Circus Maximus, and Ovid, *Fasti* VI, 209, notes that Herakles was denoted *magnos custos* at the Circus Flaminius. This association between the hero and the circus was maintained into Late Antiquity. Fifth-century contorniates from the reign of Anthemius

Prokopius show Herakles on the *verso* framed by the legend "Herakles Hyppodromos." See Alföldi, 1952.

38. See Peirce, 1989, and Ruysschaert, 1963.

39. For a full account of the ceremony in the Hippodrome, see Guilland 1965.

40. *Chron. Pasch.* 528; Whitby/Whitby, 16.

41. Pausanias X, 16; Strabo, IX, 3, 6.

42. See Tertullian *de spec.* VIII; Lyle, 1984, and Kiilerich, 1998: 153–59

43. Guilland, 1965, and Humphreys, 1986: 55 and 581.

44. Humphreys, 1986: 475.

45. On the Forum of Constantine in general, see Reinach, 1896; Müller-Wiener, 1977: 255–57; Janin, 1964: 62–64; and Bauer, 1996: 167–87.

46. The sources for the Forum of Constantine are largely those of the Hippodrome. See note 31, this chapter, especially Niketas Choniates. Important references are also found in Arethas. See cat. no. 107.

47. The area around the Column of Constantine has only been excavated cursorily. See N. Firatli, 1964, and Barsanti, 1990: 34.

48. Various sources attest the divinity and history of the Palladion. See Ovid, *Fasti*, VI, 419–60, and Dion. Hal. I, 68–9. For the canonical Roman version in which Aeneas transports the Palladion to Lavinium, see Virgil, *Aen.* II, 162–79.

49. The Palladion was kept in the inner sanctum of the Temple of Vesta from Rome's earliest history (Livy XXVI, 27, 14). Although Augustus may have placed the statue or a copy of it temporarily in the Vesta chapel at his house on the Palatine, Herodian (I, 14, 4) reports that the statue was still there in A.D. 191. The last known chief vestal was Coelia Concordia who took up the position in 380. The cult appears to have endured until 394.

50. On nymphaea, see: Boethius and Ward-Perkins, 1970: 405–06; Gros, 1996: 418–442.

51. Hülsen, 1919, and Kleiner, 1968: 114–15.

52. Herkenrath in Hülsen, 1919: 55–72; Lange, 1920; and Hanfmann, 1975: 66–67.

53. See Ferguson, 1970: 13–31; Vermaseren, 1977: 38–69; and Roller, 1999: 263–46.

54. Magna Mater protected Aeneas on his flight from Troy, and her symbols adorned his ships as apotropaia. Virgil, *Aen.* IX, 77–83; 107–22/X, 156–58. Aeneas himself prayed frequently to the

goddess (*Aen.* VII, 139; X, 251–55) and it was she who guaranteed Rome's glorious future (*Aen.* VI, 784–87).

55. On the Augustan restoration of the Palatine temple, see Ovid, *Fasti* IV, 347–48, and *Mon. Ancyr.* IV, 8.

56. On Livia and her assimilation of Kybele see Vermaseren, 1977: 177, and Bartman, 1999: 85, 95, 103, 222.

57. On the history of Tyche/Fortuna and various aspects of her Roman cult see Champeaux, 1982.

58. Prokop. *De Aed.* I, 2,1.

59. Mango, 1959: 46.

60. This idea was first proposed by Maass, 1891, who believed that the horoscope was one commissioned by Constantine for the church. Preger, 1902bis, in a review of Maass rejected the notion outright, claiming that the statuary was purely decorative.

61. For a succinct overview of astrology and astrological practices in the Hellenistic and Roman worlds, see Barton, 1994. An older but still useful and far more exhaustive discussion of Roman astrological practice may be found in two studies: Bouché-Leclercq, 1879, and Bouché-Leclerq, 1899. Both Bouché-Leclercq and Barton point out that it was Augustus who first embraced horoscopes as means to legitimate individual rule as predestined. Further, the systematic use of astrology appears to have been an elite practice from the first century B.C. on; although this conclusion derives largely from the fact that testimony regarding more popular types of astrological practice, if it existed, do not survive. Augustus's own use of astrology developed out of earlier, Greek precedent, especially that of Hellenistic kings. As Barton, 42, notes, such predictions were risky in that they invited others to follow with counter-predictions. In an attempt to stifle such activity the first Roman emperor banned private astrological practice and divinations related to the prediction of death. In the fourth century, Constantine banned exactly the same type of activity (*CTh* IX, 16), probably not because of any inherent incompatibility that he felt with his Christian leanings as has been suggested (Barton, 1994: 71) but for purposes of scotching any potential objections to or challenges to his rule. Christian attitudes toward

astrology were mixed. On the one hand, heavenly interaction with the life of Jesus was acknowledged: the star that brought the Magi to the infant's side and the solar eclipse that followed his death all reflect a belief in the intimate and legitimate connection between earthly activity and the heavens. On the other hand, the idea of astrology was condemned on the grounds that it offered a view into the future that circumvented divine will. See Barton, 1994: 64–85, on astrology and Christianity. Legislation regulating the astrological practice under Constantine (*CTh* IX, 16, 1–3) imposes restrictions for very definite types of activities. *CTh* IX, 16, 1, and IX, 16, 2, outlaw private divinations by soothsayers, making the offense punishable by death, while at the same time permitting them to be performed publicly. *CTh* IX, 16, 3, provides for the punishment of those who practice magic for evil purposes, but permits benevolent acts, such as the conjuring of rains for drought afflicted areas. In none of these edicts or any of the later fourth-century proclamations is the legal question framed in terms of Christianity. Rather, the overwhelming issue seems to be intent and the private nature of the activity. Overwhelmingly the concern is to prohibit private, potentially subversive acts and acts that are considered contrary to the public good. It is only in the later fourth century, under Valentinian and Valens, that all astrological practice including teaching as well as private and public divination is outlawed. See *CTh* IX, 16, 7 (A.D. 373).

62. Barton, 1994: 64–68, and Pingree, 1976.

63. For general considerations relevant to urban historiography, see Veyne, 1988: 71–93. For Late Antique ideas about the appropriate way to introduce and discuss cities, see the treatises of Menander Rhetor. For text, translation, and commentary on these rhetorical treatises, see Menander Rhetor.

64. Libanios, *Or* XI, 44–58.

65. Menander Rhetor: 50–51.

### CHAPTER FOUR

1. On population, see Mango, 1985: 19, 51, 53, and Jacoby, 1961.

2. On the late-fourth-century development of the city, see Mango, 1985: 37–50. Construction

appears to have been limited to isolated examples. Julian added a port, referred to in the *Notitia Dignitatum* as "portus novus" and later known as the Sophien, on the Propontis (Mango, 1985: 39). He also built the Senate House in the Augusteion (Bauer, 1996: 149). A cistern named for Domitius Modestus, city prefect between 363 and 369 (*PLRE* I, 605–07: s.v. "Modestus 2") may also have been added at this time (*Notitia*). Maintenance of the water supply remained a concern, as evidenced by Valen's 373 restoration of the Hadrianic aqueduct. See Jerome, *Chronicle*, 379, and Mango, 1985: 20. For imperial portraits and their urban setting see generally Bauer, 1996: 148–254.

3. On Theodosian developments, see the remarks included in discussion of later fourth- and fifth-century city history in Mango, 1985: 37–50, and Müller-Wiener, 1977: 19–23.

4. For text, see Seeck, 1876: 229–43.

5. See proposal by Berger, 1997.

6. Arkadios and Honorius were the titular sponsors of baths in the first and fifth regions (Seeck, 1876: 230, 233). Service buildings also made up part of the ongoing development of the old city as indicated by the construction of a cistern dedicated to Theodosios in the fifth region (Seeck, 1876: 233).

7. Although the Forum of Trajan inspired the elements of the Forum of Theodosios, they were arranged in a completely different way. On the Forum of Theodosios, see most recently, Bauer, 1996: 187–203, who addresses this specific issue, and Mango, 1985: 43–45. For outline of history and bibliography to 1977, see Müller-Wiener, 1977: 258–65. See also, Janin, 1964: 72, 81–82; Guilland, 1969: 2. 56–9.

8. On the Forum of Arkadios, see most recently Bauer, 1996: 203–12, and Mango, 1985: 45. For outline of history and bibliography, see Müller-Wiener, 1977: 250–53, as well as, Guilland, 1969: 2. 59–62; Janin, 1964: 71–72, 82–84; Millet, 1948: 361–65; and Tiftixoglu, 1973.

9. On the question of function, see Bauer, 1996: 202–03, for the Forum of Theodosios.

10. See *Notitia* regions six through thirteen for list of buildings in the new territories. No less than eight church foundations are included in the list.

11. See *CTh* XVI.1 for the establishment of Christianity as the religion of state.

12. See Seeck, 1876: 230 and 233 for imperial baths dedicated to Arkadios and Honorius in the first and fifth regions respectively. Mango, 1985: 41, discusses the fifth-century (427) dedication of the Constantinian baths.

13. For the early history of Hagia Sophia, see Mathews, 1977: 11–19, and Müller-Wiener, 1977: 84–96.

14. For references to the palaces, see Seeck, 1876: 230–32, and Janin, 1964: 135–37.

15. On the land walls, see Müller-Wiener, 1977: 286–307, and Meyer-Plath/Schneider, 1943.

16. Mango, 1985: 49; Whitby, 1985; Mango, 1995: 16.

17. On late Roman circuses, see Humphrey, 1986: 579–638.

18. On the Augustan and Constantian obelisks, see Iversen, 1972: I, 55–64, (Constantian from Thebes) and 65–75 (Augustan from Heliopolis).

19. On the Built Obelisk, see Müller-Wiener, 1977: 65 and 71.

20. The date of the erection of the Built Obelisk is unknown. A base inscription indicating that Constantine VII Porphyrogenitos undertook its restoration in the tenth century, covering its shaft with bronze plaques, provides a *terminus ante quem*. In an earlier article I have suggested that the Built Obelisk was installed at the same time as the Theban obelisk, with the distinct end of creating a visual reminder of Rome. See Guberti Bassett, 1996: 93–4. In a similar spirit, Mango, 1997, suggests that Constantine erected the monument originally with the same mimetic end in mind. Kiilerich, 1998: 75–76, suggests that the obelisk was added only after the Arab conquests of Egypt when true obelisks became impossible to obtain. Because the obelisk base depicts the circus with two obelisks, Kiilerich's hypothesis must be discarded, leaving either the Constantinian or Theodosian date of installation as possibilities, unless, of course, the relief is taken to refer directly to Rome rather than Constantinople. In this case a later date would be possible, if unlikely.

21. *Chron. Pasch.* 528.

22. On the obelisk base see most recently Kiilerich, 1998; Effenberger, 1996: 207–84; and the still crucial early publication by Bruns, 1935.

23. On the Constantinopolitan Senate as an institution, see Dagron 1974: 119–210; on the Senate

House in the Augusteion, see Mango, 1959: 56–60; Berger, 1995; and, most recently, Bauer, 1996: 151. For accounts of the fire and the building's destruction, see Zosimos V, 24 (see cat. no. 17 for text); Socrates VI, 18; *Chron. Pasch.* 568. Zosimos's account of the destruction is the most detailed and suggests that a raised portico fronted the building, rich in polychrome marbles.

24. Zosimos III, 11.

25. On the expansion of the Senate see Dagron, 1974: 119–210, and Ridley, 1982: 174, n. 48.

26. On the conflict between paganism and Christianity in the later Roman world, see Geffcken, 1978, and Trombley, 1994.

27. For the range of antipagan legislation, see *CTh* XVI, 10. On the closure of temples, see especially XVI, 10, 10; XVI, 10, 11; and XVI, 10, 13.

28. *CTh* XVI, 10, 25.

29. *PECS*, 280 on Dodona.

30. On Lindos, see Dyggve, 1960: I, 130 and II, 524. The last known inscription from Lindos dates to around A.D. 300 and refers to the planting of olive trees in honor of Athena by her local priest Aglocharos. Several other inscriptions are associated with this one. See Dyggve and Trombley, 1994: I, 103–04.

31. *CTh* X, 10,19.

32. *Or.* XIV, 3–4.

33. *Or.* XVIII, 159–62.

34. On the Athenaeum see *LTUR* I: 131–2 (Athenaeum), and 265–6 (Chalcidicum). The topographical questions relating to the identification of the Athenaeum, which has also been identified by some as the Atrium Minervae, are complex and need not concern us here. What is important is the equation not only between the building and the Senate, but also between the Senate and Athena/Minerva. Berger, 1995, believes that the Athena statue in Constantinople occupies the same position as a Minerva statue in Rome. He offers no locus classicus for the source of this opinion, nor does his source, Gerkan, 1941: 33–44. Nonetheless, statue or not, as the architectural and topographical evidence for Rome indicate there is a long-standing association between Minerva and the Senate.

35. For the relationship to the Forum of Trajan, see Kollwitz, 1941: 7–8, and Becatti, 1960:

88–89; and Mango, 1985: 45, who suggests that the measurements of the complex may have followed those of the Roman forum.

36. On the Column and its reliefs, see Becatti, 1960: 81–150, and Kiilerich, 1993: 51–55.

37. For the removal of statuary from established positions in front of the Hagia Sophia, see Augusteion in the catalogue.

38. For outline of history and bibliography, see Müller-Wiener, 1977: 297–300. For excavation of the site, see Macridy and Casson, 1931: 63–84. Müller-Wiener assigns the Gate to Theodosios II, as does the bulk of more recent scholarly literature. For a reassessment of that date and assignation to Theodosios I, see most recently Bardill, 1999: 671–96, and discussion later.

39. For the Nike, see Kedrenos II, 173; and *Theoph Cont.*, 197. For the Tyche see Patria II, 58a. For the statue of Theodosios, see Theophanes, 412; *Patria* I, 73; and Zonaras III, 263.

40. The gate has been associated with both Theodosios I and Theodosios II. Although initially associated with Theodosios I, recent scholarship has preferred to link the portal with Theodosios II. Reassessment of the archaeological evidence by Bardill has reopened the question by arguing persuasively for a date in the reign of Theodosios I. For an overview of the various positions, see Bardill, 1999.

41. The location of the Porta Triumphalis is open to discussion (Kleiner, 1985: 201–04); however, its appearance is documented by Martial (VIII, 65) who describes the decoration of the gate under Domitian with two elephant chariots. Although the location of the Roman gate remains unclear, it appears, like its later Constantinopolitan counterpart, to have been an arched entry that was built into the city wall. See *LTUR* s.v "Murus Servii Tulli."

42. On Caracalla and the use of elephant quadriga, see Dio Cassius LXXVII. 7.4 and Scullard, 1974: 258. For numismatic evidence, see Bastien, 1994: plate 173, n. 2, and Scullard, 1974: 256–57. Evidence for Theodosian use of elephants in triumph derives from the graphic record of the Column of Arkadios preserved in the Freshfield Album. See Freshfield, 1922.

43. *Anth. Gr.* IX, 285. Aristotle, *Historia animalium*, also supports this sentiment. IX, 46, which

describes the elephant bowing before monarchs in acknowledgment of their power.

44. For the themes of Theodosian iconography, see Kiilerich, 1993, and Kiilerich, 1998.

45. On the individual columns, see Kiilerich, 1993, as well as Becatti, 1960: 83–288, and Giglioli, 1952.

### CHAPTER FIVE

1. The material presented in this chapter and the accompanying catalogue entries is largely consistent with Guberti Bassett, 2000. For another study of the Lausos collection, see Mango Vickers Francis, 1992. The collection is also considered in the following: Corso, 1991: 128–42. The earliest mention is by Gilles (Gyllius). See Gilles, 1561 bis: 129–32. Gilles's discussion is essentially a recapitulation of the eleventh-century inventory given by Georgios Kedrenos. Other references to the collection proceed in the same spirit and include: *RE* supp. 7, 365–66 s.v. "Lausos" (Nagl); Guilland, 1962, 1969: 2/32. Bowra, 1960, associates the collection with *Anth. Gr.* IX, 528 and the late-fourth-century struggle between paganism and Christianity.

2. On Kedrenos and Zonaras, see Hunger, 1978: I, 393–94, 416–18.

3. See the entries under Lausos Collection in the catalogue for texts and translations. A glance at these passages reveals them as a potentially rich source of information; however, because of the chronological gap between the destruction of the ensemble and its description they have remained problematic. More than five hundred years separate the testimony of Kedrenos and Zonaras from the loss of the Lausos gathering in 475, with the result that their observations regarding the collection have often been dismissed as fiction. Kedrenos's harshest critic has been Christian Blinkenberg, who scorned the notion of the collection's existence and characterized the relevant passage in the *Synopsis* as nothing less than "ein Gewebe von Fabeln," a tissue of lies. See Blinkenberg, 1933: 32–34. Recent scholarship has, however, established the legitimacy of the texts. See Mango Vickers Francis, 1992, and Guberti Bassett, 2000.

4. On Lausos, see PLRE II, 660–61 s.v. "Lausus"; Mango Vickers Francis, 1992: 89, 93–94, 95, and Bardill, 1997: 67–68.

5. For text, see Palladios. For analysis and commentary, Magheri Catalluccio, 1984.

6. Palladios, 18.

7. Palladios, 19.

8. Mango Vickers Francis, 1992: 95. Contrast Bowra, 1960: 5–6, who dates the collection's formation to the 380s, and Corso, 1991: 129, who places it after 392.

9. See generally, Jaeger, 1939: 95–100. On the role of the paideia in Late Antiquity, see Kaster, 1988, and Brown, 1992: 35–70, especially.

10. Corso, 1991: 129.

11. Elsner, 1995: 214–15, and Arafat, 1996: 11.

12. On Pausanias, see Habicht, 1985; Elsner, 1995: 125–55; and Arafat, 1996. On Egeria see Wilkinson, 1981.

13. *HN*, XXXVI, 9.

14. *HN*, XXXVI, 11.

15. *HN*, XXXVI, 20–23.

16. *HN*, XXXIV, 63.

17. On Pliny, see Ferri, 1946; Becatti, 1951; Pollitt, 1974: 73–84; Isager, 1971, 1991.

18. See *RE* XL: 430–32, s.v. "Plinius Nachleben," (Kroll); Sillig, 1833; and Cranz and Kristeller, 301–02.

19. Pliny XXXIV, 66–67, and XXXIV, 67–68, mentions Xenokrates as a source together with Antigonus.

20. Donohue, 1998: 195.

21. *HN* XXXV, 15–16.

22. Athenagoras, 17.

23. Themistios *Or 26.* 316 as quoted in Donohue, 1998: 451.

24. For the range of Roman attitudes toward nature, see Beagon, 1992, and Sorabji, 1993.

25. Arist. *HA* VI, 5; VIII, 5; IX, 12, remarks on the alien origins of vultures as well as their mating habits and carnivorous nature.

26. See, for example, Aelian VIII, 1, and XVII, 45.

27. Cosmas Indicopleustes, XI, 7.

28. On pans: Roscher: s.v. "Pan." For centaurs: *RE:* s.v. "Kentauren," and Roscher: s.v. "Kentauren."

29. See Jennison, 1937: 36, n. 1, for Cape Buffalo, and Auguet, 1972: 81–119.

30. Dunbabin, 1978: 76–77.

31. Auguet, 1972: 112–13.

32. For Paphos, see Kondoleon, 1994. For Piazza Armerina, see Carandini, Ricci, and de Vos, 1982; Dunbabin, 1978: 196–212; and Wilson, 1983. Auguet, 1972: 115–19, discusses the hunt mosaics in terms of animal acquisition.

33. The bibliography regarding the mosaic is vast and its dating controversial. Suggestions range from the fifth century to the seventh century. For a summary of arguments, see Trilling, 1989. More recently, see Jobst Erdal Gurtner, 1997, which sets the date between 485 and 550. This date is based on secure coin and ceramic evidence from the excavation immediately below the pavement and should therefore be considered definitive. Trilling interprets the mosaic's complex combination of natural images as a metaphor for the struggle between the civilized and the uncivilized.

34. *VC* III, 54.

35. Athenagoras, 17.

36. See, for example, the remarks in Eusebios, *DE* VI, 20 as cited by Donohue, 1998: 306.

37. See note 9, this chapter.

38. On the equation among muteness, stupidity, and barbarism, see Donohue, 1998: 122–23. For ancient views regarding speech and animals, see Sorabji, 1993: 7–16, 80–86. For remarks by Eusebios on dumb *xoana* and irrational animals, see *PE* I, 4, 12 a–c as cited by Donohue, 1998, 308.

39. For the notion of a mediating Kairos, see Bassett Clucas, 1986, and Mango Vickers Francis, 1992; and Guberti Bassett, 2000.

40. Plutarch, "On Listening to Lectures," 45C in Plutarch, *Moralia* I: 242–43.

41. Stewart, 1987.

42. See Bartman, 1988, 1991.

43. *CTh* XVI, 1, 2.

44. Bowra, 1960, first considered the collection in this context, an approach taken up by Mango Vickers Francis, 1992, and Corso, 1991: 131. On the conflict between paganism and Christianity, see Geffcken, 1978, and Trombley, 1994.

45. On the preservation of temples, see *CTh* XVI, 10, 8; XVI, 10, 15; XVI, 10, 18.

46. On the destruction of temples, see *CTh* XVI, 10, 25.

47. Translation Pharr, *CTh*, 473.

48. On the Theodosian desire to safeguard the artistic patrimony of the Roman Empire, see Lepelley, 1994. The pursuit of this policy in official sectors was not limited to sculpture. For a similar approach with respect to architecture, see Alchermes, 1994.

49. Prudentius, *Contra Symmachum* I, 499–505: "deponas iam festa velim puerilia, ritus/ridiculos tantoque indigna sacraria regno./Marmora tabenti respergine tincta lavate,/o procures: liceat statuas consistere puras,/artificum magnorum opera: haec pulcherrima nostrae/ ornamenta fiant patriae, nec decolor usus/in vitium versae monumenta coninquinet artis." Translation, Alchermes, 1994: 171.

50. On Roman public collections and their display, see Becatti, 1973: 18–54; Strong, 1973: 247–64; Pollitt, 1978: 155–74. For the location of the Lausos portico in particular, see Guilland, 1962, and Bardill, 1997, who convincingly relocates the collection immediately to the east of the Forum of Constantine.

51. For a topographical list of Greek statuary and other works of art on display in Rome, see Pollitt, 1978: 170–71; and Ridgway, 1984: 109–11.

52. On the Porticus Metelli itself, see Pollitt, *Greece*: 144, 146; Pollitt, *Rome*: 45, 55, 74, 109; Nash, 2/254 s.v. "Porticus Metelli"; *NTDAR* s.v. "Porticus Metelli"; *LTUR* s.v. "Porticus Metelli" and Favro, 1996: 100, 170–71.

53. Ridgway, 1984: chapters 4, 5, and 6. The great and glaring exception to this rule is of course the example of the Knidian Aphrodite, which survives in over two hundred copies. Ridgway, 1984: 76, accounts for this selective phenomenon of copying on the basis of subject matter, arguing that temple statues in public settings, and especially gods such as Aphrodite/Venus with statue cults at Rome, were the images of choice. On the phenomenon of Knidia copying, see Havelock, 1995.

54. See Bowra, 1960, and Mango Vickers Francis, 1992.

55. Elsner, 1995: 132–34, 144–50.

56. See Socrates I, 16, and Sozomen II, 5, 4.

57. For general discussion, see Lane Fox, 1986: 27–261. The notion of monolithic religious practice on the part of the pagan communities of the Roman Empire is not valid. Pagan religion was made up of a wide range of overlapping and

coexisting cults and cult practices. There was no single creed or doctrine that constituted pagan religion. State cults existed at the imperial and civic level. Most cults were purely regional and local, as in the case of Egypt and Syria. Others, such as the Mithras cult, had an international following but were essentially personal in nature and had no public manifestation. Nor were the cults static. New practices were introduced and older ones changed with the passage of time. The vitality and variety of religious experience in the later Roman world thus made it likely that although viewers might agree on the antiquity and venerability of the Lausos cult images, they might also have a sense of detachment from them.

58. See, for example, Belting, 1994, in which the possibility for the formal and aesthetic appreciation of images in the premodern period is dismissed.

59. Athenagoras, 17.

60. Elsner, 1995: 18.

61. On the Palace of Marina, see Palace of Marina entries in the catalogue and Magdalino, 1984; Magdalino, 1988; and Mango, 1991. Magdalino believes the bath to have been constructed by Leo VI the Wise in the tenth century and considers it an example of the cultural phenomenon known as the "Macedonian Renaissance." By contrast, Mango claims the bath and its décor for the fifth century, arguing that Leo's work at the baths was one of restoration.

62. See Trombley, 1994: I, 129–36.

63. See Trombley, 1994: I, 187–245.

### CHAPTER SIX

1. The restoration is presumed on the basis of *Chron. Pasch.* 527, which refers to the dedication of new sculpture. It is thought that Christodorus of Koptos's ekphrasis must have been declaimed orally on the occasion.

2. For the destruction of the Augusteion and the Senate, see Zosimos V, 24. For text and translation, see cat. no. 17.

3. For the destruction of the Basilika, see Kedrenos I, 564; Kedrenos I, 616; Zonaras III, 131. For texts, see Lausos Collection entries in the catalogue.

4. See Prokop. *De Aed.* I for an account of Justinian's building activity in the capital. On Prokopios, see Averil Cameron, 1985: 84–112, especially on *De Aedeficia.*

5. See Prokop. *De bello pers.* I, 14, 9 for the destruction during the Nika rebellion.

6. Prokop. *De Aed.* I, 10. 5–I, 11, 25.

7. The exact number of Constantinian church foundations remains a matter of controversy. As with practically all questions of Constantinopolitan topography, evidence is unclear. Sources agree that Hagia Eirene and Hosios Mokios were Constantinian in date. Hagia Eirene, in the center, functions as an episcopal church. Hosios Mokios, outside the walls, appears to have been a cemetery church. Less clear are the dates of the actual church of Holy Apostles (as opposed to the Mausoleum), and the foundation of Hagia Sophia. Eusebios (*VC* IV, 58–60) reports that Constantine built his own mausoleum. On the basis of this reference Krautheimer believes that the church was constructed at the same time. See most recently his arguments in Krautheimer, 1983: 53–60. Mango, 1990, by contrast and with reason, links the actual foundation of the church to the reign of Constantius, arguing that the building would have been added to the Mausoleum to accommodate the relics of Timothy, Andrew, and Luke that were conveyed to the site in 356 and 357 (*Chron. Pasch.* 542 Philostorgios III, 2). The foundation and construction of Hagia Sophia also is open to discussion. The church may well have been planned by Constantine (Kedrenos I, 498); however, it was only under Constantius that the church was built (Socrates II, 10). Its dedication by the city's Arian bishop took place in 360 (*Chron. Pasch.* 544). Krautheimer believes that the church was Constantinian. Mango, 1985: 24, more reasonably, prefers a Constantan date, linking the dedication of the church to the establishment of the city's urban prefecture. For history and bibliography, see Müller-Wiener, 1977: 84–96 (Hagia Sophia) and 405–11 (Holy Apostles/Fatih Camii). On the reconstruction of the early churches see Mathews, 1977: 11–19 (Hagia Sophia) and 77–88 (Hagia Eirene).

8. See *Notitia Urbis Constantinopolitanae* in Seeck, 1876: 229–43. The summary tally of buildings at the end of the document (242) notes fourteen churches.

9. For a detailed account of Justinianic church-building, see Prokop. *De Aed.* I, 1–9.

10. Prokop. *De Aed.* I, 11.6–7.

11. *Par.* 11. For text, see Augusteion entries in the catalogue.

12. Prokop. *De bello pers.* I, 19, 37.

13. This is not to say that Justinian and his advisors had no instinct for collecting or any sense of materials and their symbolic value. The rich array of marbles at Hagia Sophia may have been conceived as a kind of collection. In a manner consistent with Roman imperial usage, the marbles from around the Empire were deployed in the decoration of the church. Implicit in their use was the expression of imperial dominion. For a sixth-century discussion of the building's decor and its evocation of empire, see Paul the Silentiary in Mango, *Sources:* 80–91. For a study of the *ekphrasis*, see Macrides and Magdalino, 1988. On the late antique viewer's capacity for abstract viewing see Onians, 1980.

14. On the Chalke Gate in general, see Mango, 1959. For the sculptured decoration, see Mango, 1959: 98–107. Berger, 1988: 242–50, and Bauer, 1996: 165.

15. For attribution to Constantine, see *Patria* III, 15 and III, 20. On the name see Mango, 1959: 21.

16. On Aitherios, see: *Anth. Gr.* IX, 656, and Mango, 1959: 26–30.

17. Prokop. *De Aed.* I, 10, 12–15 describes the vestibule's architecture.

18. On the mosaics see Prokop. *De Aed.* I, 10, 15–20.

19. Mango 1959: 98–107 discusses the appearance of the façade, suggesting that the entrance would have looked similar to the Porta Aurea of Diocletian's palace at Split or the façade of the Palace of the Exarchs at Ravenna. On the image of Christ, see Mango, 1959: 135–42.

20. For other discussions of the sculpture and its installation see Mango, 1959: 98–107; Berger, 1988: 242–50; and Bauer, 1996: 165. Mango's remarks are largely descriptive of what was there, making no attempt to reconstruct the display, while Berger, followed by Bauer, attempts to locate the individual statues in precise locations, a labor that the evidence does not permit.

21. On crowns in Late Antique portraiture, see Delbrueck, 1933: 53–66. The *corona radiata* does not appear to have been worn after the Constantinian age; although Calza, 1972: 390–91, includes an Iranian relief representation of an unknown Roman figure that some have identified with Julian. The example, dating to the later fourth century, is the only known use of the *corona radiata* after 350.

22. Berger, 1988: 245, places the statues in the Regia between the Milion and the entrance to the Chalke and also attempts a display order.

23. On the image of Christ Chalkites, see Mango, 1959: 108–48, esp 135–42 for iconography.

24. Eusebios, *VC* I, 6 as translated by Drake, 2000: 85.

25. Eusebios, *VC* III, 3 describes the image. See also Mango, 1959: 23–24.

26. See Chapter Four and cat. nos. 16–19 for discussion of the sculpture at the Senate in the Augusteion.

27. On the mosaics, see Prokop. *De Aed.* I, 10. 12–19. For placement, see Mango, 1959: 32–33.

28. Malalas, 479, says that the Chalke was completed sometime after 535. Mango, 1959: 34, argues for completion after 340 on the basis of the dates of the Vandal campaigns.

29. See especially the collection of statuary in the Forum of Arkadios: cat. nos. 102–05. Individual statues in other collections that appear inconsistent with the overall imagery of a given space may also reflect reinstallation. See, for example, cat. no. 20, an elephant in the Basilika; cat. no. 111, an elephant in the Forum of Constantine; and the various figures in the Amastrianon (cat. nos. 1–5).

30. For documentation on the suppression of Hellenic religion, see generally Trombley, 1994. On specific pagan persecutions see Jones, 1964: I, 91–92 (Constantine, after 324); I, 113–14 (Constans, 341, and Constantius, 353); I, 285–86 (Justinian, 529); I, 296 (Justinian, 562). For the specific date of the last Justinianic persecution, see Stein, 1949–59: 799–800.

31. Malalas, 491.

32. See Casson, 1928, for the excavation in general, and Casson, 1929: 18, for reuse of base as paving stone.

33. For Aphrodisias, see Roueché, 1989: esp xx–xxv, for remarks surveying the overall state of the epigraphical and sculptured evidence.

34. For a general sense of the nature of later Roman sculptural production through the period of Constantine, see Kleiner, 1992: 357–463. For the Theodosian age, see Kollwitz, 1941, and Kiilerich, 1993. For portraiture in particular, see Delbrueck, 1933. For the period of the fifth and sixth centuries, see the examples in Weitzmann, 1979.

35. Rouché, 1989: 15–59 (fourth century); 60–122 (fifth century).

36. For the display of imperial statuary in the individual spaces of fourth-, fifth-, and sixth-century Constantinople see Bauer, 1996: 148–268.

37. On the reduction in private liturgies, see Liebeschuetz, 1972: 132–36. Rouché, 1989: 35, confirms a similar trend for Aphrodisias observing the dominance of activity by imperial government officials in the epigraphical evidence.

38. Liebeschuetz, 1972: 136.

39. Saradi, 1995: 37–56.

40. For a list of Hippodrome monuments, by and large statues of victorious charioteers, see *Anth. Gr.* XV, 41–50 and Cameron, 1973.

41. See Chapter Five.

42. *Praeparatio Evangelica* V, 2.

43. See legislation limiting and prohibiting sacrifice: *CTh* XVI, 10, 6; XVI, 10. 8; XVI, 10, 10.

44. For a discussion of the relationship between antiquity and contemporary thought in the sixth century, see Maas, 1992.

45. The bibliography on Hagia Sophia is vast. For a survey of the church and its history see Müller-Wiener, 1977: 84–96, which includes a complete bibliography to 1976. Subsequent studies include Van Nice, 1986; Mainstone, 1988; Mark and Cakmak, 1992.

46. On the cosmic nature of the Hippodrome, see Tertullian, *De spect.* IX; Cassiodorus, *Var* III, 51; Malalas, 173–76; and Lyle, 1984. For the Christian sense of the church as a microcosm of the universe, see Paul the Silentiary's descriptions of Hagia Sophia and its church furnishings, which introduce and sustain the metaphor of the church as a repository for the world as cited in Mango, *Sources* 1976: 80–96. For the liturgical implications of this imagery see Taft, 1995.

47. *Diegesis peri tes Hagias Sophias*, 27 in Preger, 105.

48. On the translation of the relics see Mango, 1990.

49. Among the remains brought to Constantinople at this time were those of John the Baptist (Sozomen VII, 21; *Chron. Pasch.* 564); Samuel (*Chron. Pasch.* 569); and St. Stephen (Migne, *PG* 63, 933). Major relics of the Virgin, including her cincture and her funerary shroud, were also translated at this time. Verina, the wife of Leo I, deposited the shroud in the Blachernae Church, and her cincture was brought to the Church of the Theotokos in Chalkoprateia during the same period. For discussion and bibliography, see Holum, 1982: 142, n. 120.

50. The bibliography on the subject is enormous. Classic studies include Baynes, 1949; Baynes, 1951; Kitzinger, 1954. More recent studies include Pelikan, 1990; Av. Cameron, 1992; Belting, 1994 (with substantial bibliography).

51. On the creation of sacred ground and the portability and transference of sanctity, see Geary, 1978; Brown, 1980; Maraval, 1985: 23–104. See also the collected essays in Ousterhout, 1990.

## INTRODUCTION TO THE CATALOGUE

1. On the issue of copies and copying, see Bieber, 1977; Marvin, 1977; Vermeule, 1977; Ridgway, 1984; and Bartman, 1992.

2. On the Knidia and its legacy in copying and representation, see Havelock, 1995.

# SELECT BIBLIOGRAPHY

Albrecht, Michael van
　1997. *A History of Roman Literature from Livius Andronicus to Boethius with Special Regard to its Influence on World Literature* 2 vols. (Leiden)
Alchermes, Joseph
　1994. "Spolia in the Roman Cities of the Late Empire: Legislative Rationales and Architectural Reuse," *DOP* 48: 167–78
Alcock, Susan E.
　1989. "Archaeology and Imperialism: Roman Expansion and the Greek City," *JMA* 2/1: 87–135
Alföldi, Andreas
　1934. "Die Ausgestaltung des monarchischen Zeremoniells," *RM* 49: 1–118
　1952. "Zu den römischen Reiterscheiben," *Germania* 30: 187–90
Alzinger, W.
　1972. *Die Ruinen von Ephesos* (Berlin)
Amelung, W.
　1899. "Kybele Orans," *RM* 14: 8–12
Anastos, Milton
　1967. "The Edict of Milan," *REB* 25: 13–41
Andreae, Bernard
　1974. "Die römischen Repliken der mythologischen Skulpturengruppen von Sperlonga," *AntPl* 14 (Berlin): 63–105
Angel de Elvira, Miguel
　1984. "La escultura clasica en los epigramas bizantinos de la Antologia," *Erytheia* 4: 25–41
　1986. "Las estatuas animadas de Constantinopla," *Erytheia* 8: 99–115
Arafat, Karin W.
　1996. *Pausanias' Greece* (Cambridge)

Arias, P. E.
　1952. *Skopas* (Rome)
Auguet, Roland
　1972. *Cruelty and Civilization: The Roman Games* (London)
Aurigemma, Salvatore
　1956. "Lavori nel Canopo di Villa Adriana-III," *BdA* 41: 57–71
Babelon, Ernst and J-A Blanchet,
　1895. *Catalogue des bronzes antiques à la Bibliothèque Nationale* (Paris)
Bagnall, Roger S.
　2001. "Archaeological Work on Hellenistic and Roman Egypt, 1995–2000," *AJA* 105: 227–43
Bammer, A.
　1988. *Ephesos: Stadt am Fluss und Meer* (Graz)
Bardill, Jonathan
　1997. "The Palace of Lausus and Nearby Monuments in Constantinople: A Topographical Study," *AJA* 101: 67–68
　1999. "The Golden Gate in Constantinople: A Triumphal Arch of Theodosius I," *AJA* 103: 671–96
Barnes, Timothy D.
　1981. *Constantine and Eusebius* (Cambridge, MA and London)
Barrett, J. C.
　1997. "Romanization: A Critical Comment," in *Mattingly*, 1997: 51–66
Barsanti, Claudia
　1990. "Note archeologiche su Bisanzio Romana," *Milion* 2: 11–50

Bartman, Elizabeth
1988. "Decor et duplicatio: Pendants in Roman Sculptural Display," *AJA* 92: 211–25
1991. "Sculptural Collecting and Display in the Private Realm," in Elaine Gazda, ed. *Roman Art in the Private Sphere* (Ann Arbor): 71–88
1992. *Ancient Sculptural Copies in Miniature* (Leiden)
1999. *Portraits of Livia* (Cambridge)

Bartoccini, R.
1929. *Le terme di Lepcis* (Bergamo)
1931. "L'arco quadrifonte dei Severi a Lepcis," *Africa italiana* 4: 32–151
1960. "Il porto romano di Leptis Magna," *Boll-Centro* (suppl. 13)

Barton, Tamsyn
1994. *Ancient Astrology* (London)

Bassett, Sarah
1985. "*Paene Omnium Urbium Nuditate:* The Reuse of Antiquities in Constantinople, Fourth through Sixth Centuries" (diss. Bryn Mawr College)

Bassett Clucas, Sarah
1986. "The Lausos Collection in Constantinople," *The 17th International Byzantine Congress: Abstracts of Short Papers* (Washington, D.C.)

Bastien, Pierre
1994. *Le buste monétaire des empereurs Romains* (Welteren, Belgium)

Bauer, Franz Alto
1996. *Stadt, Platz und Denkmal in der Spätantike* (Mainz)
2001. "Urban Space and Ritual: Constantinople in Late Antiquity," *ActaAArtHist* 15: 27–61

Baumgarten, P.
1881. *De Christodoro Poeta Thebano* (Bonn)

Baynes, Norman
1949. "The Supernatural Defenders of Constantinople," *AnalBoll* 67: 165–77
1951. "The Icons before Iconoclasm," *HTR* 44: 93–106

Baxandall, Michael
1991. "Exhibiting Intention: Some Preconditions of the Visual Display of Culturally Purposeful Objects," in *Karp and Lavine,* 1991: 33–41

Beagon, Mary
1992. *Roman Nature* (Oxford)

Becatti, Giovanni
1951. *Problemi fidiaci* (Milan)
1960. *La Colonna Coclide Istoriata* (Rome)
1973. "Opera d'arte greca nella Roma di Tiberio," *ArchCl* 25: 18–53
1977. *Arte e gusto negli scrittori latini* (Florence)

Beck, Hans-Georg
1973. "Großstadt-Probleme: Konstantinopel vom 4.–6. Jahrhundert," *Studien zur Frühgeschichte Konstantinopels* (Munich): 1–26

Belting, Hans
1994. *Likeness and Presence. A History of the Image before the Era of Art,* trans. Edmund Jephcott (Chicago)

Berger, Albrecht
1982. *Das Bad in der byzantinische Zeit* (Munich)
1987. "Die Altstadt von Byzanz in der vorjustinianischen Zeit," *Varia II* (*Poikila Byzantina,* 6) Bonn: 7–30
1988. *Untersuchungen zu den Patria Konstantinopoleos, Poikila Byzantina* 8 (Bonn)
1995. "Die Senate von Konstantinopel," *Boreas* 18: 131–42
1997. "Regionen und Straßen im frühen Konstantinopel," *IstMitt.* 47: 349–414
2000. "Streets and Public Spaces in Constantinople," *DOP* 54: 161–72

Bergmann, Marianne,
1999. *Chiragan, Aphrodisias, Konstantinopel. Zur mythologischen Skulptur der Spätantike* (Wiesbaden)

Berlo, J. et al.
1995. "The Problems of Collecting and Display, Part 1," *ArtBull* 77: 6–24

Bernoulli, J. J.
1881–94. *Römische Ikonographie* 2 vols. (Stuttgart)

Bieber, Margarete
1961. *The Sculpture of the Hellenistic Age* (New York)

Blank, Horst
1969. *Wiederverwendung alter Statuen als Ehrendenkmäler bei Griechen und Römern* (Rome)

Blinkenberg, Christian
1917–18. *L'Image d'Athana Lindia* (Copenhagen)
1933. *Knidia: Beitrage zur Kenntnis der praxitelischen Aphrodite* (Copenhagen)

Boase, T. S. R.
1979. *Giorgio Vasari: The Man and the Book* (Princeton)

Boethius, Axel and John B. Ward-Perkins

1970. *Etruscan and Roman Architecture* (Harmondsworth)

Bosio, Luciano

1983. *La Tabula Peutingeriana* (Rimini)

Bouché-Leclercq, A.

1879. *Histoire de la divination dans l'antiquité* (Paris)

1899. *L'Astrologie grecque* (Paris)

Bowra, C. M.

1960. "Palladas and the Converted Olympians," *BZ* 53: 1–7

Bréhier, Louis

1915. "Constantin et la fondation de Constantinople," *RHist* 119: 241–72

Brett, Gerard, Günter Martiny, and R. B. K. Stevenson

1947. *The Great Palace of the Byzantine Emperors, being a First Report on the Excavations carried out in Istanbul on behalf of the Walker Trust (The University of St. Andrews 1935–38)* (London)

Brinkerhoff, Dericksen

1970. *A Collection of Sculpture in Classical and Early Christian Antioch* (New York)

Brown, Peter

1980. *The Cult of the Saints: Its Rise and Function in Latin Christianity* (Chicago)

1992. *Power and Persuasion in Late Antiquity* (Madison)

Bruns, G.

1935. *Die Obelisk und seine Basis auf dem Hippodrome zu Konstantinopel* (Istanbul)

1948. *Staatskameen des 4. Jahrhunderts nach Christi Geburt* (Berlin)

Buckton, David, ed.

1984. *The Treasury of San Marco, Venice* (Milan)

1994. *Byzantium. Treasures of Byzantine Art and Culture from British Collections* (London)

Bury, J. B.

1912. "The Great Palace," *BZ* 21: 210–25

Cagiano de Azevedo, M.

1962. "I cosidetti Tetrarchi di Venezia," *Commentari* 3/4: 160–81

1966/67. "Nota sui 'Tetrarchi' di Venezia," *RendPontAcc* 39: 153–59

Calza, Raissa

1972. *Iconografia romana imperiale* 3 vols. (Rome)

Cameron, Alan

1973. *Porphyrius the Charioteer* (Oxford)

1983. "The Foundation of Constantinople: Myths Ancient and Modern," *Abstracts of Papers, Ninth Annual Byzantine Studies Conference Nov. 4–6, 1983* (Durham, NC): 33–34

Cameron, Alan and Roger Bagnall

1987. *Consuls of the Later Roman Empire* (Atlanta)

Cameron, Averil

1992. "The Language of Images: The Rise of Icons and Christian Representation," in Diana Wood, ed. *The Church and the Arts* (Oxford): 1–42

Carandini, Andrea, Andreina Ricci, and Mariette de Vos

1982. *Filosofiana, la villa di Piazza Armerina: immagine di un aristocratico romano al tempo di Costantino* (Palermo)

Casson, Stanley

1928. *Preliminary Report upon the Excavations Carried out in and Near the Hippodrome of Constantinople in 1927* (London)

1929. *Second Report upon the Excavations Carried out in and Near the Hippodrome of Constaninople in 1928* (London)

1930. "Les fouilles de l'hippodrome de Constantinople," *GBA* 30/1: 215–42

Champeaux, Jacqueline

1982. *Fortuna. recherches sur le culte de la fortune à Rome et dans le mond romain des origines à la morte de César* 2 vols. (Rome)

Charbonneaux, J.

n.d. *La sculpture grecque au Museé du Louvre* (Paris)

Christiensen, T.

1984. "The So-Called Edict of Milan," *ClMed* 35: 129–75

Cicogna, E. A.

1844. *I due gruppi di porfido sull'angolo del tesoro della Basilica di S. Marco in Venezia* (Venice)

Clifford, James

1988. "On Collecting Art and Culture," in *The Predicament of Culture* (Cambridge, MA/London): 215–51

Clark, Graeme, ed.

1990. *Reading the Past in Late Antiquity* (Rushcutters Bay, Australia)

Clinton, Kevin

1974. "The Sacred Officials of the Eleusinian Mysteries," *TAPA* n.s. 64: 3–143

Cook, A. B.
    1914. *Zeus, a Study in Ancient Religion* 3 vols. (Cambridge)

Conticello, Baldassare
    1974. "I gruppi scultorei di soggetto mitologico a Sperlonga," *AntPl* 14 (Berlin): 7–59

Corso, Antonio
    1991. *Prassitele: fonti epigrafiche e letterarie; vita e opera* 3 vols. (Rome)

Croke, Brian
    1990. "City Chronicles of Late Antiquity," in *Clark*, 1990: 165–203

Crome, Johann Friedrich
    1963. "Die goldenen Pferde von S. Marco und der goldene Wegen der Rhodier," *BCH* 87: 209–28

Curran, John
    2000. *Pagan City and Christian Capital. Rome in the Fourth Century* (Oxford)

Cutler, A.
    1968. "The *De Signis* of Nicetas Choniates, a Reappraisal," *AJA* 72: 113–18

Dagron, Gilbert
    1974. *Naissance d'une capitale. Constantinople et ses institutions de 330* (Paris)
    1984. *Constantinople imaginaire, Études sur le recueil des Patria* (Paris)

Dalleggio D'Alessio, E.
    1930. "Fouilles et découvertes I," *EchOr* 29: 339–41

Davies, O.
    1944. "The Golden Gate at Istanbul," *JRS* 34: 74–75

Dawkins, R. M.
    1924. "Ancient Statues in Medieval Constantinople," *Folklore* 35: 209–48

Deichmann, Friedrich Wilhelm and A. Tschira
    1957. "Das Mausoleum der Kaiserin Helena und die Basilika der Heiligen Marcellinus und Petrus an der Via Labicana vor Rom," *JdI* 72: 44–100

Delbreuck, Richard
    1932. *Antike Porphyrwerke* (Berlin/Leipzig)
    1933. *Spätantike Kaiserporträts* (Berlin/Leipzig)

Demus, Otto
    1960. *The Church of San Marco in Venice: History, Architecture, Sculpture* (Washington, D.C.)

Devambez, Pierre
    1937. *Grands bronzes du Musée de Stamboul* (Paris)

Donohue, A. A.
    1988. *Xoana and the Origins of Greek Sculpture* (Atlanta)

Dörig, José
    1957. "Lysipps letztes Werke," *JdI* 72: 19–43

Downey, Glanville
    1971. "Ekphrasis" *Reallexikon für Byzantinische Kunst* II (Stuttgart): 32–77

Drake, H. A.
    2000. *Constantine and the Bishops* (Baltimore)

Du Cange, Charles Du Fresne
    1680. *Historia byzantina duplici commentario illustrata* (Paris; reprint edition, Brussels, 1964)
    1688. *Glossarium ad scriptores mediae et infirmae-graecitatis Graocitatis* (Lyon; reprint edition, Graz, 1958)

Dück, Johannes
    1903/04. "Die Erdbeben von Konstantinopel," *Die Erdbebenwerke* 3 nr. 6–12

Dunbabin, Katherine
    1978. *The Mosaics of Roman North Africa* (Oxford)

Duncan-Jones, Richard
    1982. *The Economy of the Roman Empire* 2nd edition (Cambridge)
    1990. *Structure and Scale in the Roman Economy* (Cambridge)

Dygvve, Einar
    1960. *Lindos, Fouilles de l'Acropole 1902–14 et 1952 III. La sanctuaire d'Athana Lindia et l'architecture lindienne* (Copenhagen)

Ebersolt, Jean
    1910. *Le Grand Palais de Constantinople* (Paris)
    1918. *Constantinople byzantine et les voyageurs du Levant* (Paris)

Edwards, Charles
    1986. "The Running Maiden from Eleusis and the Image of Hekate," *AJA* 90: 307–18.

Effenberger, A.
    1996. "Überlegungen zur Aufstellung des Theodosios-Obelisken im Hippodrome von Konstantinopel," in B. Brenk, ed. *Innovation in der Spätantike* (Wiesbaden): 207–84

Elsner, J.
    1995. *Art and the Roman Viewer* (Cambridge)

Elsner, J. and R. Cardinal, eds.
    1994. *The Cultures of Collecting* (London)

Empereur, Jean-Yves
1998. *La Gloire d'Alexandrie* (Paris)
Engemann, J.
1989. "Melchior Lorichs Zeichnung eines Saulensockels in Konstantinopel," *Quaeritur, inventus colitur. Miscell. in onore di U. M. Fasola* I (Vatican City): 249–65.
Erim, Kenan T.
1986. *Aphrodisias, City of Venus Aphrodite* (London)
Fant, J. Clayton ed.
1988. *Ancient Marble Quarrying and Trade* (Oxford)
Favro, Diane
1996. *The Urban Image of Augustan Rome* (Cambridge)
Fenster, E.
1968. *Laudes Constantinopolitanae* (Munich)
Fentress, Elizabeth, ed.
2000. *Romanization and the City* (Portsmouth, R. I.)
Fentress, James and Chris Wickham
1988. *Social Memory* (Oxford)
Ferguson, John
1970. *Religions of the Roman Empire* (Ithaca, NY)
Ferri, S.
1946. *Plinio il Vecchio, Storia delle Arti antiche* (Roma)
Finley, M. I.
1999. *The Ancient Economy* (Berkeley)
Firatli, N.
1964. "Short Report on Finds and Archaeological Activities outside the Museum, I. Finds from the Çemberitaş District," *IstArkMüzYil* 11/12: 207–09
1990. *La sculpture byzantine figurée au musée archéologique d'Istanbul* (Paris)
Firatli, N. and T. Ergil
1969. "The 'Milion' Sounding," *IstArkMüzYil* 15–16: 199–212
Fittschen, Klaus
1991. "Zur Reconstruktion Griechischer Dichterstatuen. 1. Teil: Die Statue des Menander," *AM* 106: 243–79
Flinders Petrie, W. M.
1886. *Naukratis, part 1, 1884–85* (London)
Floren, J.
1981. "Zu Lysipps Statuen des sitzenden Herakles," *Boreas* 4: 47–60

Foss, Clive
1979. *Ephesus after Antiquity: A Late Antique, Byzantine, and Turkish City* (New York)
Fowden, Garth
1991. "Constantine's Porphyry Column: the earliest Literary Allusion," *JRS* 81: 119–31
Francis, E. D.
1984. "Amasis and Lindos," *Bulletin of the Institute of Classical Studies* 31: 119–30
Francis, E. D. and Michael Vickers
1984. "Green Goddess: A Gift to Lindos from Amasis of Egypt," *AJA* 88: 68–69
Franz, Alison
1988. *Late Antiquity: 267–700. Athenian Agora* 24 (Princeton)
Freeman, P. W. M.
1997. "Mommsen through to Haverfield: the origins of Romanization studies," in *Mattingly*, 1997: 27–50
Freshfield, E. H.
1922. "Notes on a Vellum Album Containing Some Original Sketches of Public Buildings and Monuments, Drawn by A German Artist who Visited Constantantinople in 1574," *Archaeologia* 72: 87–104
Frick, O.
1859. "Das Plataeische Weihgeschenk zu Konstantinopel" *Jb. f. ClassPhilologie Suppl. Bd.* III: 487–512
Frickenhaus, A.
1915. "Der Eros von Myndos," *JdI* 30: 127–29
Frowlow, A.
1944. "La dédicace de Constantinople dans la tradition byzantine," *RHR* 64: 61–127
Führer, J.
1892. "Zur Geschichte des Elagabalus und der Athena Parthenos der Pheidias," *RM* 7: 158–65
Fullerton, Mark
1986. "The Location and Archaism of the Hekate Epipyrgidia," *AA*: 669–74.
Gauer, W.
1995. "Konstantin und die Geschichte. Zu den 'Spolien' am Konstantinsbogen und zur Schlangensäule," in *Panchaia. Fest. K. Thraede* (Münster): 131–40
Geary, Patrick
1978. *Furta Sacra: Theft of Relics in the Central Middle Ages* (Princeton)

Geffcken, Johannes
 1978. *The Last Days of Greco-Roman Paganism*
  trans. Sabine MacCormack (Amsterdam)
Gerkan, A. von
 1941. "Die römische Curia," in Fritz Krischen,
  ed. *Antike Rathäuser* (Berlin): 33–44
Giglioli, Giulio Quirinio
 1952. *La Colonna di Arcadio a Costantinopoli*
  (Naples)
Gilles, Pierre
 1532. *Lexicon graecolatinum* (Basle)
 1533. *Liber unus de Galicis et Latinis nominibus pis-
  cium* (Lyon)
 1561. *De Bosporo Thracio libri tres* (Lyon)
 1561 bis. *De topographia Constantinopoleos et de
  illius antiquitatibus libri quatuor* (Lyon; reprint
  edition, Athens, 1967)
 1729. *The Four Books of the Antiquities of Constantinople* (London; reprint, New York, 1988)
Grace, V. R.
 1932. "Scopas in Chryse," *JHS* 52: 228–32
Graindor, Paul
 1924. "Constantin et le dadouque Nicagoras,"
  *Byzantion* 3: 209–14
Gros, Pierre
 1996. *L'Architecture romaine 1: les monuments
  publics* (Paris)
Guberti Bassett, Sarah
 1991. "The Antiquities in the Hippodrome of
  Constantinople," *DOP* 45: 87–96
 1996. "*Historiae custos*: Sculpture and Tradition
  in the Baths of Zeuxippos," *AJA* 100: 491–
  506
 2000. "'Excellent Offerings': The Lausos Collection in Constantinople," *ArtB* 82: 6–25
Guidoboni, E., ed.
 1989. *I terremoti prima del Mille in Italia e nell'area
  mediterranea* (Bologna)
Guilland, Rodolphe
 1959. "Les trois places (forum) du Théodose le
  Grand," *JÖB* 8: 53–55
 1962. "Études sur la topographie de Constantinople byzantine: Le Palais de Lausos,"
  *Helleniki* 17: 95–104
 1965. "Études sur l'Hippodrome de Byzance
  III & IV: Rôle de l'empereur et des diverses
  fonctionnaires avant et pendant les courses.
  Les courses de l'Hippodrome," *Byzantinoslavica* 26: 1–39

1969. *Études de Topographie de Constantinople
  Byzantine* 2 vols. (Berlin and Amsterdam)
1970. "Les Hippodromes de Byzance:
  l'hippodrome de Sévère et l'Hippodrome de
  Constantin le Grand," *Byzantinoslavica* 31:
  182–88
Gundel, Hans Georg
 1992. *Zodiakos. Tierkriesbilder in Altertum* (Mainz
  am Rhein)
Gurlitt, W.
 1893. "Die grosse eherne Athena des Pheidias,"
  *Analecta Graecensiana Festschrift zur 42 Ver-
  sammlung deutscher Schulmanner in Wien 1893*
  (Graz): 99–121
Habicht, Christian
 1985. *Pausanias' Guide to Ancient Greece* (Berkeley)
Hanfmann, George M. A.
 1975. *From Croesus to Constantine. The Cities of
  Western Asia Minor and their Arts in Greek and
  Roman Times* (Ann Arbor)
Hannestad, Niels
 1994. *Tradition in Late Antique Sculpture. Conser-
  vation, Modernization, Production* (Aarhus)
Harbeck, Hans
 1910. "Zwei neue Zeichnungen von Melchior
  Lorichs," *JdI* 25: 28–32
Harrison, E. B.
 1965. *Archaic and Archaistic Sculpture. Athenian
  Agora 9* (Princeton)
 1988. "Lemnia and Lemnos: sidelights of a
  Pheidian Athena," in Margot Schmidt, ed.
  *Kanon, Festschrift Ernst Berger* (Basel): 101–
  07
Havelock, Christine
 1995. *The Aphrodite of Knidos and Her Successors:
  A Historical Review of the Female Nude in Greek
  Art* (Ann Arbor)
Helbig, W.
 1963–72. *Führer durch die Öffentlichen Sammlun-
  gen Klassicher Altertümer in Rom* 4th edition,
  Supervised by H. Speier (Tübirgen)
Heyne, Gottfried Christian
 1790–91. "Priscae artis opera quae Constanti-
  nopoli extitisse memorantur," *Commenta-
  tiones Societatis Regiae Scientiarum Gottingensis*
  11: 3–38
Hogarth, D. C.
 1980. *Excavations at Ephesus* (London)

Holum, Kenneth

1982. *Theodosian Empresses* (Berkeley)

Hülsen, Julius

1919. *Milet V. Das Nymphaeum* (Berlin and Leipzig)

Humphrey, John

1986. *Roman Circuses* (London)

Hunger, Herbert

1978. *Die hochsprachliche profane Literatur der Byzantiner* 2 vols. (Munich)

Inan, Jale

1975. *Roman Sculpture in Side* (Ankara)

Inan, Jale and Elizabeth Alföldi-Rosenbaum

1979. *Römische und byzantinische Portraitplastik aus der Türkei* (Mainz am Rhein)

Isager, Jacob

1971. "The Composition of Pliny's Chapters on the History of Art," *ARID* 6: 49–62

1991. *Pliny on Art and Society* (London)

Iversen, Erik

1972. *Obelisks in Exile* 2 vols. (Copenhagen)

Jacoby, David

1961. "La population de Constantinople à l'époque byzantine: un problème de demographie urbaine," *Byzantion* 31: 81–109

Jaeger, W.

1939. *Paideia: The Ideals of Greek Culture*, trans. Gilbert Highet (Oxford)

Jahn, Otto

1848. "Athena Parthenos," *ArchZeit* 6: 239

James, Liz

1996. "'Pray not fall into temptation and be on your guard': Pagan Statues in Christian Constantinople," *Gesta* 35: 12–20

James, Liz and Ruth Webb

1991. "To understand ultimate things and enter secret places: ekphrasis and art in Byzantium," *Art History* 14: 1–17

Janin, R.

1953. *La Géographie ecclésiastique de l'empire byzantine* vol. 3: *Les églises et les monastères* (Paris)

1955. "Du Forum Bovis au Forum Tauri: étude de topographie," *REB* 13: 85–109

1964. *Constantinople byzantin* (Paris)

Jashemski, Wilhelmina F.

1979. *Gardens of Pompei*, vol. 1 (New Rochelle)

1993. *Gardens of Pompei*, vol. 2 (New Rochelle)

Jenkins, Romily

1947. "The Bronze Athena at Byzantium," *JHS* 67: 31–33

1951. "Further Evidence Regarding the Bronze Athena at Byzantium," *BSA Annual* 46: 72–74

Jennison, George

1937. *Animals for Show and Pleasure in Ancient Rome* (Manchester)

Jobst, Werner

1987. "Die Kaiserpaläste von Konstantinopel und seine Mosaiken," *AntW* 18: 2–22

Jobst, Werner, Behcet Erdal, and Christian Gurtner

1997. *Istanbul: The Great Palace Mosaic* (Istanbul)

Johnson, F. P.

1927. *Lysippos* (Durham, NC)

Johnson, Mark

1986. "Late Antique Imperial Mausolea" (diss. Princeton University)

Jones, A. H. M.

1940. *The Greek City from Alexander to Justinian* (Oxford)

1964. *The Later Roman Empire, 284–602* 3 vols. (Oxford)

1971. *Cities of the Eastern Roman Provinces* (Oxford)

1974. *The Roman Economy*, P. A. Brunt, ed. (Totowa, NJ)

Kapossy, Balázs

1969. *Brunnenfiguren der hellenistischen und römischen Zeit* (Zurich)

Karayannopoulos, J.

"Konstantin der Grosse und der Kaiserkuct," *Historia* 5: 341–57

Karp, Ivan and Steven D. Lavine

1991. *The Poetics and Politics of Museum Display* (Washington D.C./ London)

Kaster, R. A.

1988. *Guardians of Language: The Grammarian and Society in Late Antiquity* (Berkeley)

Keller, O.

1887. *Thiere des classischen Alterthums* (Innsbruck)

1909. *Die Antike Tierwelt* (Leipzig)

Kiilerich, Bente

1993. *Late Fourth-Century Classicism in the Plastic Arts. Studies in the So-Called Theodosian Renaissance* (Odense)

1998. *The Obelisk Base in Constantinople: Court Art and Imperial Ideology* (Rome)

Kinney, Dale
1995. "Rape or Restitution of the Past? Interpreting Spolia," *The Art of Interpreting*, ed. Susan C. Scott (University Park): 53–67
1997. "Spolia. *Damnatio* and *Renovatio Memoriae*," *MAAR* 42: 117–48
2001. "Roman Architectural Spolia," *Proceedings of the American Philosophical Society* 145/2: 138–50

Kitzinger, Ernst
1954. "The Cult of Images in the Age Before Iconoclasm," *DOP* 8: 83–150

Klauser, Theodore
1944. "Aurum Coronarium," *RM* 59: 144–53

Kleiner, Diana
1992. *Roman Sculpture* (New Haven)

Kleiner, F. S.
1985. "The Study of Roman triumphal Arches 50 Years After Kähler," *JRA* 2: 195–206

Kleiner, Gerhard
1968. *Die Ruinen von Milet* (Berlin)

Kollwitz, Johannes
1941. *Oströmische Plastik der theodosianische Zeit* (Berlin)

Kondoleon, Christine
1994. *Domestic and Divine: Roman Mosaics in the House of Dionysios* (Ithaca)

Kostof, Spiro
1991. *The City Shaped. Urban Patterns and Meanings through History* (Boston, Toronto, and London)
1992. *The City Assembled. The Elements of Urban Form through History* (Boston, Toronto, London, 1992)

Krautheimer, Richard
1981. *Early Christian and Byzantine Architecture* (Harmonsdworth, Middlesex/New York)
1983. *Three Christian Capitals* (Berkeley)

Kreisis, A.
1960. "Über den Wohnhaustyp der frühen Konstantinopel," *BZ* 53: 322–27

Lane Fox, Robin
1987. *Pagans and Christians* (New York)

Lange, Erna
1920. "Die Entwicklungen der antiken Brunnenplastik," *JdI* 35: 100–102

Lathoud, David
1924. "La consécration et la dédicace de Constantinople," *EchOr* 23: 289–314
1925. "La consécration et la dédicace de Constantinople," *EchOr* 24: 180–201

Lattimore, Steven
1976. *The Marine Thiasos in Greek Sculpture* (Los Angeles)

Lauer, J. Ph. and Charles Picard
1955. *Les statues ptolémaiques du Serapeion du Memphis* (Paris)

Le Goff, Jacques
1992. *History and Memory*, trans. Steven Rendall and Elizabeth Claman (New York)

Lehmann, Phyllis Williams
1959. "Theodosius or Justinian? A Renaissance Drawing of a Byzantine Rider," *AB* 41: 39–57

Lehmann-Hartleben, Karl
1941. "The *Imagines* of the Elder Philostratus," *ArtBull* 23: 16–44

Lehmann-Haupt, C. F.
1918. "Aus und um Konstantinopel I," *Klio* 15: 434–39

Leppelley, Claude
1994. "Le musée des statues divines: la volonté de sauvegarde le patrimoine artistique paeien à l'epoque théodosienne," *CahArch* 42: 5–15

Leppin, Harmut
1996. *Von Constantin dem Großen zu Theodosius II. Das christliche Kaisertum bei den Kirchenhistorikern Socrates, Sozomenus und Theodoret* (Göttingen)

Levi, Annalena and Mario
1967. *Itineraria Picta* (Rome)

Levi, Doro
1923. "Il Kairos attraverso la letteratura greca," *Rendiconti della Real'Accademia Nazionale dei Lincei; classe di scienze morali, storiche e filologiche* 5th ser. 32: 260–80.
1924. "Il concetto di Kairos e la filosofia di Platone," *RendLinc.* 5th ser 33: 7–117.

Liebeschuetz, J. H. W. G.
1972. *Antioch. City and Imperial Administration in the Later Roman Empire* (Oxford)

Linfert, Andreas
1982. "Athenen des Pheidias," *AM* 97: 57–77
1989. "Keine Athena des Pheidias in Konstantinopel," *Boreas* 12: 137–40

Lippold, Georg
  1939. *Handbüch der Archäologie* (Berlin)
  1956. *Die Skulpturen des Vatikanischen Museums* (Berlin)

Loeffler, E.
  1950–53. "Lysippos' Labors of Herakles," *Marsyas* 6: 8–24

L'Orange, H. P.
  1932. *Studien zur Geschichte des spätantiken Porträts* (Oslo)
  1962. "Kleine Beiträge zur Ikonographie Konstantins der Grossen," *Opuscula Romana* 41: 101–05
  1965. *Art Forms and Civic Life in the Later Roman Empire* (Princeton)
  1984. *Das spätantike Herrscherbild von Diokletian bis zu den Konstantin-Söhnen 284–361 n Chr.* (Berlin)

Lorenz, T.
  1966. *Polyklet: Doryphoros* (Stuttgart)
  1972. *Polyklet* (Wiesbaden)

Lyle, Emily B.
  1984: "The Circus as Cosmos," *Latomus* 43: 827–41

Lynch, Kevin
  1960. *The Image of the City* (Boston)

Maas, Michael
  1992. *John Lydus and the Roman Past* (London and New York)

Maass, Ernst
  1891. *Analecta sacra e profana* (Marburg)

MacCormack, Sabine
  1981. *Art and Ceremony in Late Antiquity* (Berkeley)
  1998. *The Shadows of Poetry: Vergil in the Mind of Augustine* (Berkeley)

MacDonald, William L.
  1986. *The Architecture of the Roman Empire, II: An Urban Appraisal* (New Haven/London)

MacMullen, Ramsay
  1976. *The Roman Government's Response to Crisis A.D. 235–337* (New Haven/London, 1976)

MacPherson, C. B.
  1962. *The Political Theory of Possesive Individualism* (Oxford)

Mackprang, Mogens B.
  1938. "Eine in Jütland vor 200 Jahren gefunden Kaiserstatuette," *ActaArch* 9(1938): 135–51

Macridy Bey, T. and S. Casson
  1931. "Excavations at the Golden Gate," *Archaeologia* 81: 63–84

Madden, Thomas F.
  1992. "The Serpent Column of Delphi in Constantinople: placement, purposes, and mutilations," *BMGS* 16: 111–45

Madigan, Brian
  1975. "The Theme of Lysippos' Tarentum Herakles and its Philosophical and Political Context," (M.A. thesis, Rutgers University)

Magdalino, Paul
  1984. "The Bath of Leo the Wise," *Maistor: Classical, Byzantine, and Renaissance Studies for Robert Browning*, ed. Ann Moffat (Canberra): 225–40
  1988. "The Bath of Leo the Wise and the Macedonian Renaissance Revisited," *DOP* 42: 97–118
  1996. *Constantinople médiévale. Études sur l'évolution des structures urbaines* (Paris)

Magheri Cataluccio, E.
  1984. *Il Lausaïkon di Palladio tra semiotica e storia* (Rome)

Maguire, Henry
  1974. "Truth and Convention in Byzantine Descriptions of Works of Art," *DOP* 28: 111–40
  1977. "The Depiction of Sorrow in Middle Byzantine Art," *DOP* 31: 125–74
  1981. *Art and Eloquence in Byzantium* (Princeton)
  2000. "Gardens and Parks in Constantinople," *DOP* 54: 251–64

Mainstone, R. J.
  1988. *Hagia Sophia: Architecture, structure and liturgy of Justinian's Great Church* (New York)

Majeska, George
  1984. *Russian Travelers to Constantinople in the Fourteenth and Fifteenth Centuries* (Washington, D.C., 1984)

Mamboury, Ernst
  1934. *Die Kaiserpaläste von Konstantinopel* (Berlin/Leipzig)
  1934 bis "Un nouvel élément pour la topographie de l'antique byzance," *ArchAnz*: 50–62
  1936. "Les fouilles byzantins à Istanbul," *Byzantion* 11: 266–67
  1938. "Ancien emplacement du Palais du Justice Ottoman," *Byzantion*, 13: 306–07

Manderscheid, H.
1981. *Die Skulpturenausstattung der kaiserzeitlichen Thermenanlagen* (Berlin)

Mango, Cyril
1949. "L'Euripe de l'Hippodrome de Constantinople," *REB* 7: 180–93
1959. *The Brazen House. A Study of the Vestibule of the Imperial Palace of Constantinople* (Copenhagen)
1959 bis "Letter to the Editor: A Response to Lehmann," *AB* 41: 351–56
1963. "Antique Statuary and the Byzantine Beholder," *DOP* 17: 55–75
1965. "Constantinopolitana," *JdI* 80: 305–36
1981. "Constantine's Porphyry Column and the Chapel of St. Constantine," *Deltion,* ser 4. 10: 103–10
1985. *Le développement urbain de Constantinople (VIe–VIIe siècles)* (Paris)
1990. "Constantine's Mausoleum and the Translation of Relics," *BZ* 83: 51–62
1991. "The Palace of Marina, the Poet Palladas, and the Bath of Leo VI," *Euphrosynon: Apheiroma ston Manole Chatzedake* vol. 1(Athens): 321–30
1993. "Constantine's Column," *Studies on Constantinople* (Aldershot) III: 1–6
1995. "The Water Supply of Constantinople," in Cyril Mango and Gilbert Dagron, eds. *Constantinople and its Hinterland* (Aldershott): 9–18
1997. "The Palace of the Boukoleon," *Cahiers archaeologiques* 45: 41–50

Mango, Cyril, Michael Vickers, and E. D. Francis
1992. "The Palace of Lausus at Constantinople and its Collection of Ancient Statues," *Journal of the History of Collections* 4: 89–98

Maraval, Pierre
1985. *Lieux saints et pelerinages d'orient* (Paris)

Mark, Robert and Ahmet S. Cakmak
1992. *Hagia Sophia from the Age of Justinian to the Present* (Cambridge)

Marrou, H.
1956. *A History of Education in Antiquity* (London)

Martiny, Günter
1938. "The Great Theater, Byzantium," *Antiquity* 12: 89–93

Marvin, Miranda
1983. "Freestanding Sculptures from the Baths of Caracalla," *AJA* 87: 347–84

Mathews, Thomas
1977. *The Early Churches of Constantinople, Architecture and Liturgy* (University Park and London)

Mattingly, D. J.
1997. *Dialogues in Roman Imperialism. Power, discourse, and discrepant experience in the Roman Empire* (Portsmouth, R.I.)

Mattingly, H.
1923–62. *Coins of the Roman Empire in the British Museum* 6 vols. (London)

Maurice, Jules
1904. "Les origines de Constantinople," *Société Nationale des Antiquaires de France. Centenaire 1804–1904 Recueil de Mémoires* (Paris): 281–2
1911. *Numismatique constantinienne* (Paris)

Ménage, V. L.
1964. "The Serpent Column in Ottoman Sources," *AnatSt* 14: 169–73

Mendel, Gustav
1912. *Catalogue des sculptures grecques, romaines, et byzantines* (Constantinople)

Metropolitan Museum of Art
1979. *The Horses of San Marco, Venice* (New York)

Metzler, Dieter
1981. "Oekonomische Aspekte des Religionswandels in der Spätantike," *Hephaistos* 3: 27–40

Meyer-Plath, B. and A. M. Schneider
1938. *Die Landmauer von Konstantinopel 1* (Berlin)

Meyer-Plath, B. and A. M. Schneider
1943. *Die Landmauer von Konstantinopel 2* (Berlin)

Michon, E.
1903. "Deux colonnes de porphyr ornées de bustes au Musée du Louvre," *Mélanges Boissier* (Paris): 371–81

Millet, Gabriel
1948. "Le forum d'Arcadius, la dénomination, les statues," *Memorial Louis Petit* (Bucharest): 361–65

Miranda, Salvatore
1976. *Études de topographie du Palais Sacré du Byzance* 2nd ed. (Mexico City)

Mitchell, S.

1987. "Imperial buildings in the eastern provinces," in S. Macready and F. H. Thompson, eds. *Roman Architecture in the Greek World* (London): 18–25

Momigliano, Arnaldo

1963. *The Conflict between Paganism and Christianity in the Fourth Century* (Oxford)

Mordtmann, A. D.

1892. *Esquisse topographique de Constantinople* (Lille)

Müller-Wiener, Wolfgang

1977. *Bildlexikon zur Topographie Istanbuls* (Tübingen)

1988. "Milet, 1976–86," *Antike Welt* 19/4: 31–42

Nash, Ernest

1961–62. *Pictorial Dictionary of Ancient Rome* 2 vols. (New York)

Naumann, R.

1966. "Der antike Rundbau beim Myrelaion," *IstMitt* 16: 209–11

Nelson, Robert S. and Richard Shiff

1996. *Critical Terms for Art History* (Chicago)

Nibby, A.

1825. *Del circo volgarmente detto di Caracalla* (Rome)

1838. *Roma nell'anno MDCCCXXXVIII, I Roma antica* (Rome)

Nielsen, Inge

1990. *Thermae et Balnea. The Architecture and Cultural History of Roman Public Baths* 2 vols. (Aarhus)

Onians, John

1980. "Abstraction and Imagination in Late Antiquity," *Art History* 3/1: 1–23

1988. *Bearers of Meaning. The Classical Orders in Antiquity, the Middle Ages, and the Renaissance* (Princeton)

Oster, R. E.

1987. *A Bibliography of Ancient Ephesos* (Metuchen, N.J.)

Ostrogorsky, George

1969. *History of the Byzantine State* (New Brunswick)

Ousterhout, Robert, ed.

1990. *The Blessings of Pilgrimage* (Urbana, IL)

Pape, Magrit

1975. "Griechische Kunstwerke aus Kriegsbeute und ihre öffentliche Aufstellung in Rom" (Diss. Hamburg)

Parapetti, Roberto

1983–84. "Architectural and Urban Space in Roman Gerasa," *Mesopotamia* 18–19: 37–84

Pascal, Louis

1857. "Pierre Gilles," *Nouvelle Biographie Générale* (Paris)

Pearce, Susan

1993. *Museums, Objects, and Collections* (Washington, D.C.)

Peirce, P.

1989. "The Arch of Constantine: Propaganda and Ideology in Late-Roman Art," *Art History* 12: 387–418

Pelikan, Jaroslav

1990. *Imago Dei: The Byzantine Apologia for Icons* (Princeton)

Peschlow, U.

1977. *Die Irenenkirche in Konstantinopel* (Tübingen)

Petsas, Ph.

1972. "An Aegiochus from Aegion," *Athens Annual of Archaeology* 5: 469–502

Pfeiffer, R.

1941. "The Measurements of the Zeus at Olympia," *JHS* 61: 1–5

Picard, Charles

1935–66. *Manuel de l'archéologie grecque: la sculpture* 5 vols. (Paris)

Pingree, David

1976. "Political horoscopes from the reign of Zeno," *DOP* 30: 133–50

Pisani Sartorio, Giuseppina and R. Calza

1976. *La villa di Massenzio sulla via Appia: il palazzo, le opere d'arte* (Rome)

Pollitt, J. J.

1978. "The Impact of Greek Art on Rome," *TAPA* 108: 155–74

Poulsen, Frederik

1951. *Catalogue of Ancient Sculptures in the Ny Carlsberg Glyptotek* (Copenhagen)

Preger, Th.

1901. "Das Gründungsdatum von Konstantinopel," *Hermes* 36: 336–42

1902. "Noch einmal die Gruendung Constantinopels," *Hermes* 37: 316–18

1902 bis. review of E. Maas, *BZ* 11: 164–68

1910. "Studien zur Topographie Konstantinopels. Die Konstantinsmauer," *BZ*: 450–61

Press, Gerald A.
1982. *The Development of the Idea of History in Antiquity* (Kingston and Montreal)

Prinzig, Gunter and Paul Speck
1973. "Fünf Lokalitäten in Konstantinopel," in Hans-Georg Beck, ed. *Studien zur Frühgeschichte Konstantinopels* (Munich): 179–227

Ragogna, A.
1963. *I Tettrarchi dei gruppi porfirei di S. Marco in Venezia* (Caltagirone)

Rasch, Jürgen J.
1984. *Das Maxentius-Mausoleum an der Via Appia in Rom* (Mainz)

Reinach, Solomon
1895. "Constantinople," *RA* 2: 345
1896. "Archaeological News, Turkey," *AJA* 9: 509–10

Reinach, Th.
1896. "Commentaire archéologique sur le poème de Constantin le Rhodien," *REG*: 66–103

Reulos, Michel and Peter G. Bietenholz
1985–87. *Contemporaries of Erasmus* 3 vols. (Toronto/Buffalo/London)

Reusch, A.
1908. *Guida Illustrata del Museo Nazionale di Napoli* (Naples/Munich)

Richter, G. M. A.
1965. *The Portraits of the Greeks* (London)
1970. *The Sculpture and Sculptors of the Greeks* (New Haven)

Richter, G. M. A. and R. R. R. Smith
1984. *The Portraits of the Greeks* (Ithaca, NY)

Ridgway, Brunilde S.
1964. "The date of the so-called Lysippan Jason," *AJA* 68: 113–28
1981. *Fifth-Century Styles in Greek Sculpture* (Princeton)
1984. *Roman Copies of Greek Sculpture: The Problem of the Originals* (Ann Arbor)

Ridley, Ronald T.
1982. *Zosimus' New History* (Sydney)

Robert, Louis
1969. "Théophane de Mytilène a Costantinople," *CRAI*: 42–64

Roller, Lynne E.
1999. *In Search of God the Mother. The Cult of Anatolian Cybele* (Berkeley)

Rose, C. Brian
1991. "The Theater of Ilion," *Studia Troica* 1: 69–77
1998. "The 1997 Post-Bronze Age Excavations at Troia," *Studia Troica* 8: 71–113

Roueché, Charlotte
1989. *Aphrodisias in Late Antiquity* (London)

Rubin, Patricia
1995. *Giorgio Vasari: Art and History* (New Haven)

Runciman, Steven
1969. *The Fall of Constantinople, 1453* (Cambridge)

Saradi, Helen
1995. "The *kallos* of the Byzantine City: The development of a Rhetorical *Topos* and Historical Reality," *Gesta* 34: 37–56

Schede, M.
1929. "Archäologische Funde," *AA*: 340–342

Schiering, W.
1969. *Die Bronzestatuette des Zeus von Dodona* (Stuttgart)

Schneider, A. M.
1939. "Die Grabung im Gebiet des ehemaligen Justizpalastes," *AA*: 187
1941. "Brande im Konstantinopel," *BZ* 41: 382–403
1950. "Strassen und Quartiere Konstantinopels," *MdI* 3: 68–79

Schweinfurth, P.
1952. "L'ancienne Constantinople et sa Porte Dorée," *Belleten* 16: 261–71

Scullard, H. H.
1974. *The Elephant in the Greek and Roman World* (London/New York)

Seeck, Otto
1891. "Das sogenannte Edikt von Mailand," *Zeitschrift fur Kirchengeschichte* 12: 381–86

Segal, Arthur
1997. *From Function to Monument. Urban Landscapes of Roman Palestine, Syria, and Provincia Arabia* (Oxford)

Sillig, J.
1833. "Über des Ansehen Naturgeschichte des Plinius im Mittelalter," *Allegemeine Schulzeitung* 9 nos. 52–53: 409–20

Smith, A. H.
1892–1904: *A Catalogue of Greek Sculpture in the British Museum* (London)

Smith, R. R. R.
1988. *Hellenistic Royal Portraits* (Oxford)

Sorabji, Richard
1993. *Animal Minds and Human Morals, the Origins of Western Debate* (Ithaca)

Speck, Paul
1995. "Urbs quam Deo donavimus. Konstantins des Großen Konzept für Konstantinopel," *Boreas* 18: 143–73

Spieser, J.-M.
1984. *Thessalonique et ses monuments du IVe au VIe siècle* (Athens and Paris)

Squariciapino, M. F.
1966. *Leptis Magna* (Basle)

Stein, Ernst
1949. *Histoire du Bas-Empire* 2 vols. (Paris)

Stewart, Andrew
1977. *Skopas of Paros* (Park Ridge, NJ)
1978. "Lysippan Studies I: the Only Creator of Beauty," *AJA* 82: 163–71
1990. *Greek Sculpture* (New Haven)
1993. *Faces of Power: Alexander's Image and Hellenistic Politics* (Berkeley)

Stichel, R.
1988. "Eine Athena des Phidias in Konstantinopel?" *Boreas* 11: 155–64
1997. "Die Schlangensäule im Hippodrome von Istanbul," *IstMitt* 47: 315–48
2000. "Sechs kolossale Säulen nahe der Hagia Sophia und die Curia Justinians am Augusteion in Konstantinopel," *Architectura* 30: 1–25

Stillwell, Richard
1961. "Houses of Antioch," *DOP* 15: 45–57

Stirling, Lea
1996. "Divinities and heroes in the Age of Ausonius: a Late-antique Villa and Sculptural Collection at Saint-Georges-de-Montagne (Gironde)," *RA*: 103–43

Strong, D. E.
1973. "Roman Museums," *Archaeological Theory and Practice* (New York): 247–63

Strocka, V. M.
1977. *Ephesos VIII.1: Die Wandmalerei der Hanghäuser in Ephesos* (Vienna)

Strube, Christine
1973. "Der Begriffe Domus in der Notitia Urbis Constantinopolitanae," *Studien zur Frühgeschichte Konstantinopels*, Hans-Georg Beck, ed. (Munich): 1 21–34

Stryzgowski, Josef
1893. "Das Goldene Thor in Konstantinopel," *JdI* 8: 1–39
1899. *Der Bilderkreis des griechischen Physiologus* (Leipzig)
1902. "Die Porphyrgruppen von S. Marco in Venedig," *Klio* 2: 105–24

Stupperich, R.
1982. "Das Statuenprogramm in der Zeuxippos-Thermen. Überlegungen zur Beschreibung der Christodorus von Koptos," *IstMitt* 32: 210–35

Talbot, Alice Mary
1994. "The Posthumous Miracles of St. Photeine," *Analecta Bollandiana* 112: 85–104

Talbot Rice, David
1958. *The Great Palace of the Byzantine Emperors: Second Report* (Edinburgh)

Thompson, Homer
1959. "Athenian Twilight," *JRS* 49: 61–72

Tiftixoglu, Victor
1973. "Die helenianae nebst einigen anderen Besitzungen im Vorfeld des früheren Konstantinopel," in Hans-Georg Beck, ed. *Studien zur Frühgeschichte Konstantinopels* (Munich): 49–122

Toynbee, J. M. C.
1947. "Roma and Constantinopolis in Late Antique Art from 312 to 365," *JRS* 37: 135–44

Trilling, James
1989. "The Soul of Empire: Style and Meaning in the Mosaic Pavement of the Byzantine Imperial Palace in Constantinople," *DOP* 43: 27–71

Trolle, Stefan
1978. "An Egyptian Head from Camirus, Rhodes," *ActaArch* 49: 139–50

Trombley, Frank R.
1994. *Hellenic Religion and Christianization, c. 370–529* 2 vols (Leiden)

Trouillot, Michel-Rolph

    1995. *Silencing the Past. Power and the Production of History* (Boston)

Unger, Fr. W.

    1897. "Über die vier Kolossal-Säulen in Constantinopel," *RepKunstW* 2: 8–37

Van der Vin, J. P. A.

    1980. *Travellers to Greece and Constantinople, Ancient Monuments and Old Traditions in Medieval Travellers' Tales* 2 vols. (Leiden)

Van Milligan, Alexander

    1899. *Byzantine Constantinople. The Walls of the City and Adjoining Historical Sites* (London)

Van Nice, Robert

    1986. *Saint Sophia in Istanbul: an architectural survey* (Washington, D.C.)

Vermaseren, Maarten J.

    1977. *Cybele and Attis the Myth and the Cult* (London)

Vermeule, Cornelius

    1968. *Roman Imperial Art in Greece and Asia Minor* (Cambridge, MA)

    1977. *Greek Sculpture and Roman Taste* (Ann Arbor)

Verzone, P.

    1958. "I due gruppi in porfido di San Marco in Venezia ed il Philadelphion di Costantinopoli," *Palladio* 1: 8–14

Veyne, Paul

    1988. *Did the Greeks Believe in their Myths?: an essay on the constitutive imagination*, trans. Paula Wissing (Chicago)

Vickers, M.

    1972. "The Hippodrome at Thessaloniki," *JRS* 62: 25–32

Viljamaa, J.

    1963. *Studies in Greek Encomiastic Poetry of the Early Byzantine Period* (Helsinki)

Walters, H. B.

    1899. *Catalogue of the Bronzes, Greek, Roman, Etruscan in the Department of Greek and Roman Antiquities, British Museum* (London)

Ward-Perkins, Bryan

    1999. "Re-using the Architectural Legacy of the Past, entre idéologie et pragmatisme," in G. P. Brogiolo and B. Ward-Perkins, eds. *The Idea and Ideal of the Town* (Leiden): 225–44

Ward-Perkins, J. B.

    1948. "Severan Art and Architecture at Leptis Magna," *JRS* 38: 59–80

Wartena, J. R.

    1927. *Inleidung op een uitgave der Tabula Peutingeriana* (Amsterdam)

Weitzmann, Kurt ed.

    1979. *The Age of Spirituality* (New York)

Wharton, Annabel Jane

    1995. *Refiguring the Post Classical City* (Cambridge)

Whitby, Michael

    1985. "The Long Walls of Constantinople," *Byzantion,* 55: 560–83

Whittaker, C. R.

    1997. "Imperialism and culture: the Roman initiative," in *Mattingly*, 1997: 143–64

Wiegand, Ernst

    1914. "Neue Untersuchungen über das Goldene Tor in Konstantinopel," *AM* 39:1–64

Wilkinson, John

    1981. *Itinerarium Egeriae: Egeria's Travels to the Holy Land* (Warminster)

Wilson, R. J. A.

    1983. *Piazza Armerina* (London)

Wittkower, Rudolph

    1937–38. "Chance, Time and Virtue," *JWI* 1: 313–21

Woolf, Greg

    1992. "The unity and diversity of Romanization," *JRA* 5: 349–52

    1995. "Becoming Roman, staying Greek: Cultural Identity and the Civilizing Process in the Roman East," *ProcCambPhilSoc* 40: 116–43

    2001. "Inventing Empire in Ancient Rome," in Susan E. Alcock, Terence N. D'Altroy, Kathleen D. Morrison, Carla M. Sinopoli, eds. *Empires. Perspectives from Archaeology and History* (Cambridge): 311–322

Wrede, Henning

    1966. "Zur Errichtung des Theodosius Obelisken in Istanbul," *IstMitt* 16: 178–98

    1972. *Die spätantike Hermengalerie von Welschbillig* (Berlin)

Wroth, Warwick

    1894. *Catalogue of the Greek Coins of Troas, Aeolis, and Lesbos in the British Museum* (London)

Wulff, O.

    1898. "Die sieben Wunder von Byzanz und die

Apostelkirche nach Konstantinos Rhodios,"
*BZ* 7: 319

Wurch-Kozelj, Manuela

1988. "Methods of Transporting Blocks in Antiquity," in N. Herz and M. Waelkens, eds. *Classical Marble: Geochemistry, Technology, Trade* (Dordrecht/Boston/London): 55–64

Yegül, Fikret

1992. *Baths and Bathing in Classical Antiquity* (New York/Cambridge, MA/London)

2000. "Memory, Metaphor, and Meaning in the Cities of Asia Minor," in *Fentress*, 2000: 133–54

Zanker, Paul

1995. *The Mask of Socrates,* trans. Alan Schapiro (Berkeley)

2000. "The City as Symbol: Rome and the Creation of an Urban Image," in *Fentress*, 2000: 25–41

Zucker, Martin

1887. "Zur ältern griechischen Kunstgeschichte I: die angebliche Athenastatue des Dipoinos und Skyllis," *NJbb* 135: 785–91

# INDEX